THE NEW
MANNERS &
CUSTOMS
OF THE
BIBLE

THE NEW MANNERS & CUSTOMS OF THE BIBLE

By James M. Freeman
Edited by Harold J. Chadwick

Bridge-Logos *Publishers*

Gainesville, Florida 32614 USA

The New Manners and Customs of the Bible
by James M. Freeman
International Standard Book Number: 0-88270-745-0
Library of Congress Catalog Card Number: 97-0770836
Copyright ©1998 by Bridge-Logos Publishers

Reprinted 2004

Published by:
Bridge-Logos *Publishers*
Gainesville, Florida FL 32614, USA
bridgelogos.com

CONTENTS

EXODUS 99

LEVITICUS 143

1 KINGS 233

2 KINGS 255

MARK 493

LUKE 497

ACTS 525

JOHN 513

FOREWORD

Harold J. Chadwick is Editorial Director of Bridge-Logos Publishers. Among recent achievements, he rewrote *FOXE'S BOOK OF MARTYRS* into modern English and updated it to include martyrs from A.D. 37 to 1997. The new best-seller version is titled *THE NEW FOXE'S BOOK OF MARTYRS*, and is available from Bridge-Logos Publishers. He also edited, expanded, and rewrote *THE REAL FAITH* by Dr. Charles Price. The new version is titled *THE REAL FAITH FOR HEALING*, and is available from Bridge-Logos Publishers.

He is the author of *WE SHALL JUDGE ANGELS*, a book that explores the fall of Lucifer, God's reason for creating humanity, His eternal purpose in Christ, and the part that Christians have in that purpose in this age and in the ages to come. He also writes a monthly back page—USA TODAY, Stateside Comment—for the *European Christian Bookstore Journal*.

Harold began his writing career in 1961 when he took a correspondence course from Writer's Digest School while working as a flight simulator crew chief at Loring Air Force Base in Maine. He then worked five years as a technical writer for various companies, including General Electric and the Philco Corporation. While working in Philadelphia, Pennsylvania, he freelanced studio greeting card ideas, and was hired as editor of a greeting card company in Cincinnati, Ohio.

While there he wrote *The Greeting Card Writer's Handbook*, which was published by *Writer's Digest Magazine* in 1968. He was subsequently hired as Director of Writer's Digest Correspondence School for Writers, where he remained for eight years. During that time he directed the activities of twenty-eight writing instructors, wrote all of the school's direct mail material, wrote several courses on writing fiction and nonfiction, and lectured on writing at various writing conferences.

After leaving Writer's Digest he worked for a while as Writing Manager for American Greetings contemporary card department, and then left there in 1976 to enter the ministry with his wife Beverlee. For several years they pastored a church they founded, and then in 1986 founded Omega Faith Ministries, a teaching fellowship dedicated to teaching the truth of the Scriptures and proclaiming the sovereignty of God and the all-sufficiency of Christ. To this end they maintain a web site at: *http://www.omegafaith.org.*

In 1989, Harold started work on his book *WE SHALL JUDGE ANGELS* and finished it in 1994. It was accepted for publication by Bridge Publishing (now Bridge-Logos Publishers), and was published in February 1995. Just prior to publication he was hired as an editor for Bridge, elevated to Senior Editor the same year, and then to Editorial Director in early 1996, a position he maintains today. He is currently working on another book, *CHRIST IS GOD'S EVERYTHING FOR YOU*, which will be published by Bridge-Logos Publishers when it's completed.

PREFACE

James M. Freeman wrote his original *Manners and Customs of the Bible* in the late 1800s. In editing and updating his book, my first thought was to remove all of his material that was dated to his period, especially since much of his research material and references went back to as early as the late 1600s. In reading through his material, however, it became apparent that many of the biblical manners and customs were still practiced during those years in the nations that Freeman referred to as Oriental or the East (since the British renamed it during World War II, that area has been known as the Middle East). Due to the rapid technological progress since the beginning of this century, however, many of those manners and customs are no longer practiced as various means of transportation and communication have reached into those areas and changed many of the ways of doing things.

It became obvious, therefore, that if all of Freeman's "dated material" was removed, priceless information from those years would be lost and might never be recovered or available again, and it was information that provided great insight into many of the manners and customs in the Bible. For that reason, most of the material was left in and simply rewritten to reflect that it was from a historically rich past and not "current" and "modern" as Freeman often referred to it.

To Freeman's material we added considerable new material that reflects some of the world changes and information available since he wrote his book, such as the completion of the Aswan High Dam on the Nile River in 1970, statistics concerning Mount Ararat and the Ararat Massif, and fascinating background information on what is called "The Lord's Prayer." We also added a number of sayings from the Bible that are considered essential knowledge for anyone who wishes to be culturally literate. There were several reasons for doing so.

The Bible is the most widely known book in the English-speaking world, and no English-speaking person can be considered literate without a basic knowledge of the Bible. All educated speakers of English need to understand what is meant when someone speaks of another as having "The mark of Cain," or describes a contest as being between David and Goliath, or says "My cup runs over," or asks, "Am I my brother's keeper?"

Those who cannot use or understand such allusions cannot fully participate in literate English. The New Testament parables and sayings of Jesus, such as "Blessed are the meek, for they shall inherit the earth" and His story of the "Good Samaritan," are so often alluded to that they need to be known by all English-speaking people regardless of their religious beliefs. The linguistic and cultural importance of the Bible is an undeniable fact, and so we have included in this rewritten and updated edition biblical information that will aid the reader in those areas.

At the end of James Freeman's original Preface to his book he wrote: "Should this volume aid the student in obtaining a better understanding of the Bible, the labor of the writer will not have been in vain." All of us at Bridge-Logos Publishers heartily agree with his sentiment, and pray that you will enjoy *The New Manners and Customs of the Bible* for many years, and that it will enrich you both spiritually and culturally.

Harold J. Chadwick, Editorial Director

GENESIS

2:8 "GARDEN OF EDEN"

Now the LORD God had planted a garden in the east, in Eden; and there he put the man he had formed.

God created a beautiful Garden that contained the tree of life, and there put the man whom he had created. In the Garden, God also placed the tree of the knowledge of good and evil, and commanded the man not to eat of it, "for when you eat of it you will surely die" (Genesis 2:17). Then "the LORD God said, "It is not good for the man to be alone. I will make a helper suitable for him" (Genesis 2:18), and so He created from the man a woman to be his companion. In the Garden the man and woman—Adam and Eve—were to live in peaceful and contented innocence, effortlessly reaping the fruits of the earth. But they disobeyed and ate of the forbidden fruit, and so God drove them out and "placed on the east side of the Garden of Eden cherubim and a flaming sword flashing back and forth to guard the way to the tree of life" (Genesis 3:24). See illustration on page 3. Adam and Eve's sin and consequent

Adam and Eve in the Garden

loss of God's grace and of their paradise is called the fall of man, or simply "the Fall." When used figuratively as a metaphor, a "Garden of Eden"—or "the Garden" or "Eden"—is any condition or place of complete peace and happiness.

2:16-17 "Forbidden fruit"

And the LORD God commanded the man, "You are free to eat from any tree in the garden; but you must not eat from the tree of the knowledge of good and evil, for when you eat of it you will surely die."

The forbidden fruit is the fruit of the tree of knowledge of good and evil in the Garden of Eden, often pictured as an apple, that God commanded Adam—and through Adam, Eve—not to eat. Their disobedience brought on the Fall. Today, the expression "forbidden fruit" is used commonly to refer to anything that is tempting but potentially dangerous. It's often associated with sexual matters.

Somewhere in history, a story was started that when Adam took the first bite of the "apple" and tried to swallow it, the piece of forbidden fruit stuck in his throat because he felt so guilty. So ever since then the slight projection at the front of the throat formed by the largest cartilage of the larynx, which is usually more prominent in men than in women, has been called the "Adam's apple."

3:6-7 "Fall of man"

When the woman saw that the fruit of the tree was good for food and pleasing to the eye, and also desirable for gaining wisdom, she took some and ate it. She also gave some to her husband, who was with her, and he ate it. Then the eyes of both of them were opened, and they realized they were naked; so they sewed fig leaves together and made coverings for themselves.

When Adam and Eve disobeyed God, they lost God's grace and the peace and happiness of the Garden of Eden. When they ate the forbidden fruit of the knowledge of good and evil, the LORD God told Eve, "I will greatly increase your pains in childbearing; with pain you will

Adam and Eve driven from Eden

give birth to children." To Adam he said, "Because you listened to your wife and ate from the tree about which I commanded you, 'You must not eat of it,' "Cursed is the ground because of you; through painful toil you will eat of it all the days of your life. It will produce thorns and thistles for you, and you will eat the plants of the field. By the sweat of your brow you will eat your food until you return to the ground, since from it you were taken; for dust you are and to dust you will return." (Genesis 3:16-19)

The LORD God then drove them out of the garden and into the world, where they would be subject to sickness, pain, and eventual death. From obedience they fell to disobedience. From innocence they fell to knowledge of good and evil. From happiness and peace they fell to sorrow and pain. From effortless enjoyment of the fruits of the Garden they fell to eating what they could produce from the ground by their own work and sweat. From life they fell to death. All the consequences of falling from God's grace. Today, one of the common definitions of "fall" is "to experience defeat or ruin."

4:1-2 "Am I my brother's keeper?"

Adam lay with his wife Eve, and she became pregnant and gave birth to Cain. She said, "With the help of the LORD I have brought forth a man." Later she gave birth to his brother Abel. Now Abel kept flocks, and Cain worked the soil.

The saying, "Am I my brother's keeper," comes from the story of Cain and Abel, who were the first children of Adam and Eve after their expulsion from the Garden. About them this is recorded, "In the course of time Cain brought some of the fruits of the soil as an offering to the LORD. But Abel brought fat portions from some of the firstborn of his flock" (Genesis 4:3-4).

God was pleased with Abel's sacrifice but not with Cain's. When Cain saw this he became angry. Then the LORD said to Cain, "Why are you angry? Why is your face downcast? If you do what is right, will you not be accepted? But if you do not do what is right, sin is crouching at your door; it desires to have you, but you must master it" (Genesis 4:6-7). But Cain would not heed God's words

Cain and Abel

and jealousy got the best of him and he murdered his brother Abel. Then the LORD said to him, "Where is your brother Abel?" "I don't know," he replied. "Am I my brother's keeper" (Genesis 4:9)?

Cain's sarcastic and uncaring words now symbolize people's unwillingness to accept responsibility for the welfare of others—their "brothers" in the extended sense of the term. That Christians do have this responsibility was taught by Jesus when he said the second greatest commandment was, "Love your neighbor as yourself" (Matthew 22:39).

4:15 "The mark of Cain"

But the LORD said to him, "Not so; if anyone kills Cain, he will suffer vengeance seven times over." Then the LORD put a mark on Cain so that no one who found him would kill him.

For the crime of murdering his brother Abel, Cain was exiled by God to a life of wandering in a distant land. Cain protested the punishment and said to the LORD, "My punishment is more than I can bear. Today you are driving me from the land, and I will be hidden from your presence; I will be a restless wanderer on the earth, and whoever finds me will kill me" (Genesis 4:13-14). So the LORD set a mark upon Cain to protect him in his wanderings. What the "mark" was, the Bible doesn't tell us, but the "mark of Cain" now refers to an individual's or mankind's sinful nature. In the past, perhaps more than now, the expression was used to speak of a person's evil nature, such as, "He has the mark of Cain on him."

4:20-21 Use of the Term "Father"

Adah gave birth to Jabal; he was the father of those who live in tents and raise livestock. His brother's name was Jubal; he was the father of all who play the harp and flute.

In the above verses, the term father is used to denote the author or beginner of something. It is frequently used this way throughout the Bible. Undoubtedly Jabal was the first to dwell in tents and have cattle, therefore he is called the father of all those who dwell in tents and have cattle. In other words, he was the progenitor of tent dwellers and herdsmen, and probably was a nomad and lived a wandering life.

In the same way, Jubal was considered to be the first to play the harp and organ, and so he was the father of those who played such instruments— possibly he was also the inventor of them. Arched harps, the most ancient of all harps, were known in Sumer (an ancient country of western Asia, corresponding approximately to Babylonia of biblical times) and Egypt between about 3000 and 2000 B.C., and Jubal would predate those times, having been not far descended from Cain.

In the KJV, the term organ (NIV, flute) is used to designate any wind instrument. It was probably a kind of Pan's pipe; that is, a wind instrument consisting of seven or eight reeds of unequal length. The modern pipe organ was not known in biblical days. The earliest organ, the hydraulis, was developed by the Greek inventor Ctesibius in about the 3rd century B.C. The hydraulis utilized a large chamber partly filled with water. The wide mouth of a funnel-like extension from the wind chest was set in the top of the water; as air pressure in the wind chest fell, water rose in the funnel and compressed the air, thus keeping the air pressure constant. This organ was used in the Jerusalem Temple after 100 B.C., and for public entertainment in ancient Rome and Byzantium.

A similar use of the term father to mean the author or beginner of something is found in Job 38:28: "Does the rain have a father? Who fathers the drops of dew?" It is also used this way in Isaiah 9:6, where the Messiah is called "the Everlasting [or eternal] Father," which means that He is the author of eternal life. In John 8:44 where the devil is called "the father of lies," meaning he is the originator of all lies. In 2 Corinthians 1:3 (KJV) where God is called "the father of mercies," meaning that all mercy begins in Him. And in Ephesians 1:17 (KJV) God is called "the father of glory," meaning that He is the beginning of all glory.

Noah preaching by his ark

6:14-16 "NOAH'S ARK"

Make thee an ark of gopher wood; rooms shalt thou make in the ark, and shalt pitch it within and without with pitch. And this is the fashion which thou shalt make it of: The length of the ark shall be three hundred cubits, the breadth of it fifty cubits, and the height of it thirty cubits. A window shalt thou make to the ark, and in a cubit shalt thou finish it above; and the door of the ark shalt thou set in the side thereof; with lower, second, and third stories shalt thou make it (KJV).

This was Noah's ark. It was built of gopher-wood, which is now an unknown wood but was probably cypress or cedar, and was covered with pitch—a tar-like substance—to seal the wood and make the ark watertight. The boat was 300 cubits long, 50 cubits wide, and 30 cubits high. The cubit is an ancient unit of linear—straight line—measure, originally equal to the length of the forearm from the tip of the middle finger to the elbow, or about 17 to 22 inches (43 to 56 centimeters). Today a cubit is generally translated as being 18 inches, or a little under 46 centimeters. But since Moses, who wrote Genesis, was educated in Egypt it's possible he used the Egyptian cubit of approximately 20.5 inches to indicate the size of the ark. Using the shorter cubit, the ark would have been about 450 feet long, 75 feet wide, and 45 feet high. Not until the late 19th century was another ship built anywhere near this size.

The ark had a ratio (length x width x height) of 30 x 5 x 3. According to modern shipbuilders, this ratio represents an advanced knowledge of shipbuilding since it is the optimum design for stability in rough seas. The ark, as designed by God, was virtually impossible to capsize—to do so, it would have to be tilted over 90 degrees.

The ark was a three-story, oblong, floating cargo vessel and house, probably with a flat bottom, and with a door in the side and a window in the roof or side. The Hebrew word translated "window" in the KJV version above occurs only here in the Old Testament, and its precise meaning is unknown. Some translate it "roof" and interpret it as the roof of the vessel, which was one cubit above the walls. Others say that it was a cubit high space for light and air that circled the top edge of the ark, and not a window that could be opened. Traditionally, however, the term has been interpreted as the window mentioned later in Genesis 8:6: "And it came to pass at the end of forty days, that Noah opened the window of the ark which he had made."

Some attempts at illustrating the ark have shown both the circular space for light and air and a hinged window in the side of the ark. The NIV, however, does not refer to a window in its version of Genesis 6:14-16: "So make yourself an ark of cypress wood; make rooms in it and coat it with pitch inside and out. This is how you are to build it: The ark is to be 450 feet long, 75 feet wide and 45 feet high. Make a roof for it and finish the ark to within 18 inches of the top. Put a door in the side of the ark and make lower, middle and upper decks."

With the shorter cubit the ark would have an internal volume of 1,518,750 cubic feet, or the equivalent of 569 standard railroad boxcars. If the average sized animal was the size of a sheep it means the ark could hold over 125,000 sheep. (Assuming the shape of the ark to be rectangular there would have been over 100,000 sq. ft of floor space!)

It took Noah 100 years to build the ark—he was about 500 years old when he started (Genesis 5:32), and 600 years old when he finished (Genesis 7:6). (Some say he was 480 years old when he started the ark, which would mean it took 120 years to finish it.) The ark's purpose was to keep safe certain persons and animals from the deluge that God was about to bring upon the earth. The ark became known as a symbol of Noah's faith and a symbol of God's mercy. Today "ark" is also used as a term for a shelter or refuge.

7:11-12 "The Flood"

In the six hundredth year of Noah's life, on the seventeenth day of the second month—on that day all the springs of the great deep burst forth, and the floodgates of the heavens were opened. And rain fell on the earth forty days and forty nights.

The Flood

used in Genesis 1:2—"Now the earth was formless and empty, darkness was over the surface of the deep, and the Spirit of God was hovering over the waters." The word has the sense of an almost immeasurable depth. Where the NIV uses the expression "burst forth," the KJV uses "broken up." The Hebrew word so translated could also be expressed by "split" or "ripped open." So everything in the verse indicates that there were two great sources of the flood waters: a massive downpour from above the earth, and gigantic geysers shooting up from within the earth. Rather than it being only a simple rain pouring down from above, the Flood was also a violent upheaval of the earth that undoubtedly caused extensive changes in the geographical structure of the earth.

The exact date of the Flood is not known, but it lasted for 12 months and 11 days. The exact dating of its length adds proof to the reality of the Flood. The "springs of the great deep" refer to subterranean waters that burst forth from the earth and added to the rain. The word "deep" that is used here is the same word that is

Some believe that prior to the Flood it had not rained upon

the earth, but the earth was covered by a water canopy that protected the earth's inhabitants from the harmful, aging, rays of the sun, and every day a mist came upon the ground to water it. Genesis 1:6-7 say, "And God said, 'Let there be an expanse between the waters to separate water from water.' So God made the expanse and separated the water under the expanse from the water above it." This seems to indicate that God suspended a great quantity of water above the earth in a vapor form, which would create conditions upon the earth similar to those within a greenhouse. All this would account for the extreme ages of those prior to the Flood, and the rapid decline in longevity after the Flood when humanity was no longer protected from the harmful rays of the sun.

Methuselah lived 969 years, Noah lived 950 years, Noah's son Shem lived 600 years, but Shem's son Arphaxad—born two years after the Flood—lived only 438 years. Arphaxad's son Shelah lived 433 years, his son Eber lived 464 years, but Eber's son Peleg lived only 239 years. Peleg's son Reu also lived 239 years, and Reu's son Serug lived 229 years. Terah, who was the father of Abram (Abraham) lived 205 years, and Abraham died when he was only 175 years old. (See Genesis 11:10-26, 32; 25:7.)

As can be seen from biblical records, as humanity moved further from the time of the Flood, and the breaking up of the water canopy surrounding the earth, their life span decreased—Moses died when he was 120 year's old, and Joshua when he was 110. This water canopy around the earth would also account for the source of the water above the earth that was so great that "rain fell on the earth forty days and forty nights." During that time, the quantity of water that poured down from heaven and gushed up from within the earth was so great that the Scriptures record that: "They [the waters] rose greatly on the earth, and all the high mountains under the entire heavens were covered. The waters rose and covered the mountains to a depth of more than twenty feet" (Genesis 7:19-20).

Some years ago during a trip to the Smoky Mountains, the editor and his family visited the Sequoia Caverns in northern Georgia, just across the border

8:3-4 "MOUNT ARARAT"

Noah's Ark comes to rest on Ararat

The water receded steadily from the earth. At the end of the hundred and fifty days the water had gone down, and on the seventeenth day of the seventh month the ark came to rest on the mountains of Ararat.

Mount Ararat consists of two volcanic peaks in extreme eastern Turkey, near the border with Armenia and Iran, on which the ark rested after the Flood subsided. The name Ararat is the Hebrew form for *Urartu*, the Assyrian name of an Assyrian-Babylonian kingdom that flourished between the Aras and the Upper Tigris rivers from the 9th to the 7th century B.C. Ararat is a sacred place to the Armenian people. The Persian people call it *Koh-i-nuh*, "Noah's Mountain," and have a legend that refers to Ararat as the cradle of the human race.

from Chattanooga, Tennessee. Inside the caverns, the guide pointed out fish bones of all sizes that were pressed into the ceiling of a passageway between two caverns. He said the same kind of fossils could be seen in the ceiling of the main cavern, which was about 50 feet high. Among the fish fossils in the passageway was the imprint of the bottom of a human foot. The guide, a strong Christian who used the tour to proclaim Christ, said that nothing could have pressed the fish and the human foot into the ceiling except the pressure of a tremendous flood of unprecedented depth. That flood, he said, could only have been Noah's Flood.

From the lowlands of the Aras River, Ararat rises to a height of nearly 17,000 feet. It has two conical peaks: Little Ararat and Great Ararat. Except for a 7000-foot spur on the northwest that merges with a long ridge, the mountain is completely isolated by surrounding plains that rise about 2500 to 4500 feet above sea level. From an elevation of about 8800 feet, Little Ararat rises to 12,840 feet, and Great Ararat rises to 16,854 feet. (Three encyclopedias give different elevations for both mountains. They list Little Ararat from 12,782 feet [3896 meters] to 12,840 feet [3925 meters], and Great Ararat from 16,804 feet [5122 meters] to 16,854 feet [5137 meters]).

Above the 14,000-foot level, Great Ararat is covered with perpetual snow. Considering the high elevations of the areas surrounding the peaks, the region is remarkably fertile and pasturable. Some archaeologists believe that Ararat received more rainfall in biblical times than it does today. If so, the pasturable areas may have been even more productive in ancient times.

The first successful climb of Great Ararat in modern times was in 1829 by a German, Johann Jacob von Parrot. On July 2, 1840, an earthquake struck the mountain and tore off great masses that avalanched down and destroyed a village, a convent, and a chapel—the last settlements on the mountain. In the summer of 1949, an American expedition ascended Mount Ararat in an unsuccessful attempt to search for evidence of the existence of Noah's ark. Recent expeditions, one headed by a former American astronaut, have reported finding timbers that some believe came from the ark.

Modern Mount Ararat, however, is neither excluded nor specifically identified in the Scriptures as the resting place of the ark. The phrase, "came to rest on the mountains of Ararat," places it in the range of mountains in which Ararat is located. It's not wrong to attempt to discover the location of the ark, or whatever remains of it, but the truth of Noah's Flood doesn't depend upon locating the ark or its remains. The Scriptures are sufficient evidence in themselves.

The dove returns to the ark

in the ark. He reached out his hand and took the dove and brought it back to himself in the ark. He waited seven more days and again sent out the dove from the ark. When the dove returned to him in the evening, there in its beak was a freshly plucked olive leaf! Then Noah knew that the water had receded from the earth. He waited seven more days and sent the dove out again, but this time it did not return to him.

8:6-12 RAVEN AND DOVE

After forty days Noah opened the window he had made in the ark and sent out a raven, and it kept flying back and forth until the water had dried up from the earth. Then he sent out a dove to see if the water had receded from the surface of the ground. But the dove could find no place to set its feet because there was water over all the surface of the earth; so it returned to Noah

Noah's raven and dove are symbols of Satan and the Holy Spirit, and the ark is a symbol of heaven. The raven sent out of the ark finds no place to rest its foot, and so it roams endlessly and restlessly over the earth. It is as Daniel Defoe wrote in *The*

History of the Devil: "Satan, being thus confined to a vagabond, wandering, unsettled condition, is without any certain abode; for though he has, in consequence of his angelic nature, a kind of empire in the liquid waste or air, yet this is certainly part of his punishment, that he is . . . without any fixed place, or space, allowed him to rest the sole of his foot upon."

The dove is sent out three times. The first time he finds no place to stay. This symbolizes the dispensation of the Holy Spirit in the Old Testament, where he never stayed with anyone but resided only temporarily upon them and then returned to heaven; he was not permanently upon the earth.

The second time the dove is sent out, he returns with an olive leaf in his mouth. This symbolizes the dispensation of the Holy Spirit at the time of Jesus. He came out from heaven in the specific form of a dove and resided within Jesus while the Prince of Peace ministered upon the earth. About this event, John the Baptist testified, "I saw the Spirit come down from heaven as a dove and remain on him" (John 1:32). The Holy Spirit did not return to heaven until the time of Jesus' ascension.

The third time the dove is sent out, he does not return to the ark but remains in the world. This symbolizes the dispensation of the Holy Spirit when Jesus sent Him down on the day of Pentecost to remain with His Church until God's purpose in Christ is fulfilled. The Holy Spirit, the dove that descended on Jesus at the Jordan River, came and stayed—and is still here in the world.

8:10-11 "OLIVE LEAF"

He *[Noah]* waited seven more days and again sent out the dove from the ark. When the dove returned to him in the evening, there in its beak was a freshly plucked olive leaf! Then Noah knew that the water had receded from the earth.

The olive leaf brought by a dove to Noah's ark signified that the Flood was receding, that God's destruction of the corrupt people of the earth was completed, and that God's creation was once more at peace with Him. Today, an olive branch is regarded as a sign of peace, as is the dove, and so the combination of a dove with an olive branch in it's mouth is often used as a symbol of peace.

11:3 BABYLONIAN BRICKS

They said to each other, "Come, let's make bricks and bake them thoroughly." They used brick instead of stone, and tar for mortar.

The soil of Babylonia, which was an ancient empire of Mesopotamia in the Euphrates River valley, was an alluvial deposit, rich and tenacious, and well suited for making bricks. While many of the bricks in that country were merely sun-dried, others were baked in kilns, such as those used for the tower of Babel. The bricks normally were about a foot square and three to four inches thick.

Babylonian builders constructed ziggurats, palaces, and city walls of sun-dried brick and covered them with more durable kiln-baked, often

Olives

brilliantly glazed, brick arranged in decorative pictorial friezes—horizontal bands, as along the upper part of a wall in a room. A ziggurat was a temple tower of

Babylonian brick

the ancient Assyrians and Babylonians, having the form of a terraced pyramid of successively receding stories.

In the KJV, the word slime is used instead of tar: "And they had brick for stone, and slime had they for mortar." The slime referred to is bitumen, which literally bubbled from the ground in the area of ancient Babylon. Bitumens are naturally occurring mixtures of hydrocarbons, such as crude petroleum, asphalt, and tar. Bitumen was used as mortar to cement the bricks together.

11:4 "Tower of Babel"

Then they said, "Come, let us build ourselves a city, with a tower that reaches to the heavens, so that we may make a name for ourselves and not be scattered over the face of the whole earth."

The descendants of Noah spread over the earth as far as they could travel, and some of them moved eastward and found a plain in Shinar, the area between the Tigris and Euphrates rivers, and there began to build a tower. At that time they were all of one language, and thus working together could accomplish whatever they set their minds to. But their error was that in their arrogance they intended that their tower would reach up to heaven itself, make a name for themselves, and make them godlike. God stopped the building of the tower by confusing their language so that they could no longer understand each another. "That is why it was called Babel—because there the LORD confused the language of the whole world. From there the LORD scattered them over the face of the whole earth" (Genesis 11:9).

Tower of Babel

The word "Babel" is a transliteration of an Akkadian word that the Scripture writer linked by a play on words with the Hebrew verb that means "to confuse." The Babylonians, however, understood it to mean something more acceptable to them —"the gate of God." Today, "babel" stands for a confusion of sounds or voices, or a scene of noise and confusion.

12:10 EGYPT

Now there was a famine in the land, and Abram went down to Egypt to live there for a while because the famine was severe.

Egypt is a country of northeast Africa on the Mediterranean Sea. In ancient times Egypt was confined to the Nile River valley, which is a long, narrow, band of fertile land surrounded by uninhabitable desert. Ancient Egypt was a flourishing kingdom and one of the earliest kingdoms of which we have any record. It produced magnificent structures and delicate works of art. After about 800 B.C. the kingdom declined, falling to various conquerors ranging from the Assyrians, Alexander the Great in 332 B.C., the Romans, Turks, French, and finally British. Ancient Egypt is one of the major countries in the Bible, and figures significantly in many of its events, including the stories of Joseph and his brothers, and of Moses and the Exodus. The ancient Egyptians were a white race, and their place of origin is still unknown. It's kings were usually given the title of Pharaoh.

12:15 PHARAOH

When Pharaoh's officials saw her, they praised her to Pharaoh, and she was taken into his palace.

Pharaoh was the common title of the kings in ancient Egypt. In Egyptian the name means "great house." Originally it was used for the palace of the king, but about the beginning of the Egyptian 18th Dynasty, which is considered to be from 1570 to 1293 B.C., it was applied to the king himself. The word is familiar to Bible readers because Scripture writers used it to designate Egyptian kings, usually with no other identification.

Pharaoh in his court

14:16 USE OF THE TERM "BROTHER"

And he brought back all the goods, and also brought again his brother Lot, and his goods, and the women also, and the people *(KJV)*.

In Genesis 11:31, it shows that Lot was Abram's nephew, not his brother. In the same way, in Genesis 29:12, Jacob tells Rachel that he is her father's brother, but in actuality he is her father's nephew, as shown in Genesis 28:5—Rebekah and Laban being sister and brother. This use of the word brother to show various kinds of relationship is quite common in the Bible. In essence, the term means a person who shares a common ancestry, allegiance, character, or purpose with another or others, especially a kinsman or a fellow man.

In the Old Testament, *brother* is used to signify kinsmen, allies, fellow countrymen. In Genesis 13:8 it's used to describe the relationship of Abram and his nephew Lot: "So Abram said to Lot, "Let's not have any quarreling between you and me, or between your herdsmen and mine, for we are brothers." After Solomon and Hiram of

Tyre entered into political alliance with one another, they were called brothers: "What kind of towns are these you have given me, my brother?" he asked. And he called them the Land of Cabul, a name they have to this day" (1 Kings 9:13). In the New Testament it's used to signify a near relation, such as a cousin, as in Matthew 12:46, John 7:3, Acts 1:14, and Galatians 1:19. Also simply a fellow-countryman, as in Matthew 5:47, Acts 3:22, and Hebrews 7:5.

14:22 UPLIFTED HAND

But Abram said to the king of Sodom, "I have raised my hand to the LORD, God Most High, Creator of heaven and earth, and have taken an oath."

This was Abram's way of taking a solemn oath. It is a method still used today in every court room in the country, where the right hand is raised when an oath to tell the truth is taken. Almost every oath in the government and the military today is taken the same way. In Isaiah 62:8, it tells of the Lord taking an oath in a similar way, "The LORD has sworn by his right hand and by his mighty arm." The combination of a raised right hand when taking an oath is also shown in Daniel 12:7: "The man clothed in linen, who was above the waters of the river, lifted his right hand and his left hand toward heaven, and I heard him swear by him who lives forever, saying, "It will be for a time, times and half a time. When the power of the holy people has been finally broken, all these things will be completed"; and in Revelation 10:5-6, "Then the angel I had seen standing on the sea and on the land raised his right hand to heaven. And he swore by him who lives for ever and ever . . ."

17:10-11 CIRCUMCISION

"This is my covenant with you and your descendants after you, the covenant you are to keep: Every male among you shall be circumcised. You are to undergo circumcision, and it will be the sign of the covenant between me and you."

Circumcise means *cutting around*. Circumcision was appointed by God to be the special mark of His chosen people, an abiding sign of their consecration to Him, and His covenant with them. He established it as a national ordinance. In compliance with the divine command, Abraham, although ninety-nine years of age, was circumcised on the same day with Ishmael, who was thirteen years old (Genesis 17:24-27). Slaves, whether born in the household or purchased, were circumcised (Genesis 17:12, 13). It was later decreed that all foreigners must have their males circumcised before they could enjoy the privileges of Jewish citizenship (Exodus 12:48). During the journey through the wilderness, the practice of circumcision fell into disuse, probably because the Israelites were under God's judgment during that time, but was resumed by Joshua's command before they entered the Promised Land (Joshua 5:2-9). It was observed always afterwards among the tribes of Israel, although it's not expressly mentioned from the time of the settlement in Canaan until the time of Christ, about 1,450 years later.

The Jews prided themselves in the possession of this covenant distinction (see Judges 14:3, 15:18; 1 Samuel 14:6, 17:26; 2 Samuel 1:20; and Ezekiel 31:18).

As a rite of the Church, circumcision ceased when the New Testament times began; ceased so completely, in fact, that Paul told the Galatians that if they were circumcised in belief that it was a requirement of their salvation they would fall from grace and Christ would be of no use to them. (See Galatians 5). Paul resolutely resisted the Jewish Christians who sought to impose circumcision on his Gentile converts (Acts 15:1-2). Our Lord would have been circumcised, for He was a Jew and it became him to "fulfill all righteousness" (Matthew 3:15), as of the seed of Abraham, according to the flesh; and Paul "took and circumcised" Timothy (Acts 16:3) to avoid giving offense to the Jews. Being circumcised would render Timothy's labors more acceptable to the Jews. But Paul would by no means consent to the demand that Titus should be circumcised (Galatians 2:3-5). The great point for which he contended was the free admission of uncircumcised Gentiles into the Church. He contended successfully in behalf of Titus, even in Jerusalem.

In the Old Testament a spiritual idea is attached to circumcision. It was the symbol of purity (Isaiah 52:1). We read of uncircumcised lips (Exodus 6:12, 30), ears (Jeremiah 6:10), hearts (Leviticus 26:41). The fruit of a tree that is unclean is spoken of as uncircumcised (Leviticus 19:23). Circumcision was a sign and seal of the covenant of grace as well as of the national covenant between God and the Hebrews. It sealed the promises made to Abraham, which related to the commonwealth of Israel, national promises. But the promises made to Abraham included the promise of redemption (Galatians 3:14), a promise that has come upon us. The covenant with Abraham was a dispensation or a specific form of the covenant of grace, and circumcision was a sign and seal of that covenant. It had a spiritual meaning. It signified purification of the heart, inward circumcision effected by the Holy Spirit (Deuteronomy 10:16, 30:6; Ezekiel 44:7; Acts 7:51; Romans 2:28; Colossians 2:11).

Under the Jewish dispensation, Church and state were identical. No one could be a member of the one without also being a member of the other. Circumcision was a sign and seal of membership in both. Every circumcised person bore thereby evidence that he was one of the chosen people, a member of the Church of God as it then existed, and consequently also a member of the Jewish commonwealth.

18:2-3 BOWING

Abraham looked up and saw three men standing nearby. When he saw them, he hurried from the entrance of his tent to meet them and bowed low to the ground. He said, "If I have found favor in your eyes, my lord, do not pass your servant by."

In biblical times bowing was a method of showing respect, the lesser bowing to the greater, or a method of demonstrating humility or showing acquiescence. In certain Asiatic countries it is a way of salutation, just as shaking hands is in Western countries. Bowing is also used to express an attitude of deference or homage.

Abraham bowed before the Lord to show respect and reverence. In Genesis 23:7,

"Abraham rose and bowed down before the people of the land, the Hittites" to express thankfulness. In Genesis 33:3, Jacob bowed to Esau seven times—the bowing was undoubtedly to express respect and humility, and the seven times may have been to express repentance and seek forgiveness. This would be in keeping with what the Lord said as recorded in Luke 17:4, "If he sins against you seven times in a day, and seven times comes back to you and says, 'I repent,' forgive him." And in Genesis 43:28, the brothers of Joseph bowed before him to honor him as the governor of the land: "They replied, "Your servant our father is still alive and well." And they bowed low to pay him honor."

Where the soil is dry and dusty and sandals or similar footwear is worn, frequent washing of the feet is not only a luxury, but a necessity for comfort and health. It is, also, extremely refreshing, as anyone knows who has bathed their feet in cool water when they're dusty and hot. Under such circumstances, it's great hospitality and consideration to see that the feet of guests are washed with cool water. Just as important as feeding them when they're hungry, or giving them a place to rest when they're tired. Not to do so would be discourteous and even insulting.

In Genesis 24:32, it tells how Rebekah's family gave Abraham's servant and the men

18:4 FEET WASHING

"Let a little water be brought, and then you may all wash your feet and rest under this tree."

Jesus washed the feet of His disciples

who were with him water to wash their feet, "So the man went to the house, and the camels were unloaded. Straw and fodder were brought for the camels, and water for him and his men to wash their feet." In Genesis 43:24 it tells how Joseph's servant gave water to Joseph's brothers, "The steward took the men into Joseph's house, gave them water to wash their feet and provided fodder for their donkeys."

It is this courtesy of providing water for washing that Jesus refers to when He mildly reproves Simon the Pharisee, at whose house He was a guest, for not giving Him water to wash his feet: "Then he turned toward the woman and said to Simon, "Do you see this woman? I came into your house. You did not give me any water for my feet, but she wet my feet with her tears and wiped them with her hair" (Luke 7:44).

When the apostle Paul wrote to Timothy about the qualifications necessary for a widow be provided for by the Church, he listed foot washing among them: ". . . and is well known for her good deeds, such as bringing up children, showing hospitality, washing the feet of the saints, helping those in trouble and devoting herself to all kinds

of good deeds" (1 Timothy 5:10). All of these were signs that the person had committed her life to serving others. If she had done this, then it was the responsibility of the Church to provide for her.

These signs of a servant give force to the beautiful symbolic action of our Lord, Who washed the feet of His disciples, so that His disciples might see how they were to act toward each other after He was gone. No one was to be master or lord it over another, each was to be a servant of the other. (John 13:4-15)

18:7-8 MEALS

Then he ran to the herd and selected a choice, tender calf and gave it to a servant, who hurried to prepare it. He then brought some curds and milk and the calf that had been prepared, and set these before them. While they ate, he stood near them under a tree.

Normal meals consisted of a vegetable or lentil stew made in a large cooking pot, and seasoned with herbs and salt. Only on special occasions such as a sacrifice or festival day, or in the case of special guests, was meat added to the stew. Rarely was the meat roasted or game or fish eaten. When it was time to eat, the pot was placed on the floor, usually on a rug, with all those eating sitting around the pot. A blessing or thanksgiving was always given, and each person used a piece of bread as a scoop to take up some of the stew from the common pot, because there were no eating utensils. For this reason, it was essential that everyone's hands be washed before the meal. At some point in biblical history, a table and benches, or simply a low table, began to replace the rug on the floor, but everyone still dipped into the common eating pot in the center. This common pot or dish is what is referred to in John 13:26—"Jesus answered, 'It is the one to whom I will give this piece of bread when I have dipped it in the dish.' Then, dipping the piece of bread, he gave it to Judas Iscariot, son of Simon."

After Abraham killed the calf to feed the Lord and his servants, he would have immediately roasted it, for it would have taken too long to boil it. To serve such a rare delicacy to unexpected guests in the middle of the day showed that Abraham well knew who had come to visit him, for almost never was a meal eaten in the heat of the day (Genesis 18:1). His knowledge of the nature of his visitors is shown also by the fact that he apparently did not consider himself worthy to eat with them, and stood by and watched while they ate (Genesis 18:8).

The milk that was served at the meal would probably have been goats milk, and the butter (KJV) would have been curdled milk—Hebrew: *hemah*, (see Judges 5:25, 2 Samuel 17:29), or butter in the form of the skim of hot milk or cream, a semifluid (see Job 20:17, 29:6; Deuteronomy 32:14). Proverbs 30:33 speaks of butter being made into cheese.

19:1 GATEWAY

The two angels arrived at Sodom in the evening, and Lot was sitting in the gateway of the city. When he saw them, he got up to meet them and bowed down with his face to the ground.

The gateways of walled cities, as well as the open spaces near them, were popular places for

City Gate

meeting or gathering, and often the elders of the city met there to judge the affairs of the city (see Genesis **29:18 Dowry**), as shown in Genesis 34:20, "So Hamor and his son Shechem went to the gate of their city to speak to their fellow townsmen."

Some gates had arched structures that provided shade, and often open tents for shade were placed around the outside area. Seats were also provided to sit upon, most especially for the elders and judges. Eli the prophet was sitting at the gate to Shiloh when he learned that his sons Hophni and Phinehas had been killed by the Philistines and the ark of God taken. "When he mentioned the ark of God, Eli fell backward off his chair by the side of the gate. His neck was broken

and he died, for he was an old man and heavy. He had led Israel forty years" (1 Samuel 4:18).

Anyone at the gate of a city could easily see all who came in and went out, and could easily spot strangers to a small city, and so Lot readily saw the two angels when they came to Sodom. In a similar sense, when the Jews in Damascus were trying to capture the newly converted Saul, they set watch at the city gates: "After many days had gone by, the Jews conspired to kill him, but Saul learned of their plan. Day and night they kept close watch on the city gates in order to kill him" (Acts 9:23-24).

By command of God, courts of justice were established at the gates of every city: "Appoint judges and officials for each of your tribes in every town the LORD your God is giving you, and they shall judge the people fairly" (Deuteronomy 16:18). The courts were usually presided over by elders of the city, as shown in Deuteronomy 21:18-19: "If a man has a stubborn and rebellious son who does not obey his father and mother and will not listen to them when they discipline him, his father and mother shall take hold of him and bring him to the elders at the gate

of his town," and in
Deuteronomy 25:6-7: "The first
son she bears shall carry on the
name of the dead brother so that
his name will not be blotted out
from Israel. However, if a man
does not want to marry his
brother's wife, she shall go to the
elders at the town gate and say,
'My husband's brother refuses to
carry on his brother's name in
Israel. He will not fulfill the duty
of a brother-in-law to me.'" Lot
sitting at the gate may have
meant that he was an elder or
judge in the city.

19:4 Houses

**Before they had gone to
bed, all the men from every
part of the city of Sodom—
both young and old—
surrounded the house.**

In Mesopotamia, Abraham
lived in houses made of mud
brick (see Genesis 11:3), but
then became a tent dweller
because God gave him no
permanent place of his own to
live. "By faith he made his home
in the promised land like a
stranger in a foreign country; he
lived in tents, as did Isaac and
Jacob, who were heirs with him
of the same promise" (Hebrews

11:9). Tents were normally made
of goat hair, which shed water
and could be easily bundled and
carried to the next camp site.
They were quite suitable for a
wandering life.

Except for individuals like
Lot who joined themselves with
a people other than those of
Abraham, it wasn't until the
Israelites went to Egypt in
Joseph's time that they lived in
houses, and at some point during
the 400 years there probably had
to build the houses they lived in.
At the time of the Exodus we
can see that they lived in houses,
"Then they are to take some of
the blood and put it on the sides
and tops of the door frames of
the houses where they eat the
lambs" (Exodus 12:7). When
they left Egypt, however, and
wandered in the wilderness for
40 years they once more lived in
tents. "Who went in the way
before you, to search you out a
place to pitch your tents in, in
fire by night, to show you by
what way ye should go, and in a
cloud by day" (Deuteronomy
1:33, KJV).

It wasn't until the time of
Joshua, however, when they
captured Canaan, that they
began to build houses like the
Canaanites. In those areas where
stone was plentiful, they built

stone houses, and where there were no stones, they built mud-brick houses, and where trees were plentiful, they built wood houses. They used whatever building materials were plentiful or available where they lived. "The bricks have fallen down, but we will rebuild with dressed stone; the fig trees have been felled, but we will replace them with cedars" (Isaiah 9:10).

19:24 "SODOM AND GOMORRAH "

Then the LORD rained down burning sulfur on Sodom and Gomorrah—from the LORD out of the heavens.

Sodom and Gomorrah were filled with evilness and sexual perversion: "Then the LORD said [to Abraham], 'The outcry against Sodom and Gomorrah is so great and their sin so grievous that I will go down and see if what they have done is as bad as the outcry that has reached me. If not, I will know'" (Genesis 18:20- 21).

God sent two angels in the form of men to advise all good men to leave the evil towns, but they found only one good man, Lot, Abraham's nephew, and so God destroyed the cities. Before the destruction, the angels guided Lot and his wife and two daughters out from Sodom into the countryside, and warned them not to look back. When Lot's wife failed to heed the warning and looked back, perhaps to see what was going

The burning of Sodom

to happen to the cities or perhaps in longing, she was turned into a pillar of salt. The sexual perversion of sodomy that male homosexuals practice derives its name from the city of Sodom.

19:30 CAVES

Lot and his two daughters left Zoar and settled in the mountains, for he was afraid to stay in Zoar. He and his two daughters lived in a cave.

There are numerous natural caves in many of the geographical areas identified in the Bible. Some were used for dwellings, some for burial places, and some for storing or hiding provisions or other goods. The first mention of a cave in the Bible is in the story of Lot after he fled from Sodom. "And Lot went up out of Zoar, and dwelt in the mountain, and his two daughters with him; for he feared to dwell in Zoar: and he dwelt in a cave, he and his two daughters" (Genesis 19:30).

Abraham bought the cave of Machpelah as a tomb for Sarah: "And he [Abraham] communed with them, saying, If it be your mind that I should bury my dead out of my sight; hear me, and entreat for me to Ephron the son of Zohar, That he may give me the cave of Machpelah, which he hath, which is in the end of his field; for as much money as it is worth he shall give it me for a possession of a burying place amongst you" (Genesis 23:11-16, 19).

In the time of Gideon the Israelites took refuge from the Midianites in dens and caves, such as those in the mountain regions of Manasseh: "And the hand of Midian prevailed against Israel: and because of the Midianites the children of Israel made them the dens which are in the mountains, and caves, and strong holds" (Judges 6:2). David used the cave of Adullam for refuge: "David therefore departed thence, and escaped to the cave Adullam: and when his brethren and all his father's house heard it, they went down thither to him" (1 Samuel 22:1). And so did the five Canaanite kings at Makkedah: "But these five kings fled, and hid themselves in a cave at Makkedah" (Joshua 10:16), which did them no good at all.

23:14-16 BURIAL

Ephron answered Abraham, "Listen to me, my lord; the land is worth four hundred shekels of silver, but what is that between me and you? Bury your dead." Abraham agreed to Ephron's terms and weighed out for him the price he had named in the hearing of the Hittites: four hundred shekels of silver, according to the weight current among the merchants.

The first burial recorded in the Bible is that of Sarah in the 23rd chapter of Genesis. In that account, there is also recorded the first commercial transaction, in which Abraham paid Ephron "four hundred shekels of silver" for a burial place for Sarah. By that, Abraham became the owner of a small parcel of the land of Canaan, which was all of Canaan that he ever possessed. When he died, "his sons Isaac and Ishmael buried him in the cave of Machpelah" (Genesis 25:9) beside Sarah, his first wife.

Sarah was probably buried immediately after she died because of the warm climate of that area, and because of the wild animals and many birds that were about. A body left in the heat for more than twenty-four hours would begin to decay, and if left unprotected would be devoured by the animals. To allow a body to decay or be desecrated above the ground was considered dishonorable and an insult to the

Burial in a tomb

dead person. In addition to Sarah and Abraham, eventually, Isaac, Rebekah, Leah, and Jacob (Israel) were buried in the cave of Machpelah. (see Genesis 49:31 and 50:13). In the time of Jesus, Lazarus was buried in a cave: "Jesus therefore again groaning in himself cometh to the grave. It was a cave, and a stone lay upon it" (John 11:38, KJV).

24:2-8 Manner of Swearing an Oath

He said to the chief (*eldest, KJV*) servant in his household, the one in charge of all that he had, "Put your hand under my thigh. I want you to swear by the LORD, the God of heaven and the God of earth, that you will not get a wife for my son from the daughters of the Canaanites, among whom I am living, but will go to my country and my own relatives and get a wife for my son Isaac." The servant asked him, "What if the woman is unwilling to come back with me to this land? Shall I then take your son back to the country you came from?" "Make sure that you do not take my son back there," Abraham said. "The LORD, the God of heaven, who brought me out of my father's household and my native land and who spoke to me and promised me on oath, saying, 'To your offspring I will give this land'—he will send his angel before you so that you can get a wife for my son from there. If the woman is unwilling to come back with you, then you will be released from this oath of mine. Only do not take my son back there." So the servant put his hand under the thigh of his master Abraham and swore an oath to him concerning this matter.

This strange manner of swearing an oath has been found also in the culture of the Babylonians. Abraham's eldest or chief servant was undoubtedly Eliezer, who is referred to in Genesis 15:2-3—But Abram said, "O Sovereign LORD, what can you give me since I remain childless and the one who will inherit my estate is Eliezer of Damascus?" And Abram said, "You have given me no children; so a servant [born] in my household will be my heir." In speaking of Eliezer as being part of his household, Abraham is saying to the Lord that if they remain childless, he and Sarai will adopt Eliezer as their son and heir. Archeologists have discovered writings that show it was the custom for childless, wealthy, couples to adopt their chief servant, one born in their household, and make him their heir.

The word thigh—Hebrew, *yarek*—is a euphemism; that is, a mild or indirect word that is substituted for one that is considered too harsh, blunt, or offensive. Without question, the servant's hand was placed beneath Abraham's *procreative organs* (these words are also euphemisms). Whether the placement of the hand had to do with the act of circumcision instituted by God, and thus gave a covenant solemnity to the oath, is not known. It has been said by some that it had reference to the long-range effects that the servant's mission would have

upon Abraham's descendants, or that it symbolized that even his yet unborn children would avenge any violation of the act. But neither of these explanations seem to fit Israel's request to his son Joseph to take his body out of Egypt and bury it where his fathers are buried, when the same manner of swearing an oath was used (see Genesis 47:29).

Whatever the origin and basis, the requests in both instances, and the results of the fulfilled oaths, denote that this manner of swearing an oath placed great importance and solemnity upon it.

24:3-4 BRIDE CHOSEN BY PARENTS

"I want you to swear by the LORD, the God of heaven and the God of earth, that you will not get a wife for my son from the daughters of the Canaanites, among whom I am living, but will go to my country and my own relatives and get a wife for my son Isaac."

It was the custom for the parents, especially the father, to chose whom their offspring would marry (see also Genesis 38:6). Sometimes proposals were initiated by the father of the maiden (Exodus 2:21). At times, the maiden's brothers were consulted (Genesis 24:51, 34:11), but her consent was not required. In all cases, the son or daughter was expected to agree with the choice the parents made. Once the marriage agreement had been made, the man paid a bride-price for the maiden to her father (Genesis 31:15, 34:12; Exodus 22:16, 17; 1 Samuel 18:23, 25; Ruth 4:10; Hosea 3:2).

Young men who choose wives for themselves without their parents mediation usually afflicted their parents by so doing (Genesis 26:34-35, 27:46). Occasionally, however, a son had the privilege of suggesting his personal preference to his parents, and would be allowed to marry the girl of his choice if his parents approved of her and the marriage (Judges 14:1-3). These are still the customs in many lands and some religions. Because the "daughters of the Canaanites" did not know the true God, Abraham did not want his servant to choose a wife for Isaac from among them, but from the people of his homeland. He was so set in this that he made his servant swear an oath to that effect.

Hebron, or Mamre, where Abraham lived is about nineteen miles south of Jerusalem and fifteen miles west of the Dead Sea—it is still called Hebron today and is one of the most ancient cities still in existence. The journey from there to Abraham's homeland of Mesopotamia was slightly over 500 miles. The trip would have taken almost two months there and the same time back to Hebron. Abraham's servant traveled to the city of Nahor, which was about twenty-five miles from Haran, both cities being named after Abraham's brothers, Nahor and Haran: "After Terah had lived 70 years, he became the father of Abram, Nahor and Haran" (Genesis 11:26).

24:11 Wells

He had the camels kneel down near the well outside the town; it was toward evening, the time the women go out to draw water.

Many years ago a visitor to Palestine wrote, "A modern guidebook could hardly furnish a truer picture of what occurs at the close of every day in the vicinity

At the well

of Eastern villages than this description, written in the Scriptures so many years ago." Because of the hot, dry, climate in that area, a reliable water supply was essential, both for the people and the animals. Often wells were dug to obtain water, and when a good supply of water was found, a city would develop around it. Early in the morning, women would come to the well for a supply of water for the day, and again in early evening for water for that night. Abraham's servant, who was undoubtedly

Eliezer, arrived in Nahor in early evening, and went directly to the town's well to water his camels and refresh his men and himself. He knew also, of course, that it was the time of day when the town's women customarily came to the well to get water.

24:15 PITCHERS

Before he had finished praying, Rebekah came out with her jar *[pitcher, KJV]* on her shoulder.

Pitchers and bottles

This was an earthenware water jar or pitcher with one or two handles that women used to carry water, usually on the head or shoulder. In the home, the water would be poured into a larger pot for household use—the pot would hold from 20 to 30 gallons. In John 2:6, the KJV speaks of a water pot holding two or three firkins; a firkin is about 9 gallons. If only one woman was in the home, she might have to make several trips to the well before the pot was filled—unless she had servants to get the water for her. There was an advantage, therefore, for the town to be built close to the well, but not so close that the dust stirred up in the town's streets would dirty the water. (See also the story of the Samaritan woman at the well in John 4:4-28.)

24:16 CONSTRUCTION OF WELLS

The girl was very beautiful, a virgin; no man had ever lain with her. She went down to the spring, filled her jar and came up again.

The wells were usually cut out of solid limestone rock, sometimes with steps to descend down into them, such as is indicated in the above verse. Around the well itself would be a brim or low wall so that nothing would fall into the well, including people. It would be this kind of brim that Jesus sat on: "Now Jacob's well was there. Jesus therefore, being wearied with his journey, sat thus on the well" (John 4:6, KJV). The usual method for drawing water from the well was to lower a bucket or jar into the well with a rope. Many of the brims of ancient wells that are still in existence have furrows that were worn in them by the ropes used to draw water.

24:20 WATERING ANIMALS

So she quickly emptied her jar into the trough, ran back to the well to draw more water, and drew enough for all his camels.

These troughs were near the wells for convenience in watering animals. They were made of wood or stone. Some troughs were hollowed out of a long stone block so that several animals could drink from the same trough. Sometimes smaller troughs that would accommodate only one animal were used and several of them were placed around the well. If machinery, such as wheels and pulleys, was used to draw the water and fill the troughs, it was operated by men, otherwise it was the responsibility of the women to keep water in the troughs.

If a well was out in an open area and subject to dust blown by the wind, then it was customary to cover it with a flat stone, as shown in Genesis 29:2-3: "There he [Jacob] saw a well in the field, with three flocks of sheep lying near it because the flocks were watered from that well. The stone over the mouth of the well was large. When all the flocks were gathered there, the shepherds would roll the stone away from the well's mouth and water the sheep. Then they would return the stone to its place over the mouth of the well."

24:22 EARRINGS

And it came to pass, as the camels had done drinking, that the man took a golden earring of half a shekel weight, and two bracelets for her hands of ten shekels weight of gold _(KJV)_.

The "earring" (Hebrew, _nezem_) spoken of in the KJV text is actually a nose ring, as shown in the NIV text: "When the camels had finished drinking, the man took out a gold nose ring." It is so translated in the NKJV, and in most other modern-day versions. In verse 47, Eliezer says, "I put the earring upon her face. . . ." Obviously, except for

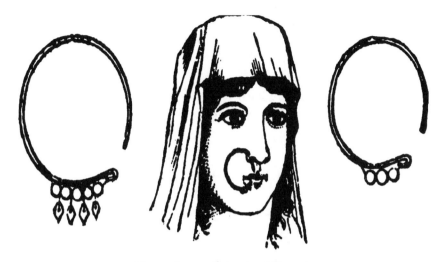

Nose-rings of Ancient Egypt

the nose, there is no place on the face to put an earring. Thus the NIV text reads, ""Then I put the ring in her nose. . . .""

In the same way, the two bracelets were arm bracelets and would not have been put on Rebekah's hands but on her arms. For this reason, the NKJV text in Genesis 24:22 says, ". . . and two bracelets for her wrists weighing ten shekels of gold." A shekel is an ancient Hebrew unit of weight equal to about half an ounce.

In verse 24:30, the KJV says, "And it came to pass, when he saw the earring and bracelets upon his sister's hands . . ." But the NIV says, "As soon as he had seen the nose ring, and the bracelets on his sister's arms . . ."

And the NKJV says, "So it came to pass, when he saw the nose ring, and the bracelets on his sister's wrists . . ."

Many of the nose rings and bracelets had inscriptions on them and were quite ornate. The larger nose rings and earrings worn by the women, and there was little difference between the two designs, would often be decorated with precious gems. So would the earrings that were sometimes worn by the men. Thus they were a handsome present to someone or a goodly offering to God (Numbers 31:50).

Pagans who wore earrings often had inscriptions on them invoking the protection of their gods, and so we find in Genesis

35:4 that when Jacob told his household to "Put away the strange gods that are among you," they surrendered to him their earrings along with their idols: "And they gave unto Jacob all the strange gods which were in their hand, and all their earrings which were in their ears." In Isaiah 3:20, the KJV translates the Hebrew word *lehashim* as earrings, but it is more properly translated amulets or charms, as it is in more modern translations, for the word means whispering or incantations.

24:53 BRIDAL PRESENTS

Then the servant brought out gold and silver jewelry and articles of clothing and gave them to Rebekah; he also gave costly gifts to her brother and to her mother.

Apparently Rebekah's father was not alive because the dowry or bride-price (see Genesis **29:18 Dowry**), was given to her brother and mother. The gifts given to Rebekah were wedding gifts, but the dowry paid to her brother and mother was to secure her financial future in case Isaac should forsake her or he should die. The dowry was actually hers, and was to kept for her by her brother and mother. If the dowry was used for other purposes, the bride had full right to protest, as Rachel and Leah did about their father: "Does he not regard us as foreigners? Not only has he sold us, but he has used up what was paid for us" (Genesis 31:15). The wedding gifts to the bride were also a token of her future husband's ability to provide for

Isaac and Rebekah

her, and his respect and desire for her. To not give gifts would be the highest of insults, just as would be the refusal to accept the gifts.

24:59 NURSE

So they sent their sister Rebekah on her way, along with her nurse and Abraham's servant and his men.

The nurse in ancient families was often the woman who breast-fed a child, and they were often nursed for up to three years. In Exodus 2:7, this is written about the baby Moses, "Then his sister asked Pharaoh's daughter, "Shall I go and get one of the Hebrew women to nurse the baby for you?" When the child was finally weaned, it was often a time of celebration. Genesis 21:8 says, "And the child grew, and was weaned: and Abraham made a great feast the same day that Isaac was weaned." Even after the child was grown, a nurse would often stay with the family as the child's tutor, counselor, helper, friend. Rebekah's nurse, Deborah, stayed until she died: "Now Deborah, Rebekah's nurse, died and was buried under the oak below

Bethel. So it was named Allon Bacuth" (Genesis 35:8).

24:64-65 COVERING THE FACE WITH A VEIL

Rebekah also looked up and saw Isaac. She got down from her camel and asked the servant, "Who is that man in the field coming to meet us?" "He is my master," the servant answered. So she took her veil and covered herself.

Although Rebekah undoubtedly covered her face as a sign of modesty and respect, in later years Hebrew woman normally did not wear veils. When Abraham's servant first met Rebekah at the well she was not wearing a veil, for he could see that "The girl was very beautiful" (Genesis 24:16). This is similar to what is said about Sarai in Genesis 12:14: "When Abram came to Egypt, the Egyptians saw that she was a very beautiful woman." Obviously Sarai was not wearing a veil. And in 1 Samuel 1:12, this is written: "As she [Hannah] kept on praying to the LORD, Eli observed her mouth." Eli could not have seen Hannah's mouth,

Veil

garments off from her, and covered her with a veil, and wrapped herself, and sat in an open place, which is by the way to Timnath; for she saw that Shelah was grown, and she was not given unto him to wife. When Judah saw her, he thought her to be an harlot; because she had covered her face."

Some say that the Hebrew word, *tzaiph*, translated veil in Genesis 24:65 and in Genesis 38:14, did not mean simply a face covering, but a large wrap, or loose flowing robe, that was worn outdoors. The upper part could be used to cover the head and face, similar to the wraps worn now by women in fundamentalist Muslim countries like Iran.

25:29-33 Birthright

Once when Jacob was cooking some stew, Esau came in from the open country, famished. He said to Jacob, "Quick, let me have some of that red stew! I'm famished!" (That is why he was also called Edom.) Jacob replied, "First sell me your birthright." "Look, I am about to die," Esau said. "What good is the birthright to

of course, if she had been wearing a veil.

At some point in Hebrew history, it became the prostitutes, or harlots, who wore veils. In Genesis 38:14-15, it tells how Judah thought his daughter-in-law Tamar was a harlot because she wore a veil: "And she [Tamar] put her widow's me?" But Jacob said, "Swear to me first." So he swore an oath to him, selling his birthright to Jacob.

The "birthright" was a special privilege accorded a firstborn. It has to do with the law of primogeniture, which is the right of the eldest child, especially the eldest son, to inherit the entire estate of one or both parents. But it was more than that, it included a number of other privileges and responsibilities. The firstborn son also inherited the leadership and priesthood of the family or tribe, and he received a double portion of the inheritance (Deuteronomy 21:17). For example, if there were only two sons, the firstborn would receive two-thirds of the inheritance, if there were three sons, he would receive three-fourths of the inheritance. It was as if the firstborn were two persons instead of one. Any portion of the firstborn's inheritance could, however, be transferred to another by God or by his father, or he could transfer it himself as Esau did for a portion of red stew.

Reuben was the firstborn of the twelve sons of Jacob, and so should have inherited the priesthood of the tribes, but God transferred that honor to his brother Levi: "And I have taken the Levites for all the firstborn of the children of Israel. And I have given the Levites as a gift to Aaron and to his sons from among the children of Israel, to do the service of the children of Israel in the tabernacle of the congregation, and to make an atonement for the children of Israel: that there be no plague among the children of Israel, when the children of Israel come nigh unto the sanctuary" (Numbers 8:18-19).

Although four other sons were born to King David before Solomon, David chose Solomon over Adonijah who was his fourth and apparently only living son born previous to Solomon. When his father was stricken and dying, Adonijah expected he would soon be king and so declared himself as such: "Then Adonijah the son of Haggith exalted himself, saying, I will be king: and he prepared him chariots and horsemen, and fifty men to run before him" (1 Kings 1:5). But David, in keeping with God's Word about Solomon and his promise to Bathsheba, made Solomon king instead of Adonijah: "Even as I sware unto thee [Bathsheba] by the LORD

God of Israel, saying, Assuredly
Solomon thy son shall reign after
me, and he shall sit upon my
throne in my stead; even so will I
certainly do this day" (1 Kings
1:30). "And Jonathan answered
and said to Adonijah, Verily our
lord king David hath made
Solomon king" (1 Kings 1:43).
The tablets of ancient Nuzi
(modern Yorgham Tepe) in
northern Iraq have provided
scholars with information
concerning legal customs of the
15th century B.C., customs with
parallels in the patriarchal
narratives. Among them was the
revelation that the birthright
could be sold or changed from
one son to another by the father.

25:34 POTTAGE

**Then Jacob gave Esau
some bread and some lentil
stew (pottage of lentiles,
KJV). He ate and drank,
and then got up and left. So
Esau despised his
birthright.**

Pottage is the Hebrew word
nazid, meaning "boiled." It's a
thick soup or stew usually made
with lentils and vegetables and
spiced with various herbs. Lentils
are small, pea-like, plants that are
still widely used for food in soup
and bread. At Gilgal, Elisha used
meal (flour) to heal a group of
prophets who had been made sick
from wild vegetable used in the
pottage: "Elisha returned to
Gilgal and there was a famine in
that region. While the company
of the prophets was meeting with
him, he said to his servant, 'Put
on the large pot and cook some
stew (pottage, KJV) for these
men.' One of them went out into
the fields to gather herbs and
found a wild vine. He gathered
some of its gourds and filled the
fold of his cloak. When he
returned, he cut them up into the
pot of stew (pottage, KJV),
though no one knew what they
were. The stew was poured out
for the men, but as they began to
eat it, they cried out, 'O man of
God, there is death in the pot!'
And they could not eat it. Elisha
said, 'Get some flour.' He put it
into the pot and said, 'Serve it to
the people to eat.' And there was
nothing harmful in the pot" (2
Kings 4:38-41).

The bread that Esau served
was most likely made of wheat,
which would have been ground
into a course meal by a mortar
and pestle or with millstones
turned by an animal or human

being (Proverbs 27:22). The meal would then be mixed with water, salt, olive oil, leaven or yeast, and then baked by one of three ways. If an iron oven was not available, the bread would be baked on heated rocks covered with ashes, or in a clay or iron pan or on a griddle. Bread baked by the latter two methods was usually about 12 inches in diameter and about half an inch thick.

"If you bring a grain offering baked in an oven, it is to consist of fine flour: cakes made without yeast and mixed with oil, or wafers made without yeast and spread with oil. If your grain offering is prepared on a griddle, it is to be made of fine flour mixed with oil, and without yeast." (Leviticus 2:4-5)

26:26-31 PEACE MEAL

Meanwhile, Abimelech had come to him from Gerar, with Ahuzzath his personal adviser and Phicol the commander of his forces. Isaac asked them, "Why have you come to me, since you were hostile to me and sent me away?" They answered, "We saw clearly that the LORD was with you; so we said, 'There ought to be a sworn agreement between us'—between us and you. Let us make a treaty with you that you will do us no harm, just as we did not molest you but always treated you well and sent you away in peace. And now you are blessed by the LORD." Isaac then made a feast for them, and they ate and drank. Early the next morning the men swore an oath to each other. Then Isaac sent them on their way, and they left him in peace.

Abimelech may have been fearful that he had made an enemy of Isaac by sending him away, and that Isaac with his larger force might attack him. So he came to Isaac's encampment to make peace with him. It was customary that when a binding agreement (covenant) of friendship, or at least peace, was made between individuals or tribes, they would eat a meal together to demonstrate or seal that friendship. This custom was probably what developed into the covenant meal that later became part of the covenant-making process.

When Laban and Jacob made a covenant (binding agreement) of peace with each other at Galeed, also called Mizpah, they ate a meal together: "He offered a sacrifice there in the hill country and invited his relatives to a meal. After they had eaten, they spent the night there" (Genesis 31:54). The Passover meal that the Lord ate with his disciples was actually a covenant meal, because His death on Calvary would bring peace between God and those who believed in Christ: "In the same way, after the supper he took the cup, saying, "This cup is the new covenant in my blood, which is poured out for you" (Luke 22:20). (See Genesis **31:44-54 Covenant Stones**.)

26:14-17 Stopping Up Wells

He *[Isaac]* had so many flocks and herds and servants that the Philistines envied him. So all the wells that his father's servants had dug in the time of his father Abraham, the Philistines stopped up, filling them with earth. Then Abimelech said to Isaac, "Move away from us; you have become too powerful for us." So Isaac moved away from there and encamped in the Valley of Gerar and settled there.

In a pastoral land, stopping up the wells of someone would prevent them from watering their flocks or herds, and so they would have to either re-dig the wells or leave the area. In this case, the Philistines were still few in number, and so they began to fill up the wells that were essential to Isaac's continued prosperity. Although stopping up someone's wells was always an act of hostility, Isaac knew that it was God who was prospering him because of the covenant He had made with his father, Abraham, and so rather than going to war over wells God had provided him, he simply moved to another land when Abimelech asked him to, knowing that God would remain faithful to the covenant and prosper him there, also. He eventually moved to Beersheba, where during the night the LORD appeared to him and said, "I am the God of your father Abraham. Do not be afraid, for I am with you; I will bless you and will increase the number of your descendants for the sake of my servant Abraham."

"your firstborn, Esau." Isaac trembled violently and said, "Who was it, then, that hunted game and brought it to me? I ate it just before you came and

Isaac blesses Jacob

27:30-38 DEATHBED BEQUEST

After Isaac finished blessing him and Jacob had scarcely left his father's presence, his brother Esau came in from hunting. He too prepared some tasty food and brought it to his father. Then he said to him, "My father, sit up and eat some of my game, so that you may give me your blessing." His father Isaac asked him, "Who are you?" "I am your son," he answered,

I blessed him—and indeed he will be blessed!" When Esau heard his father's words, he burst out with a loud and bitter cry and said to his father, "Bless me—me too, my father!" But he said, "Your brother came deceitfully and took your blessing." Esau said, "Isn't he rightly named Jacob ? He has deceived me these two times: He took my birthright, and now he's taken my blessing!" Then he asked, "Haven't you reserved any blessing for me?" Isaac answered Esau, "I have made him lord over you and have made all his relatives his servants, and I have sustained him with grain and new wine. So what can I possibly do for you, my son?" Esau said to his father, "Do you have only one blessing, my father? Bless me too, my father!" Then Esau wept aloud.

Even though Esau had bartered away his birthright and married heathen women, Isaac still favored him over Jacob: "Isaac, who had a taste for wild game, loved Esau, but Rebekah loved Jacob" (Genesis 25:28). Isaac must also have known God's Word to Rebekah: "Two nations are in your womb, and two peoples from within you will be separated; one people will be stronger than the other, and the older will serve the younger" (Genesis 25:23). God had declared that it was His will that the second-born son take the inheritance position of the first son, yet Jacob went against all of this because he favored Esau who

brought him fresh meat to eat. Deathbed bequests were legally binding, and if Isaac had blessed Esau instead of Jacob, then God's will would have been overthrown and the Messianic line would have been cut.

27:41 Days of Mourning

Esau held a grudge against Jacob because of the blessing his father had given him. He said to himself, "The days of mourning for my father are near; then I will kill my brother Jacob."

This alludes to the period of formal mourning for the dead, which usually lasted seven days: "Then they took their bones and buried them under a tamarisk tree at Jabesh, and they fasted seven days" (1 Samuel 31:13).

"When Job's three friends, Eliphaz the Temanite, Bildad the Shuhite and Zophar the Naamathite, heard about all the troubles that had come upon him [among other things the deaths of his sons and daughters], they set out from their homes and met together by agreement to go and sympathize with him and comfort him. When they saw him from a distance, they could hardly recognize him; they began to weep aloud, and they tore their robes and sprinkled dust on their heads. Then they sat on the ground with him for seven days and seven nights. No one said a word to him, because they saw how great his suffering was" (Job 2:11-13).

Jacob's ladder

28:12 "JACOB'S LADDER"

He had a dream in which he saw a stairway resting on the earth, with its top reaching to heaven, and the angels of God were ascending and descending on it.

Jacob's ladder represents the blessings of God descending from heaven. The dream assured Jacob that despite his deceit he was the corridor of the blessings of the Abrahamic covenant. Jesus later used this same description of the ladder from Jacob's dream to convey to Nathaniel and the others who were there that the blessed works of God would be done through Him and thereby prove that He was the Messiah: "Nathanael declared, 'Rabbi, you are the Son of God; you are the King of Israel.' Jesus said, 'You believe because I told you I saw you under the fig tree. You shall see greater things than that.' He then added, 'I tell you the truth, you shall see heaven open, and the angels of God ascending and descending on the Son of Man'" (John 1:49-51).

Today, "climbing Jacob's ladder" is sometimes used to denote someone who is "climbing the ladder of success," which is also an expression derived from the scriptural account of Jacob's dream.

Jacob's ladder is also used today as a name for a nautical rope or chain ladder with rigid rungs. According to the American Heritage Dictionary, Jacob's ladder is also: "Any of various plants of the genus *Polemonium*, especially *P. caeruleum*, having blue flowers and alternate, pinnately compound leaves with numerous leaflets." Certainly Jacob never dreamed that his ladder would someday be used as a name for flowering plants.

28:17-19 MEMORIAL STONES

He *[Jacob]* was afraid and said, "How awesome is this place! This is none other than the house of God; this is the gate of heaven." Early the next morning Jacob took the stone he had placed under his head and set it up as a pillar and poured oil on top of it. He called that place Bethel *[house of God]*, though the city used to be called Luz.

A memorial is something that serves as a reminder. In the Scriptures, memorials witness to God's redemptive participation in history for the salvation of His chosen people. The memorials were landmarks of an important stage in the development of the relationship between God and a person or persons, or they marked a turning point in the history of that relationship. They also helped to strengthen the faith of those involved, and often provided opportunities to teach future generations about what took place and why.

God had appeared to Jacob in a dream, and the next morning Jacob set up a memorial of stones to serve as a reminder of what had taken place that night. Thirty years later he repeated this solemn act in the same place: "And Jacob set up a pillar in the place where he talked with him, even a pillar of stone: and he poured a drink offering thereon, and he poured oil thereon" (Genesis 35:14).

God's covenant name, the LORD (Yahweh) was to be a memorial name, one that He was to be remembered by forever: "God also said to Moses, 'Say to the Israelites, "The LORD, the God of your fathers—the God of

Abraham, the God of Isaac and the God of Jacob—has sent me to you." This is my name forever, the name by which I am to be remembered from generation to generation'" (Exodus 3:15). At Mount Sinai, Moses built an altar of twelve stones as a memorial: "Moses then wrote down everything the LORD had said. He got up early the next morning and built an altar at the foot of the mountain and set up twelve stone pillars representing the twelve tribes of Israel" (Exodus 24:4). Forty years later when the Israelites finally crossed over the Jordan into the Promised Land, twelve stones were set in the Jordan as a memorial to God's provinces of passage across the Jordan and the keeping of His covenant promises to Abraham and Moses. "So Joshua called together the twelve men he had appointed from the Israelites, one from each tribe, and said to them, 'Go over before the ark of the LORD your God into the middle of the Jordan. Each of you is to take up a stone on his shoulder, according to the number of the tribes of the Israelites, to serve as a sign among you. In the future, when your children ask you, "What do these stones mean?" tell them that the flow of the

Jordan was cut off before the ark of the covenant of the LORD. When it crossed the Jordan, the waters of the Jordan were cut off. These stones are to be a memorial to the people of Israel forever.' So the Israelites did as Joshua commanded them. They took twelve stones from the middle of the Jordan, according to the number of the tribes of the Israelites, as the LORD had told Joshua; and they carried them over with them to their camp, where they put them down. Joshua set up the twelve stones that had been in the middle of the Jordan at the spot where the priests who carried the ark of the covenant had stood. And they are there to this day. Now the priests who carried the ark remained standing in the middle of the Jordan until everything the LORD had commanded Joshua was done by the people, just as Moses had directed Joshua. The people hurried over, and as soon as all of them had crossed, the ark of the LORD and the priests came to the other side while the people watched (Joshua 4:4-11).

As can be seen from the KJV translation of Joshua 4:9, two memorials were set up—one on the Promised Land side of the Jordan, and one in the middle of the river: "And Joshua set up twelve stones in the midst of Jordan, in the place where the feet of the priests which bare the ark of the covenant stood: and they are there unto this day." Some say that the twelve stones in the river are symbols of the principle of substitution—the twelve tribes about to enter the Promised Land of Canaan buried in the waters of the Jordan, Christians about to enter the promised land of Christ buried into his death (Romans 6:4). They could also have been a reminder that when God brought His people out of Egypt He buried Pharaoh's army in the Red Sea.

Many years later at Shechem, Joshua set a large stone under an oak tree as a witness against the people if they should break God's laws, for it was there that He gave them His decrees and laws: "And Joshua recorded these things in the Book of the Law of God. Then he took a large stone and set it up there under the oak near the holy place of the LORD. 'See!' he said to all the people. 'This stone will be a witness against us. It has heard all the words the LORD has said to us. It will be a witness against you if you are untrue to your God'" (Joshua 24:26-27).

When the Philistines attacked God's people and He fought against them and gave His people victory, the prophet Samuel set up a memorial to remind them of God's intervention on their behalf. "While Samuel was sacrificing the burnt offering, the Philistines drew near to engage Israel in battle. But that day the LORD thundered with loud thunder against the Philistines and threw them into such a panic that they were routed before the Israelites. The men of Israel rushed out of Mizpah and pursued the Philistines, slaughtering them along the way to a point below Beth Car. Then Samuel took a stone and set it up between Mizpah and Shen. He named it Ebenezer, saying, 'Thus far has the LORD helped us'" (1 Samuel 7:10-12). *Ebenezer* literally means stone of help. It was a memorial or testimony to God's intervention on behalf of His chosen people. As such, it symbolizes God's New Covenant grace toward those in Christ.

All the memorial stones were erected as testimonies of God's intervention into the lives of His people, even those that were erected as a witness against the people if they did not obey God's commands. So it has been suggested that Paul had such memorials and witnesses in mind when he wrote Timothy that God's household, the Church, was *the pillar and foundation of the truth*: "Although I hope to come to you soon, I am writing you these instructions so that, if I am delayed, you will know how people ought to conduct themselves in God's household, which is the church of the living God, the pillar and foundation of the truth" (1 Timothy 3:14-15).

29:1-2 Well-Stones

Then Jacob continued on his journey and came to the land of the eastern peoples. There he saw a well in the field, with three flocks of sheep lying near it because the flocks were watered from that well. The stone over the mouth of the well was large.

The stone was to protect the well from impurities, such as blowing sand and birds or other wilderness animals who might fall into the well. Some of the stones were so large and heavy that it would take a strong man or several men to remove it. This was undoubtedly the case with the stone that Jacob removed so Rachel could water the sheep. The custom of covering a well with a stone is probably what is alluded to in Job 38:30—"The waters are hid as with a stone, and the face of the deep is frozen" (KJV).

29:3 Opening Wells

When all the flocks were gathered there, the shepherds would roll the stone away from the well's mouth and water the sheep. Then they would return the stone to its place over the mouth of the well.

Because it was impossible to uncover a well without some sand and other debris falling into the water, it was customary for all the flocks to gather at the well the same time of the day, and the well to be opened only once, rather than several times a day. It also guaranteed that everyone was sharing equally from the well, and that no one was taking excessive water and carrying it back to their camp. In the hot and arid wilderness a single well often had to serve the needs of several tribes, and it was important that no tribe take more than their share of water, least they should deplete the water supply and leave none for the other tribes until the well refilled.

29:9 SHEPHERDESS

While he was still talking with them, Rachel came with her father's sheep, for she was a shepherdess.

Men were usually the shepherds, but Laban apparently had no sons at this time (see Genesis 29:16 and 31:1) and so it was the responsibility of his youngest daughter, Rachel, to shepherd his flock.

29:13 MEN KISSING

As soon as Laban heard the news about Jacob, his sister's son, he hurried to meet him. He embraced him and kissed him and brought him to his home, and there Jacob told him all these things.

This custom of embraces and kisses among men, though strange to us and often having a different connotation today,

is common in many European and Eastern countries. Jacob kissed his father: "So he went to him and kissed him. When Isaac caught the smell of his clothes, he blessed him and said, "Ah, the smell of my son is like the smell of a field that the LORD has blessed" (Genesis 27:27).

Esau embraced and kissed Jacob: "But Esau ran to meet Jacob and embraced him; he threw his arms around his neck and kissed him. And they wept" (Genesis 33:4). Joseph kissed all his brothers: "And he kissed all his brothers and wept over them. Afterward his brothers talked with him" (Genesis 45:15).

Moses kissed Jethro: "So Moses went out to meet his father-in-law and bowed down and kissed him. They greeted each other and then went into the tent" (Exodus 18:7).

David and Jonathan kissed: "After the boy had gone, David got up from the south side of the stone and bowed down before Jonathan three times, with his face to the ground. Then they kissed each other and wept together—but David wept the most" (1 Samuel 20:41). And the elders at

Miletus embraced Paul and kissed him: "They all wept as they embraced him and kissed him" (Acts 20:37).

Any television news or other broadcasts of certain European and Eastern countries will often show that this custom in still much in vogue in those countries.

29:17 WEAK EYES

Leah had weak eyes, but Rachel was lovely in form, and beautiful.

"Leah was tender eyed; but Rachel was beautiful and well favoured" (KJV). The tender eyes of Leah, as so translated in the KJV, were actually eyes that were visually weak or lacked luster—dull and unimpressive eyes. This was considered to be a great defect among those who admired sparkling eyes that were lively and flashing. That Leah's eyes were compared to Rachel's beauty obviously meant there was no beauty in them and that Leah herself was probably plain in face and form compared to her sister.

Two other patriarchs' wives are mentioned as being beautiful—Sarai (Sarah): "As he [Abram] was about to enter Egypt, he said to his wife Sarai, "I know what a beautiful woman you are" Genesis 12:11), and Rebekah: "The girl [Rebekah] was very beautiful, a virgin; no man had ever lain with her. She went down to the spring, filled her jar and came up again" (Genesis 24:16).

29:18-19 MARRYING RELATIVES

Jacob was in love with Rachel and said, "I'll work for you seven years in return for your younger daughter Rachel." Laban said, "It's better that I give her to you than to some other man. Stay here with me."

In those days of barbarity it was preferable to give a daughter in marriage to those within your own tribe, customs, or blood line, which normally meant a near relative. This was true also of obtaining a wife. Thus Abraham told his servant: I want you to swear by the LORD, the God of heaven and the God of earth, that you will not get a wife for my son from the daughters of the Canaanites, among whom I am living, but will go to my country and my own relatives and get a wife for my son Isaac." (Genesis 24:3-4). The Canaanites were barbaric idol worshippers, and Abraham wanted no wife for his son from among them.

Esau married two women from the warlike Hittites, and not women from his own tribe, and "They were a source of grief to Isaac and Rebekah" (Genesis 26:35). It has been suggested by some that the Hittites were a people with yellow skins, receding foreheads, oblique eyes, and protruding upper jaws. If this was true of Esau's wives, then it may have more than the fact that they were Hittites that grieved his parents.

29:18 Dowry

Jacob was in love with Rachel and said, "I'll work for you seven years in return for your younger daughter Rachel."

Usually the father of a bride-to-be would set a price for her to compensate him for the cost of raising her and for the loss of her services, which the hopeful bridegroom would have to pay if he wanted to marry her. If the bridegroom did not have the means to give a dowry or bride-price, then he could perform some kind of service in its place, such as Jacob did for Rachel—although he got Leah instead (Genesis 29:15-30), and as Caleb required for marriage to his daughter Acsah (Joshua 15:16-17).

In a similar way, Saul offered his daughter in marriage to any man who killed Goliath: "Now the Israelites had been saying, 'Do you see how this man keeps coming out? He comes out to defy Israel. The king will give great wealth to the man who kills him. He will also give him his daughter in marriage and will exempt his father's family from taxes in Israel'" (1 Samuel 17:25). So if a young man wanted to marry a certain girl, or become part of an important family through marriage, and did not have the financial means to pay an adequate dowry, he could often find a way to perform a service of some type in place of the dowry.

If the dowry is paid before the official marriage ceremony, the marriage is still considered to be a legal fact. Many ancient Eastern texts attest to this. Once Abraham's servant had paid the dowry for Rebekah, she and Isaac were as much married as when she arrived in Hebron several weeks later. The act of paying the dowry, Rebekah leaving her father's home and going to Hebron to Isaac, and the consummation of the marriage, were apparently sufficient to seal the marriage, for there is no indication of a wedding ceremony being performed at any time. The Scripture simply states: "And Isaac brought her into his mother Sarah's tent, and took Rebekah, and she became his wife; and he loved her: and Isaac was comforted after his mother's death" (Genesis 24:67, KJV).

It was also required in God's laws that if a man seduced a virgin who was not pledged to be married, he must pay the father the bride-price and marry the girl if the father agreed. This law is recorded in Exodus 22:16-17: "If a man seduces a virgin who is not pledged to be married and sleeps with her, he must pay the bride-price [KJV, endow her], and she shall be his wife. If her father absolutely refuses to give her to him, he must still pay the bride-price [KJV, dowry] for virgins."

The centuries-old customs concerning the dowry or bride-price have changed, however, since biblical times. In countries today where a dowry is customarily given, it is the parents of the bride-to-be who must pay a dowry to the potential bridegroom. That is now the dictionary definition of dowry: "Money or property brought by a bride to her husband at marriage." This custom is often abused by the potential bridegroom in countries where women are considered to be nothing more than chattel—a slave or piece of personal property to use as they wish—and is a great burden on poor families.

So much so that in countries like India it's considered a great misfortune when a daughter is born to a poor family, for she will not bring money to them when she marries; instead, they will have to pay money out for her. At the same time, because the "men consider them lower than the shoes they wear," the new husband, who most often is chosen by the parents and not known to the bride until they marry, may do to her whatever he wishes without fear of consequences. As of this time,

1997, more than 5,000 women are killed every year in India because their in-laws consider their dowries inadequate. Only a tiny percentage of the killers are ever punished, because hundreds of thousands of cases in which women have been beaten, tortured, and killed await trial in courts.

Only a few year's ago in Firozpur Namak, India, a young bride was burned to death because of her poor dowry. Although in the past, victim's families have been reluctant to seek justice for fear of having what is considered their shame publicized, the woman's family sought justice from the council of village elders—that ancient system of village courts that still remains strong in India. The government's legal system that was borrowed from British colonialism has little authority in the tradition-bound villages. The verdict of the council of elders was that the victim's husband must return the dowry and pay her family the money they spent on the wedding. Life for him and those who assisted him in burning his wife went on as usual.

See also Genesis **24:53 Bridal Presents**.

29:20-22 MARRIAGE FEAST

So Jacob served seven years to get Rachel, but they seemed like only a few days to him because of his love for her. Then Jacob said to Laban, "Give me my wife. My time is completed, and I want to lie with her." So Laban brought together all the people of the place and gave a feast.

The usual duration of a wedding feast was a week. Thus, "Finish this daughter's bridal week" in Genesis 29:27 meant to complete the week of festivities for the bride and groom. This was also the duration of Samson's marriage feast: "'Let me tell you a riddle,' Samson said to them. 'If you can give me the answer within the seven days of the feast, I will give you thirty linen garments and thirty sets of clothes'" (Judges 14:12).

29:26 OLDEST FIRST

Laban replied, "It is not our custom here to give the younger daughter in marriage before the older one.

The deceiver Jacob had asked for the younger Rachel's hand, but was deceived by Laban and tricked into marrying Leah. Thus the ancient Near Eastern tradition of the older daughter marrying first was preserved. This custom is still adhered to in many countries, and when a younger daughter has an opportunity to marry, everything is done to get the older daughter married first. Even in countries where this custom is not observed, there is still somewhat of a social stigmatism attached to a woman whose younger sisters all marry before she does. Undoubtedly a carry-over from the ancient custom.

29:32 Significance of Names

Leah became pregnant and gave birth to a son. She named him Reuben, for she said, "It is because the LORD has seen my misery. Surely my husband will love me now."

Rueben means *look* or *see, a son*. When Leah's next son was born she named him Simeon, which means *hearing*, "Because the LORD heard that I am not loved, he gave me this one too" (Genesis 29:33). When her third son was born she named him Levi, which means *attachment*, saying, ""Now at last my husband will become attached to me, because I have borne him three sons" (Genesis 29:34). And when her fourth son was born, she said, "This time I will praise the LORD." So she named him Judah" (Genesis 29:35), which means *praise*. It is from the royal line of Judah that King David and Jesus were born (see Matthew 1:1-16).

The scriptural custom of naming a child came from the ancient world's belief that a name expressed the basic character of the person. As in Leah's case, the name sometimes expressed what they believed was the purpose or reason for the birth of the child. This often involved what they felt was their relationship to God, or God's intervention into their lives through the child. Sometimes the child's name expressed what they hoped was the future of the child.

When Eve gave birth to her first child, she said, "With the help of the LORD I have brought forth a man" (Genesis 4:1) and she named him Cain, which means *acquisition* or *possession* or sounds in the Hebrew much like the verb *I acquired.* Possibly Eve believed that Cain was the fulfillment of the LORD's statement about the seed that would come from her.

Later, when her second son was born, she named him Abel, which means *breath, vapor,* or *vanity,* and seems to relate to shortness of life. Some suggest that Cain and Abel may have been twins, because in the Hebrew, Genesis 4:2 literally translates: "and she continued to bear his brother Abel."

When Jesus saw Simon, he declared, "Thou art Simon the son of Jona: thou shalt be called Cephas, which is by interpretation, A stone" (John 1:42, KJV). Cephas is an Aramaic name corresponding to the Greek *Petros,* which means "a mass of rock detached from the living rock," or "a piece of the rock." The name Cephas doesn't occur again in the gospels, although Paul used it three times in his first letter to the Corinthians. The name Peter gradually replaced the old name Simon, yet Jesus always used the name Simon when addressing him (see Matthew 17:25; Mark 14:37; Luke 22:31-32).

Naming a child for significant reasons dates back to ancient superstitions from many lands. Examples can easily be found in the history of the North American Indians. To what degree it was superstition or divine influence in the naming of children in the Bible, no one can tell, except in those instances that the Scriptures clearly tell us that God directed the naming of the child. Such as in the naming of Jesus and John the Baptist: "You will be with child and give birth to a son, and you are to give him the name Jesus" (Luke 1:31). "But the angel said to him: 'Do not be afraid, Zechariah; your prayer has been heard. Your wife Elizabeth will bear you a son, and you are to give him the name John'" (Luke 1:13).

31:19 IMAGES

And Laban went to shear his sheep: and Rachel had stolen the images that were her father's.

These "images" (Hebrew: *teraphim*) appear to have been figurines, rude representations of the human form, or even statuettes of deceased ancestors. Most often, however, they were of female deities. They were usually made of wood but sometimes of silver: "So he returned the silver to his mother, and she took two hundred shekels of silver and gave them to a silversmith, who made them into the image and the idol. And they were put in Micah's house" (Judges 17:4). Whatever they were, in this particular case they could not have been very large or Rachel would not have been able to hide them so easily.

Teraphim

Those who kept idols believed they were responsible for human happiness when worshiped, and human misery when ignored. As such they were worshiped as gods and often consulted for advice: "For the king of Babylon will stop at the fork in the road, at the junction of the two roads, to seek an omen: He will cast lots with arrows, he will consult his idols, he will examine the liver" (Ezekiel 21:21). (See also Zechariah 10:2.)

The significance of the images to Rachel and her family isn't clear. Several suggestions have been given as to why Rachel took them. Some Jewish writers believe that the teraphim were supposed, on consultation, to be able to give any information desired, and that Rachel was afraid that Laban would learn from them what route Jacob and his family had taken. If she believed that, Rachel may have wanted them for purposes of divination. It's also possible that the images were made of silver and so were valuable if sold. And then there is the possibility that they were gods of fertility and Rachel took them for that reason.

Whatever the reasons, Jacob, who was more knowledgeable in the ways of God than his wives or Laban, later removed them from his household: "So Jacob said to his household and to all who were with him, 'Get rid of the foreign gods you have with you, and purify yourselves and change your clothes. Then come, let us go up to Bethel, where I will build an altar to God, who answered me in the day of my distress and who has been with me wherever I have gone.' So they gave Jacob all the foreign gods they had and the rings in their ears, and Jacob buried them under the oak at Shechem" (Genesis 35:2-4).

31:27 TABRET AND HARP

Wherefore didst thou flee away secretly, and steal away from me; and didst not tell me, that I might have sent thee away with mirth, and with songs, with tabret, and with harp?

The Hebrew word *toph*, here and in other places translated "tabret," and in a number of verses translated "timbrel," represents a very ancient musical instrument of percussion. There are three varieties depicted on Egyptian monuments: one circular, another square or oblong, and a third consisting of

two squares separated by a bar. Parchment was stretched over one of these frames, and small bells or pieces of tinkling brass were inserted in the rim. The toph was generally played by women, used on festive occasions of great joy such as victory processions (1 Samuel 18:6), the procession of the ark to Jerusalem (2 Samuel 6:5), and times of drinking and merrymaking (Isaiah 5:12), with the music often accompanied by dancing. Our modern tambourines are derived from the ancient toph.

The Hebrew word *kinnor*, which frequently appears in the

Babylonian harp

Old Testament and is translated "harp" has given rise to considerable discussion. It was invented by Jubal, and was undoubtedly the earliest musical instrument made by anyone. Some believe the word *kinnor* denotes the whole class of stringed instruments. It was the national musical instrument of the Hebrews and was used as an accompaniment to joyful songs and songs of praise to God (see 1 Samuel 16:23; 2 Chronicles 20:28; Psalms 33:2, 137:2). What the instrument looked like is uncertain, which probably means that it had a number of different shapes, depending on the type of wood available and the sound the instrument maker wanted. Different writers have represented it shaped like the lyre, a triangular shape, or shaped like the modern guitar or harp. There is equal variety of opinion as to the number of strings: 7, 10, 24, and 47 have been expressed. It has also been asserted by some that it was played by means of a plectrum, like that sometimes used to play a guitar, while others say the ancient harp was played by hand.

These conflicting statements are easily harmonized if we suppose that the shape varied at different times, or the word *kinnor* was the generic term for all lyre-type instruments. There is also the probability that the number of strings varied at different periods or with the size of the instrument, that the instruments were of different sizes, and that they were sometimes played with a plectrum and sometimes by hand. Supposing allows us to harmonize all kinds of things.

31:44-54 COVENANT STONES

Come now, let's make a covenant, you and I, and let it serve as a witness between us." So Jacob took a stone and set it up as a pillar. He said to his relatives, "Gather some stones." So they took stones and piled them in a heap, and they ate there by the heap. Laban called it Jegar Sahadutha *[Aramaic, heap of witnesses]*, and Jacob called it Galeed. Laban said, "This heap is a witness between you and me today." That is why it was called Galeed *[Hebrew, heap of witness]*. It was also called

Mizpah *[Hebrew, watchtower]*, because he said, "May the LORD keep watch between you and me when we are away from each other. Laban also said to Jacob, "Here is this heap, and here is this pillar I have set up between you and me. This heap is a witness, and this pillar is a witness, that I will not go past this heap to your side to harm you and that you will not go past this heap and pillar to my side to harm me. May the God of Abraham and the God of Nahor, the God of their father, judge between us." So Jacob took an oath in the name of the Fear of his father Isaac. He offered a sacrifice there in the hill country and invited his relatives to a meal.

Jacob and Laban made a covenant and set up stones not only as a witness, or reminder, of the covenant but also as a borderline—one that neither one of them was to cross for the purpose of harming the other. The use of stones as a witness, or a reminder to those who made the covenant, is mentioned several times in the Scriptures, also the use of stones as memorials (see Genesis **28:17-19 Memorial Stones**).

In the making of a covenant, such as that between Jacob and Laban, several other things were often done, especially if it was a blood covenant.

After agreeing to make the covenant, the two involved would detail the conditions of the covenant and tell what would happen to the other person if they broke the covenant. If it was a covenant in which they were binding themselves together as partners, they would also list what the other would receive from the covenant. These were called the "blessings and cursings." You can see an example of these in Deuteronomy 28 when God made covenant with His people concerning His laws.

Each party would then cut himself somewhere on his hand where the cut would be visible, often on the fat part of the thumb. He would then rub fresh ashes into the cut so that it would form a dark scar that could easily be seen. This was the mark of the covenant, and showed that each person had a covenant partner somewhere.

The modern wedding ring is derived from this custom.

To demonstrate that what each partner had was now available to the other partner whenever needed, they would then exchange some article of clothing. After that they would exchange weapons of some type to demonstrate that each would come to the other's aid whenever they were being attacked by an enemy and needed help. An enemy of one was now the enemy of the other. Thus Christ said to Saul, "Saul, Saul, why do you persecute me?" when Saul was actually persecuting Christians (Acts 9:4).

At the end of all they did, they would then have a meal together to demonstrate their friendship (see Peace Meal), and take into themselves what the other had provided, for it was customary for each to provide something for the covenant meal. The covenant meal was the final binding and demonstration of the newly made covenant. It was a covenant meal that the Lord and His disciples ate together in the upper room. It started as an Old Testament Passover meal, and was changed by the Lord into a New Testament covenant meal: And he took bread, gave thanks and broke it, and gave it to them, saying, "This is my body given for you; do this in remembrance of me." In the same way, after the supper he took the cup, saying, "This cup is the new covenant in my blood, which is poured out for you. (Luke 22:19-20)

33:10 Giving Gifts

"No, please!" said Jacob. "If I have found favor in your eyes, accept this gift from me. For to see your face is like seeing the face of God, now that you have received me favorably.

In biblical days it was customary to give gifts of all kinds for a myriad of reasons: to win a bride, to pay a dowry, to bind a friendship, to appease an enemy, to feed someone hungry, to express love, and many more. In many countries today gift giving is still a common way of life.

Not many years ago in this country it was the same. Not only were gifts given at expected occasions, like birthdays, anniversaries, Christmas, etc., but suitors gave gifts to the girls they were courting, husbands brought gifts home to their wives—without ulterior motives, invited guests brought gifts to their hostess. To not give a gift displayed stinginess or thoughtlessness, and to refuse a gift displayed enmity. Thus Jacob was particularly anxious that Esau accept his gift.

Gift giving is an excellent and useful custom, for Proverbs 18:16 says, "A gift opens the way for the giver and ushers him into the presence of the great." (See also Genesis 43:11; Judges 3:18; 1 Samuel 9:7, 10:27; 2 Samuel 17:27-29; 1 Kings 10:2, 14:3; 2 Kings 5:5, 15, 8:9; 2 Chronicles 9:24; Psalms 72:10, 76:11; Matthew 2:11.)

35:14 Offerings

And Jacob set up a pillar in the place where he talked with him, even a pillar of stone: and he poured a drink offering thereon, and he poured oil thereon.

From the beginning God put into the awareness of His people that they were to offer to Him in worship something that was part of themselves, something that they had produced with their own labor or purchased with the money they had earned by their labor. Whatever they offered to Him, it was never to be second-best (Malachi 1:7-8), nor was it be something without cost or concern—convenient and easy to give. The giving of the work of their hands and minds to God in worship would represent the giving of themselves to Him, and so the giving must always be sacrificial, even as the manner in which they conducted their lives, in both the Old and New Testament, must be sacrificial: "Therefore, I urge you, brothers, in view of God's mercy, to offer your bodies as living sacrifices, holy and pleasing to God—this is your spiritual act of worship" (Romans 12:1). If it was easy and convenient to give a hin (about five liters) of wine, than two should be given. Only when the giving becomes sacrificial does it truly become an offering of worship.

Throughout the Old Testament, you see God's people giving Him an offering of whatever they had when they wanted to worship Him by sacrificing, or when the law required them to sacrifice. Wine, animals, grain flour, olive oil, gold, jewelry, cloth—whatever they had that they could give, or the products of their labor that God required for sacrifice, or what was needed for God's work: "With the first lamb offer a tenth of an ephah of fine flour mixed with a quarter of a hin of oil from pressed olives, and a quarter of a hin of wine as a drink offering" (Exodus 29:40).

"Then the whole Israelite community withdrew from Moses' presence, and everyone who was willing and whose heart moved him came and brought an offering to the LORD for the work on the Tent of Meeting, for all its service, and for the sacred garments. All who were willing, men and women alike, came and brought gold jewelry of all kinds: brooches, earrings, rings and ornaments. They all presented their gold as a wave offering to the LORD. Everyone who had blue, purple or scarlet yarn or fine linen, or goat hair, ram skins dyed red or hides of sea cows brought them. Those presenting an offering of silver or bronze brought it as an offering to the LORD, and everyone who had acacia wood for any part of the work brought it. Every skilled woman spun with her hands and brought what she had spun—blue, purple or scarlet yarn or fine linen. And all the women who were willing and had the skill spun the goat hair. The leaders brought onyx stones and other gems to be mounted on the ephod and breastplate. They also brought spices and olive oil for the light and for the anointing oil and for the fragrant incense. All the Israelite men and women who were willing brought to the LORD freewill offerings for all the work the LORD through Moses had commanded them to do" (Exodus 35:20-29).

The people of willing hearts brought so many offerings to Moses for the building of God's tabernacle in the wilderness that the artisans came to Moses and said: "'The people are bringing more than enough for doing the work the LORD commanded to be done.' Then Moses gave an order and they sent this word throughout the camp: 'No man or woman is to make anything else as an offering for the sanctuary.' And so the people were restrained from bringing more, because what they already had was more than enough to do all the work" (Exodus 36:5-7).

God's people gave of themselves, more than enough for God's work.

33:19 MONEY

For a hundred pieces of silver *[money, KJV]*, he bought from the sons of Hamor, the father of Shechem, the plot of ground where he pitched his tent.

In ancient times, pieces of gold and silver of various shapes and weights were widely used in trade, and were usually exchanged for other goods by weight. Because there was no uniformity to the size or quality of the metal, the weight and purity of it had to be tested every time it was exchanged. It wasn't until about 600 B.C. that the Lydians in Asia Minor thought of shaping electrum, which is a natural alloy of gold and silver, into bean-shaped lumps of fixed weight and purity and stamping them with official symbols.

The idea quickly caught on with everyone, and within 50 years the practice of striking coins was established in all the important trading centers throughout the known world. National philosophies often showed up in the official symbols on the coins: Greek coins were stamped with images of gods or goddesses, while Roman Empire coins, from about 100 B.C. to A.D. 500, were stamped with images of emperors.

37:3 "COAT OF MANY COLORS"

Now Israel loved Joseph more than any of his other sons, because he had been born to him in his old age; and he made a richly ornamented robe *(a coat of many colors, KJV)* for him.

The "coat of many colors" that Jacob made Joseph was a varicolored tunic, which was probably a long-sleeved, ornamented, coat. Wool was the most commonly used raw material, and by the time of Joseph wool spinning was advanced enough so that it wasn't necessary to describe it in the Scriptures—its instruments and process were common knowledge. Natural wool tones range from white to yellow to gray, and so lend themselves to a multiple of

Cisterns under Solomon's temple

37:24 CISTERNS

So when Joseph came to his brothers, they stripped him of his robe—the richly ornamented robe he was wearing—and they took him and threw him into the cistern. Now the cistern was empty; there was no water in it.

color possibilities using natural dyes.

For whatever reason, it appears that the coats of Joseph's brothers had not been colored and had probably been left in their natural wool colors, which may have been a common practice with work coats. Thus Joseph's multicolored coat would have been a strong contrast to their plain coats. Whatever the difference in the appearance of their coats, the special appearance of Joseph's coat indicated a favored position in his father's eyes, and that caused strong jealousy and resentment in his brothers.

Today, the expression a "coat of many colors" is sometimes used to describe a person whose personality and character change to fit the occasion.

Cistern is the translation of the Hebrew word *bor*, which means hole, pit, or more often well. The difference between cistern and well is not always clear in the Scriptures. *Bor* denotes a receptacle of some type that holds water that is conveyed to it, normally by the surrounding area being slanted down toward it, such as for a man-made lake. The Hebrew word *beer* denotes a place where water rises or springs up on the spot—a fountain or spring (see Jeremiah 2:13). Cisterns are often mentioned in the Scriptures. The lack of natural springs in Palestine made it necessary to collect rainwater in cisterns, and the number of them that dot Palestine are clear evidence of the efforts the ancient people made to supplement the natural water supply. The cisterns were usually pear-shaped reservoirs, having relatively small openings at the top and larger hollowed-out areas below to hold the water—although some of them were simply round or square holes in the ground.

Many of the earliest cisterns were hollowed out of limestone, and the porous rock allowed much of the water to escape. Where limestone was not available, a hole was sometimes dug in the ground and large rocks were then used to form a floor and wall. Naturally, even more water escaped from this type of construction. Somewhere after 1300 B.C., plaster, probably made of lime, was used to cover the floor and wall of both types of cisterns, and considerably less water was lost. To keep out dust and debris, the openings of some cisterns were constructed so they could be covered with a stone and still allow water to run into the cistern when it rained. Some cisterns had crude filters on them to trap the debris.

Sometimes dry cisterns were used for other purposes than holding water. Joseph's jealous brothers threw him into one: "'Come now, let's kill him and throw him into one of these cisterns and say that a ferocious animal devoured him. Then we'll see what comes of his dreams.' When Reuben heard this, he tried to rescue him from their hands. 'Let's not take his life,' he said. 'Don't shed any blood. Throw him into this cistern here in the desert, but don't lay a hand on him.' Reuben said this to rescue him from them and take him back to his father. So when Joseph came to his brothers, they stripped him of his robe—the richly ornamented robe he was wearing—and they took him and threw him into the cistern. Now the cistern was empty; there was no water in it" (Genesis 37:20-24).

The prophet Jeremiah was also imprisoned by Malchiah (Malkijah, NIV) King Zedekiah's son, in a cistern that had been dug in the courtyard of a prison: "So they took Jeremiah and put him into the cistern of Malkijah, the king's son, which was in the courtyard of the guard [prison, KJV]. They lowered Jeremiah by ropes into the cistern; it had no water in it, only mud, and Jeremiah sank down into the mud" (Jeremiah 38:6). The word that is translated *dungeon* in the

KJV, "And in the dungeon there was no water, but mire: so Jeremiah sunk in the mire," is the Hebrew word *boor*, which in other places is translated pit or cistern.

In Jeremiah 2:13, God speaks of His people as having dug their own cisterns, broken cisterns. This is a picture of cisterns that have been plastered on the inside, and the plaster has cracked and water is leaking out: "My people have committed two sins: They have forsaken me, the spring of living water, and have dug their own cisterns, broken cisterns that cannot hold water."

In addition to holding water, cisterns appear to have also been a convenient place to deposit bodies: "When they went into the city, Ishmael son of Nethaniah and the men who were with him slaughtered them and threw them into a cistern" (Jeremiah 41:7). The cistern was one that stored the city's water in case of an attack, so Ishmael effectively ruined it: "Now the cistern where he threw all the bodies of the men he had killed along with Gedaliah was the one King Asa had made as part of his defense against Baasha king of Israel.

Ishmael son of Nethaniah filled it with the dead" (Jeremiah 41:9). Throwing the bodies into the city's cistern may also have been a way of ruining that cistern for any future use.

37:25 CARAVAN

As they sat down to eat their meal, they looked up and saw a caravan of Ishmaelites coming from Gilead. Their camels were loaded with spices, balm and myrrh, and they were on their way to take them down to Egypt.

A caravan consists of a company of travelers journeying together, as across a desert or through hostile territory. The caravan of Ishmaelites were merchants on their way to Egypt with products that were used for incense and perfume, to flavor food or make tea, and possibly for healing and embalming. They probably traveled together more for protection than for any other reasons. Deserts bandits would hesitate to attack a large caravan because of its combined strength, but would readily attack the smaller and weaker ones.

Many years ago, before other means of transporting goods across the deserts developed, a visitor to Palestine wrote a description of a caravan that was journeying to Mecca on a religious pilgrimage. (Mecca is a city of modern Saudi Arabia near the coast of the Red Sea. The birthplace of Mohammed, it is the most sacred city of Islam and a pilgrimage site for all devout believers of that religion.) This caravan was undoubtedly larger than the Ishmaelites caravan, yet it may have been set up on a similar plan. "They travel four camels abreast, which are all tied one after the other, like as in teams. The whole body is called a caravan, which is divided into several cottors, or companies, each of which has its name, and consists, it may be, of several thousand camels; and they move, one cottor after another, like distinct troops."

The writer also said that the camels had bells about their necks, and many of the camel drivers sang as they traveled. Altogether it made a pleasant musical sound. Though there was great confusion when the caravan started out, he said, the various cottors soon settled into an orderly condition. It was

undoubtedly a caravan that Joseph and Mary were traveling with when they missed their active Son: "Thinking he was in their company, they traveled on for a day. Then they began looking for him among their relatives and friends" (Luke 2:44). Considering the size of some caravans, and that often groups of relatives and friends traveled together for safety, it's easy to see how they could have thought their 12-year-old Son was with others in the caravan.

37:34 Rending Garments and Wearing Sackcloth

Then Jacob tore *(rent, KJV)* **his clothes, put on sackcloth and mourned for his son many days.**

Tearing the clothes is a symbol of the inward anguish the mourner is feeling, a violent expression of emotional pain, an outward sign to others that the person is suffering great inner turmoil. In moments of great anguish, the grief-stricken person might tear whatever clothing they were wearing and put ashes on their head, such as Tamar did about being raped by her brother Amnon: "Tamar put ashes on her head and tore the ornamented robe she was wearing. She put her hand on her head and went away, weeping aloud as she went" (2 Samuel 13:19). Her actions were those of a widow mourning for her lost husband.

Sackcloth was a rough cloth made of camel's hair, goat hair, hemp, cotton, or flax. Revelation 6:12 refers to sackcloth made of goat's hair: "I watched as he opened the sixth seal. There was a great earthquake. The sun turned black like sackcloth made of goat hair." Garments made of sackcloth, which was often loosely woven like burlap, were worn as a sign of mourning or penitence. The garments were sometimes worn in place of regular clothing, or were loose-fitting sacks put over the shoulders, or simply a loin cloth. Sometimes the person put the sackcloth on an ash heap and laid upon both instead of wearing the cloth as shown in Isaiah 58:5. In Nineveh, the king commanded that both "man and beast be covered with sackcloth" (Jonah 3:8) as a sign of national repentance. See also 2 Samuel 3:31, 1 Kings 21:27, 2 Kings 19:1, Esther 4:1-2, Job 16:15, and Psalm 30:11 for other references to sackcloth. Those descended from Isaac and from Ishmael are people of passionate emotions, and even today they often tear their clothing to express their great anguish or grief.

37:36 CAPTAIN OF THE GUARD

Meanwhile, the Midianites sold Joseph in Egypt to Potiphar, one of Pharaoh's officials, the captain of the guard.

The Hebrew word *sar* is sometimes rendered chief (Genesis 40:2, 41:9), prince (Daniel 1:7, KJV), ruler or governor (Judges 9:30, 1 Kings 22:26). This same Hebrew word denotes a military leader, official, commander, or captain (Exodus 18:21; Deuteronomy; 1:15; 1 Samuel 18:13, 1 Samuel 22:2, 2 Samuel 23:19; 2 Kings 1:9), the "captain of the body-guard" or "the captain of the guard" (Genesis 39:1, 41:10), or, as sometimes shown in marginal references, it may be rendered "chief of the executioners." The "captain of the guard" or "captain of the body-guard," both titles meaning the same thing, was responsible for the security of the king's prisoners and for executing their sentences upon them. He was also the official guardian of the person, or body, of the king—the chief of the king's bodyguard.

The officers of the king's bodyguard often performed the duty of executioners. In Jeremiah 39:13 it's recorded that in Babylon, Nebuzaradan held the position of captain or commander of the guard, and Daniel 2:14 tells us that Arioch held a similar position and acted as executioner: "When Arioch, the commander of the king's guard, had gone out to put to death the wise men of Babylon, Daniel spoke to him with wisdom and tact."

39:20 Prison

Joseph's master took him and put him in prison, the place where the king's prisoners were confined.

This is the first time in the Scriptures where we read of a prison. The Hebrew word *sohar* that is here translated

In prison

prison more precisely means a round tower or fortress. The one in which Joseph was imprisoned appears to have been a part of Potiphar's house—probably a part of the palace, isolated from the residential area, that had been specially constructed to confine the king's prisoners.

A similar prison in the king's residence is mentioned in Jeremiah 32:2—"The army of the king of Babylon was then besieging Jerusalem, and Jeremiah the prophet was confined in the courtyard of the guard in the royal palace of Judah." At other times, the prison was in the residence of one of the king's officials: "They were angry with Jeremiah and had him beaten and imprisoned in the house of Jonathan the secretary, which they had made into a prison" (Jeremiah 37:15).

40:11 EGYPTIAN USE OF WINE

Pharaoh's cup was in my hand, and I took the grapes, squeezed them into Pharaoh's cup and put the cup in his hand.

Based on this verse, it has been suggested by some that the ancient Egyptians did not drink fermented wine, or that at least the Pharaoh's, who were believed to be gods, did not. It was evidently a part of the duty of Pharaoh's butler to press the grapes into the cup that the king might drink, perhaps that way to assure that the juice had not been poisoned—but it doesn't follow that because of this, no fermented wine was drunk in Egypt. There are old monuments that have representations of different articles employed in wine making, winepresses in operation, and what appears to be inebriated men and women.

Wine was used for sacramental purposes in Egypt no later than the start of about 3000 B.C., but archaeological evidence indicates that it wasn't produced there for general consumption until about 1000 B.C. Since the name Pharaoh was not applied to the king until the beginning of the 18th Dynasty (1570-1293 B.C.), it's doubtful if there would have been any fermented wine for about 600 years after that.

40:20-22 BIRTHDAY FEAST

Now the third day was Pharaoh's birthday, and he gave a feast for all his officials. He lifted up the heads of the chief cupbearer and the chief baker in the presence of his officials: He restored the chief cupbearer to his position, so that he once

again put the cup into Pharaoh's hand, but he hanged the chief baker, just as Joseph had said to them in his interpretation.

The Eastern kings celebrated their birthdays by holding feasts and granting pardons to offenders. This was a common practice in many lands that had kings. On the occasion referred to in the text, Pharaoh availed himself of this custom to pardon the chief butler, but for reasons untold he refused to grant clemency to the chief baker.

41:8 EGYPTIAN MAGICIANS

In the morning his mind was troubled, so he sent for all the magicians and wise men of Egypt. Pharaoh told them his dreams, but no one could interpret them for him.

The magicians of Egypt are frequently referred to in the history of the Exodus. Magic was an inherent part of the ancient Egyptian religion, and entered largely into their daily life. These particular magicians (Hebrew, *chartom*), were an order of Egyptian priests who supposedly understood and could interpret sacred writings. They cultivated a knowledge of art and science, interpreted dreams, and practiced divination and sorcery: "Then Pharaoh also called for the wise men and the sorcerers, and they also, the magicians of Egypt, did the same with their secret arts. For each one threw down his staff and they turned into serpents" (Exodus 7:11-12).

The magicians were men of great influence in Egypt, and were much esteemed and highly honored. They were sought out for direction and assistance on any subjects that required knowledge far out of the ordinary. Thus Pharaoh sent for them when he desired an interpretation of his strange dreams. Moses encountered similar men many years later, and even more years later there were others like them in Babylon: "Then the king gave orders to call in the magicians, the conjurers, the sorcerers and the Chaldeans, to tell the king his dreams. So they came in and stood before the king" (Daniel 2:2). See also Daniel 1:20.

41:14 SHAVING AMONG THE EGYPTIANS

So Pharaoh sent for Joseph, and he was quickly brought from the dungeon. When he had shaved and changed his clothes, he came before Pharaoh.

Egyptians were known for their careful attention to personal cleanliness, and contrary to the customs of the Hebrews and others, the Egyptians only allowed a beard and hair to grow as a sign of mourning, which was the reverse of the custom of the Hebrews, who shaved both as a sign of mourning. "They have gone up to the temple and to Dibon, even to the high places to weep. Moab wails over Nebo and Medeba;

Everyone's head is bald and every beard is cut off" (Isaiah 5:2). The Egyptians normal custom was to shave both for reasons of cleanliness. Strangely, however, while so careful to shave their beards, the Egyptians apparently wore false beards at times, for we have a number of pictures and statues of Pharaohs showing them with beards, which we now know were fake.

41:1 NILE RIVER

When two full years had passed, Pharaoh had a dream: He was standing by the Nile.

The Nile is the longest river it in the world and flows 4,132 miles (6,650 kilometers) north through eastern Africa from its remotest head stream, the Ruvyironza River, in present-day Burundi to a delta and the mouth of the river at the Mediterranean Sea in northeast Egypt. For thousands of years the source of the Nile was unknown, and was

Shaving among ancient Egyptians

considered to be one of the last great mysteries on earth that was still unsolved. Then in the 1850s, a party of Europeans discovered Lake Victoria and its outflow. Later explorers traced the Nile's ultimate source to the Ruvyironza River, which is one of the upper branches of the Kagera River in modern Tanzania. The Nile has been used for irrigation in Egypt since at least 4000 B.C., a function that now is largely regulated by the Aswan High Dam, constructed in the 1960s in southern Egypt, near the city of Aswan.

41:41 PROMOTION OF SLAVES

So Pharaoh said to Joseph, "I hereby put you in charge of the whole land of Egypt."

Slaves were often promoted in biblical days. They were sometimes made state officials, ranking members of the army, king's confidants, and at times were given an estate and slaves of their own. Many Roman gladiators were made honored and respected members of Caesar's army—and even officers if they had distinguished themselves as gladiators. Daniel was a slave, but after he interpreted Nebuchadnezzar's vision, "the king placed Daniel in a high position and lavished many gifts on him. He made him ruler over the entire province of Babylon and placed him in charge of all its wise men" (Daniel 2:48).

So it was also with Joseph when he interpreted Pharaoh's dream. In these two cases, however, it was not slaves being promoted because of their own abilities, but two slaves being promoted because God intervened and imparted knowledge and wisdom to them. They are those who have difficulty accepting Joseph's promotion from a slave to second-in-command in all Egypt, second to only Pharaoh himself. But the promotion was the result of the great importance put on dreams and visions in antiquity and God's control over all rulers and governments, and all circumstances and situations. This was the same reason for Daniel's promotion.

41:42 SIGNET RING

Then Pharaoh took his signet ring from his finger and put it on Joseph's finger. He dressed him in robes of fine linen and put a gold chain around his neck.

Although not shown in the KJV version of the first sentence of this text, "And Pharaoh took off his ring from his hand, and put it upon Joseph's hand," the ring that Pharaoh gave Joseph was a signet ring, as shown in most other versions. A signet is a seal, especially one used to authenticate official documents. A signet ring is a finger ring that bears an engraved seal. The ring was used much like a signature today, although seals are still sometimes used for important documents, and most often are impressed with a signet. At times it also identified the official position or level of the person who wore it.

A Pharaoh's ring carried the highest authority in Egypt and empowered subordinates to act for the king; in their positions of authority, they literally were the king. King Ahasuerus (or Xerxes) first gave his ring to Haman, who used it to seal a letter commanding the governors in every province to kill the Jews (Esther 3:10-13), and then gave the ring to Mordecai after Haman was hanged: "The king took off his signet ring, which he had reclaimed from Haman, and presented it to Mordecai" (Esther 8:2).

When Daniel was thrown into the lions' den, King Darius sealed the den with his signet ring and the rings of his nobles: "A stone was

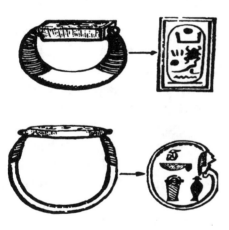

Rings and signets

brought and placed over the mouth of the den, and the king sealed it with his own signet ring and with the rings of his nobles, so that Daniel's situation might not be changed" (Daniel 6:17). In the King James version of that verse, the word "signet" properly denotes a ring.

In his 1889 Bible Dictionary Matthew Easton says, "Some years ago, the impression of a signet ring on fine clay was discovered among the ruins at Nineveh. It bears the name and title of an Egyptian king. Two actual signet rings of ancient Egyptian monarchs, Cheops and Horus, have also been discovered. When digging a shaft close to the south wall of the temple area, the engineers of the Palestine Exploration Fund, at a depth of 12 feet below the surface, came upon a pavement of polished stones, formerly one of the streets of the city. Under this pavement they found a stratum of 16 feet of concrete, and among this concrete, 10 feet down, they found a signet stone bearing the inscription, in Old Hebrew characters, 'Haggai, son of Shebaniah.' It has been asked if this might not be the actual seal of Haggai the prophet. He was in Jerusalem after the Captivity; and he alone of all the minor prophets refers to a signet ring" (Haggai 2:23).

41:43 SECOND CHARIOT— HERALD

And he made him to ride in the second chariot which he had; and they cried before him, Bow the knee: and he made him ruler over all the land of Egypt *(KJV).*

The "second chariot" would have been a chariot that followed immediately after Pharaoh's chariot in state processions, or was so designed that it designated that the one riding in it was second-in-command to Pharaoh. The NIV version of this verse reads: "He had him ride in a chariot as his second-in-command, and men shouted before him, 'Make way!' Thus he put him in charge of the whole land of Egypt." The person running before the chariot and shouting "Bow the knee!" or "Make way!" would be similar to a herald who goes before royalty and notifies all along the travel

Egyptian Granary

route that royalty is coming, and everything should be cleaned and cleared for his or her passage. Thus it was that John the Baptist came as a herald to Jesus, "calling in the desert, 'Make straight the way for the Lord'" (John 1:23).

41:48 GRANARIES

Joseph collected all the food produced in those seven years of abundance in Egypt and stored it in the cities. In each city he put the food grown in the fields surrounding it.

A granary was a facility for storing threshed and winnowed grain. The granaries varied in size and structure and were used extensively in Egypt and wherever grain was grown. Some were large structures with numerous rooms, such as Hezekiah's storehouse in 2 Chronicles 32:28, or those that were probably used by Joseph. Other granaries were silos in the form of round or square pits in the ground, often walled with rocks and plastered or unplastered. At ancient Megiddo there is still the remains of a large pit-type silo walled with rocks and with steps leading down into it. At the site of ancient Beersheba, a multi-structured grain storehouse has been excavated.

42:25-26 Sacks of Two Kinds

Joseph gave orders to fill their bags with grain, to put each man's silver back in his sack, and to give them provisions for their journey. After this was done for them, they loaded their grain on their donkeys and left.

This was probably two different kinds of bags. The first bag or sack was quite large and was used to carry grain—it is mentioned several times in the Scriptures. The Hebrew word for this bag is the same word that is translated as sackcloth that is worn during times of humiliation, mourning, or great anguish. The second bag or sack mentioned here was probably the bag that was often used by shepherds and travelers to carry their personal supplies while on a short journey—it would normally hold enough supplies for a day or two. It was usually made of animal skins and carried across the shoulders, much like a woman's purse today. These smaller bags would not have held enough grain to feed Israel's tribe of seventy people (Genesis 46:27), and so the grain was undoubtedly put into larger sacks. Possibly Joseph's brothers brought the larger sacks with them, hoping they would be filled in Egypt.

43:10 Slaying Animals for Dinner

When Joseph saw Benjamin with them, he said to the steward of his house, "Take these men to my house, slaughter an animal and prepare dinner; they are to eat with me at noon."

The ancients had the animals they desired for food slaughtered in the courtyard of their dwelling, or, if they lived in a tent, in a nearby area. Some Egyptian monuments have illustrations of poulterers' shops, but none illustrate butcher's shops, and show all slaughtering of animals as being done in private houses. The reason for this is not known. Since poultry, fish, vegetables, and bread formed their principal food, perhaps there wasn't sufficient demand to warrant butcher shops.

The method of slaying animals is well illustrated. Depending on the size of the animal, it was either held or tied in some way, while the butcher cut its throat. The blood was sometimes drained into a basin and kept for some other use. The animal was then skinned, dressed, cut into pieces, and the pieces carried on trays to the cooking area, where it was immediately prepared for dinner so that there wasn't sufficient time for the meat to begin to go bad. Since there was no way to preserve meat in those days, the animal was not killed until it was time to cook it. In our verse-text Joseph orders his steward to "slaughter an animal and prepare dinner (slay, and make ready, KJV), so that little time passed between the slaughter and the eating. This is similar to when the LORD and two angels visited Abraham and "he ran to the herd and selected a choice, tender calf and gave it to a servant, who hurried to prepare it" (Genesis 18:7). Also like what is written in 1 Samuel 28:24—"The woman had a fattened calf at the house, which she butchered at once."

43:31 Bread, Principal Food

And he washed his face, and went out, and refrained himself, and said, Set on bread *(KJV)*.

In the KJV the word *bread* appears 281 times in the Old Testament and 80 times in the New Testament; however, the 7 Hebrew words that refer to bread are not always translated as such. In the NIV, the word *bread* appears 188 times in the Old Testament and 83 times in the New Testament. The frequency with which the word is mentioned indicates that bread, not vegetables or meat, was the basic food of ancient people. It is probably for this reason that in most Bible translations several of the seven Hebrew words for bread are translated *food* or *meal*. For example, the KJV says that after Joseph's brothers cast him into the pit, "they sat down to eat bread," but the NIV says, as do other versions, "they sat down to eat their meal" (Genesis 37:25).

43:32 Abomination

They served him by himself, the brothers by themselves, and the Egyptians who ate with him by themselves, because Egyptians could not eat with Hebrews, for that is detestable *(an abomination, KJV)* to Egyptians.

The Egyptians believed that they would be defiled if they ate with the Hebrews, who were shepherds, for shepherds were detested by the Egyptians. This can be seen from Joseph's advice to his brothers and father's household: When Pharaoh calls you in and asks, 'What is your occupation?' you should answer, 'Your servants have tended livestock from our boyhood on, just as our fathers did.' Then you will be allowed to settle in the region of Goshen, for all shepherds are detestable to the Egyptians" (Genesis 46:33-34).

This aversion may have come from the fact that Lower and Middle Egypt had once been held in subjective oppression by the *Hyksos*, a tribe of nomad shepherds. The Hyksos established themselves in Egypt and had a succession of kings. They fought the Egyptians, burned some of their principal cities, committed great cruelties, and were not driven out until they and their descendants had occupied the country for hundreds of years. It's believed they weren't driven out until just before the time of Joseph.

The Egyptians also detested what they considered the lawless ways of wandering shepherds who had no fixed home, and moved from place to place with each change of the season in search of food, water, and grazing land.

Joseph skillfully used the Egyptians distaste for shepherds to provide his family an area where they and their flocks could flourish and Jacob's people could

Shepherds—detested by Egyptians

retain their cultural and spiritual uniqueness. Goshen was a pastoral region of ancient Egypt on the eastern delta of the Nile River, where rich black soil had been deposited by the river. There Joseph's family was isolated from most of the Egyptians, and had little daily contact with them.

As often happens, many years later those who had been detested now detested others and made it a law that no Jew could eat with a Gentile because they considered them unclean: "He [Peter] said to them: "You are well aware that it is against our law for a Jew to associate with a Gentile or visit him. But God has shown me that I should not call any man impure or unclean" (Acts 10:28).

44:2 Joseph's Cup

"Then put my cup, the silver one, in the mouth of the youngest one's sack, along with the silver for his grain." And he did as Joseph said.

The cup referred to by Joseph would have been a drinking vessel. Some were made of pottery, and others of various metals—usually bronze, silver, or gold. During ancient times cups came in two shapes; some looked

like modern cups, and others were shaped like shallows bowls and came in various sizes. A silver cup like Joseph's would be quite valuable, and so when it was found in Benjamin's sack, it enabled Joseph's steward to act quite indignant over the seeming theft. Strangely, Joseph apparently also used the cup for divination, although there are no Scriptures referring to his doing so, for he told his steward to say to his brothers: "Isn't this the cup my master drinks from and also uses for divination" (Genesis 44:5)? It is also possible that Joseph had his steward speak of divination to add significance to the cup, and to test whether his brothers would stand with Benjamin or turn him over to others as they had Joseph.

44:5 Divining Cup or Bowl

Isn't this the cup my master drinks from and also uses for divination?

Whether Joseph actually practiced divination, or only pretended to do so, or merely instructed his steward to ask an ironical question, or whether the original words may have a different interpretation from that

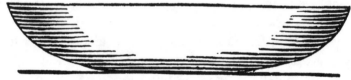

Divining cup

which the translators have put upon them, is one that concerns the commentator rather than the archaeologist. It's a fact that divining cups were used among the Egyptians and other nations. The cups were engraved or painted with magical inscriptions, and when used were filled with pure water. Most authorities agree with this, but they differ in opinion as to what use was made of the cup after the water was poured in. Here are the opinions of various writers, and it's possible that they are all correct, and that different methods were used at different times.

1. The divination was performed by means of the figures that were reflected by the rays of light that were permitted to fall on the water.

2. Melted wax was poured into the water, and the will of the gods was interpreted by the various shapes formed by the wax.

3. The cup was shaken, and the position, size, or number of the bubbles that rose to the surface was considered.

4. Small plates of silver or gold and precious stones and carved with magical characters were thrown into a divining bowl, and an incantation was said over the bowl. The reflections of the stones in the water were then interpreted, or a voice was supposedly heard, or a likeness of the deceased person about whom the inquiry was made supposedly appeared in the water.

5. The diviner fixed his or her eyes on a specific point in the cup or bowl until a trance-like state was entered, at which time the diviner was purported to be able to see strange and otherworldly things.

45:2 Loud Weeping

And he wept so loudly that the Egyptians heard him, and Pharaoh's household heard about it.

As previously said, the physical descendants of Isaac and Ishmael are passionate and expressive people, with seemingly supercharged emotions that often appear excessive to those of other cultures. Their weeping is loud whether it comes from joy or grief, and equally loud is their laughter or wails.

Their joy is exuberant, often full of unrestrained enthusiasm, and their grief is depressive, filled with almost hopeless despair. Their love is deep and demonstrative, and their hate is violent and destructive. The angel of the LORD said to Sarah's servant Hagar about her son Ishmael: "He will be a wild donkey of a man; his hand will be against everyone and everyone's hand against him, and he will live in hostility toward all his brothers" (Genesis 16:12). It was true through the days of the Bible and it is true today.

45:19 Wagons

"You are also directed to tell them, 'Do this: Take some carts (wagons, KJV) from Egypt for your children and your wives, and get your father and come.

These wagons were vehicles of transportation, usually with two or four wooden wheels, depending on their size—the two-wheelers were normally called carts. The wagons were used to transport people and goods, and were usually pulled by oxen. Differently fitted, they could also be used as war vehicles: "They will come against you with weapons, chariots and wagons and with a throng of people; they will take up positions against you on every side with large and small shields and with helmets" (Ezekiel 23:24). In war use, they were probably used to haul troops or weapons or supplies for the army. A *chariot* was a horse-drawn two-wheeled vehicle used in war, races, and processions.

45:22 CHANGES OF RAIMENT

To each of them he gave new clothing, but to Benjamin he gave three hundred shekels of silver and five sets of clothes *(changes of raiment, KJV).*

For reasons not expressed, Joseph was treating his older half-brothers kindly, and his youngest full-brother, Benjamin, as a rich man. Whether it was because of the difference in blood relationship, or because his half-brothers, who were born of Leah, had treated him so badly, is not said. But Joseph definitely gave preferential treatment to Benjamin, starting with Benjamin's share at the dinner table: "When portions were served to them from Joseph's table, Benjamin's portion was five times as much as anyone else's" (Genesis 43:34). Some have said that Joseph was testing his brothers at the table to see if they would resent the portion he gave to the youngest as they had resented the love and favor he had with his father: "Now Israel loved Joseph more than any of his other sons, because he had been born to him in his old age; and he made a richly ornamented robe for him. When his brothers saw that their father loved him more than any of them, they hated him and could not speak a kind word to him" (Genesis 37:3-4). If so, perhaps his giving five changes of raiment to Benjamin was a continuation of this test, for so many changes of clothes were in those days the signs of a rich man, and the desire of many. Clothing was often given as gifts to kings and prophets and for great deeds done—see 2 Kings 5:5, 22-23; 2 Chronicles 9:24; Esther 6:8-9; and Daniel 5:29.

46:4 CLOSING EYES

"I *[God]* will go down to Egypt with you, and I will surely bring you back again. And Joseph's own hand will close your eyes."

It was an ancient custom that the nearest relative should close the eyes of a deceased person, and give a parting kiss to the corpse. It was a comforting assurance to Jacob that God would go with him to Egypt and that his beloved Joseph, whom he had mourned for many years as dead, would perform this filial custom for him. At Jacob's death, we are told that "Joseph threw himself upon his father and wept over him and kissed him" (Genesis 50:1). Without question, he also closed the eyes of the patriarch as God promised, for God's promises contain the power of their fulfillment, and "the Scripture cannot be broken" (John 10:35).

49:8 TOKEN OF TRIUMPH

"Judah, your brothers will praise you; your hand will be on the neck of your enemies; your father's sons will bow down to you."

Judah (Judah means praise) would be praised by his brothers and lead them, and would defeat all his enemies. The expression "your hand on the neck of your enemies" was a token of superiority and triumph. Job makes use of a similar metaphor when he represents God as taking him by the neck and shaking him: "He seized me by the neck and crushed me" (Job 16:12). David wrote, "Thou hast also given me the necks of mine enemies, that I might destroy them that hate me" (2 Samuel 22:41, KJV). The implication of the expression is much like the later action of victorious soldiers putting their feet on the necks of their enemies: "When they had brought these kings to Joshua, he summoned all the men of Israel and said to the army commanders who had come with him, 'Come here and put your feet on the necks of these kings.' So they came forward and placed their feet on their necks" (Joshua 10:24).

The Franks, who were a group of Germanic tribes that dwelt along the middle and lower Rhine River about A.D. 350, had a custom of putting an arm around another person's neck as a sign of superiority over that person. When an insolvent debtor gave himself up to his creditor as a slave, he would put the arm of his new master around his neck as a token of submission to him.

49:10 Scepter

The scepter will not depart from Judah, nor the ruler's staff from between his feet, until he comes to whom it belongs and the obedience of the nations is his.

A scepter (Hebrew *shebet*; Greek *skeptron*) is simply a staff or rod that is a symbol of rule and authority, such as denoted in Isaiah 15:5—"The LORD has broken the rod of the wicked, the scepter of the rulers." The symbol of the scepter derived from the thought that a ruler was the shepherd of his people, and so at times a scepter was also used as a symbol for a ruler or shepherd. We can see this in Numbers 24:17—"A star will come out of Jacob; a scepter [ruler] will rise out of Israel," in Psalm 45:6—"Your throne, O God, will last for ever and ever; a scepter [perhaps *ruler*] of justice will be the scepter [perhaps *shepherd*] of your kingdom."

There is no record, however, either in the Scriptures or in ancient writings, of a scepter having ever been actually used by a Jewish king

49:10 Shiloh

The scepter shall not depart from Judah, nor a lawgiver from between his feet, until Shiloh come; and unto him shall the gathering of the people be *(KJV)*.

Shiloh is generally understood as being a prophetic title for the Messiah, "the peaceful one" as the word signifies. The Vulgate version translates Shiloh as "he who is to be sent," thus pointing to the Messiah. Some say that the word means "until he who is to come has come." The NIV says, "until he comes to whom it [the ruler's staff] belongs." Most versions, however, such as the KJV, the NKJV, express it in its most simple form as does the NASB: "Until Shiloh comes." In each version interpreting Shiloh as a proper name and capitalizing it because of the divinity of Him whose name it is. This is much in keeping with the words in Isaiah

6:9—"For to us a child is born, to us a son is given, and the government will be on his shoulders. And he will be called Wonderful Counselor, Mighty God, Everlasting Father, Prince of Peace."

49:12 MILK SYMBOLIZES WEALTH

His eyes will be darker than wine, his teeth whiter than milk.

In this use, milk does not symbolize health, but *wealth*. This is the Old Testament's most extensive use of the word *milk*, and when combined with the word *honey* symbolizes abundance and blessing. Thus the Promised Land was known as a land of milk and honey: "Hear, O Israel, and be careful to obey so that it may go well with you and that you may increase greatly in a land flowing with milk and honey, just as the LORD, the God of your fathers, promised you" (Deuteronomy 6:3). The Israelites were then admonished: "But remember the LORD your God, for it is he who gives you the ability to produce wealth, and so confirms his covenant, which he swore to your forefathers, as it is today" (Deuteronomy 8:18). Yet when

they entered the Promised Land they did exactly what God said they would do: "When I have brought them into the land flowing with milk and honey, the land I promised on oath to their forefathers, and when they eat their fill and thrive, they will turn to other gods and worship them, rejecting me and breaking my covenant" (Deuteronomy 31:20). Paul wrote: "These things happened to them as examples and were written down as warnings for us." So we should ask ourselves: *How often in our own lives do the things that God gives us become more important to us than God?*

50:2-3 EMBALMING

Then Joseph directed the physicians in his service to embalm his father Israel. So the physicians embalmed him, taking a full forty days, for that was the time required for embalming.

Among the ancient Egyptians, embalming was a method of preserving a body by using various aromatic substances like myrrh, cassia, and cinnamon. Embalming is believed to have

Various Egyptian burial methods

originated with them about 4000 B.C., and was in common use for well over 3000 years. The custom apparently had a religious origin and was used so that the person's body and soul could be reunited after death. Eventually the practice of embalming spread to others, such as the Assyrians, Persians, Scythians, and Jews.

The Egyptian form of embalming became more complicated over the years, and reached such a stage that bodies embalmed thousands of years ago are still in an excellent state of preservation today. The soles of the feet of some mummies unwrapped after as much as 3000 years were still soft and elastic.

Historians estimate that the Egyptians embalmed approximately 730-million bodies, and although many of the mummies disintegrated in the intense heat of northern Africa, archaeologists estimate that many millions are still preserved in undiscovered tombs and burial places.

The Egyptians method of embalming consisted removal of the viscera—the soft internal organs of the body—and the brains. (Some say the heart and kidneys were left in place, or removed and prepared for preservation and then replaced— or put into vases and placed in the burial tomb.) A mixture of balsamic herbs and other substances like bitumen and salt were then used to fill the body cavities, balsams were injected into the arteries and veins, and the incisions were sewn up. The body was then steeped in niter (carbonate of soda) for a period of forty to seventy days.

The length of time may have increased from forty days to seventy as the Egyptians learned how to better preserve the bodies, or, as some say, it may have taken forty days to embalm the body properly and thirty days to soak it. After the steeping, the body was wound with long strips of linen and similar clothes. The strips were often seven or eight inches wide and as long as six or seven hundred feet, and were saturated with herbs and other substances similar to those used to fill the body cavities.

Only the Egyptians perfected the art of embalming to the degree that mummies have been preserved in excellent condition for thousands of years, and that may be because only they embalmed for the religious purpose of preserving the body for life after death. That was probably also why methods of

embalming varied in different cultures. The Assyrians used honey in embalming, the Persians used wax, and the Jews used spices and aloes. Alexander the Great was embalmed with honey and wax.

Joseph had his father embalmed, seemingly according to the Egyptian custom: "Then Joseph directed the physicians in his service to embalm his father Israel. So the physicians embalmed him, taking a full forty days, for that was the time required for embalming. And the Egyptians mourned for him seventy days" (Genesis 50:2-3). Historians say that Egyptian embalmers banded together as a guild, so it's a moot question as to whether the physicians spoken of here were also the embalmers, or, as some say, whether Jacob was embalmed by physicians because he was not an Egyptian, and so was not subject to their customary practices. When Joseph died, he also was embalmed: "So Joseph died at the age of a hundred and ten. And after they embalmed him, he was placed in a coffin in Egypt" (Genesis 5:26). Many years later, "Moses took the bones of

Joseph with him because Joseph had made the sons of Israel swear an oath. He had said, "God will surely come to your aid, and then you must carry my bones up with you from this place" (Exodus 13:19).

The Scriptures record that a form of embalming was used for two others: Asa and Jesus. "They buried him [Asa] in the tomb that he had cut out for himself in the City of David. They laid him on a bier covered with spices and various blended perfumes, and they made a huge fire in his honor" (2 Chronicles 16:14).

In the case of the Lord, the form of preparing the body externally was much like that of the Egyptians, and, as the Scripture tells us, was a Jewish custom: "He was accompanied by Nicodemus, the man who earlier had visited Jesus at night. Nicodemus brought a mixture of myrrh and aloes, about seventy-five pounds. Taking Jesus' body, the two of them wrapped it, with the spices, in strips of linen. This was in accordance with Jewish burial customs" (John 19:39-40). Obviously, seventy-five pounds of myrrh and aloes

were enough to completely cover his body and to saturate the linen strips in which He was wrapped. (It should be noted, also, that since the Scripture tells us that Jesus' body was wrapped in "*strips* of linen cloth," that eliminates the possibility that the "Shroud of Turin" came from the Lord's body, since a shroud is a *single* winding sheet.)

50:4-5 WHY JOSEPH COULD NOT SEE THE KING

When the days of mourning had passed, Joseph said to Pharaoh's court, "If I have found favor in your eyes, speak to Pharaoh for me. Tell him, 'My father made me swear an oath and said, "I am about to die; bury me in the tomb I dug for myself in the land of Canaan." Now let me go up and bury my father; then I will return.'"

Without question, the reason Joseph, who was second-in-command in Egypt, did not speak directly to Pharaoh was because of the Hebrew custom of allowing their beards and hair to grow during the days of mourning.

Joseph had not yet taken the body of his father into the land of Canaan to bury it, and so his time of mourning was not finished: "When they reached the threshing floor of Atad, near the Jordan, they lamented loudly and bitterly; and there Joseph observed a seven-day period of mourning for his father" (Genesis 50:10). Thus an unshaved Joseph, who was

50:9 LARGE FUNERALS

Chariots and horsemen also went up with him. It was a very large company.

This not only shows the high esteem in which Joseph was held, but it also furnishes an illustration of the Egyptian fashion of large and stately funeral processions for their nobles. This custom existed in every province in Egypt, and in every age of its ancient history.

Ancient Egyptian funeral procession

probably also wearing sackcloth, would have been a great offense to Pharaoh if he had appeared before him. When Joseph returned to Egypt, he would have shaved his head and beard and put back on his normal Egyptian clothing, and so could once more appear before Pharaoh.

50:11-12 THRESHING FLOORS

When they reached the threshing floor of Atad, near the Jordan, they lamented loudly and bitterly; and there Joseph observed a seven-day period of mourning for his father. When the Canaanites who lived there saw the mourning at the threshing floor of Atad, they said, "The Egyptians are holding a solemn ceremony of mourning." That is why that place near the Jordan is called Abel Mizraim.

The threshing floor was not in a shed or a building or any place covered with a roof and surrounded by walls, but normally an open-air circular piece of slightly elevated ground from fifty to one-hundred feet in diameter, that was smooth, hard, and clean. Following the harvest, the threshing floor was the center of the economic activity of the village and surrounding area. The sheaves of dried cereal grass from the harvested fields were brought here to be trampled by oxen or broken down by threshing sledges (vehicles mounted on low runners). The grain was further separated from the grass and chaff with winnowing forks, which were used to toss the trampled products into the air so that the wind would blow away the light grass and chaff and the grain would fall to the ground. After that, sieves were used to strain out the grain from whatever products still remained with it.

Once all this was done, the separated grain was closely guarded until it could be distributed. Sometimes the villages had communal granaries, but most people kept their personal supply of grain in home storage pits or private granaries. For Scripture references see: Deuteronomy 25:4; Ruth 3:2-7; 2 Samuel 24:22; Isaiah 41:15-16; Jeremiah 15:7; Joel 2:24; Amos 2:13, 9:9; Luke 22:31.

Atad, which means *thorn*, is the name of the person who owned a threshing floor, east of the Jordan and north of the Dead Sea, where Jacob held a formal seven-day period of mourning for his father. Because the Egyptians who were with him joined in the mourning, the Canaanites who lived there called the place *Abel-mizraim*, which means "mourning of Egypt."

50:26 Joseph's Coffin

So Joseph died at the age of a hundred and ten. And after they embalmed him, he was placed in a coffin in Egypt.

Although Joseph was embalmed by the Egyptians, it is probable that he was not embalmed in their customary manner for the purpose of preserving his body so that it could be united with his soul after death. This would have been against his religious beliefs. It is also probable that the coffin they put him in was a *sarcophagus*, which is a stone coffin, often decorated, and located above ground. This would be in keeping with his telling the sons of Israel, "you must carry my bones up from this place" (Genesis 50:25). This would be a lot easier to do if the coffin were not buried in the ground.

Also, note that Joseph did not request that his "body" be carried up, which he probably would have done if he was going to be embalmed in the normal Egyptian way, but that his "bones" be carried up. This would seem to denote that he was going to be buried in a *sarcophagus* (coffin) that was made of limestone.

The word *sarcophagus* is a gruesome name and comes to us from Latin and Greek, having been derived in Greek from *sarx* (flesh) and *phagein* (to eat). The Greek word *sarkophagos* meant

Sarcophagus

"eating flesh," and in the phrase "*lithos* (stone) *sarcophagos*" denoted a limestone that was thought to decompose the flesh of corpses that were put in it. The Greek word *sarkophagos* used by itself as a noun then came to mean "coffin." The term was carried over into Latin, where *sarcophagus* was used in the phrase *"lapis* (stone) *sarcophagus,"* referring also to the same limestone. *Sarcophagus* used as a noun in Latin meant "coffin of any material." The Latin word was then brought over into English, with the first recorded use being in 1601 to mean the flesh-consuming stone, and then in 1705 to mean any stone coffin. Considering that in Exodus 13:19 it's written that "Moses took the *bones* of Joseph with him," it's most likely that Joseph's coffin was made of a limestone that consumed his flesh between the time of his burial and the time when his "bones" were taken by Moses.

EXODUS

2:3 MOSES' ARK

But when she could hide him no longer, she got a papyrus basket (ark of bulrushes, KJV) for him and coated it with tar (slime, KJV) and pitch. Then she placed the child in it and put it among the reeds along the bank of the Nile.

The Hebrew word translated *ark* in the KJV is better translated *basket*, the word is the same for both. Also the KJV bulrushes were actually papyrus plants. Moses' basket was make of the leaf of the papyrus, which is a reedy plant that in those days grew plentifully on the banks of the Nile, and which was used by the Egyptians for making garments, shoes, cords, baskets, boats, sails, and a variety of other things. The roots were dried and used for fuel. The pith of the stem was boiled and eaten, but it was used mainly in making papyrus paper. The inside bark was cut into strips, which were sewn together and dried in the sun, forming the papyrus used for writing. Papyrus grows today in Egypt, in Ethiopia, in the Jordan River valley, and in Sicily.

The tar or slime that the Levite woman mixed with pitch to coat the ark is brittle when cold, but melts easily and runs freely when heated. Together they are tenacious when set and make a firm cement. In preparing the small vessel for the infant Moses, his mother probably plaited the papyrus leaves together, and then coated them with a mixture of hot tar and pitch. When the coating cooled, it would have been firm and waterproof.

2:5 BATHING IN THE NILE

Then Pharaoh's daughter went down to the Nile to bathe, and her attendants were walking along the river bank.

Scripture language doesn't distinguish between washing, partial bathing, and full bathing.

This was undoubtedly because the dry climate of the Middle East made full bathing virtually impossible except where there was a sufficient source of water, such as the Nile River. When the word "bathe" appears in a Scripture verse, therefore, it usually refers to washing or partial bathing. There are, however, two significant exceptions: Pharaoh's daughter in the Nile River, and Bathsheba on her rooftop. One evening David got up from his bed and walked around on the roof of the palace. From the roof he saw a woman bathing" (2 Samuel 11:2).

2:21 UNCOMMON MARRIAGE CUSTOM

Moses agreed to stay with the man, who gave his daughter Zipporah to Moses in marriage.

Usually the proposal of marriage came from the family of the bridegroom, but it appears that on occasion this custom was reversed, as with Moses and with others. Caleb gave his daughter Achsah to Othniel: And Caleb said, "'I will give my daughter Acsah in marriage to the man

who attacks and captures Kiriath Sepher.' Othniel son of Kenaz, Caleb's brother, took it; so Caleb gave his daughter Acsah to him in marriage" (Joshua 15:16-17). In a similar manner, Saul gave his daughter Michal to David (1 Samuel 18:25-27), although it wasn't really Saul's intention that David marry his daughter but that he be killed by the Philistines.

3:1 HOREB, THE MOUNTAIN OF GOD

Now Moses was tending the flock of Jethro his father-in-law, the priest of Midian, and he led the flock to the far side *(back side, KJV)* **of the desert and came to Horeb, the mountain of God.**

It is our custom to give geographical directions by facing north, but the Semites (Arabs, Arameans, Babylonians, Carthaginians, Ethiopians, Hebrews, and Phoenicians) faced east when giving directions. Thus the Hebrew phrase translated "the far side" or "the back side" might be better translated "the west side."

Leading the flock to this area of the mountain was undoubtedly not a special occasion for Moses

Exodus

God, are another scriptural example of different names for the same mountain. Or perhaps, as some have suggested, Horeb may be the mountain range and Mount Sinai a peak of that

Moses encountering the burning bush at Horeb

but something he did regularly, for shepherds often moved their flock as the seasons and pasture varied. So he was not looking for God in this place but for better feeding for his flock. Horeb, therefore, is only called the mountain of God as Moses thought and wrote about the event many years later.

In Exodus 3:12 God said to Moses: "When you have brought the people out of Egypt, you will worship God on this mountain," and in Deuteronomy 5:2 Moses said to the Israelites: "The LORD our God made a covenant with us at Horeb." Based on these two passages, it is generally believed that Horeb and Sinai, where Moses received the Law from

range. The belief that Horeb, where Moses encountered the burning bush, and Sinai are two names for the same mountain is further strengthened, however, by the possibility that the name Sinai came from the Hebrew word *seneh*, the name for a native bush.

3:5 Sandals Removed

"Do not come any closer," God said. "Take off your sandals *(shoes, KJV)*, for the place where you are standing is holy ground."

Removing one's sandals was a sign of respect toward a superior, or toward a person's dwelling.

101

Sandals were often removed before entering someone's home, or before entering a sacred place like a temple. Also, those who were slaves or destitute often did not wear sandals, as can be seen from Luke 15:22: "But the father said to his servants, 'Quick! Bring the best robe and put it on him. Put a ring on his finger and sandals on his feet.'"

God telling Moses in Genesis 3:5 to take off his sandals, and the "commander of the Lord's army" telling Joshua in Joshua 5:15 to "Take off your sandals, for the place where you are standing is holy," may have been on the basis of demanded respect or worship as some have suggested, but there may have been a more spiritual reason.

When God descended on Mount Sinai, the mountain itself became so holy because of his presence that He told Moses: "Put limits around the mountain and set it apart as holy," and tell the people: "Be careful that you do not go up the mountain or touch the foot of it. Whoever touches the mountain shall surely be put to death" (Exodus 19:23, 12). At the bush, God told Moses to take off his sandals because: "where you are standing is holy ground." The commander (captain, KJV) of the

Lord's army told Joshua: "Take off your sandals, for the place where you are standing is holy." Same reason as with Moses: the place or ground where they were standing was holy—made holy by the presence of God. So it is probable that being told to take off their sandals was not because of demanded respect, and certainly not worship on their part because they had been told to do it, but because nothing man-made—and therefore unclean—was to be between the feet of God's creature and the holiness that God's presence made the ground.

3:22 SILVER AND GOLD TAKEN FROM EGYPTIANS

"Every woman is to ask *(shall borrow of, KJV)* her neighbor and any woman living in her house for articles of silver and gold and for clothing, which you will put on your sons and daughters. And so you will plunder the Egyptians."

The Israelites "borrowed" from the Egyptians in accordance with a divine command, but the

Hebrew word, *sha'al*, that is translated "borrow" in the KJV, means simply and always to "request" or "demand."

Determining God's purpose in this has always caused considerable controversy among commentators and a multitude of opinions. Some have even compared it to ancient Eastern customs of putting on jewelry to go to a sacred festival, and that those who did not have much would often borrow from their neighbors so they wouldn't appear in the temples before their gods improperly dressed. The most common interpretation of God's reason, however, is that since the Egyptians had forced the Israelites to work as slaves for many years, God was seeing to it that they received some pay for their labors. So they simply asked their neighbors for silver, gold, and clothing, and God opened the Egyptians' hearts to their pleas. There is only one thing wrong with this interpretation, however; except for the clothing, the Israelite's had no use for the silver and gold in the wilderness.

So it's more likely that God's reason was not for the purpose of increasing the Israelites' material wealth, but for a spiritual purpose of His own: the building of the tabernacle in the wilderness. Consider these verses: "All who were willing, men and women alike, came and brought gold jewelry of all kinds: brooches, earrings, rings and ornaments. They all presented their gold as a wave offering to the LORD. Everyone who had blue, purple or scarlet yarn or fine linen, or goat hair, ram skins dyed red or hides of sea cows brought them. Those presenting an offering of silver or bronze brought it as an offering to the LORD" (Exodus 35:22-24). Where did these former slaves get their gold jewelry, colored yarn and fine linen, and silver and bronze? From the Egyptians, of course. God knew that He was going to have His people build a tabernacle in the wilderness, so He had them collect what they would need for the tabernacle before they left Egypt—if He had not, they never could have built it.

5:7 Egyptian Bricks

"You are no longer to supply the people with straw for making bricks; let them go and gather their own straw."

The ancient Egyptian bricks were made of clay moistened with water and then put into molds. After they were sufficiently dry to be removed from the molds, they were laid in rows on a flat surface and exposed to the sun, which gradually dried and hardened them. When strengthened with straw, sun-dried mud bricks were a sturdy building material so long as they could be protected from direct rain. Some bricks were made with straw and some without. Many had chopped barley and wheat straw, while others contained bean haulm (stems) and stubble. This crude brick was generally used in Egypt for dwellings and other ordinary buildings, tombs, walls of towers, fortresses, temple enclosures, and sometimes small temples. Archaeologists in Egypt have found examples of bricks such as these, with and without straw.

Egyptian bricks were frequently stamped with the name of the king during whose reign they were made. Their size is different than the Babylonian bricks. They range from 14½ to 20 inches long, and from 6½ to 7 inches thick. Several bricks bearing the name of Thutmose III, and plainly showing the chopped straw used in their manufacture, are in the Abbott Collection,

Egyptian brick

which also contains some of the ancient implements that were used in brick-making. Thutmose III was the father of Amenhotep II, the 7th king of the 18th dynasty, who ruled Egypt from 1450 to 1425 B.C., and who probably was Pharaoh at the time of the Exodus, which is considered to have taken place around 1441 B.C.

5:11 HARDER LABOR A PUNISHMENT

"Go and get your own straw wherever you can find it, but your work will not be reduced at all."

Many years ago, M. Chabas, a French Egyptologist, discovered a papyrus with hieroglyphics on it. When deciphered, the writings proved to be the work of a scribe who was reporting that twelve workmen who had been employed at brick-making had failed in their tasks, and that as punishment they had been given harder work to do. There was no evidence that these workmen were Hebrews, but the report did show that the cruelty inflicted on the Hebrews by their taskmasters was in keeping with the customs of ancient Egypt.

7:19 IRRIGATION

The LORD said to Moses, "Tell Aaron, 'Take your staff and stretch out your hand over the waters of Egypt— over the streams and canals (rivers, KJV), over the ponds and all the reservoirs (pools of water, KJV).'"

Irrigation is the storage and transportation of water by man-made dams, cisterns, reservoirs, aqueducts, and canals. In ancient Egypt and other countries like Mesopotamia, the dry climate made the storage and transportation of water essential. Extensive canal systems crisscrossed the lands and provided the large quantities of water that were necessary for the crops during the rainless months of March to October. Since a Pharaoh's second-in-command usually was overseer of the irrigation system and the distribution of water, it's probable that Joseph filled this position while he was in Egypt.

Historically, every summer the Nile flooded large portions of the desert, thereby providing ideal farming land and sufficient water trapped in reservoirs and cisterns to last through the growing season. Outside the flood region, Egypt's vast irrigation system enabled them to use the desert land that wasn't watered by the flood. The black sediment brought down by the Nile during this annual flooding settled in the Nile delta and made it extremely fertile (compare Genesis **43:32 Abomination**). The opening of the Aswan High Dam in the early 1970s, however, allowed for control of the flooding and so reduced sedimentation deposits.

Water was drawn from the Nile or canals and reservoirs by waterwheels or by a *shaduf*, which is a device consisting of a long suspended pole weighted at one end and with a hanging bucket at the other end. It is still used in the Middle East and especially Egypt for raising water.

During the time of the exile to Babylon (Matthew 1:11), which was the capital of ancient Babylonia in Mesopotamia on the Euphrates River, and was located about 50 miles south of present Bagdad, there were huge canals up to seventy-five feet wide and several miles long that carried water from the Euphrates to the city and farm lands surrounding it. Some of these huge irrigation canals were so wide and deep that small ships could travel them and carry produce from outlying farms to major cities.

7:19 RECEPTACLES FOR NILE WATER

"Blood will be everywhere in Egypt, even in the wooden buckets and stone jars."

The water needed for daily use was kept in these receptacles,

even as was done in Nahor where Rebekah lived (see Genesis **24:15 Pitchers**). Some of the stone jars had filtering pots of white sand through which the water was poured into the jars. There were also stone reservoirs on street corners and other places for common use, much like public drinking fountains today. Even though these receptacles were not connected to the Nile, God turned the water in them into blood, also, which eliminates the possibility that the Nile turned red because of the reflection of the setting sun or some natural biological problem—as some say today.

7:20-21 WORSHIP OF THE NILE

Moses and Aaron did just as the LORD had commanded. He raised his staff in the presence of Pharaoh and his officials and struck the water of the Nile, and all the water was changed into blood. The fish in the Nile died, and the river smelled so bad that the Egyptians could not drink.

Many ancient cultures had great reverence for the rivers that

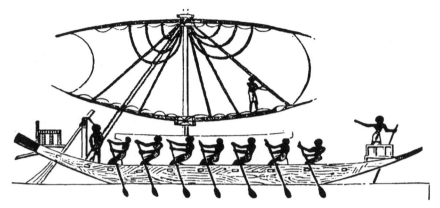

Boat on the Nile

watered their lands and were literally the lifeblood of their nations—their source of life. It was the same with the Egyptians. They considered the Nile to be the sacred bloodstream of the god *Osiris*, who was the ruler of the realm of the dead in the mysterious region below the western horizon. *Sothis* and *Khnum* were the gods of the Nile and watched over it and protected it. When God turned the Nile into blood and filled it with death, He was actually showing the Egyptians His power over all their gods and that He alone was God.

Whether the water became blood-like, bloody, or actual blood is not known and Bible scholars differ widely in their opinions. Only exposed water seems to have been affected. Regardless of how the change was affected, it turned Egypt's water into something nauseating and unusable, filled with death, and would have been looked upon by the Egyptians, and especially Pharaoh and the priests, as a great offense to their pagan gods that they believed

Nile emblem

gave life to their land by means of the river.

9:8-9 Ashes Used in Cursing

Then the LORD said to Moses and Aaron, "Take handfuls of soot from a furnace and have Moses toss it into the air in the presence of Pharaoh. It will become fine dust over the whole land of Egypt, and festering boils will break out on men and animals throughout the land."

In a book written many years ago, a visitor to India wrote: "When the magicians pronounce an imprecation [curse] on an individual, a village, or a country, they take ashes of cow-dung, or those from a common fire, and throw them in the air, saying to the objects of their displeasure, 'Such a sickness or such a curse shall surely come upon you.'"

This pagan ritual that developed through the years may actually have been taken from what God did in Egypt as recorded in the Book of Exodus, since the devil attempts to counterfeit and pervert everything that God does, even as the Egyptian magicians turned their staffs into snakes (Exodus 7:11) and a little water dug out of the River bank into blood (Exodus 7:22).

The ashes, from wherever they came, were a visual sign that it was the God of the Israelites who was causing the disease that came upon the Egyptians because of Pharaoh's stubbornness. Boils broke out on every person and their animals, and nothing could stop it. Whether God put power into the dust itself to cause the boils or whether the dust was strictly a sign, doesn't matter. It was Almighty God coming against the Egyptians because Pharaoh would not let His "people go."

10:21 Darkness That Could Be Felt

Then the LORD said to Moses, "Stretch out your hand toward the sky so that darkness will spread over Egypt—darkness that can be felt."

Once the editor and his family were deep in a cavern in Georgia, and the guide told everyone that he was going to turn off the lights so they could experience true darkness. He warned everyone to stand still and not to panic, that the lights would be off for only a few seconds. When he turned off the lights, the darkness was so absolute that it literally could be felt—it pressed against your eyes as you strained to see a minuscule of light somewhere, and surrounded you like some black, living, thing. The increasingly heavy breathing of those in the cavern became the breathing of something monstrous drawing near. The impulse to panic was almost overwhelming and it took all your mental discipline to fight it. Seconds that were hours passed, and then somewhere in the dark there was a broken sob, and the guide turned the lights back on. There were great sighs of relief from everyone, and embarrassed grins on every face, for all had been afraid of this darkness that they had never before known.

The darkness that God brought upon Egypt, so thick and heavy that it could be felt, was like that—a living darkness that swallowed the light and blinded every person and animal in the land. Fear and panic raced through Egypt and thousands of voices cried out and begged for help from *Ra*, their Egyptian god of the sun. But Ra could not help them, he had been challenged by Yahweh and found to be no god at all. This the Egyptians learned, and their fear of the God of the Israelites increased.

12:12 Gods of Egypt

"On that same night I will pass through Egypt and strike down every firstborn—both men and animals—and I will bring judgment on all the gods of Egypt. I am the LORD."

(Items in parenthesis are other possibilities.)

Aker - Earth-god, Helper of the dead - two lion heads.

Amon - life and reproduction (Wind-god, god Thebes, Helper of the pious) - Man with ram's head (ram and goose sacred).

Anubis - Conducts dead to judgment, Son of Osiris - Jackal-headed, black skinned.

Apis - Ensures fertility - Sacred bull.

Aton - Sun-god [during reign of Akhenaton regarded as the only god].

Atum - Primordial creature-god - Serpent-human.

Bes - Music and revelry (Protection at birth, Dispenser of virility) - Group of demons.

Edjo - Goddess of Delta/ Lower Egypt - Uraeus serpent.

Geb - Earth-god, Consort of Nut, Begetter of Osiris - Human.

Hathor - Sky-goddess, Goddess of love, dance, alcohol - Cow.

Heket - Primordial goddess - Frong.

Horus - Sun-god (Sky-god), Son of Osiris and Isis - Hawk (Falcon).

Isis - Goddess of fertility (life, healing, Daughter of Geb), Wife and sister (Consort/sister) of Osiris, Mother of Horus - Human.

Khepri - Primordial god, Rising sun - Scarabaeus.

Khnum - Giver of the Nile, Creator of mankind - Human with ram's head.

Khons - Moon-god - Human.

Maat - Justice, Daughter of Ra - Human.

Meskhenet - Goddess protector of newborns and of destiny.

Min - God of virility and reproduction.

Mut - "Eye of the sun," consort of Amon - Vulture or human.

Nekhbet - Goddess of Upper Egypt.

Nut - Sky-goddess, Consort of Geb, Mother of Osiris and Seth, Mother of heavenly bodies.

Osiris - Annual death and resurrection personified the self-renewing vitality and fertility of nature (Dead Pharaohs, Ruler of dead, life, vegetation).

Ptah - Creator-god, Lord of artisans.

Ra - Supreme deity, God of sun, earth, and sky, Father of Matt, National god - Man with head of a hawk crowned with a solar disk and uraeus (Human with falcon head).

Sekhmet - Goddess of war and sickness - Human with lion head.

Selket - Guardian of life, Protector of dead - Scorpion.

Seshat - Goddess of writing and books.

Seth - God of chaos, desert and storm, crops, Brother of Osiris.

Shu - God of air, bearer of heaven.

Sobek - Creator-god - Crocodile.

Sothis - God of Nile floodwaters.

Themuthis - Goddess of fertility and harvest, fate - Serpent.

Thoth - God of wisdom, moon, learning (chronology, Messenger of gods) - Ibis or Baboon.

Thoueris - Goddess of fertility and women in labor - Hippopotamus.

12:34 Kneading Trough

So the people took their dough before the yeast was added, and carried it on their shoulders in kneading troughs wrapped in clothing.

The unleavened dough that they took with them could have been some that they had previously prepared and had only to add the leaven (yeast) to begin the fermentation process, or it could have been a "starter' piece of dough from the previous day's batch. To make bread, they would usually combine flour, water, oil, and yeast (leaven) or the "starter," and knead it with their hands—knead means to work the mixture into a uniform mass by folding, pressing, and stretching the dough. This was done, of course, in a kneading trough or bowl. The mixture would then be left in the trough to ferment and rise.

Kneading was customarily the work of the women, as shown in Genesis 18:6—"So Abraham hurried into the tent to Sarah. 'Quick,' he said, 'get three seahs of fine flour and knead it and bake some bread,'" and 1 Samuel 28:24—"She took some flour, kneaded it and baked bread without yeast." With no yeast in the dough, it wouldn't raise and would make a flat bread that could be used to wrap around other foods. People of nobility often had cooks and bakers (see

Kneading trough

Genesis **14:20 Birthday Feast),** and so in those cases it would be men who prepared the bread and baked it. The kneading bowls were often of various shapes and made of wood, earthenware, or bronze.

In Deuteronomy 28:5, Moses told the people: "Your basket and your kneading trough will be blessed" if they obeyed God. Then in verse 17 he said, the basket and kneading trough would be cursed if they disobeyed God. In Exodus 8:3, Moses tells the Egyptians that God's plague of frogs will affect their means of baking and kneading bread, which in those days was the basic food in most countries: "The Nile will teem with frogs. They will come up into your palace and your bedroom and onto your bed, into the houses of your officials and on your people, and into your ovens and kneading troughs."

14:6-7 Chariots of Egypt

So he had his chariot made ready and took his army with him. He took six hundred of the best chariots, along with all the other chariots of Egypt, with officers over all of them.

The chariot was a vehicle generally used for warlike purposes. Rarely is it spoken of as being used for peaceful purposes. The Egyptian chariot was a framework of wood, nearly semicircular in front, and with straight sides and open back. The front was of wood, and the sides were strengthened and ornamented with leather and metal bindings. The floor was a rope network to give a springy footing. The fittings on the inside and the harness were of rawhide or tanned leather. On the sides, quivers and bow cases were fastened,

Egyptian chariot

crossing each other. The wheels were low to provide a low center-of-balance, had six spokes, and were kept on the axle by a leather thong or linchpin. There was no seat in the chariot. The chariot was usually drawn by two horses.

The chariots of the king and his second-in-command did not differ materially from ordinary war-chariots. The king, however, usually rode alone into battle, having the reins fastened around his waist so that both hands were free to use his weapons. Jehu, the king of Israel, seems to have imitated the custom of Egyptian monarchs in driving his own chariot: "The driving is like that of Jehu son of Nimshi—he drives like a madman" (2 Kings 9:20).

14:7 THIRD MEN

He took six hundred of the best chariots, along with all the other chariots of Egypt, with officers *(captains, KJV)* over all of them.

The word translated officers or captains is literally "third men." Usually each war-chariot carried two men: the charioteer who drove the chariot, and the warrior who did the actual fighting. Sometimes, however,

there was a third man, an officer, who had charge over the other two men. The strength or size of Pharaoh's chariot force is seen then in this: that he had, besides the usual pair of men to each chariot, a third man or "captain." Thus if needed, one could act as charioteer, one as warrior, and one as shield-bearer. Although, more likely, the purpose of the "captain" was to keep track of the battle and direct the actions of the charioteer and the warrior so that they would be most effectively used.

14:24 NIGHT WATCHES

During the last watch of the night *(morning watch, KJV)* the LORD looked down from the pillar of fire and cloud at the Egyptian army and threw it into confusion.

Before the captivity, the Hebrews divided the night into three watches. The first was from sunset to 10 P.M., the second from 10 P.M. to 2 A.M.; the third from 2 A.M. to sunrise. The first was called the "beginning of the watches" (Lamentations 2:14). The second was called the "middle watch" (Judges 7:19). The third was called the "morning watch" (last watch of the night, NIV), as in our verse-text, and in 1 Samuel 11:11) This method of dividing time is also referred to in Psalms 63:6 and 119:48. The Psalmist meditated on God and His Word in or through the "night watches."

15:1 EGYPTIAN CAVALRY

Then Moses and the Israelites sang this song to the LORD: "I will sing to the LORD, for he is highly exalted. The horse and its rider he has hurled into the sea."

Most say that this passage refers to men who are "masters of a horse," and as such means "mounted men" who rode in chariots. They further say that Egypt did not develop cavalry for another 500 years, and these are the horsemen referred to in 1 Chronicles 12:3—"With twelve hundred chariots and sixty thousand horsemen and the innumerable troops of Libyans, Sukkites and Cushites that came with him from Egypt." Obviously, 60,000 horsemen are too many to ride in 1200 chariots, so they were a separate fighting force. So Egypt apparently developed a massive cavalry force in later years. Archaeologists, however, do not agree among themselves as to the existence of cavalry among the ancient Egyptians because there are no representations of cavalry on Egyptian monuments.

15:20 DANCING

Then Miriam the prophetess, Aaron's sister, took a tambourine in her hand, and all the women followed her, with tambourines and dancing.

In some places, the word rendered *dancing* refers to the whirling motion of Oriental sacred dances, in other places it means to skip or leap for joy. Dancing is referred to throughout the Bible—it was a basic part of Jewish life. Ecclesiastes 3:4 says there is: "a time to mourn and a time to dance." So dancing was used to express joy and excitement in every kind of occasion.

At first, dancing was performed on sacred occasions only. It was part of the religious ceremonies of the Egyptians as

Women dancing

only of the honor of God, and forgot himself.

The ancient Hebrew form of dancing was much like our folk dancing, or square dancing, today. One difference is that the men and women danced separate from each other, in groups of their own. Dancing was usually performed outdoors in the daytime, and for many reasons and occasions. When Jephthah returned from his conquest over the Ammonites, he was met by "his daughter, dancing to the sound of tambourines" (Judges 11:34)! When the men of Benjamin surprised the daughters of Shiloh, the latter were dancing at "the annual festival of the LORD" (Judges 21:19-21). When David returned after killing Goliath, "the women came out from all the towns of Israel to meet King Saul with singing and dancing, with joyful songs and with tambourines and lutes" (1 Samuel 18:6).

well as the Hebrews, and was engaged in by many idolatrous nations, often accompanied with debauchery. Among the Hebrews, however, it was accompanied with sacred song, and was usually performed by the women only (this passage in Exodus is the first recorded song in the Bible). Thus the peculiarity of David's conduct in dancing before the ark of the Lord when it was brought home to Jerusalem (2 Samuel 6:14). The women took part in it with their timbrels. Michal should, in accordance with the example of Miriam and others, have herself led the female choir, instead of keeping aloof on the occasion and watching "from a window" (2 Samuel 6:16). David led the dancing choir wearing only the ephod or linen tunic. He thought

In several places in the Scriptures, and especially in the Psalms, God's people are exhorted to praise the LORD by dancing. For example, Psalm 149:3—"Let them praise his name with dancing and make music to him with tambourine and harp," and Psalm 150:4—"praise him with tambourine and dancing, praise him with the strings and flute."

16:3 Flesh Pots

The Israelites said to them, "If only we had died by the Lord's hand in Egypt! There we sat around pots of meat *(flesh pots, KJV)* and ate all the food *(bread, KJV)* we wanted, but you have brought us out into this desert to starve this entire assembly to death."

The flesh pot was a three-legged vessel of bronze that the Egyptians used for cooking. The ancient Egyptians were fond of meat. They chiefly ate beef and goose, and had an abundance of fish from the Nile River. Cows were sacred and so were not eaten, but ox were. The complaining of the Israelites against Moses, however, was foolish exaggeration. It was not the custom in Egypt for slaves to sit around flesh pots and eat all the bread and vegetables that they wanted. In ancient Egypt meat was not even a customary part of the common people's diet. It is doubtful, also, that they really wished they had died by the LORD's hand when the destroyer passed over Egypt. Often in the wilderness these former slaves acted like foolish and whiny children rather than God's people headed for the Promised Land—much like we often act today.

16:31 "Manna from heaven"

The people of Israel called the bread manna. It was white like coriander seed and tasted like wafers made with honey.

God miraculously gave food to the Israelites in the Exodus after the food they had brought with them from Egypt had run out. "When the dew was gone, thin flakes like frost on the ground appeared on the desert floor" (Exodus 16:14). Not knowing what it was, they called it "manna," which means "What is it?" In the centuries since then, the expression "manna from heaven" has been used to mean any unexpected good fortune.

16:36 Omer - Ephah

(An omer is one tenth of an ephah.)

An *omer* is an ancient Hebrew unit of dry measure equal to about 3.7 quarts (3.5 liters). An *ephah* is also a unit of dry measure and is equal to about one bushel (35 liters). The word *omer* is used only in this chapter.

19:10 Cleanliness in Worship

And the LORD said to Moses, "Go to the people and consecrate them today and tomorrow. Have them wash their clothes."

To meet the LORD, the people had to be spiritually and physically clean. This is not only a Hebrew custom, pagans have similar ceremonies in connection with their worship. Many years ago, a writer who observed pagans worshiping in their temple wrote: "No man can go to the temple wearing a dirty cloth—he must either put on a clean one, or go himself to a tank and wash in it, if it is soiled, or he must put on that which is quite new. Near the temples men may often be seen washing their clothes in order to prepare themselves for some religious ceremony." When Jacob was going up to Bethel to build an altar to the LORD, he commanded his household: "Get rid of the foreign gods you have with you, and purify yourselves (be clean, KJV) and change your clothes" (Genesis 35:2).

22:6 Thorn Bush Fires

"If a fire breaks out and spreads into thornbushes so that it burns shocks (stacks, KJV) of grain (corn, KJV) or standing grain or the whole field, the one who started the fire must make restitution."

A stock, or stack, was a number of sheaves of grain stacked upright in a field for drying. Thorn bushes often grew plentifully around the edges of the fields, and at times intermingled with the wheat. Sometimes they were also planted as hedges to protect the wheat field. By harvest time the bushes and other grasses that grew up with the grain were as dry as the grain itself. If the bushes were deliberately set on fire, it would spread throughout the grain field so rapidly that it was virtually impossible to extinguish it. In Judges 15:4-5, it tells how Samson burned up the stocks and standing grain of the Philistines by tying torches to the tails of foxes and letting them loose in the grain fields.

As the stocks of grain dried, the farmers had to be exceedingly careful of fires, and often a person was put to death for setting a grain field on fire, even if done accidentally. After the harvest, and before the autumn rains started, the dry thorn bushes and other grasses were commonly set on fire to clear the land for plowing, and to provide a fertilizer from the ashes.

23:5 BEASTS TO BE HELPED

"If you see the donkey of someone who hates you fallen down under its load, do not leave it there; be sure you help him with it."

Because of the roughness of the lands, it was an easy matter for an overburdened animal to fall to the ground. Obviously, if the load he was carrying fell on top of him, it would be difficult, if not impossible, for him to extricate himself without help, especially if he fell into a hollow or among stones. The law intended that even if the owner of the animal was trying to free the animal, you should help him to do so, even though the owner is someone you hate. The mercy you were showing was not toward the owner, but toward the animal, and it was not God's way that you leave the animal to die under its burden because of your hate for its owner. This law sets the conduct of the priest and the Levite in Jesus' parable of the Good Samaritan in Luke 10:31-32, in a most unenviable light. It shows that they treated a fellow human with less regard than one of their own laws required them to treat an enemy's donkey.

23:10 THREE GREAT FESTIVALS

"Three times a year you are to celebrate a festival (feast, KJV) to me."

The three great festivals or feasts were Passover, Pentecost, and the Feast of Tabernacles. On each of these occasions every male Israelite was commanded "to appear before the Lord" and bring a gift offering with him: "Three times a year all your men must appear before the LORD your God at the place he will choose: at the Feast of Unleavened Bread, the Feast of Weeks and the Feast of Tabernacles. No man should appear before the LORD empty-handed. Each of you must bring a gift in proportion to the way the LORD your God has blessed you" (Deuteronomy 16:16-17). The attendance of women was voluntary, but many women often accompanied their husbands (see 1 Samuel 2:19 and Luke 2:41).

In Exodus 34:23-24, God promised to protect their land while the men were at the feasts: "Three times a year all your men are to appear before the Sovereign LORD, the God of Israel. I will drive out nations before you and enlarge your territory, and no one will covet your land when you go up three times each year to appear before the LORD your God." This promise was always fulfilled, as someone wrote long ago: "During the whole period between Moses and Christ we never read of an enemy invading the land at the time of the three festivals. The first instance on record is thirty-three years after they had withdrawn from themselves the divine

protection by staining their hands with the Savior's blood. In A.D. 66, Cestius, the Roman general, slew fifty of the people of Lydda while all the rest had gone up to the feast of Tabernacles."

Besides their religious purpose, these three festivals had an important bearing on developing a sense of national unity among the people—it was a time to renew old acquaintances, make new friends, and refresh their awareness that God had called them forth as His own peculiar people. In God's providence, the times fixed for the festivals were arranged so that they interfered as little as possible with the people's work. Passover was just before the harvest commenced, Pentecost was at the conclusion of the corn harvest and before the vintage (wine harvest), and the Feast of Tabernacles was after all the crops of the soil had been gathered in.

23:10 Preparation for Festivals

"Three times a year you are to celebrate a festival *(feast, KJV)* to me."

In these times of calendars and set days of the year, and with the same days being observed at the same time all over the world—allowing for time differences, of course—it's hard to appreciate the difficulties that the ancient Hebrews had in finding the right time at which to observe their required feast days. The first appearance of the new moon was the starting point. To determine this the Sanhedrin in Jerusalem took the deposition of two impartial witnesses as to the time they had seen the new moon. A person with a bundle of brushwood or straw was then sent to the top of Mount Olivet, where he kindled his torch and waved it back forth until he was answered by similar torches from the surrounding hills. Those who responded would then signal with their torches to others further out in the regions—who would then do the same thing—until the entire land was notified.

After a time, the Samaritans imitated the signs, thus causing great confusion. This made it necessary to send messengers, who were usually fast runners, all over the country—sort of a human pony express. These messengers, however, did not go out at every new moon, but only seven times during the year. In this way all the people were notified of the times for these three great festivals—Passover,

Pentecost, and Tabernacles.

These three festivals were preceded by a season of preparation, called *peres*, which lasted fifteen days. During this time, each person was expected to meditate on the solemnity of the feast, and to undergo whatever legal purifications might be required. This is what John 11:55 refers to: "When it was almost time for the Jewish Passover, many went up from the country to Jerusalem for their ceremonial cleansing before the Passover." For the convenience of the people who were traveling, all the necessary roads, bridges, streets, and public water tanks would be repaired.

All the males of Israel were expected to attend these festivals. The only ones excused were the aged, the infirmed, and infants who could not walk alone. Each who attended had to bring offerings with them.

23:15 Passover (Feast of Unleavened Bread)

"Celebrate the Feast of Unleavened Bread; for seven days eat bread made without yeast, as I commanded you.

Do this at the appointed time in the month of Abib, for in that month you came out of Egypt. No one is to appear before me empty-handed."
(See also Deuteronomy 16:1)

The first of the three great festivals is called Passover in commemoration of the destroying angel "passing over" the houses of the Israelites when the first-born of the Egyptians were slain.

The ancient Jewish canons, or laws, distinguish between what they term "the Egyptian Passover" and "the Permanent Passover." The former refers to the feast in its original form, and the latter refers to the feast as it was modified in the subsequent years of the history of the Israelites. For example, the original Passover meal had no wine, but by the time of Jesus wine was a part of the meal, having been added about a hundred years before His birth. The essential parts of the feast, however, remained the same.

Passover took place during the month of *Abib*, or, as it was subsequently called, *Nisan*, which corresponds closely with April of our calendar year. While the festival lasted, great care was taken to abstain from leaven. A

he-lamb or kid of the first year was selected by the head of the family and was slain. Its blood was then sprinkled first on the door posts and then on the bottom of the family altar. The animal was then roasted whole with fire, and eaten with unleavened bread and a salad of bitter herbs. It could not be boiled, nor must a bone of it be broken (see John 19:36). When they first ate the Passover in Egypt, the Israelites had their loins girded and their shoes on, ready for a journey, and they ate standing up, as if in a hurry to be away. In later years, they ate sitting or reclining. Not fewer than ten, nor more than twenty, persons were admitted to one of these meals.

Some have suggested that in addition to the foreshadowing of Christ in the original Passover, there were in some of its ceremonies an intentional divine rebuke of the idolatry of heathen nations, and especially that of the Egyptians. Two of the Egyptian gods, *Amon* and *Khnum*, were each represented by a human body with a ram's head. To have a lamb slain, and its blood sprinkled on the doorposts, was an act of contempt against these gods. Some heathen people ate raw flesh in connection with their festivities. The Passover lamb was to be cooked. This cooking was by roasting, for the Egyptians and Syrians sometimes boiled the flesh of their sacrifices in water or milk. The lamb was to be roasted with fire, for the Egyptians, Chaldeans, and ancient Persians are said to have roasted their sacrifices in the sun. It was to be roasted whole, even to the intestines, for the heathen customarily looked into intestines for omens, and sometimes even ate them raw. All of these are, of course, only conjectures about the Passover ceremonies, for the Scriptures only tell us that the Passover lamb was a foreshadow of Jesus, and indicate that the blood on the lintel and doorposts was as His blood on Calvary's Cross.

23:16 Pentecost (Feast of Harvest)

"Celebrate the Feast of Harvest with the firstfruits of the crops you sow in your field."

The *Feast of Harvest* is also called the *Feast of Weeks* because of the "seven weeks" by which its time is determined: "Count off seven weeks from the time you begin to put the sickle to the standing grain. Then celebrate the Feast of Weeks to the LORD your God by giving a freewill offering in proportion to the blessings the LORD your God has given you" (Deuteronomy 16:9-10). It is also referred to as the Day of Firstfruits (Numbers 28:26), because on that day the first loaves made from the wheat harvest were offered to the Lord. Later it was called *Pentecost* (fiftieth day), because it occurred fifty days after Passover. Pentecost is the name most familiar to us today. These fifty days began with the offering of the first sheaf of the barley harvest during Passover week (see Leviticus 23:10), and ended with the Feast of Harvest. This feast took place after the grain harvest, and before the vintage (wine harvest).

The purpose of the Feast of Harvest was to express gratitude to God for the harvest that had been gathered, and thereby acknowledge that it was God who gave them the harvest. Some Jews assert that, in addition to this, it was intended to celebrate the giving of the law on Sinai, which took place fifty days after the Passover. It is further said that the Feast occupied only one day because that was all the time it took God to give Moses the law.

On this day the people rested from all labor. Two loaves, made of the new wheat were offered before the Lord. These were leavened (Leviticus 23:17), in contrast to the Passover bread, which was unleavened. This was because Passover is a memorial of the haste in which they departed from Egypt, when they had not time to leaven their bread, and the Feast of Harvest is a celebration of thankfulness to God for their ordinary food. In addition to this offering of the loaves, every person was required to bring in a basket a portion of the firstfruits of all they produced from the soil and offer it to the Lord (Deuteronomy 26:1-10). At the same time, there was a burnt offering of seven young lambs, one young bullock, and two rams. A kid was given as a sin offering, and two young lambs for a peace, or fellowship, offering (Leviticus 23:18-19).

23:16 FEAST OF TABERNACLES (FEAST OF INGATHERING)

"Celebrate the Feast of Ingathering at the end of the year, when you gather in your crops from the field."

The Feast of Ingathering is more generally known as the Feast of Tabernacles (Leviticus 23:34). It was instituted to remind the Israelites that their fathers dwelt in tents or booths in the wilderness (Leviticus 23:43), and to be an annual thanksgiving after all the crops of the land were gathered for the year (Leviticus 23:39). The feast was held in the seventh month, *Tizri* or *Ethanim*, corresponding to our October, and lasted for eight days, during which the people dwelt in booths made of the branches of palm, willow, and other trees (Leviticus 23:39-43). On each day there were offered in sacrifice two rams, fourteen lambs, and a kid for a burnt-offering.

During the observance of the feast, seventy bullocks were offered: thirteen on the first day, twelve on the second, eleven on the third, and so on—the number decreasing by one each day until the seventh day when only seven bullocks were offered. The eighth day was a day of peculiar solemnity, and had for its special offerings a bullock, a ram, and seven lambs for a burnt offering, and a goat for a sin offering (Numbers 29:12-38). Altogether there were 199 animals offered each year at the Feast of Tabernacles.

On the Sabbatical year (seventh year), the Feast of Tabernacles was further celebrated by a public reading of the law (Deuteronomy 31:10-13). Whether this was intended to include the whole law or only certain portions of it are a matter of debate.

23:17 ANNUAL PILGRIMAGES

"Three times a year all the men are to appear before the Sovereign LORD."

This great and sudden increase in the population of the sacred city—for it was to Jerusalem that the men went, after they were settled in the Promised Land—could be accommodated much easier than at first might be supposed. Three times a year these pilgrims were looked for, and every provision was made for their reception. Those who could not find room in inns and private homes could pitch their tents in the streets or in the areas surrounding the city.

Many years ago, travelers to that land watched Mohammedans, in countless numbers, make their great pilgrimage to Mecca (today a modern city of western Saudi Arabia near the coast of the Red Sea). The pilgrims carried with them provisions enough to last during the journey both ways, and also during their stay in the city. They took from their homes butter, honey, oil, olives, rice, and bread, besides provisions for camels and donkeys. They dwelt in tents until their return. Undoubtedly, the ancient Israelites traveling to Jerusalem during the three great feasts traveled much the same way.

23:19 FORBIDDEN COOKING

"Bring the best of the firstfruits of your soil to the house of the LORD your God. "Do not cook *(seeth, KJV, or boil)* a young goat in its mother's milk."

It's supposed by most that the reason for this command, also given in Exodus 34:26 and Deuteronomy 14:21, is that there were some Canaanite sacrificial customs in which this was done and the Lord wished to avoid any comparison to them. But recent archaeological investigations don't support this theory. Others believe that it was because of the maternal relationship between the mother and offspring, and that this was the reason for the command forbidding the killing of a cow and its calf on the same day (Leviticus 22:28) and the taking together of a bird with its young (Leviticus 22:26). Perhaps the intention is to teach that anything that blunts moral sensitivity is to be avoided. Whatever the reason, God's rule not to boil a kid in its mother's milk remains one of the more puzzling commands in the Scriptures, and the exact reason for it will not truly be known until the Lord Himself explains it.

25:10 CUBIT

"Have them make a chest of acacia wood—two and a half cubits long, a cubit and a half wide, and a cubit and a half high."

The word *cubit* is from the Latin word *cubitus*, the lower arm. The Hebrew word is *ammah*, the *mother of the arm*, which is the forearm. Even after all these years, no one is quite certain as to the exact length of a cubit. The American Heritage Dictionary refers to it as "An ancient unit of linear measure, originally equal to the length of the forearm from the tip of the middle finger to the elbow, or about 17 to 22 inches (43 to 56 centimeters)." It is probable, however, that there were two cubits, one shorter than the other, and that the shorter one was measured from the root of the hand at the wrist to the elbow.

Deuteronomy 3:11 speaks of "the cubit of a man (KJV), and 2 Chronicles 3:3 says: "The foundation Solomon laid for building the temple of God was sixty cubits long and twenty cubits wide (using the cubit of the old standard)." (The KJV calls it "cubits after the first measure.") Then in Ezekiel 41:8 we are told about "great cubits," which Ezekiel 40:5 tells us were a "cubit and an hand breadth" (KJV). But it is impossible to determine the exact length of any of these cubits.

Various estimates of the Mosaic cubit have been made, ranging from twelve to twenty-two inches. The ancient Egyptian cubit was nearly twenty-one inches (now set at 21.888 inches), which some of the best authorities now estimate to be the length of the Mosaic cubit. Other authorities, however, claim that the length of the Mosaic cubit, as applied to the Tabernacle and Temple, was eighteen inches, and that the Israelites did not use the

25:30 TABLE OF SHOWBREAD

"Put the bread of the Presence *(showbread, KJV)* on this table to be before me at all times."

The table of showbread was on the north side of the Holy Place: "Place the table outside the curtain on the north side of

Table of the showbread

cubit of twenty-one inches, which was Babylonian as well as Egyptian, until after the captivity.

the tabernacle" (Exodus 26:35). It was made of acacia wood overlaid with gold, and was two cubits long (3'), one cubit wide (1½'), and a cubit and a half high

(2¼'). It had an ornamental cornice of gold around the top, and was furnished with rings of gold and gilded staves for carrying it (Exodus 25:23-28). On it were placed twelve loaves of bread in two rows or piles, and frankincense was put on each row. The bread was changed every Sabbath (Leviticus 24:5-9) There were also golden vessels of various kinds (Exodus 25:29), probably for the bread, frankincense, and wine.

27:20 BEATEN OLIVE OIL

"And thou shalt command the children of Israel, that they bring thee pure oil olive beaten for the light, to cause the lamp to burn always" *(KJV)*.

Oil obtained from fresh, ripe olives beaten in a mortar rather than crushed in a press, would be of a finer quality, burn with a bright, clean flame, and produce little smoke. Even today the oil from lightly pressed olives is of a higher quality than that produced from heavily pressed olives. Every year Solomon gave Hiram a present of about 120,000 gallons (440 kilo-liters) of "pure oil" (1 Kings 5:11), which was the higher quality oil obtained

from beaten olives, as can be seen from our text-verse, and from Leviticus 24:2—"Command the children of Israel, that they bring unto thee pure oil olive beaten for the light, to cause the lamps to burn continually."

28:16 SPAN

It is to be square—a span long and a span wide—and folded double.

The American Heritage Dictionary defines a span (Hebrew *zereth*) as "The distance from the tip of the thumb to the tip of the little finger when the hand is fully extended, formerly used as a unit of measure equal to about nine inches (23 centimeters)." In biblical use, it is also half a cubit.

32:4 METALLIC IDOLS

And he received them at their hand, and fashioned it with a graving tool, after he had made it a molten calf *(KJV)*.

The word *molten* is an adjective that means "made by melting and casting in a mold." So the inference is that the gold earrings that the people gave Aaron were melted down and then formed around a mold. It is highly unlikely that the calf was made of solid gold because of the quantity of gold it would have taken, and since only earrings were used, it would have required thousands of them. Most of the large idols worshiped by the ancients were first made of wood and then covered with plates of metal, and that is undoubtedly how Aaron made this golden calf. Isaiah 30:22 refers to making idols in this manner, as does Isaiah 40:19—"As for an idol, a craftsman casts it, and a goldsmith overlays it with gold and fashions silver chains for it." Sometimes the idols were carved out of wood or stone and then covered with gold or silver, as indicated in Habakkuk 2:19—"Woe to him who says to wood, 'Come to life!' Or to lifeless stone, 'Wake up!' Can it give guidance? It is covered with gold and silver; there is no breath in it."

A wooden or stone image was first prepared, and the gold was then cast into a flat sheet that the goldsmith hammered and spread out into plating, which was then shaped and fastened around the image. Thus the goldsmith first melted the gold, and then used a "graving tool" to fashion it to the shape of the image. Aaron's molten calf seems to have been made in this manner. This is evident from the way in which it was destroyed. It was first burned (gold doesn't burn, wood does), and then ground to powder. In Deuteronomy 9:21, Moses describes what he did with the golden calf: "Also I took that sinful thing of yours, the calf you had made, and burned it in the fire. Then I crushed it and ground it to powder as fine as dust and threw the dust into a stream that flowed down the mountain."

32:6 Calf Worship

So the next day the people rose early and sacrificed burnt offerings and presented fellowship offerings. Afterward they sat down to eat and drink and got up to indulge in revelry *(rose up to play, KJV)*.

The Hebrew verb *sahaq*, translated "play" in the KJV rendering of this verse, is highly suggestive of sexual activities. It is the same verb used in Genesis 26:8 that is translated "caressing" in the NIV, and "sporting" in the

Calf idol

KJV. Considering the drinking that was taking place, and the nakedness, the worship of the calf may have turned into a drunken sex orgy, which was not uncommon among the pagans. More than likely some of the Israelites had picked up these ways of worshiping while slaves of the Egyptians, and had even worshiped with them or as they did.

The Egyptian idolaters worshiped deity under animal forms, thus differing from many other nations whose deities were in human form. They kept live animals in some of their temples, and had statues and illustrations of them in others. The calf idol was almost certainly inspired by *Apis*, the sacred bull of Egypt, who ensured fertility. The Egyptians' worship of their fertility gods was often accompanied with lascivious dances and other obscene

practices. This is probably what is referred to in Exodus 38:25— "And when Moses saw that the people were naked; (for Aaron had made them naked unto their shame among their enemies)" (KJV).

Reference is made to the Egyptian origin of this calf worship in Ezekiel 20:6-8. When Jeroboam, who had lived in Egypt for some time (1 Kings 12:2), was made king of Israel, he set up two golden calves, probably also inspired by Apis and patterned after Aaron's calf (1 Kings 12:28).

38:8 MIRRORS

They made the bronze basin and its bronze stand from the mirrors of the women who served at the entrance to the Tent of Meeting.

Ancient mirrors were metallic. The mirrors of the Egyptians, whose mirrors these had been, were made of a mixed metal such as bronze, and were brightly polished. They were usually small, about the size of what we now call hand mirrors. They were created with great skill, and the handles, which were of wood, stone, or metal, were artistically shaped and highly ornamented. The Egyptian women customarily carried a mirror in one hand when they went into their temples to worship. It may be that the Hebrew women imitated this custom when they brought their mirrors to "the door of the tabernacle of the congregation" (KJV). Someone who visited northwest Africa in the 19th century reported seeing Moorish women who had made mirrors a part of the ornaments of their clothing, hanging them from the front where they could easily be reached. Reference is made to a "molten looking glass" (KJV) in Job 37:18, which the NIV translates as "a mirror of cast bronze."

38:24 TALENTS

The total amount of the gold from the wave offering used for all the work on the sanctuary was 29 talents and 730 shekels, according to the sanctuary shekel.

A silver talent is estimated to have weighed about 80 pounds,

and a gold talent weighed twice that amount, about 160 pounds. Thus the gold that the people willingly gave for the work of the tabernacle would have weighed about 4560 pounds, or slightly over two tons of gold. At today's gold prices of around $250 an ounce, the total value of that much gold would be over $18,000,000. The silver that was given totaled 100 talents 1,775 shekels, which would be about 8000 pounds of silver. Also given were 70 talents 2,400 shekels of brass. (Exodus 38:24-31)

40:2 TABERNACLE IN THE WILDERNESS

Set up the tabernacle, the Tent of Meeting, on the first day of the first month.

The tabernacle was thirty cubits long, ten cubits wide, and ten cubits high (Exodus 36:20-30). Considering a cubit to be18 inches, by today's measurements this would make the tabernacle 45 feet long, 15 feet wide, and 15 feet high. Its two sides and its western end were made of boards of acacia wood (shittimwood, KJV)—the eastern end was left open. Every board was ten cubits

Tabernacle in the wilderness

symbolic cherubim were wrought with needlework in blue, purple, and scarlet threads, and probably also with threads of

long, and a cubit and a half wide (Exodus 36:21). The thickness isn't mentioned in the Bible, but the Jewish historian Josephus says that each of these boards was four fingers thick, excepting the two corners of the west end, which were each a cubit in thickness. Each board had two tenons or projections at the base (Exodus 36:22) that fit into silver mortises (sockets) (Exodus 36:24). These mortises, in turn, were fastened to the ground by means of brass (or bronze) pins (Exodus 38:20), which, according to Josephus, were each a cubit in length. The boards were held together by means of wooden bars covered with gold (Exodus 36:31-34).

The framework was covered with four coverings, the first of fine linen, in which figures of the gold (Exodus 26:1-6; 36:8-13). Above this was a second covering of twelve curtains of black goat hair cloth, reaching down on the outside almost to the ground (Exodus 26:7-11). The third covering was of ram skins dyed red, and the fourth was of badger (sea cows, NIV) skins (Exodus 25:5; 26:14; 35:7, 23; 36:19; 39:34). Precisely what animal is meant by that name is unknown. Badger, or sea cows, is translated from the Hebrew word *tahash*, which is the *dugong*, a species of seal.

Internally the tabernacle was divided by a veil into two chambers. The exterior chamber was called the "holy place," also "the sanctuary" (Hebrews 9:2) and the "first tabernacle" (Hebrews 9:6). The interior chamber was called the "holy of holies," "the most holy place," "the holiest of all," the "second tabernacle" (Exodus 28:29; Hebrews 9:3, 7). The veil separating these two chambers was a double curtain of the finest workmanship, which was never passed except by the high priest once a year, on the great Day of Atonement. The holy place was separated from the outer court that enclosed the tabernacle by a curtain, which hung over the six pillars that stood at the east end of the tabernacle, and by which it was entered. The order as well as the typical character of the services of the tabernacle are recorded in Hebrews 9; 10:19-22.

The holy of holies, a cube of 10 cubits (15' x 15' x 15'), contained the "ark of the testimony," the oblong chest that contained the two tables of stone, the pot of manna, and Aaron's rod that budded. The holy place was the western and larger chamber of the tabernacle. Here were placed the table for the consecrated bread (showbread, KJV), the golden lamp stand (candlestick, KJV), and the golden altar of incense.

Round about the tabernacle was a court, enclosed by curtains hung upon sixty pillars (Exodus 27:9-18). This court was 150' long and 75' wide. Within it were placed the altar of burnt offering, which measured 7 $\frac{1}{2}$ feet in length and width and 4 $\frac{1}{2}$ feet high, with horns at the four corners, and the laver of brass (Exodus 30:18), which stood between the altar and the tabernacle.

The entire tabernacle was completed in seven months. On the first day of the first month of the second year after the Exodus, it was formally set up, and the cloud of the divine presence descended on it (Exodus 39:22-43; 40:1-38). The tabernacle was so constructed that it could easily be taken down and carried from place to place during the wanderings in the wilderness.

40:3 ARK OF THE COVENANT

Place the ark of the Testimony in it and shield the ark with the curtain.

This is called elsewhere the "ark of the covenant" (Deuteronomy 31:26, and "the ark of God" (1 Samuel 3:3). It was made of acacia wood, overlaid with gold within and without. It was two cubits and a half long (3 ¾ feet), one cubit

Ark of the Covenant and the Israelites

that this is not in accordance with 1 Kings 8:9, and that these two objects were laid by the side of the ark and accompanied it. Naturally, the passage in 1 Kings does not prove that the manna and the rod were never in the ark, but only that they were not there at the time the ark was put into Solomon's Temple—they could have once been in the ark and then somehow lost or destroyed.

It has also been supposed by some that a complete copy of the law was placed in the ark because of what is written in Deuteronomy 31:26—"Take this book of the law, and put it in the side of the ark of the covenant of the LORD your God, that it may be there for a witness against thee." Others say that "*in* the side of the ark" should have been translated "*by* the side of the

and a half wide (2' 3" wide), and the same in height. An ornamental cornice, or "crown" of gold ran around the top. In each corner of the ark was a gold ring, and through the rings were kept two gilded staves for the purpose of carrying the ark when the Tabernacle was moved (Exodus 25:10-15).

The ark was put into the Most Holy Place (Exodus 26:34). In it were placed the two tablets of the law, for which it was especially designed (Exodus 25:16). According to Hebrews 9:4, in addition to the tablets in the ark there were a golden pot of manna and Aaron's rod that budded. Some think, however,

ark." The NIV translates this passage: "beside the ark."

The cover of the ark was of solid gold, and was called the "mercy seat"

Moses with the tables of the Law

(atonement cover, NIV) (Exodus 25:17, 21). Springing from the ends of this cover were two golden cherubim with outstretched wings (Exodus 25:18-20). No specific description is given anywhere in the Scriptures of their size, shape, or general appearance. We don't know how to account for this failure to describe them, especially since all other articles associated with the Tabernacle are minutely described. Whether the form of the cherubim was so generally known as to make description unnecessary, or whether the description was purposely concealed as among the secrets of the LORD cannot now be known. Certainly a description was given to Moses at the time he was told how to build the Tabernacle, or the cherubim would have been designed after man's imagination and not God's knowledge and desire. From the account given in Ezekiel in chapter 1:4-11, the cherubim seem to have been composite figures. But these could not have been in all ways like the cherubim over the ark, for Ezekiel describes them as having four wings each, two of which covered their bodies, while Moses speaks of the wings being stretched forth on high: "covering the mercy seat." This seems to indicate that they had but two wings each.

More particular description is given of the colossal cherubim in the Temple of Solomon, which were probably patterned after those of the Tabernacle. These are distinctly stated to have had two wings each, and to have stood with their wings outstretched, and their faces turned inward (2 Chronicle 3:10-13). However composite the form, it was doubtless more human than anything else. According to Jewish tradition, the cherubim over the mercy seat had human faces—or perhaps humans have cherubim faces.

40:4 CANDLESTICK

Candlestick

Bring in the table and set out what belongs on it. Then bring in the lampstand *(candlestick, KJV)* and set up its lamps.

The candlestick consisted of a standard with three branches on each side, thus affording room for seven lamps, which were supplied with olive oil. The candlestick stood on the south side of the Holy Place, and was made of gold, as were its snuffers and tongs (Exodus 25:31-40). Nothing is known of its size, or of the formation of its base, or of the exact position of the six branches. Whether the tops of these branches were on a level, or in the form of an arch, and whether the branches extended in the same plane or in different planes so as to form a curve is not known.

40:5 GOLDEN ALTAR OF INCENSE

Place the gold altar of incense in front of the ark of the Testimony and put the curtain at the entrance to the tabernacle.

The altar was made of acacia wood covered with

gold. It was two cubits high (3'), one cubit long (1½'), and one

Altar of incense

cubit wide (1½'). It had four "horns" or projections on the four corners at the top, and like the ark and the table of showbread, it had a cornice of gold, and rings and staves for carrying it. The rings were of gold, and the staves were of acacia covered with gold (Exodus 37:25-28). Its position was in the west end of the Holy Place, near the veil that concealed the Most Holy Place (Exodus 40:26). Thus it was immediately in front of the ark of the covenant, though separated by the veil.

40:6 Altar of Burnt Offering

Place the altar of burnt offering in front of the entrance to the tabernacle, the Tent of Meeting.

This altar was placed in the court, not far from the entrance to the Tabernacle (Exodus 40:6, 29). It was made of acacia wood, and covered with bronze (brass, KJV) plates. It was five cubits long (7½'), five cubits wide, and three cubits high (4½'), and had four horns at the four corners. It had bronze rings and bronze-covered staves for moving it. It was hollow, and is believed to have been filled with earth, thus complying with the command in Exodus 20:24—"Make an altar of earth for me and sacrifice on it your burnt offerings and fellowship (peace, KJV) offerings, your sheep and goats and your cattle." (See also Exodus 38:1-7.)

Around the altar, midway from the bottom, was a projecting ledge on which the priest stood while offering sacrifice. This is represented in the Hebrew word *karkob* in

Exodus 27:5, which is translated "compass" in the KJV, and "ledge" in the NIV. It is believed that an inclined plane of earth led up to this on one side, probably the south.

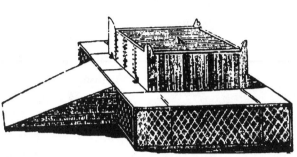

Altar of Burnt Offering

altar half way to the bottom. Both of these theories assume, of course, that the grating was in a horizontal position. Some archaeologists, however, believe this grating or network to have been perpendicular, and to have

Thus we can see how Aaron "came down" from the altar as in Leviticus 9:22 in the KJV. Some believe, however, that the ledge was low enough so that after Aaron "sacrificed the sin offering, the burnt offering and the fellowship offering, he stepped down" (NIV).

Various views have been entertained in reference to the grating or network spoken of in Exodus 27:4-5 and 38:4. Some place it at the top of the altar, believing that the fire and the sacrifice were put upon it, but if the altar was filled with earth, as some believe, there would not have been a need for a grating for such a purpose. Others believe the altar to have been only half filled with earth, and that this grating was placed inside of the

dropped from the edge of the *karkob*, or projecting ledge, to the ground. This would seem to agree with Exodus 27:5, even in the NIV: "Put it under the ledge of the altar so that it is halfway up the altar."

Many years ago, a German archaeologist, Johann Friedrich Meyer, wrote in favor of this view; in fact, he may have even been the first to suggest it. He wrote: "Under the outer edge of this bench (ledge) was the copper lattice work, which extended from it to the ground on all four sides, just as the body of the chest extended from the inner edge of the bench. It formed, with the bench or the *karkob* around, an expanding set-off, by reason of which the under half of

137

the altar, on all sides, appeared wider than the upper. On the karkob, bench, ledge, or passageway, the priest walked in order to attend to the sacrifice, to lay wood upon the altar, or to officiate in other ways. The grating served to preserve the base of the altar from the sprinkled blood of the sacrifices (see Exodus 29:12; Leviticus 4:7), and to keep away from the sacred altar men and the beasts to be offered in sacrifice."

40:7 LAVER

Place the basin *(laver, KJV)* between the Tent of Meeting and the altar and put water in it.

The laver or basin was made of women's mirrors: "They made the bronze basin and its bronze stand from the mirrors of the women who served at the entrance to the Tent of Meeting" (Exodus 38:8). It was used for the priests to wash their hands and feet (Exodus 30:17-21). So that they would be certain not to bypass washing, the laver was placed between the brazen altar and the door of the Tabernacle (Exodus 40:30-32). No description is given of its shape

or size, but it is believed to have been circular. In connection with the laver, frequent mention is made of what is called its "foot." See Exodus 30:18, 28; 31:9; 35:16; 39:39; 40:11; and Leviticus 8:11. This has led some commentators to believe that the "foot" was something more than a mere pedestal or base for the support of the laver, but that it may have been a lower basin to catch water that flowed through pipes or openings from the upper basin, thus making a convenient arrangement for washing the hands and feet of the priests.

40:8 OUTER COURT

Set up the courtyard around it and put the curtain at the entrance to the courtyard.

This outer court that surrounded and enclosed the Tabernacle was one hundred cubits long (150') and fifty cubits wide (75'). It was surrounded by a canvas wall five cubits high (7½'). The sides and ends, excepting its entrance at the east end, were made of fine linen curtains, which were hung on fillets, or, more properly, rods, made of silver. These silver rods were connected by silver hooks to supporting bronze (brass, KJV) pillars. There were twenty pillars on each side, and ten on each end, all fitted into bronze (brazen, KJV) sockets. The entrance at the east end occupied three panels, and was twenty cubits wide (30'), thus taking up two fifths of the front. The curtain at the entrance was made of the finest kind of needlework, and embroidered in colors (Exodus 27:16). The frail walls of the Tabernacle were steadied by cords that were fastened into the ground at suitable distances by tent pegs (Exodus 35:18).

The High Priest in his robes

40:13 Priestly Garments

Then dress Aaron in the sacred garments, anoint him and consecrate him so he may serve me as priest.

First we'll examine the garments that the high priest wore in common with the other priests:

1. *Linen drawers*. These reached from the waist to the thigh (Exodus 28:42). Someone has said that these were to be worn as an evidence that the divine worship sanctioned no such sexual impurities as were associated with idolatrous worship, and that this is also the reason for the command in

Exodus 20:26—"And do not go up to my altar on steps, lest your nakedness be exposed on it."

2. *Tunic or shirt.* It was made of white linen, all one piece, had sleeves, and is believed to have reached to the ankles, and to have been of a checker pattern. (Exodus 28:39, 40; 29:5)

3. *Sash or girdle.* This was wound around the tunic between the waist and the shoulders. Josephus says it was four fingers broad, and "so loosely woven that you would think it were the skin of a serpent." It was embroidered in colors. (Exodus 28:39)

4. *Turban or miter.* It was made of linen.

Now we'll examine the garments that were peculiar to the high priest:

1. *Robe.* This was woven of blue cloth, in one piece, with an opening by which it might be put on over the head. It was worn over the tunic, but whether it reached to the knees or to the ankles is uncertain. It was beautifully ornamented at the bottom with pomegranates in purple and scarlet. Little gold bells hung between these, and made a tinkling sound whenever the wearer moved. (Exodus 39:22-26).

2. *Epod.* The ordinary priest wore an epod (see 1 Samuel 22:18), but it was different in material and style from that of the high priest. This was made of made "of gold, and of blue, purple and scarlet yarn, and of finely twisted linen" (Exodus 39:2). After that they "hammered out thin sheets of gold and cut strands to be worked into the blue, purple and scarlet yarn and fine linen—the work of a skilled craftsman" (Exodus 39:3), who must have learned his skill while he was a slave in Egypt, for the art of weaving was well known to the ancient Egyptians. The epod was in two pieces, one for the back and one for the breast. The two pieces were joined by "shoulder pieces," which were a continuation of the front part of the epod (Exodus 28:7; 39:4). On the shoulder pieces were two precious stones, each having the names of six of the tribes of Israel. There stones were placed in gold settings, which some think made clasps for fastening the shoulder pieces together. (Exodus 28:9-12) The two parts of the epod were fastened around the body by means of a waistband (girdle, KJV), which was really a portion of the front

part of the epod (Exodus 28:8). The epod had no sleeves.

3. *Breastplate*. This was made of the same material as the epod. It was half a cubit wide (9") and a cubit long (18"), but when doubled it became a half cubit square (9"), and formed a pouch or pocket. On the front of this were four rows of precious stones, three in each row, and on them were engraved the names of the twelve tribes. These stones were set in gold. The breastplate was fastened to the epod by golden chains. (Exodus 28:15-29) Connected with this breastplate were the *Urim* and *Thummim*—Lights and Perfections—but precisely what these were no one knows. They were used as means of consulting the LORD in case of doubt (Numbers 27:21; 1 Samuel 28:6). How they were used is not known. Some think that the twelve stones were the Urim and Thummim, the stones themselves being the Urim, or Lights, and the names of the tribes engraved on them being the Thummim, or Perfections, because they represented the tribes in their tribal integrity. From the fact that the Urim and Thummim are said to be *in* the breastplate, others think that they were separate from the twelve stones and were put into the pocket behind them. Some believe them to have been three precious stones that were placed in this pouch of the breastplate to be used for casting lots to decided questions of doubts; and that on one of the stones was engraved *Yes*, on another *No*, the third being without inscription. The stone drawn out by the high priest would indicate the answer: affirmative, negative, or no answer to be given. This may be so, but there is no proof of it. Someone further suggested that the Urim and Thummim was a diamond, kept in the pocket of the breastplate, and having the ineffable name of the Deity inscribed on it. This one believed that this is the "white stone" referred to in Revelation 2:17. Again, there is no proof of this, and all such things are only speculations best left until the LORD clarifies it all in the ages to come.

4. *Diadem*. This was a plate of pure gold fastened around the miter or turban by a blue cord (lace, KJV), and having engraved on it the words: "HOLINESS TO THE LORD." The NIV verses read: "Make a plate of pure gold and engrave on

it as on a seal: HOLY TO THE
LORD. Fasten a blue cord to it to
attach it to the turban; it is to be
on the front of the turban"
(Exodus 28:36-37).

2:13 USE OF SALT

"Season all your grain offerings with salt. Do not leave the salt of the covenant of your God out of your grain offerings; add salt to all your offerings."

Salt stands for permanence and incorruption. Thus when salt is used in a "covenant of salt," it always signifies an everlasting covenant, with the salt being an emblem or symbol of perpetuity. The use of salt in an offering, would therefore signify the everlasting relation between God and His people—they everlastingly belong to Him, and He everlastingly belongs to them. For this reason, salt and permanence were always associated in a covenant; 2 Chronicles 13:5 states: "Don't you know that the LORD, the God of Israel, has given the kingship of Israel to David and his descendants forever by a covenant of salt?" (See also Numbers 13:19.)

LEVITICUS

2:11 FORBIDDEN OFFERINGS

"Every grain offering you bring to the LORD must be made without yeast, for you are not to burn any yeast or honey in an offering made to the LORD by fire."

It is believed that the reason yeast and honey were forbidden in this offering was that they both ferment under certain conditions. For this reason, honey may have been associated with corruption. Because yeast (leaven) also permeates, it is used almost without exception to symbolize the insidious spread of evil. In Mark 8:15, it's recorded that Jesus told his disciples: "And he charged them, saying, Take heed, beware of the leaven (yeast,

Burnt offering

6:9 BURNT OFFERING

"These are the regulations for the burnt offering: The burnt offering is to remain on the altar hearth throughout the night, till morning, and the fire must be kept burning on the altar."

The different animals for the burnt offering were bullocks, sheep, goats, turtle doves, and young pigeons. The person making this voluntary offering, laid his hand on the head of the offering so that it was accepted on his behalf as an atonement, and then slew it. The priests took the blood and sprinkled it around the great altar. In Solomon's Temple there was a red line half way up the sides of the great altar, and some of the blood was sprinkled above and some below this line. After the blood was sprinkled, the person who brought the offering skinned the animal and cut it in pieces. This was apparently changed later so that it was the priest that performed this task, sometimes helped by others when there were too many offerings, as shown in 2 Chronicles 29:34—"The priests, however, were too few to skin all the burnt offerings; so their kinsmen the Levites helped them until the task was finished and until other priests had been consecrated, for the Levites had been more conscientious in consecrating themselves than the priests had been." The entire offering was then burned by the priests. If the offering consisted of a goat, a sheep, or fowls, the ceremony was slightly changed.

The burnt offering was the only offering that was entirely burned. Thus it is sometimes called the "whole" burnt offering (Deuteronomy 33:10; Psalm 51:19). The burning was to be so gradual that it should last from morning to evening, or from one daily sacrifice to the next. It was commanded that the fire on the altar should never go out. The emphasis, however, was not on the fire, but on the continual burnt offering, which symbolized the consecration of the nation unto God.

The burnt offering is described in detail in Leviticus 1:1-17; 6:8-13. The purpose of the burnt offering is not clearly stated in the Bible, but most consider it as a symbol of entire and perpetual consecration to God. It was self-dedication, following upon and growing out of pardon and acceptance with God.

6:14 MEAT OFFERING

"These are the regulations for the grain *(meat, KJV)* offering: Aaron's sons are to bring it before the LORD, in front of the altar."

This offering was wholly vegetable in its nature, and was sometimes presented in a raw state and sometimes baked. Specific directions were given concerning the ceremonies to be observed in either case. A portion only was consumed in the fire, and the rest was given to the priest. Neither leaven (yeast) or honey was allowed to be mixed with it. It usually accompanied and was subsidiary to the sin and burnt offerings, and the quantity offered was graduated according to the animal offered as a burnt offering (Numbers 15:4-5, 6, 9).

It is believed by some that oil was used to give the grain offering a grateful relish, and frankincense to make a sweet odor in the court of the Tabernacle. Paul alludes to a fragrant offering (odor of a sweet smell, KJV) in Philippians 4:18. Full directions for the grain (meat, KJV) offering are given in Leviticus 2:1-16; 6: 14-23.

6:25 Sin Offering

"These are the regulations for the sin offering: The sin offering is to be slaughtered before the LORD in the place the burnt offering is slaughtered; it is most holy."

There were two kinds of sin offering: one for the whole congregation and the other for individuals. For the first kind, a young bullock was brought into the outer court of the Tabernacle, where the elders laid their hands upon his head and he was killed. The high priest then took the blood into the Holy Place and sprinkled it seven times before the veil, putting some on the horns of the golden altar of incense. The remainder of the blood was then poured out at the foot of the altar of burnt offering. The fat of the animal was burned upon the altar, and the rest of the body was taken outside the camp and burned (Leviticus 4:13-21).

Of the second kind of sin offering, there were three varieties. The first was for the high priest. The ceremonies only slightly varied from those just described (Leviticus 4:3-12).

The second was for any of the rulers of the people. A kid (young goat) was killed instead of a bullock. The priest did not enter the Holy Place, but merely put some of the blood on the horns of the altar of burnt offering, and poured the rest out by the foot of the altar. The fat was burned upon the altar. (Leviticus 4:22-26). The third was for any of the common people. A female kid or lamb was brought and treated as in the case just described (Leviticus 4:27-35). If poverty prevented the procuring of a young goat or lamb, two turtle doves or two young pigeons could be substituted. For the very poorest, a small offering of flour was acceptable (Leviticus 5:7-13).

What was left of the sin offering for one of the rulers or one of the common people was not burned outside the camp, as in the other instances, but was eaten by the priests and their sons. It was considered peculiarly holy, and special directions were given concerning the vessels in which it was cooked (Leviticus 6:24-30). The sin offering was offered for sins of ignorance against negative precepts (Leviticus 4: 2, 23, 22, 27).

7:1 TRESPASS OFFERING

"These are the regulations for the guilt *(trespass, KJV)* offering, which is most holy."

The trespass offering was similar to the sin offering, yet there were several important points of distinction. In the trespass offering, rams were offered, and the blood was sprinkled around the altar of burnt offering (Leviticus 5:18; 7:2). The priest was required to make a special evaluation of the offered ram (Leviticus 5: 15-16).

The trespass offering was offered in cases of trespass committed in holy things, dishonesty or falsehood in a trust, robbery coupled with deceit, and dishonesty and falsehood in reference to things found (Leviticus 5:15-6:7).

7:9 OVEN, PAN, GRIDDLE

"Every grain offering baked in an oven or cooked in a pan *(frying pan, KJV)* or on a griddle *(pan, KJV)* belongs to the priest who offers it."

The oven was a device used to bake food, especially bread indicated in our text-verse. A common oven consisted of a hole dug in the ground about four feet deep and three feet across and well plastered. A fire was built in the bottom of the hole. When the oven was thoroughly heated, the dough was rolled out no thicker than a finger and stuck against the inside of the oven, where it would instantly bake.

Another oven was made of a great stone pitcher about the same size. There would usually be a hole in the side near the bottom for the firewood, and a hole about half way up for inserted and removing the bread. Pebbles or small flints that would retain heat were placed in the bottom of the oven and the fire built on top of them. Some times the thin-rolled dough

Arab oven

was placed directly upon the heated pebbles, or against the oven walls. Some believe that reference is made to this type of oven in 2:4, and that the "unleavened cakes of fine flour mixed with oil" were to be baked inside the oven, and the "unleavened wafers anointed with oil" were to be baked outside. The "cakes" being mixed with oil, and the "wafers" only smeared with oil. Dried grass, thorny shrubs, and even animal dung were often used as fuels.

The "pan" (Hebrew *marchesheth*) was a deep vessel of iron used for boiling meat, and which could also be used for baking bread. The "griddle" was a thin flat plate of iron on which bread could quickly be baked as on modern griddles. This is the utensil referred to in Ezekiel 4:3.

7:11 Peace Offering

"**These are the regulations for the fellowship *(peace, KJV)* offering a person may present to the LORD.**"

Peace offerings were of three kinds: 1. Thank offerings. 2. Freewill offerings. 3. Offerings for vows. (Leviticus 7:12, 16)

The peace offering might be either of the herd (cattle) or of the flock (sheep), and either male or female (Leviticus 1, 7, 12). The offerings were accompanied by laying of hands on the animal, and by sprinkling blood around the great altar, on which the fat and the parts accompanying were burned (Leviticus 3:1-5). When offered for a thanksgiving, the offering was accompanied by an offering of "cakes of bread made without yeast and mixed with oil, wafers made without yeast and spread with oil, and cakes of fine flour well-kneaded and mixed with oil" (Leviticus 7:12-13). A peculiarity of the peace offering was that the breast was waved and the shoulder heaved ("heave offering" from Hebrew *terumah)*—it could mean simply "lifted up" or just presented to the Lord (Leviticus 7:34).

According to Jewish tradition this ceremony was performed by the parts on the hands of the offerer, then putting his hands again underneath, and then moving them in a horizontal direction for the waving, and in a vertical direction for the heaving. This is believed to have been intended as a presentation of the parts to God as the supreme Ruler on earth and in heaven.

The "wave breast" and the "heave shoulder" were the perquisites (payment or right) of the priests (Leviticus 7:31-34). The remainder of the offering, except for what was burned, was consumed by the offerer and his family, under certain restrictions (Leviticus 7:19-21).

In Leviticus 7:13, it states that the bread is to be made *with* leaven (yeast). Since leaven customarily symbolizes sin and evil, some have suggested that its use in this offering reflects the biblical truth that a believer can be at peace with God without attaining sinless perfection.

11:29-30, 33 EARTHENWARE UNCLEAN

"Of the animals that move about on the ground, these are unclean for you: the weasel, the rat, any kind of great lizard, the gecko, the monitor lizard, the wall lizard, the skink and the chameleon. . . . If one of them falls into a clay pot, everything in it will be unclean, and you must break the pot."

Many of the seemingly spiritual ceremonies and rituals that God gave the Israelites actually had to do with sanitation and health—this is one of them. Because of the nature of these animals, they carried many germs, and so God declared them as unclean and not to be eaten. Clothing that was touched by them was to be washed, and pots because of their porous nature were to be destroyed. The porous pots easily absorbed any uncleanness and so mere washing or scouring wasn't sufficient to clean or purify them.

For exactly the same reasons, but spiritual rather than physical, if the pots were used to cook "holy" meat, a porous clay pot must be broken, but a bronze non-porous pot could be cleaned: "The clay pot the meat is cooked in must be broken; but if it is cooked in a bronze pot, the pot is to be scoured and rinsed with water" (Leviticus 6:28).

11:35 RANGES

"Whether it be oven, or ranges for pots *(cooking pots, NIV)*, they shall be broken down" *(KJV)*.

Some think that instead of "ranges for pots," we should read "pots with lids," or as the NIV has it: "cooking pots." Others say that the words refer to some kind of structure by which two or more cooking vessels could be used at once, thus speeding up preparation of the meal and economizing fuel.

Many years ago a traveler named Rauwolff described an apparatus he saw among the Arabs that may have been similar to the "ranges" spoken of in our text-verse. A hole was dug in the ground about a foot and a half deep, into which small earthen cookware (pipkins) filled with meat and topped by lids were put. Stones were piled around the pots on three sides of the small pit. On the fourth side the Arabs placed the fuel. In a short time the heat was intense, and the meat cooked. The expression "shall be broken down," in our text-verse, probably refers to taking the rude structure apart.

14:42 MORTAR

"Then they are to take other stones to replace these and take new clay *(mortar, KJV)* and plaster the house."

There were several kinds of mortar used by the Hebrews. Sometimes they used common mud and clay, mixed with straw

chopped and beaten small. This may have been the kind especially referred to in our text-verse. The Hebrew word *aphar* (mortar) is frequently translated "dust," (material, NIV) and is so translated in Leviticus 14:41 (KJV), where reference is made to the coating of old mortar that was scraped from the outside of the house.

The Hebrews also had several varieties of calcareous earth (calcareous means composed of, containing, or characteristic of calcium carbonate, calcium, or limestone; chalky), any of which mixed with ashes made a good mortar. They likewise prepared an excellent cement of one part sand, two parts ashes, and three parts lime. These ingredients were well pounded, and were sometimes mixed with oil. At other times the oil was put on as an outer coating. Mortar was usually mixed by being trodden with the feet, but wheels were sometimes used.

16:8 "SCAPEGOAT "

"He is to cast lots for the two goats—one lot for the LORD and the other for the scapegoat."

The Old Testament records that on the day of atonement the high priest was "to lay both hands on the head of the live goat and confess over it all the wickedness and rebellion of the Israelites—all their sins—and put them on the goat's head. He shall send the goat away into the desert in the care of a man appointed for the task. The goat will carry on itself all their sins to a solitary place; and the man shall release it in the desert" (Leviticus 16:21-22).

The scapegoat was taken out of the camp into the wilderness, symbolically bearing upon itself the sins of the people, and was never allowed to return to the camp again. Certainly this dramatic ritual in which the people could vividly see their sins laid upon the scapegoat and then removed from among them, was a foreshadow of Isaiah's later statement about the Christ to come: "And the Lord has laid on Him the iniquity of us all" (Isaiah 53:6). It also symbolizes that once God removes sin because of the finished work of Christ, it is gone forever and the guilt of it never returns to the person.

Many years later, after the establishment of the temple in Jerusalem, a scapegoat that had been taken into the wilderness returned to the city. This was considered such an evil omen, that the law of Moses was modified and each year after that the scapegoat was taken to a mountain named Tzuk, about six and a half miles from Jerusalem. There he was pushed down a long, steep, slope where he could not get a footing and would fall to the bottom, breaking many bones and eventually dying. That guaranteed he could not return to Jerusalem and bring back the people's sins. The mountain is now called el-Muntar.

The term *scapegoat* has come to mean today a person or group that is made to bear the blame of others.

16:21 Offering's Head

"He *[Aaron]* is to lay both hands on the head of the live goat and confess over it all the wickedness and rebellion of the Israelites—all their sins—and put them on the goat's head."

In the ordinary sin offering, only one hand was laid on the animal's head. On the Day of Atonement, however, the high

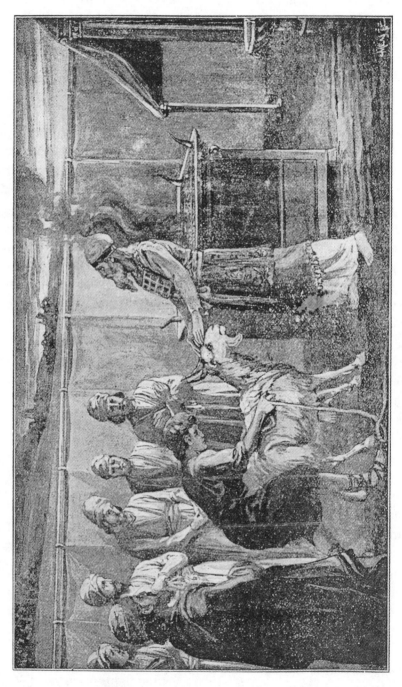

The Scapegoat

priest laid both hands upon the head of the scapegoat and confessed upon it all the iniquities, transgressions, and sins of the people. The sins of the people were thus laid upon the head of the scapegoat, and then the sin-laden goat was taken to a solitary place in the wilderness and released. This dramatic ceremony foreshadowed Isaiah's prophetic statement: "the LORD has laid on him the iniquity of us all" (Isaiah 53:6).

16:34 Day of Atonement

"This is to be a lasting ordinance for you: Atonement is to be made once a year for all the sins of the Israelites."

The Day of Atonement took place on the tenth day of the seventh month, Tisri, corresponding to our October. It was a day of great solemnity, especially designated and kept as a fast day, a day of total denial (see Leviticus 23:27; Numbers 29:7) and in later times was sometimes known by the name of the Fast (Acts 27:9).

On this day the high priest, clad in plain white linen garments, brought for himself a young bullock for a sin offering, and a ram for a burnt offering. For the people he brought two young goats for a sin offering, and a ram for a burnt offering. The two goats were brought before the door of the Tabernacle, and by the casting of lots one was designated for sacrifice and the other for a scapegoat. The high priest then slaughtered the bullock and made a sin offering for himself and family. He next entered the Most Holy Place for the first time, bearing a censer with burning coals, with which he filled the place with incense. He then came out and took the blood of the slain bullock and entered the Most Holy Place the second time, and there sprinkled the blood before the mercy seat. He came out again and killed the goat that had been designated for the people's sin offering, and, entering the Most Holy Place the third time, sprinkled its blood as he had sprinkled that of the bullock. Some of the blood of the two animals was then put on the horns of the altar of incense, and sprinkled on the altar itself.

After this the high priest, putting his hands on the head of the scapegoat, confessed the sins of the people, and then sent him off into he wilderness. After this, he washed himself and changed his garments, arraying himself in the beautiful robes of his high office, and offered the two rams as burnt offerings for himself and for the people. The garments worn while he ministered in the Most Holy Place were the "holy garments," pure white linen garments devoid of all ornamentation, signifying the highest degree of holiness and humility. When the sin offering was complete, he once more put on his garments "for glory and for beauty" (Exodus 28:2, KJV; dignity and honor, NIV).

17:7 GOAT WORSHIP

"They must no longer offer any of their sacrifices to the goat idols *(devils, KJV)* **to whom they prostitute themselves."**

The Hebrew word *se'irim* translated devils in the KJV (demons in some other versions) literally means *hairy, shaggy, rough*, or *hairy ones*, and is used for he-goats. In our text-verse it is a reference to goat-demons that were believed to inhabit the wilderness. These were probably the "satyrs" in ancient mythology. The Egyptians worshiped the goat under the name of Mendes, by which name a province in Egypt was called. The goat was worshiped as a personification of the fructifying power of nature, and was reckoned among the eight principal gods of Egypt. A splendid temple was dedicated to Mendes, and statues of the god were erected in many places. The Israelites doubtless learned the worship of the se'irim while they were slaves in Egypt. The worship was accompanied with the vilest acts of bestiality.

During the wilderness journey, the slaughter of a clean animal for food was to be done at the tabernacle as a peace offering (Leviticus 7:3-4). This requirement was undoubtedly intended to prevent the Israelites from engaging in idolatrous practices. Scriptural evidence, however, indicates that some form of Egyptian idolatry continued (see Joshua 24:14; 2 Chronicles 11:15; Ezekiel 20:6-8.) The restrictive requirement concerning the slaughter was lifted when the Israelites entered the Promised Land of Canaan (Deuteronomy 12:15, 20-21).

18:21 MOLECH

"Do not give any of your children to be sacrificed *(pass through the fire, KJV)* to Molech."

Molech (Moloch or Milcom, also Malcham in KJV) was the detestable god of the Ammonites, into whose worship the Israelites gradually were drawn. Similar rites were performed among other nations, probably varying at different times and in different places. The usual description given of this god is that of a hollow image made of brass (bronze), and having a human body with the head of an ox. The idol sat on a brazen (bronze) throne with hands extended. To prepare for sacrifices to it, the image was heated to a red-hot condition by a fire built inside it. The parents then placed their children in the heated arms, while the noise of drums and cymbals drowned the cries of the little sufferers. It's also said that there were seven chapels connected with the idol, which were to be entered according to the relative value of the offering presented. Only those who presented children were allowed to enter the seventh chapel.

Miniatures of these are thought to be the "tabernacle" (shrine, NIV) referred to in Amos 5:26 and Acts 7:43. Others think the tabernacle was a shrine or ark in which the god was carried in procession.

Some eminent writers deny that the description above refers to the Molech of the Old Testament. The Scriptures themselves give no account of the idol except to say that children were made to "pass through the fire," as so translated in the KJV. A diversity of opinion prevails as to the meaning of the expression. Most Jewish writers claim that it does not imply the actual sacrificing or burning of the children, but merely an idolatrous ceremonial purification. That is, a fire baptism, which was accomplished by carrying the children between fires, or leaping over fires with them, or causing them to do the same.

Whatever it may have been in earlier times, the Scriptures imply more than this at some periods of Jewish history. In the days of Ezekiel, God's testimony against His people was: "Is this of thy whoredoms a small matter, That thou hast slain my children, and delivered them to cause them to pass through the fire for them? (Ezekiel 16:20-21, KJV). In this passage, passing through the fire is evidently synonymous with death. As it is also in 2 Chronicles 28:3—"He burned sacrifices in the Valley of Ben Hinnom and sacrificed his sons in the fire, following the detestable ways of the nations the LORD had driven out before the Israelites." See also Psalm 106:37-38 and Jeremiah 7:31, both speak of sacrificial deaths by fire.

Frequent reference is made in the Scriptures to this heathen abomination. See 2 Kings 16:3, 17:17, 21:6, 23:10; Jeremiah 32:35, 49:1-3; Ezekiel 20:31; and Zephaniah 1:5.

19:23 Fruit of Newly Planted Trees Forbidden

"When you enter the land and plant any kind of fruit tree, regard its fruit as forbidden. For three years you are to consider it forbidden; it must not be eaten."

Like many of God's laws given to the Israelites, this one had a practical purpose rather than a spiritual one. The basic purpose of a tree's fruit is to fertilize and reproduce itself. The fertilization takes place as the fruit falls to the ground under the tree and decays; the reproduction occurs as the seeds are consumed by birds—or the fruit-seed combination consumed by ground animals—and spread to other places in their droppings. If the fruit of a newly planted tree is picked and eaten the first few years, as people even today are wont to do, then the tree's natural fertilization doesn't occur, and though the tree may grow it is considerably weakened. This is the same as human beings who don't have proper nourishment during their initial stages of growth and development.

Today, most horticultural advice is to not pick the fruit of a newly planted tree for the first 3-4 years, and allow the fallen fruit to remain on the ground and decay into natural fertilizer, but few people do. It was the same in the days of the Israelites. So to help them grow their newly planted fruit trees properly, God could either give them instantaneous horticultural knowledge, or give them a spiritual law based on his natural laws of fruit tree growth and development. Obviously, doing the first would have caused some problems, so in His wisdom He chose to do the second.

19:27 FORBIDDEN HAIR CUTTING

"Do not cut the hair at the sides of your head or clip off the edges of your beard."

This forbids shaving around the temples and ears, leaving only a crown of hair on the top of the head, as well as mutilating the beard, which were practices of the heathen. In Jeremiah 9:26 the KJV reads: "Egypt, and Judah, and Edom, and the children of Ammon, and Moab, and all that are in the utmost corners, that dwell in the wilderness: for all these nations are uncircumcised, and all the house of Israel are uncircumcised in the heart." It is believed that here the expression "all that in the utmost corners," is better translated "who clip the hair on their temples" or "who cut the corners of their hair." This was a practice honoring the gods of the heathen, and is that which is condemned in Leviticus 19:27. See also Leviticus 21:5; Jeremiah 25:23, 49:32; and Ezekiel 5:1.

19:28 TATTOOING FORBIDDEN

"Do not cut your bodies for the dead or put tattoo marks *(print any marks, KJV)* on yourselves. I am the LORD."

Both cutting and tattooing were done by the heathens, and so God forbade His people from doing so in imitation of them. Tattooing was sometimes accompanied by shaving the hair from the forehead. See Leviticus 21:5; Deuteronomy 14:1; Jeremiah 16:6, and 48:37.

19:36 HIN

"Use honest scales and honest weights, an honest ephah and an honest hin."

A hin was a unit of liquid measure considered to be one sixth of a bath. It would have been about equivalent to a gallon. (See Exodus 29:40.)

22:8 FORBIDDEN FOOD

"He must not eat anything found dead or torn by wild animals, and so become unclean through it. I am the LORD."

Like many of God's laws to the Israelites, this law was not given for spiritual reasons but for health reasons. An animal found dead most likely died from a disease that might possibly affect anyone eating the animal, even if it's cooked. We well know today that unless certain meats are cooked above a specific temperature until well done, there is a possibility of being infected by any bacteria in it—E. coli, for example— even though the animal was slaughtered under seemingly sanitary conditions. How much more then the danger of bacteria in an animal that died for unknown reasons.

The same basic reason applies to a dead animal that had been torn by wild animals. What diseases the wild animals had and passed on to the meat of the dead animal cannot be known. Rabies is transmitted by the bite of an infected animal, and so it might be possible to transfer the disease even through a dead animal that had been torn by a rabies infected wolf or wild dog. Rather than trying to teach his people all this in an age of little understanding, God in His wisdom simply gave them laws

that protected them from the transmission of such diseases.

23:18 DRINK OFFERING

"They will be a burnt offering to the LORD, together with their grain offerings and drink offerings."

Accompanying other offerings was the drink offering, which consisted of a certain quantity of wine, proportioned to the nature of the sacrifice. This was taken by the priest and poured out like the blood at the foot of the altar of burnt offering. For a bullock, half a hin (about two quarts) of wine was used. For a ram, a third of a hin. For a lamb or young goat, a fourth of a hin. (See Numbers 15:4-12.) In the temple service, the pouring out of the wine of the drink offering at the morning and evening sacrifice was the signal for the priests and Levites to begin their song of praise to God.

23:24 FEAST OF TRUMPETS

"Say to the Israelites: 'On the first day of the seventh month you are to have a day of rest, a sacred assembly commemorated with trumpet blasts.'"

This festival, commonly called the "Feast of Trumpets," is universally regarded by the Jews as the Festival of the New Year, which began with the seventh month, *Tisri*. As it occurred at the new moon, and on the first day of the month in which the Great Day of Atonement and the Feast of Tabernacles took place, it was an occasion of great interest. It has ever been observed by the Jews as connected with the Day of Atonement, and the ten days between the two are considered days of preparation for the solemn day. The silver trumpets, which were ordered to be prepared for the purpose of calling the people together (Numbers 10:1-10), were blown on this day more than at all other times, because the new year and the new month began together. Hence the name by which the feast is commonly called.

The day was kept as a Sabbath, and so no work was performed on it. The usual daily morning sacrifice was offered, then the monthly sacrifice of the new moon, and then the sacrifice peculiar to the day, which consisted of a bullock, a ram, and seven lambs for a burnt offering, and a kid for a sin offering (Numbers 29:1-6). In the New Testament the blowing of the trumpet is associated with the return of the Lord (Matthew 24:31; 1 Corinthians 15:52; 1 Thessalonians 4:16).

25:4 SABBATICAL YEAR

"But in the seventh year the land is to have a sabbath of rest, a sabbath to the LORD. Do not sow your fields or prune your vineyards."

Every seventh year was to be a time of recuperation for the soil. The spontaneous produce of this Sabbatical Year, however, was free to all comers, but especially to the poor (Exodus 23:11). It was also a time for debtors to be released by their creditors (Deuteronomy 15:1-2), thereby freeing them from their financial burdens and keeping poverty out of the nation. During the Feast of Tabernacles of this year, the law was publicly read to the people (Deuteronomy 31:10-13).

25:10 YEAR OF JUBILEE

"Consecrate the fiftieth year and proclaim liberty throughout the land to all its inhabitants. It shall be a jubilee for you; each one of you is to return to his family property and each to his own clan."

The Year of Jubilee was ushered in by the sound of trumpets through the land, every fiftieth year, on the Great Day of Atonement. Like the Sabbatical Year, it was a year of rest to the soil (Leviticus 25:11). Thus two idle years came together every fifty years, and God promised by special providence to give such a plentiful harvest during the sixth year that there should be enough until the harvest of the ninth year could be gathered (Leviticus 25:20-22). See also 2 Kings 19:29 and Isaiah 37:30. God's providence no doubt watched over the productions of the season before the Sabbatical Year, in addition to the spontaneous growth of that year.

All their transfers of real estate were made in reference to the Year of Jubilee, and the poor and unfortunate were specially favored (Leviticus 25). "Proclaim liberty throughout all the land unto all the inhabitants thereof" (Leviticus 25:10, KJV) is inscribed upon the original Liberty Bell of the United States.

26:1 STONE IDOLS

"Do not make idols or set up an image or a sacred stone for yourselves, and do not place a carved stone in your land to bow down before it. I am the LORD your God."

The Hebrew word *maskith*, here rendered "image," is translated "pictures" in Numbers 33:52 (KJV), where the word is plural. Some believe that *eben maskith*, "figure stone," is a stone formed into a figure; that is, an idol of stone as distinguished from one made of iron or wood. Others, however, regard it as referring to stones with figures or hieroglyphic inscriptions on them: "pictured" or "engraven stones," which in that age of idolatry were liable to be worshiped.

26:30 HIGH PLACES AND IMAGES

"I will destroy your high places, cut down your incense altars" *(images, KJV)*.

Frequent mention is made in the Scriptures of the "high places" of the heathen, where they were wont to worship their gods, supposing themselves there to be nearer to them, and more likely to be heard by them. This practice was imitated by the Hebrews, through denounced in their laws. They sometimes worshiped on their housetops as a substitute for hills or mountains. See Jeremiah 19:13, 32:29, and Zephaniah 1:5.

The Hebrew word *chamman*, translated "images" in the KJV can also be translated "a sun-pillar," or an "idol." In some marginal references, the "images" are called "sun images." They are supposed to have been identical with the sun-god Baal.

In the KJV Bible, 2 Chronicles 34:4 seems to indicate that these images were sometimes placed on top of the altars of Baal, and so it is thought they may have resembled rising flames. In the NIV, however, the same verse indicates that they were "incense altars" that were above the altars of Baal, which would mean they were constructed in a way that incense could be burned in or on them. In some places where their destruction is spoken of they are represented as being "cut down" (KJV), "cut to pieces" (NIV), (Ezekiel 6:4). In other places they are said to be "broke" (Ezekiel 6:6, NIV, NASB). Perhaps they were made of stone when placed

Shekel

as a fixture on the altar, and of wood when put in other positions.

27:25 SHEKEL AND GERAH

"Every value is to be set according to the sanctuary shekel, twenty gerahs to the shekel."

The shekel was the common standard both of weight and value among the Hebrews. It's estimated at 220 English grains, or a little more than half an ounce. The "shekel of the sanctuary," (Exodus 30:13; Numbers 3:47) was believed to be equal to twenty gerahs (Ezekiel 45:12). There were shekels of gold (1 Chronicles 21:25), of silver (1 Samuel 9:8), of brass (1 Samuel 17:5), and of iron (1 Samuel 17:7). A shekel eventually became a coined piece of money. Six gold shekels, according to the later Jewish system, were equal in value to fifty silver ones.

The gerah was the smallest weight known to the Hebrews, and the smallest piece of money used by them. It weighed between eleven and twelve grains (grain = 0.002285 ounce (0.065 gram).

27:32 TITHING ROD

The entire tithe of the herd and flock—every tenth animal that passes under the shepherd's rod—will be holy to the LORD.

The reference here is to the Jewish mode of tithing sheep. As the sheep passed through a narrow gate, one by one, the person counting stood by, holding in his hand a rod (probably a shepherd's rod) coated with ochre (orange-yellow color). Every tenth one he touched with his rod and put a mark on him. Jeremiah alludes to this method of counting sheep in chapter 33:13. So does Ezekiel in chapter 20:37.

NUMBERS

2:2 STANDARDS

"The Israelites are to camp around the Tent of Meeting some distance from it, each man under his standard with the banners (*ensign, KJV*) of his family."

The *degas* (Hebrew), "standard," was the large field sign that belonged to each division of three tribes, and was also the banner of the tribe at the head of that division. The *oth*, "ensign," was the small flag or banner that was carried at the head of each tribe and of each subdivision of a tribe. The Scriptures give us no indication of the shape of these emblems. According to tradition, each emblem was the same color as the stone in the breastplate worn by the high priest (Exodus 28:21), and the emblem of Judah contained a picture of a lion. Their shapes probably bore some general resemblance to the Egyptian military emblems, which are shown on a number of monuments. These emblems were not at all like our modern flags and banners. They were made of wood or metal, and ornamented with various devices, and shaped in the form of some sacred emblem.

The Israelite standards and banners were used to gather the tribes in one place, behind or around the

Egyptian standards

standard. In military battles in the past, standards were important devices to let the soldiers know where their division was. Often when the battle was going against them, they would be commanded by trumpets or other means to gather around the standard, sometimes as defense and sometimes to reform themselves for another attack. If the person carrying the standard fell to the ground and the standard was not retrieved by another soldier and lifted back to the air so that it could be seen by all, it could cause great confusion among the soldiers, and even cause them to lose the battle. Isaiah 59:19, referring to Christ, says: "So shall they fear the name of the LORD from the west, and his glory from the rising of the sun. When the enemy shall come in like a flood, the Spirit of the LORD shall lift up a standard against him."

3:6 LEVITES

"Bring the tribe of Levi and present them to Aaron the priest to assist him."

Aaron's family was set apart especially to the duties of the priesthood. The rest of the Levites were to assist the priests in serving at the tabernacle (Numbers 16:8-11), guard the tabernacle from defilement (Numbers 1:53; 3:10), redeem the firstborn of Israel (Numbers 3:12, 13, 40-43; 8:14-19), and teach the Law (Malachi. 2:4-9). Each of the three families (see Numbers 3:17-20) had its particular duties assigned. The Kohathites had charge of the sacred utensils of the Tabernacle. They saw that they were properly removed when on the march, and that they were put into their appropriate places when the encampment was again fixed (Numbers 4:4-15). The Gershonites took care of the hangings and curtains of the Tabernacle (Numbers 4: 21-2). The Merarites were assigned to look after the boards, sockets, pillars, pins, and cords of the Tabernacle (Numbers 4:29-33). Moses also gave the Levites judicial authority (Deuteronomy 17:8-12), and made them keepers of the book of the law (Deuteronomy 31:9, 25-26). After the temple was built they acted as porters, musicians, and assistants to the priests.

The first Levites who were appointed began their service when they were thirty years old

(Numbers 4:23, 30, 35), but later it was ordered that they should begin their service at age twenty-five (Numbers 8:24). In David's time they began serving at age twenty (1 Chronicles 23:24-27). They were released from all obligation to serve when at age fifty (Numbers 8:25). Forty-eight cities were set apart for their residence in the Promised Land. Six of these were also cities of refuge, and thirteen of them were shared with the priests. See Numbers 35:1-8; Joshua 21:13-19; and 1 Chronicles 6:54-60.

19:2 RED HEIFER

"This is a requirement of the law that the LORD has commanded: Tell the Israelites to bring you a red heifer without defect or blemish and that has never been under a yoke."

The sacrifice of the red heifer was a peculiar ceremony designed to purify from the ceremonial defilement resulting from contact with a corpse (Numbers 19:11-16). A heifer perfectly red, and which had never borne the yoke, was selected by the people, and brought to Eleazar the priest. The heifer was then taken outside the camp and slaughtered. Eleazar then sprinkled the heifer's blood seven times before the Tabernacle, after which the entire carcass was burned, the priest throwing into the fire cedar, hyssop, and scarlet. The ashes were then carefully collected and laid up in a suitable place for future use. (Numbers 19:1-10). When purification from the defilement of a corpse became necessary, the ashes were made into a lye by means of running water, and the water was sprinkled from a bunch of hyssop on the person, the tent, the bed, or the utensils that had been defiled (Numbers 19:17-19).

This sacrifice differed from all others in several important particulars. The offering was not slaughtered in the court or burned on the altar. It was killed and burned outside the camp. Neither the high priest nor any ordinary priest officiated, but the presumptive successor of the high priest. The animal chosen was not a bullock, as in other sacrifices, but a heifer, and the precise color was specified. The ashes were carefully preserved.

Much has been written on these subjects, and various attempts have been made to give full explanations of all the minutia of the ceremonies, but some things connected with them are not easily understood or explained. Some ancient Jews have said that not even Solomon, with all his wisdom, fully understood them.

The general design was undoubtedly intended to keep in remembrance the awful fact of sin, which brought death into the world, and the necessity of purification from its pollution. The writer makes reference to this in Hebrews 9:13-14. Dr. J. H. Kurtz, writing in 1873 about the *Sacrificial Worship of the Old Testament*, said: "This ideas of an antidote against the defilement of death was the regulating principle of the whole institution, determining not only the choice of the sacrificial animal, but what should be added to it, and all that should be done with it."

20:28 PROPHET'S MANTLE

Moses removed Aaron's garments and put them on his son Eleazar. And Aaron died there on top of the mountain. Then Moses and Eleazar came down from the mountain.

Aaron died at the age of 123 in the fortieth year after the Exodus. Just before he died, Moses transferred the sacred office of the high priest to his son Eleazar. This was done by taking the priestly garments off Aaron and putting them on Eleazar. In a similar fashion, Elijah threw his cloak (mantle, KJV) over Elisha when, in obedience to divine command, he called him to the prophet's work (1 Kings 19:19). Elisha took up the mantle as soon as Elijah was translated in the chariot of fire (2 Kings 2:13-14). In a like manner Eliakim was appointed the successor of Shebna (Isaiah 22:15, 20-21).

21:29 CHEMOSH

Woe to you, O Moab! You are destroyed, O people of Chemosh! He has given up his sons as fugitives and his daughters as captives to Sihon king of the Amorites.

Chemosh—destroyer, subduer, or fishgod— was the national god of the Moabites, and hence they are called in our text-verse, and in Jeremiah 48:46, "the people of Chemosh. He was also worshiped by the

Ammonites (Judges 11:24). The worship of this god, "the abomination of Moab," and the worship of Molech, was introduced at Jerusalem by Solomon (1 Kings 11:7), but was abolished by Josiah (2 Kings 23:13). Nothing definite is known concerning this god, or the mode of his worship. There is, however, an old Jewish tradition that says his worshipers went bareheaded and refused to wear garments that were made by use of a needle. Chemosh is also mentioned in Jeremiah 48:7, 13, 46.

22:41 BAAL

The next morning Balak took Balaam up to Bamoth Baal (high places of Baal, KJV), **and from there he saw part of the people.**

The "high places of Baal" (Hebrew *bamot-ba`al*), was an elevation somewhere in the

Baal

Transjordan plateau, probably near Mount Nebo, which was important to the worship of Baal. Ancient worshipers felt that high places elevated them closer to their gods. Each locality had its special Baal, and the various local Baals were summed up under the name of Baalim, or "lords." The word Baal signifies lord, not so much in the sense of ruler, as possessor or owner. The name was given to the principal male deity of the Phoenicians, corresponding to Bel or Belus of the Babylonians. The female deity associated with Baal was Astarte.

The worship of Baal was of great antiquity, and was accompanied with splendid ceremonies. Priests and prophets were consecrated to his service (2 Kings 10:19). Incense (Jeremiah 7:9) and prayers (1 Kings 18:26) were offered to him. The worshipers prostrated themselves before the idol and kissed it (1 Kings 19:18), perhaps at the same time kissing Baal's hand that was elevated toward the sun. They danced with shouts and cut themselves with knives (1 Kings 18:26-28). The offerings were sometimes vegetable (Hosea 2:8), and sometimes animal (1 Kings 18:23). Human sacrifices were also offered (Jeremiah 19:5).

Efforts have been made to identify Baal with one of the gods of classical mythology, but the results are by no means satisfactory. The Greek Zeus; the Roman Jupiter, Cronos, Saturn, Ares, Mars, or Hercules have each been supposed by different writers to be the same as Baal. In reference to the astrological nature of the worship, the most prevalent opinion is that Baal represented the sun, while Astarte his companion represented the moon. But others assert that the two names respectively stood for Jupiter and Venus. The ordinary symbol of Baal was a bull.

25:3 BAAL OF PEOR

So Israel joined in worshiping the Baal of Peor. And the Lord's anger burned against them.

The local, heathen god, Baal, that was worshiped at Peor. Sexual immorality was part of that worship, as indicated in Numbers 25:1-2: "While Israel was staying in Shittim, the men began to indulge in sexual immorality with Moabite women, who invited them to the sacrifices to their gods." What Balak and Balaam had failed to accomplish through sorcery, they almost accomplished through the seduction of Canaanite fertility worship. Numbers 31:16 says: "They were the ones who followed Balaam's advice and were the means of turning the Israelites away from the LORD in what happened at Peor."

DEUTERONOMY

3:3 Bashan

So the LORD our God also gave into our hands Og king of Bashan and all his army. We struck them down, leaving no survivors.

When Israel entered the Promised Land, Og, king of Bashan, came out against them, but was utterly routed (Numbers 21:33-35). Bashan extended from Gilead in the south to Hermon in the north, and from the Jordan on the west to Salcah on the east. Along with the half of Gilead it was given to the half-tribe of Manasseh (Joshua 13:29-31). Golan, one of its cities, became a "city of refuge" (Joshua 21:27). Argob, in Bashan, was one of Solomon's commissariat districts (1 Kings 4:13). The cities of Bashan were taken by Hazael (2 Kings 10:33), but were soon after reconquered by Jehoash (2 Kings 13:25), who overcame the Syrians in three battles, according to the word of Elisha (2 Kings 13:19). From this time Bashan almost disappears from history, although we read about the wild cattle of its rich pastures (Ezekiel 39:18; Psalm 22:12), the oaks of its forests (Isaiah 2:13; Ezekiel 27:6; Zechariah 11:2), and the beauty of its extensive plains (Amos 4:1; Jeremiah 50:19). Soon after the conquest, the name "Gilead" was given to the whole country beyond Jordan.

3:11 Last of the Giants

(Only Og king of Bashan was left of the remnant of the Rephaites *[giants, KJV]*. His bed was made of iron and was more than thirteen feet long and six feet wide.)

Og was the last of the Rephaim, or giant race, that inhabited Palestine: "Bashan used to be known as a land of the Rephaites" (giants, KJV) (Deuteronomy 3:13). Some have said that Og's iron bedstead was like an iron-trimmed stone coffin, or perhaps an iron-decorated couch that was to be placed in his tomb. It has also been suggested that Og's bed was a monument made of an iron-bearing rock like basalt. Whatever it was, the size of the bed tells much about how huge Og was.

4:19 ASTRAL WORSHIP

And when you look up to the sky and see the sun, the moon and the stars—all the heavenly array—do not be enticed into bowing down to them and worshiping things the LORD your God has apportioned to all the nations under heaven.

Astral worship was common in the Middle East at that time, and was forbidden by God. In the last part of our text-verse, God clearly tells His people that He created the stars for the benefit of all the earth, and not as a means to determine a person's destiny or as a power controlling that destiny. Astral worship is the most ancient and widely spread form of idolatry, and frequent allusions are

made to it in the Scriptures. Some believe that many of the precepts in the Mosaic law were directed against astral worship in its various corrupt forms. Our text-verse is an illustration of this. Besides direct reference to this superstition in this and in other passages, occasional allusion to it may be found elsewhere.

The expression "host of heaven" refers to the sun, moon, and stars, as so designated in Genesis 2:1—"Thus the heavens and the earth were finished, and all the host of them" (KJV). When the Jews fell into idolatry they worshiped these, and in conjunction often worshiped Baal: "And they left all the commandments of the LORD their God, and made them molten images, even two calves, and made a grove, and worshipped all the host of heaven, and served Baal" (2 Kings 17:16, KJV— see also verse 21:3).

6:9 DOORPOSTS INSCRIPTIONS

Write them on the doorframes (posts, KJV) of your houses and on your gates.

The Jews were commanded to write the divine words on the

posts (*mezuzoth* or *mezuwzah*) of their doors, but they eventually adopted the custom of writing Exodus 13:1-10, 11-16; Deuteronomy 6:4-9; 11:13-21 on parchment and putting them in a reed or cylinder that they then fixed to the right-hand doorpost of every room in the house.

11:10 WATERING WITH THE FOOT

The land you are entering to take over is not like the land of Egypt, from which you have come, where you planted your seed and irrigated *(wateredst, KJV)* it by foot as in a vegetable garden.

Agriculture in Egypt was dependent on irrigation. Irrigating the land by foot may allude to the ancient mode of raising water from the Nile or from the canals that were cut through Egypt, which was by means of waterwheels turned by foot, or by turning the water into small channels by foot. Palestine, by contrast, is watered by rain.

In 1856, Dr. E. Robinson, who did biblical research in Palestine, saw several of these waterwheels being used to draw water from wells. In describing one he said: "On a platform was fixed a small reel for the rope, which a man, seated on a level with the axis, wound up, by pulling the upper part of the reel toward him with his hands, while he at the same time pushed the lower part from him with his feet." For crops that required frequent water, the fields were divided into square beds surrounded by raised borders of earth to keep in the water that was brought in by canals or poured in from buckets. The water could easily be transferred from one square to another by opening a hole in the soft soil of the borders with the foot.

12:23-24 EATING THE BLOOD

But be sure you do not eat the blood, because the blood is the life, and you must not eat the life with the meat. You must not eat the blood; pour it out on the ground like water.

There have been many speculations as to why God forbade the Israelites from eating (drinking) the blood of animals, and it's possible that it was a combination of several reasons. It was a custom in many pagans lands to drink the blood of sacrificed animals, and even the blood of sacrificed humans. So the command to the Israelites not to eat of the blood may have been to remove them completely from the pagan customs that resulted from many idolatrous and cruel customs.

Since we know today that most diseases are contained in the blood and transmitted by it throughout the body, the commandment not to eat the blood may have had to do with the health of the Israelites and to prevent the transmission of any diseases the animal might be carrying in its blood. We are discovering today that some ground meats, like hamburger, can transmit diseases unless they're cooked completely through. Imagine, then, how many diseases the blood of an animal could transmit. We also know today that the blood carries throughout the body the essential elements of life—all that the body needs to sustain health and life is transmitted to it via the blood. We also know that no other liquid can replace the blood and perform its

functions—only blood can be used to replace blood. So indeed the life *is* in the blood. For this reason, many pagans drank the blood of their victims, believing that by so doing they would receive the strength and power that the victims had. The Israelites must not do so; though they sacrificed the animal, they must always remember that life was from God and thus sacred, and they must not eat of that life as if it were a common food.

It's also possible that they were not to eat of the blood because the shedding of blood was an act of atonement and pointed toward the shedding of Jesus' blood on Calvary for the remission of sins. Thus, to eat blood was to profane or make common that sacred act of atonement by which man comes to God. The blood was to be carefully carried to the altar to be disposed of by the officiating priests, or it was to be quietly poured into the earth. (See Genesis 9:4, 5, Leviticus 17:10-14; Acts 15:20; Hebrews 9:22.)

Some believe that this law of prohibition was only ceremonial and temporary; while others regard it as still binding on all. Some Jewish rabbis say that this prohibition against blood was made because of an ancient custom of eating raw flesh, especially the flesh of living animals cut or torn from them, and devoured while reeking with the warm blood. Both the meat and blood of animals were eaten by the Israelites after the battle of Gilboa and the blood eating was considered a sin that required sacrifice for atonement (1 Samuel 14:31-35).

16:1 ABIB

Observe the month of Abib and celebrate the Passover of the LORD your God, because in the month of Abib he brought you out of Egypt by night.

Abib means *a green ear*—a young ear of grain. This denotes the condition of the grain in Palestine and Egypt during this month. It was the first month of the Jewish ecclesiastical year, and was later called Nisan (Nehemiah 2:1; Esther 3:7). It corresponded nearly to our month of April.

16:21 GROVE OF TREES

Thou shalt not plant thee a grove of any trees near unto the altar of the LORD thy God, which thou shalt make thee *(KJV)*.

Idol temples and altars were surrounded by thick groves and trees, which became the resort of the abandoned of both sexes, and in which, under plea of idolatrous worship, excesses of the vilest kind were committed. For this reason God forbade the planting of trees near His altars, lest His people become, or seem to be, like the heathen. Some believe, however, that the word "grove" refers to wooden pillars or a high wooden platform. This is reflected in the NIV translation: "Do not set up any wooden Asherah pole beside the altar you build to the LORD your God." But note the references to gardens, trees, or immorality in the following verses: Isaiah 57:5, 65:3, 66:17; Jeremiah 2:20, 3:6; Ezekiel 6:13, 20:28; and Hosea 4:13.

18:10-11 DIVINATION

There shall not be found among you any one that maketh his son or his daughter to pass through the fire, or that useth divination, or an observer of times, or an enchanter, or a witch, Or a charmer, or a consulter with familiar spirits, or a wizard, or a necromancer *(KJV)*.

The word divination (Hebrew *kosem kesamim*, "divining divinations") may here be taken as a generic term, of which the seven terms following represent the species or types. This might be clearly shown in the KJV by a slight change in the punctuation, and an omission of the word *or*, which was supplied by the translators; e.g., "that useth divination: an observer of times, or an enchanter, or a witch," etc.

By divination, as the term is used in the text, we understand an attempt to penetrate the mysteries of the future by using magical arts, or superstitious incantations, or by the arbitrary interpretation of natural signs. Its practice was prevalent in the times of Moses among all idolatrous nations, as it is even today. Even in our own Christian land, there is much of this going on at the present time. It became necessary, therefore, for God to warn the Hebrews against the fascinating influence of this ungodly habit. God provided certain lawful means by which His will was revealed, such as by urim and thummim, by dreams, by prophecies, and by several other modes, so that that there was no excuse for resorting to the practices of the heathen. These are spoken of under the following heads.

1. Observer of times (can also mean sorcery or soothsaying) *meonen*. This undoubtedly means one that distinguishes lucky from unlucky days, recommending certain days for the commencement of enterprises, and forbidding other days; deciding also on the good or bad luck of certain months, and even of years. These sort of diviners often made their predictions by noticing the clouds. Some would refer this to divination by means of words, of which we have illustration, in more modern times in *bibliomancy*; that is, opening a Bible at random and taking for the will of God the first word, or verses, that are seen. Still others believe that

meonen had reference to fascination by means of the so-called "evil eye."

2. Enchanter (interprets omens, NIV), *menachesh*. This may refer to divination by the cup (see Genesis **44:5 Divining Cup or Bowl**), in which passage the word *nachesh* is used. The Septuagint translators believed it to mean divination by watching the flight of birds. Some later interpreted it to mean divination by means of serpents, which were charmed by music.

3. Witch (engages in witchcraft, NIV), *mekashsheph*. This word is used in the plural in Exodus 7:11 to denote the magicians of Pharaoh, who were well versed in the arts of black magic. In Exodus 22:18, the word is used in the feminine, and is translated witch, as in our text-verse. It is said that the greater number of works of divination were practiced by women.

4. Charmer (casts spells, NIV), *chober* (from the root *chabar*, to bind). This was one who used "a type of magic that was practiced by binding magic knots." Some think it may have been one who practiced a kind of divination that drew or bound together noxious creatures for purposes of sorcery. Others

believe it was one who used a magic ring for divination.

5. Consulter with familiar spirits (medium, NIV), *shoel ob*. This may have reference to a species of divination in which ventriloquism was used. The primary meaning of the word *ob* is a leathern bottle, which as led some authorities to think that this divination was one that called up departed spirits, and that the use of the word *ob* arose from considering the conjurer to be possessed by a demon, like a bottle or vessel in which the demon was contained. Others believe that the word may have been used because these necromancers inflated themselves in the act of divination, like a skin bottle stretched to its utmost capacity (see Job 32:19). The woman of Endor who was consulted by Saul when the Philistines were about to attack him belonged to this class. Saul asked her to divine to him by the *ob*: the familiar spirit (1 Samuel 28:7-8). When Samuel himself actually appeared, however, the witch of Endor shrieked with fear, indicating that she had not expected Samuel but rather some spirit that would impersonate him. For God's own reasons, He miraculously permitted the actual

spirit of Samuel to speak and announce Saul's imminent death (1 Samuel 28:19). This is the only instance on record in the Old Testament of someone's leaving Sheol. Sheol is said to have gates that prohibit the escape of a spirit.

6. Wizard (spiritist, NIV), *yiddeoni*, the knowing one. This may have indicated anyone who was unusually expert in the various tricks of divination.

7. Necromancer (consults the dead, NIV), *doresh el hammethim*, one who seeks the dead. The necromancers had various methods of divination by the dead. They sometimes made use of a bone or a vein of a dead body, and sometimes poured warm blood into a corpse, as if to renew life. They pretended to raise ghosts by various incantations and other magical ceremonies.

19:5 Axes

For instance, a man may go into the forest with his neighbor to cut wood, and as he swings his ax to fell a tree, the head may fly off and hit his neighbor and kill him.

There were doubtless different forms of axes used among the Hebrews, just as different words are used to signify the instrument. *Garzen*, the word used in our text-verse and in Deuteronomy 20:19, 1 Kings 6:7, and Isaiah 10:15, was probably an ax for hewing large timber. Representations of ancient Assyrian and Egyptian axes have come down to us. Some of these axes are fastened to the handle by means of thongs. There is one kind, however, which is not so fastened, but which has an opening in it into which the handle is inserted, much like axes of today. It bears a strong resemblance to a modern

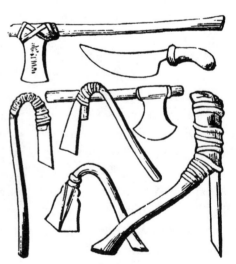

Ancient axes

ax, and from the reference to the head slipping off in our text-verse, seems to be the type of *garzen* that was used in this instance.

Egyptian axes were made of bronze, and perhaps of iron, also. That some of the axes of the Hebrews were made of iron is evident from 2 Kings 6:5-6. The NIV faces the question by directly stating that the axhead was made of iron: "As one of them was cutting down a tree, the iron axhead fell into the water. "Oh, my lord," he cried out, "it was borrowed!" The man of God asked, "Where did it fall?" When he showed him the place, Elisha cut a stick and threw it there, and made the iron float."

19:14 LANDMARKS

Do not move your neighbor's boundary stone *(landmark, KJV)* set up by your predecessors in the inheritance you receive in the land the LORD your God is giving you to possess.

The boundaries of different fields were marked by heaps of small stones about a rod apart. It was easy for a dishonest man to move these stones little by little

each year and thus gradually encroach on his neighbor's land. To do so was equivalent to stealing. This practice is alluded to in Job 24:2, and is forbidden in Proverbs 22:28 and 23:10. Those who did were in for a rude awakening. Proverbs 23:11 says: "their Defender is strong; he will take up their case against you." And Deuteronomy 27:17 says: "Cursed is the man who moves his neighbor's boundary stone." Then all the people shall say, "Amen!" A figurative allusion is made to this crime in Hosea 5:10.

20:5 DEDICATION OF HOUSES

"Has anyone built a new house and not dedicated it?"

The Scriptures don't inform us as to the ceremonies accompanying the dedication of a dwelling to God. There were probably a combination of devotional and social. Verse one of Psalm 30 says: "A Psalm and Song at the dedication of the house (temple, NIV) of David." There is some disagreement as to the occasion of this Psalm, some saying that it does not fit the time of the building of the temple, and that it was either at the occasion of the building of

David's personal house (2 Samuel 5:11), or the time of David's bringing up of the ark to Jerusalem and placing it in the tabernacle especially erected for it 2 Samuel 6:12-19), or the dedication of the threshing floor of Araunah, the future site of the temple (2 Samuel 24:18-25). The completion of the walls of Jerusalem in the time of Nehemiah was celebrated by a dedication, at which there was great rejoicing (Nehemiah 12:27). Jewish tradition says that not only was a newly built house to be dedicated, but a house lately obtained, whether by inheritance, purchase, or gift. Houses that were not suitable for habitation, and that could not be made so, were not dedicated. But buildings such as granaries and barns that were of necessity converted into dwellings were dedicated.

21:19 Gate, Place of Justice or Power

His father and mother shall take hold of him and bring him to the elders at the gate of his town.

Because the vicinity of a city gate was a place of popular gathering, it became a convenient place for the administration of justice. Here courts were held and disputes settled (Deuteronomy 16:18, KJV). See also Deuteronomy 25:7; Joshua 20:4; Ruth 4:1; Job 5:4, 31:21; Psalm 127:5; Proverbs 22:22, 31:23; Jeremiah 38:7; Lamentations 5:14; Amos 5:12; and Zechariah 8:16. From the fact that princes and judges sat at the gate in discharge of their official duties, the word "gate" became a synonym for power or authority. This is illustrated in Matthew 16:18, where the expression "gates of hell (Hades, NIV)" means *powers* of hell, or more correctly, Hades.

22:5 Clothing, Distinction in Wearing

A woman must not wear men's clothing, nor a man wear women's clothing, for the LORD your God detests anyone who does this.

In Old Testament times the distinction between male and female attire was not very marked. The statute forbidding men to wear female apparel probably referred especially to ornaments and head-dresses, but may have had other meanings upon any special occasions when there may have been distinct differences in the clothing of men and women.

In light of the final clause of our text-verse it's obvious that the entire reference is not to the principles of fashion, but to the practice of transvestitism, which is a deviant sexual behavior in which the person adopts the dress and behavior of the opposite sex. Its danger lies in its close association with the forbidden practice of homosexuality (Leviticus 18:22, 20:13) and the fact that cross-dressing was often associated with the worship of pagan gods. God created man and woman distinctively and uniquely different (Genesis 1:27), and any attempt to erase or blur that distinction is in His eyes an "abomination," and so called throughout the Scriptures.

22:8 PARAPET

When you build a new house, make a parapet (battlement, KJV) around your roof so that you may not bring the guilt of bloodshed on your house if someone falls from the roof.

The purpose of the parapet, which was a low protective wall or railing along the edge of the roof, was not for the purpose of decoration or defense as the KJV word "embattlement" infers, but to keep people from falling off the roof. The roofs were flat with a slight rise in the center to allow water to run to the edges and out holes in the parapet. Because of the heat in that climate, the family would often sleep on the roof at night (1 Samuel 9:26) and even eat meals there.

Even palaces had such roofs. It was from a roof that David saw Bathsheba bathing (2 Samuel 11:2), which she may have been doing on her roof, which was often done because of the coolness of the night and the ease of emptying water. Most of the time, however, a screen was placed around the bathing area, or bathing was only done within parapets built specially high for that purpose. Why it was so easy for David to see Bathsheba bathing is not told in the Scriptures.

179

24:10-13 Debtors Protected

When you make a loan of any kind to your neighbor, do not go into his house to get what he is offering as a pledge. Stay outside and let the man to whom you are making the loan bring the pledge out to you. If the man is poor, do not go to sleep with his pledge in your possession. Return his cloak to him by sunset so that he may sleep in it. Then he will thank you, and it will be regarded as a righteous act in the sight of the LORD your God.

Interest could not be charged on a loan to another Israelite (Deuteronomy 23:19), but a pledge of repayment could be taken. The pledge, however, could not jeopardize his livelihood or his life—for example, as shown in verse 6, a millstone by which he ground the grain for either his livelihood or his daily bread. Nor could the pledge be the mantle he used to cover himself when he slept, or his daily wage (verses 14:15).

The law in our text-verse also prevented the lender from selecting his pledge, giving the choice to the poor debtor. He could bring out as a pledge what he pleased and not what the lender could find in his house, so long as it met the claim of the lender. The lender was then compelled to accept it whether it pleased him or not.

24:12-13 Outer Garment

If the man is poor, do not go to sleep with his pledge in your possession. Return his cloak to him by sunset so that he may sleep in it *(his own raiment, KJV)*.

From our text-verse it would seem that the most common articles of pledge for a poor person was some of their clothing. The Hebrew words *salmah* and *simlah* (as in the parallel passage in Exodus 22:26) were used to denote clothing in general, but especially the large outer garment, or wrapper, which was wound around the person when worn, and then removed at night and used as a covering while sleeping. This is the *raiment* of the KJV rendering.

To keep a poor person's outer garment overnight was

Outer garment

their shoulders (Exodus 12:34).

In the New Testament the outer garment is called a *cloak* in Matthew 5:40; *clothes* by the NIV and *raiment* by the KJV in Matthew 27:31; *robe* in the NIV and *garment* in the KJV in Matthew 14:36; and *robe* in the NIV and *vesture* in the KJV in Revelation 19:13. In most of the passages where the words *robe* or *cloak* are used in the NIV and the word *garment* is used in the KJV is used, they mean the outer garment. This garment was easily and frequently laid aside (see Matthew 21:7-8, 24;18; John 13:4, 12; Acts 7:58, 22:20, 23).

considered an act of cruelty, and was forbidden by the Law. The consequences of such action are touchingly described by Job where he speaks of the poor who are afflicted by wicked men: "Lacking clothes, they spend the night naked; they have nothing to cover themselves in the cold. They are drenched by mountain rains and hug the rocks for lack of shelter."

The outer garment was often used to wrap up burdens that had to be carried, and was probably what was used by the Israelites when they wrapped the kneading troughs in the folds of their outer garments and carried them on

24:20 GLEANING

When you beat the olives from your trees, do not go over the branches a second time. Leave what remains for the alien, the fatherless and the widow.

Gleaning was the process of gathering grain or produce left in a field by reapers or on a vine or tree by pickers. God's law required a portion be left so that the poor and aliens might have a means of obtaining food. Leviticus 19:9-10 says: "When you reap the harvest of your land, do not reap to the very edges of your field or gather the gleanings of your harvest. Do not go over your vineyard a second time or pick up the grapes that have fallen. Leave them for the poor and the alien. I am the LORD your God."

This law and its benefits are beautifully illustrated in the Book of Ruth, especially chapter two. In Isaiah 17:5-9, the few grapes and olives left for gleaners is compared to the small remnant of Israel that God would leave Himself when He judged them. But as Isaiah further wrote in 27:12-13, God would one day again gather (glean) His remnant one by one and return them to "worship the LORD on the holy mountain in Jerusalem."

25:4 WAGES FOR THE LABORER

Do not muzzle an ox while it is treading out the grain.

God ordered His people not to muzzle the ox that was treading out the grain, but to leave it unmuzzled so that it might eat of the grain while it worked and thus renew its strength. Although this law had an obvious practical effect upon the laboring ox, the apostle Paul said that this law was not written exclusively for the benefit of oxen, but also for the benefit of those who minister God's word. "For it is written in the Law of Moses: "Do not muzzle an ox while it is treading out the grain." Is it about oxen that God is concerned? Surely he says this for us, doesn't he? Yes, this was written for us, because when the plowman plows and the thresher threshes, they ought to do so in the hope of sharing in the

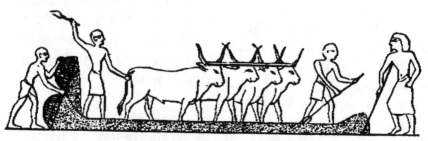

Ancient Egyptians threshing

harvest. If we have sown spiritual seed among you, is it too much if we reap a material harvest from you" (1 Corinthians 9:9-11)? He reiterates this theme in 1 Timothy 5:18—For the Scripture says, "Do not muzzle the ox while it is treading out the grain," and "The worker deserves his wages."

25:13-15 WEIGHTS, DIFFERING

Do not have two differing weights in your bag—one heavy, one light. Do not have two differing measures in your house—one large, one small. You must have accurate and honest weights and measures, so that you may live long in the land the LORD your God is giving you.

Dishonest weights were sometimes used for buying and selling, and this practice was forbidden by God. When buying, a merchant would use the heavy weight so that he would receive more than he should. When selling, he would use the light weight, which was marked the same as the heavy weight, so that he gave less than he should. The same was done with the devices used to measure out products: a large one for buying, a small one, marked the same, for selling. The implication in the final clause in our text-verse is that those who disobey this law will not live long in the land.

26:14 OFFERINGS FOR THE DEAD

I have not eaten any of the sacred portion while I was in mourning, nor have I removed any of it while I was unclean, nor have I offered any of it to the dead. I have obeyed the LORD my God; I have done everything you commanded me.

In pagan customs there was what was known as a cult for the dead that practiced many things in relation to the dead. Israel was forbidden by God to practice any of these customs. Nevertheless, the Israelites often departed from God's injunctions and engaged in the worship of pagan deities and even consulted the dead as Saul did in 1 Samuel 28. Although almost everything in relation to the dead was forbidden by God, many Christians today are literally in a cult for the dead and practice many things in relation to the dead as part of their religion, even praying to them and attributing miracles to them.

33:24 Dipping Feet in Oil

About Asher he said: "Most blessed of sons is Asher; let him be favored by his brothers, and let him bathe his feet (dip his foot, KJV) in oil.

The territory of Asher was famous for its olives (oil). This verse refers undoubtedly to the primitive method of treading the olives to extract the oil. There is a reference to this in Micah 6:15 (KJV): "thou shalt tread the olives." In recent years some have thought that this Scripture referred to an abundance of crude oil in the ground in the land given to Asher. During the 1980s, a commercial oil company funded by Christians spent millions of dollars looking for oil in that area without success, all based upon no more evidence of oil than this verse.

JOSHUA

2:6 Use of Roofs

(But she had taken them up to the roof and hidden them under the stalks of flax she had laid out on the roof.)

The flat roofs of Israelite houses were customarily used for drying anything that needed to be laid out in the sun and air. The "stalks of flax" were three- or four-foot stems that had previously been soaked in water and were then laid out on the flat roof to dry. Other things that were often laid out on the roof were fruit that needed exposure to the sun to ripen, grain that needed drying, and wet clothing.

5:2 Knives

At that time the LORD said unto Joshua, Make thee sharp knives, and circumcise again the children of Israel the second time *(KJV)*.

Knives were made of flint ("Make flint knives," NIV), bone, copper, iron, or steel. Specimens of ancient Egyptian and Assyrian knives are in several museums, and they probably have a general resemblance to those used by the Hebrews. They were made in various shapes according to their purpose.

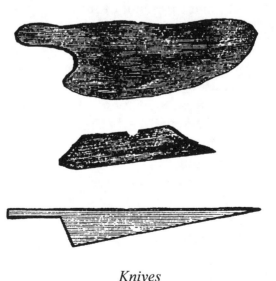

Knives

7:26 STONE HEAPS

Over Achan they heaped up a large pile of rocks *(great heap of stones, KJV)*, which remains to this day. Then the LORD turned from his fierce anger. Therefore that place has been called the Valley of Achor ever since.

Achor means "trouble." The valley is about one mile (1.6 km) south of Jericho. It was customary to heap up stones as rude monuments or memorials of important events (see Genesis 31:46 and Joshua 4:3, 6). In the case of noted criminals this was done not merely to mark the spot of their burial but as a monument of the popular abhorrence of their crimes. This case of Achan is an illustration. Another instance may be found in the case of Absalom (2 Samuel 18:17). When Joshua captured and hanged the king of Ai, he commanded that his body be thrown down at the city gate and a heap of stones piled over it (Joshua 8:29). This remained there for many years as a remembrance to all who saw it. As late as the 1800s travelers to Palestine said it was still customary to cast stones upon the graves of criminals, with many passing by adding to the heap for a long time afterward.

Second Samuel 18:18 tells about Absalom setting up a monument for himself: "During his lifetime Absalom had taken a pillar and erected it in the King's Valley (king's dale, KJV) as a monument to himself, for he thought, "I have no son to carry on the memory of my name." He named the pillar after himself, and it is called Absalom's Monument to this day." The "King's Valley" was probably the same as the Kidron Valley east of Jerusalem, or the Valley of Shaveh where Abram met Melchizedek. It is said that the Kidron Valley is where Absalom raised the pillar as a monument to himself. But the pyramid-shaped structure that now stands there is of Greek rather than Hebrew origin. Since the fourth century A.D., the Kidron Valley has been known as the Valley of Jehoshaphat; but there is no reason to believe Joel 3:2, 12 refers to the Kidron Valley. Joel may have been speaking figuratively.

10:24 ENEMIES, PUTTING FEET ON NECKS

When they had brought these kings to Joshua, he summoned all the men of Israel and said to the army commanders who had come with him, "Come here and put your feet on the necks of these kings." So they came forward and placed their feet on their necks.

Putting your feet on the necks of your enemy was a symbol of complete subjugation, and expressed total victory over them. This was also implied by the phrase to put someone "under your feet" (see Romans 16:20 and 1 Corinthians 15:25).

Assyrian king placing his foot on the neck of an enemy

JUDGES

1:6 MUTILATION OF CAPTIVES

Adoni-Bezek fled, but they chased him and caught him, and cut off his thumbs and big toes.

This ancient custom of mutilating captured enemies served two purposes: it humiliated them and it made them unfit for future warfare. According to his own confession (verse 7), Adoni-Bezek had practiced the same mutilation on seventy kings (of the many small city-states of Canaan) that he had previously captured, and said that God had now paid him back for what he did to them. The Assyrian kings were particularly addicted to such cruelties. An ancient monument bears an inscription that was put upon it by order of Asshur-izirpal, who began his reign in 883 B.C. In it he speaks of what he did in a captured city: "Their men, young and old, I took prisoners. Of some I cut off the feet and hands; of others I cut off the noses, ears, and lips; of the young men's eyes I made a heap; of the old men's I built a minaret."

3:7 BAALIM AND THE GROVES

And the children of Israel did evil in the sight of the LORD, and forgat the LORD their God, and served Baalim and the groves *(the Baals and the Asherahs, NIV) (KJV)*.

Baalim is the plural of Baal. This probably refers to the various modifications of Baal, such as Baal-Peor, Baal-Berith, Baal-Zebub, etc. This may be what is referred to in Hosea 2:17— "For I will take away the names of Baalim (names of the Baals, NIV) out of her mouth, and they shall no more be remembered by their name." Some believe, however, that Baalim is what the old grammarians called the pluralis excellentiae: a form of speech designed to describe the god in the wide extent of his influence and the various modes of his manifestation. The word Baalim frequently occurs in the Old Testament. See Judges 2:11, 8:33, 10:10; 1 Samuel 7:4, 12:10; 2 Chronicles 24:7; and Jeremiah 2:23, 9:14. See also Leviticus **26:30 High Places and Images,** Numbers **22:41 Baal,** and Numbers **25:3 Baal of Peor**.

The word *asherah*, rendered "groves" in the KJV and Asherahs in the NIV, is often found in either singular or plural form. In most places where it is used, the word "groves" is evidently inappropriate. Almost four centuries ago, a lawyer and antiquarian named Selden was the first to suggest that the word must be understood to mean, at least in most places, not groves but images of Asherah (or Astarte), a fertility goddess and mother of Baal. Most now agree with this view. If the words "images of Asherah, or Asherahs, are substituted for the word "grove" or "groves" in the following passages, the sense will be much clearer: 1 Kings 16:33; 2 Kings 17:16, 21:3; and 2 Chronicles 33:3.

Thus in 2 Kings 17:10 and 2 Chronicles 33:19 it is better understood that Asherah poles—that is, wooden images of

Asherah—were set up, in addition to the graven images also mentioned. Second Kings 23:6 tells what King Josiah did with the Asherah pole: "He took the Asherah pole from the temple of the LORD to

Symbolic tree

the Kidron Valley outside Jerusalem and burned it there. He ground it to powder and scattered the dust over the graves of the common people." In this verse it is easy to see that the KJV use of the word "grove" for Asherah is totally inappropriate: "And he brought out the grove from the house of the LORD, without Jerusalem, unto the brook Kidron, and burned it at the brook Kidron, and stamped it small to powder, and cast the powder thereof upon the graves of the children of the people." Obviously you cannot bring out a "grove" of trees from a house, nor burn "it" and stamp it to small powder. The verse is much more appropriately applied to an image than a grove of trees.

At times the Asherah apparently had over it a canopy or tent that was woven by the women, as shown in 2 Kings 23:7. This was doubtless the same image that Mannasseh put into the house of the LORD (2 Kings 21:7). From Judges 6:25-30, and other passages that speak of the Asherah as being burned or cut down, it appears that most of them, at least, were made of wood.

The Asherah is thought by some to be connected with the "sacred tree" of the Assyrians, an object that appears frequently on Assyrian monuments. If this is true, we may find in the representations of the sacred tree that have come down to us, a picture of the Asherah that the idolatrous Israelites worshiped.

According to ancient mythology, Asherah, the mother goddess, was the wife of El and mother of seventy gods—Baal being the most famous. Asherah was the fertility goddess of the Phoenicians and, and was known as "Lady Asherah of the Sea." Bible scholars who have studied ancient Middle East art work

have said that some figures in drawings could be representations of Asherah. Drawings of plain and carved poles, staffs, a cross, a double ax, a tree, a tree stump, a headdress for a priest, and several wooden images could be illustrations of an Asherah.

3:23 LOCKS

Then Ehud went out to the porch; he shut the doors of the upper room behind him and locked them.

Ancient locks consisted merely of a wooden slide drawn into its place by a string, and fastened there by teeth or catches. The lock commonly used in Egypt and Palestine is a long hollow piece of wood fixed in the door and sliding back and forth. A hole is made for it in the door post, and when it is pushed into this hole small bolts of iron wire fall into holes that are made for them in the top of the lock. The lock is placed on the inside of the door, and a hole is made in the door near the lock, through which the hand can be passed and the key inserted. This explains Song of Songs 5:4—"My lover thrust his hand through the latch-opening (put in his hand by the hole of the door, KJV); my heart began to pound for him." Some of these locks were very large and heavy.

3:25 KEYS

They waited to the point of embarrassment, but when he did not open the doors of the room, they took a key and unlocked them.

The key was usually of wood, though some have been found in Egypt of iron and bronze. The ordinary wooden key was from six inches to two feet long, and often had a handle of brass or silver that was ornamented with filigree work. At the end of the handle there were wire pins that were designed to loosen the

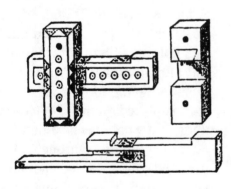

Egyptian wooden lock and key

fastenings of the lock. The key was sometimes borne on the shoulder (see Isaiah 22:22).

3:31 OXGOAD

After Ehud came Shamgar son of Anath, who struck down six hundred Philistines with an oxgoad.

The oxgoad was formidable when used as a weapon. It was about 8 feet long (2.4 meters) and two inches in diameter. At one end was a sharp point for pricking the ox when their movements became intolerably slow, and at the other end was a broad chisel-shaped blade, which was used to clear the plow blade of any roots and thorns that got caught on it and impeded it, or to clean off any sticky clay that adhered to it. It substituted nicely for a spear, and also made a long ax-like weapon. The pointed end of this instrument is alluded in Acts 26:14—"We all fell to the ground, and I heard a voice saying to me in Aramaic, 'Saul, Saul, why do you persecute me? It is hard for you to kick against the goads'" (pricks, KJV).

5:11 Ambushes Near Water

They that are delivered from the noise of archers in the places of drawing water, there shall they rehearse the righteous acts of the LORD (KJV).

This refers to the practice of lying in ambush near wells and springs for the purpose of seizing flocks and herds when brought there for water. Moses defended his future wife and sisters against shepherds who drove them away from a well (Exodus 2:17). In a book written in the 18th century, Dr. Thomas Shaw reported seeing near the coast of the western province of Algiers, a basin of Roman workmanship that received its water from a beautiful brook and that was called *Shrub we krug*—which means: Drink and away. The name was given

Windows

because of robbers who lurked near the watering place waiting for unsuspecting travelers.

5:28 Windows

Through the window peered Sisera's mother; behind the lattice she cried out.

The walls of ancient houses had few windows to the street, and those were high up from the ground. They were normally open to the air with lattice in them, which allowed air to pass through and prevented those outside from seeing in. Sometimes the windows were built outward from the wall like a modern bay-window, and so provided a good view of what was going on in the street below. The window latticework sometimes consisted of two sections that opened at the center and swung out like doors. The window spoken of in the text was evidently on the street side of the house, as was the window from which Michal saw David (2 Samuel 6:16). The window from which Jezebel was hurled may have opened into the street or into the court (2 Kings 9:30-33), and so also the window from which Eutychus fell (Acts 20:9). Windows are mentioned in several other Scriptures, such as: 2 Kings 13:17, Proverbs 7:6, Song of Songs 2:9, Daniel 6:10.

5:30 EMBROIDERED GARMENTS

"Are they not finding and dividing the spoils: a girl or two for each man, colorful garments as plunder for Sisera, colorful garments embroidered *(of needlework, KJV)*, highly embroidered garments for my neck—all this as plunder?"

The Hebrew word *rikmah*, translated "needlework" in the KJV, means work made in different colors, whether by means of the needle or the loom. Precisely how this beautiful cloth was made is not now known. The Israelites were doubtless able to make embroidered cloth either with the needle or by weaving, since there is evidence from the Egyptian monuments that both methods were very ancient. The Israelites could therefore have learned the art in Egypt. Elegant and highly ornamented garments have ever been greatly prized in Palestine and the surrounding areas. Babylon was specially famous for their manufacture, whence came the expression "Babylonish garments" as used in Joshua 7:21.

In the sacking of cities or camps varicolored cloths were considered highly desirable loot. Thus Deborah, in this fine battle-poem in Judges 5, presents the ladies who attended on the mother of Sisera as suggesting to her that her son was detained because of the valuable spoil he had taken. Sometimes gold thread was used in the creation of beautiful garments as shown in Psalm 45:13-14. The prophet Ezekiel refers to the fondness of the Assyrians for costly clothing (Ezekiel 23:12, especially in the KJV).

8:21 ORNAMENTS ON CAMELS

Zebah and Zalmunna said, "Come, do it yourself. 'As is the man, so is his strength.'" So Gideon stepped forward and killed them, and took the ornaments off their camels' necks.

Camel's ornaments

The Hebrew word *saharonim*, here translated ornaments, is translated in Isaiah 3:18 as "crescent necklaces (round tires like the moon, KJV). These were were amulets that were put on the camels as a charm against evil or injury. They were probably made of gold and had little moons, full or crescent, engraved on them— most likely in honor of the moonfaced goddess Astarte. Taking away those ornaments would thus be to remove idolatrous objects.

8:33-34 BAAL-BERITH

No sooner had Gideon died than the Israelites again prostituted themselves to the Baals. They set up Baal-Berith as their god and did not remember the LORD their God.

Baal-Berith, or the covenant Baal, was one of the numerous Baalim that the Israelites worshiped at different times. We have no definite description of this god. It was probably the god of Shechem (Judges 9:46), and was considered a local manifestation of Baal. What the worship ceremonies were we don't know. Since Shechem was an important religious site in Israel (Genesis 12:6, 7; 33:18-20; Joshua 24:32), the worship there may have been a fusion or mixture of Baal worship and Jehovah worship. It may also have been a total perversion of the worship of the LORD—an adulteration of that worship in which the Israelites put Baal in place of the LORD.

13:24-25 SAMSON

The woman gave birth to a boy and named him Samson. He grew and the

LORD blessed him, and the Spirit of the LORD began to stir him while he was in Mahaneh Dan, between Zorah and Eshtaol.

The name Samson means "of the sun," or "sunlight." He was the son of Manoah whose wife had been visited by "the angel of the LORD" in response to her prayers (Judges 13).

Samson was a "Nazarite unto God" from his birth, the first Nazarite mentioned in the Scriptures (Judges 13:3-5; compare Numbers 6:1-21). The first recorded event of his life was his marriage to a Philistine woman of Timnath (Judges 14:1-5). Such a marriage was not forbidden by the law of Moses, as the Philistines did not form one of the seven doomed Canaanite nations (Exodus 34:11-16; Deuteronomy 7:1-4).

Many have said that it was an ill-assorted and unblessed marriage, and that Samson willfully disregarded loyalty to the LORD, but the Scripture clearly says: "(His parents did not know that this was from the LORD, who was seeking an occasion to confront the Philistines; for at that time they were ruling over Israel)" (Judges 14:4). Now those whose theology will not allow them to let God be sovereign and do whatever He wants to do, say that it was not God's will for Samson to marry a pagan woman, but that He ultimately used Samson's disobedience to His purpose. But that is wresting the Scripture to fit predetermined doctrine, the Scripture clearly states that Samson's marriage to a pagan woman "was from the LORD."

Samson's wife was soon taken from him and given "to his companion" (Judges 14:20). For this Samson took revenge and "burned up the shocks and standing grain, together with the vineyards and olive groves" (Judges 15:1-8). The Philistines, in turn, took revenge upon Samson's wife and "burned her and her father to death" (Judges 15:6). Her death he terribly avenged (Judges 15:7-19). During the twenty years that followed he judged Israel but we have no record of his life. Probably these twenty years may have been simultaneous with the last twenty years of Eli's life. After this we have an account of his exploits at Gaza (Judges 16:1-3), and of his infatuation for Delilah, and her treachery (Judges 16:4-20), and then of his death (Judges 16:21-31). He perished in the last terrible destruction he brought upon his enemies: "Thus he killed many more when he died than while he lived."

16:4 DELILAH

Some time later, he fell in love with a woman in the Valley of Sorek whose name was Delilah.

Delilah is known historically as a woman in the Old Testament who was a mistress of Samson, and who betrayed him to the Philistines by having his hair shorn while he slept, thus depriving him of his strength. Her name has become synonymous with female betrayal by sexual means.

16:21 GRINDING, A PUNISHMENT

Then the Philistines seized him, gouged out his eyes and took him down to Gaza. Binding him with bronze shackles, they set him to grinding in the prison.

Grinding a hand mill was the lowest kind of slave labor. Among the Greeks and Romans, slaves were sometimes compelled to do this as a punishment. It was doubtless considered equally degrading in the day of Samson, and for this reason the Philistines condemned him to it after they destroyed his sight. Fanciful illustrations and movies have shown Samson harnessed to a large wooden pole attached to a huge millstone that he turned by pushing the pole around a circle, but nothing of the sort is referred to in the Scriptures. Samson was reduced to humiliating slave labor, doing a woman's work with an ordinary hand-mill. In Lamentations 5:13 Jeremiah laments the same fate that befell the young men of his people.

16:23 DAGON

Now the rulers of the Philistines assembled to offer a great sacrifice to Dagon their god and to celebrate, saying, "Our god has delivered Samson, our enemy, into our hands."

Dagon was the national god of the Philistines. The name is derived from the Hebrew word *dag*, meaning "little fish" or "dear," or as some say, "dear little fish," which may have had more to do with reference to affection for it than reference to its size. Although Dagon is associated with the Philistines, he originated in Mesopotamia during the third century B.C. A major temple was built for him in the maritime city of Ugarit. From there the Dagon cult was carried into Canaan when it was still part of the Egyptian empire. When the Philistines conquered the coastal region of Canaan, they adopted Dagon as their chief god.

Because the name Dagon came from a Hebrew word for fish, it has commonly been assumed that he was a sea or fish god, but modern archaeological evidence doesn't support that view. The name could have originated from a word for grain and had more to do with rapid reproduction than with fish qualities (*dagan*, Hebrew, means "grain"). As such, Dagon would be more a god of vegetation and fertility, much like Baal. In fact, in some ancient literature,

Ugaritic documents from the Fourteenth century B.C., Baal is referred to as the "son of Dagon." Little else, including his appearance, is known about his mythology or cult.

When the Philistines captured Samson, they credited Dagon with the victory: "Now the rulers of the Philistines assembled to offer a great sacrifice to Dagon their god and to celebrate, saying, 'Our god has delivered Samson, our enemy, into our hands'" (Judges 16:23). When Samson collapsed Dagon's temple, however, he proved the superiority of Israel's God (Judges 16:23-30). This was proved also when the Philistines captured the ark of God and took it into Dagon's temple and set it beside Dagon (1 Samuel 5:1-7). Even so, when the Philistines defeated the Israelite army and found the body of Saul on Mount Gilboa, "They put his armor in the temple of their gods and hung up his head in the temple of Dagon" (1 Chronicles 10:10).

RUTH

2:3 GLEANING

So she went out and began to glean in the fields behind the harvesters.

The Israelites were commanded by their law to be merciful to the poor. The corners of fields were not to be reaped, and the sheaf accidentally left behind was not to be taken away, according to the law of Moses (Leviticus 19:9, 23:22; Deuteronomy 24:21). They were to be left for the poor to glean. Similar laws were given regarding vineyards and olive yards. Basing her words on this law, Ruth the Moabitess said to her mother-in-law Naomi: "Let me go to the fields and pick up (glean, KJV) the leftover grain behind anyone in whose eyes I find favor" (Ruth 2:2).

Ruth gleaning in Boaz's field

2:4 MUTUAL SALUTATIONS

Just then Boaz arrived from Bethlehem and greeted the harvesters, "The LORD be with you!" "The LORD bless you!" they called back.

Mutual salutations were common in Bible days; the one greeting and blessing another, and the other returning the greeting and blessing. This is similar today to two people saying "Good-bye" to each other. Although not known by most, they are using an expression that once meant: "God be with you."

The American Heritage dictionary says that *good-bye* is an alteration of *God be with you.* More than one person has undoubtedly wondered exactly how *good-bye* is derived from the phrase "God be with you." To understand this, it's helpful to see earlier forms of the expression, such as *God be wy you, b'w'y, godbwye, god buy' ye,* and *good-b'wy.* The first word of the expression is now *good* and not *God,* for *good* replaced *God* by analogy with such expressions as *good day,* perhaps after people no longer had a clear idea of the original sense of the expression.

A letter written in 1573 by a Gabriel Harvey contains the first recorded use of *good-bye:* "To requite your gallonde [gallon] of *godbwyes,* I regive you a pottle of howdyes" Obviously, *howdyes* has become *howdy,* a colloquial greeting.

2:14 VINEGAR AND ROASTED GRAIN

At mealtime Boaz said to her, "Come over here. Have some bread and dip it in the wine vinegar (*KJV leaves out wine*)." When she sat down with the harvesters, he offered her some roasted grain (*parched corn, KJV*). She ate all she wanted and had some left over.

Vinegar (Hebrew *chomets*) was a beverage consisting generally of wine or strong drink turned sour. It was probably made by mixing water and new grape juice and leaving it to ferment. The Nazarites were forbidden to drink it (Numbers 6:3). It may have been excessively sour (Proverbs 10:26). It was similar to the *posea* of the Romans, which was a thin sour wine, unintoxicating, and used only by the poor. This is what is referred to under the name vinegar in the KJV (wine, wine vinegar,

NIV) in the narrative of the crucifixion of our Lord (see Matthew 27:34, 48; Luke 23:36; John 19:29-30).

The parched (roasted, NIV) corn is prepared from grains of wheat not yet fully ripe. These are sometimes roasted in a pan or on an iron plate. Sometimes the stalks are tied in small bundles and the heads of grain held over the fire until roasted. Grain thus roasted was at times eaten with bread. In Leviticus 23:14, the roasted grain is classed with bread and new grain (green ears, KJV). Jesse sent an ephah of it and ten loaves of bread to his sons in the army by the hand of David (1 Samuel 17:18). Abigail took five measures of it as part of her present to David (1 Samuel 25:18). David also received it with other provisions from the hands of his friends when he was in need, after having fled from his rebellious son Absalom (2 Samuel 17:28).

In Leviticus 2:14 it is called "green ears of corn dried by the fire" in the KJV, but more accurately in the NIV: "new grain roasted in the fire," for corn wasn't known in either Europe or the Middle East until it was brought from the Americas into Europe by Columbus and other explorers. Grain, especially rice, is the most common food element throughout the world.

2:17 RUDE THRESHING

So Ruth gleaned in the field until evening. Then she threshed *(beat out, KJV)* the barley she had gathered, and it amounted to about an ephah.

This was done by the gleaners at the close of their day's work, sticks or stones were used as convenient though rude instruments for threshing the grain they had gathered. After Ruth beat out (threshed) her barley, she had an ephah, about three-fifths of a bushel, which was enough to sustain two women for about five days.

3:2 TIME FOR WINNOWING

Tonight he will be winnowing barley on the threshing floor.

The evening was selected not only because it was cooler than the day, but because the increase of wind at night enabled the husbandmen to winnow more thoroughly. For the method of winnowing see Genesis **50:11-12 Threshing Floors**.

3:7 WATCHING THE GRAIN

When Boaz had finished eating and drinking and was in good spirits, he went over to lie down at the far end of the grain pile.

The threshing floor was usually out in the open, and so it was necessary for the owner or some trusty servant to keep watch over the grain. Boaz ate his supper and slept at the far end of the grain pile. This practice continued throughout the centuries so long as threshed grain was kept outside in the open.

3:9 SIGN OF MARRIAGE AND THE GO'EL

"Spread the corner of your garment *(skirt, KJV)* over me, since you are a kinsman-redeemer *(KJV leaves out redeemer)*."

The expression "spread the corner of your garment" implies protection, and here signifies

protection of a conjugal nature. When marriages were solemnized among the Israelites, the man threw the skirt of his *talith* or robe over his wife and covered her head with it.

The Hebrew word *go'el* or *ga'al* translates "redeemer" or, more literally, "one who redeems." When an Israelite was obliged to sell his inheritance because of poverty it was the duty of the nearest relative to redeem it for him (Leviticus 25:25). Thus the word *go'el* came to signify *kinsman*. If a kinsman became a slave, the go'el was to redeem him or her (Leviticus 25: 47-49). If brothers were living together and one died without an heir, the other brother was to redeem his name by marrying the widow and rearing a son (Deuteronomy 25:5-10). The go'el also became the recipient of property that had been unjustly kept from a deceased kinsman (Numbers 5:6-8). It was likewise the go'el's duty to avenge the blood of his next of kin by seeking the life of the murderer (Genesis 9:5-6, Numbers 35:19, 2 Samuel 14:7).

Some have supposed from the association of the go'el with marriage, as in the history of Ruth, that it was his duty to marry the widow of a deceased kinsman. But according to Deuteronomy 25:5, this duty was only obligatory on a brother-in-law, and one who was living with his deceased brother and his wife. Boaz had no such relation to Ruth, and was not obliged to marry her, so he did it for other reasons than duty. Also, there is no evidence that the unnamed kinsman spoken of by Boaz was a brother-in-law to Ruth: "Although it is true that I am near of kin, there is a kinsman-redeemer nearer than I" (Ruth 3:12). Ruth 1:1 would seem to indicate that Elimelech and Naomi had only two sons.

If the nearer go'el had been a brother-in-law, Boaz would not have begun by asking him to redeem the property (Ruth 4:4), but would instantly have demanded that he should marry the widow. If he refused to do so, he would have been liable to judicial disgrace (Deuteronomy 25:7-10). But in the case of the go'el, it was not until he redeemed the property of his relative, dying without a son, that he was under obligation to marry the widow.

In 1874, Dr. G. B. Winer wrote: "The latter was to him the consequence of the former and not the reverse, as in the case of the *levir* (brother-in-law). Should he refuse to take possession of the property he was under no obligation to marry the widow. In so refusing he incurred no judicial disgrace, because he not fail to discharge a duty but only relinquished a right. The law had expressly imposed the duty of marriage on the *levir* only, and beyond him the obligation did not extend."

Boaz had no right to redeem the property until the nearer kinsman refused, and neither he nor the other kinsman was under any obligation do it. But having once assumed the redemption, the one thus exercising his right was by that act under obligation to marry the widow.

3:15 VEIL

He also said, "Bring me the shawl *(veil, KJV)* you are wearing and hold it out." When she did so, he poured into it six measures of barley and put it on her.

The Hebrew word *mitpachath*, veil, is translated mantle (cape, NIV) in Isaiah 3:22, and some lexicographers assert that this is its meaning. They say that it doesn't signify what is commonly understood by a veil, but is simply a large outer mantle or cloak (cape), and that the grain was placed in one corner of the one that Ruth wore. Others, however, insist that a veil is meant; one made of strong cotton cloth and used for outdoor wearing.

4:7 Sign of the Shoe

(Now in earlier times in Israel, for the redemption and transfer of property to become final, one party took off his sandal [shoe, KJV] and gave it to the other. This was the method of legalizing transactions in Israel.)

There was no divine law ordaining the giving of a shoe, it was simply an ancient custom. It is not to be confused with the law in reference to livirate marriages in Deuteronomy 25:7-10. It probably originated from the fact that the right to tread the soil belonged to the owner of it, and so the transfer of a sandal was a symbol of the transfer of the property or possession. Allusion to this custom is doubtless intended in Psalm 9:8: "Moab is my washbasin, upon Edom I toss my sandal; over Philistia I shout in triumph"; that is, I will transfer it to myself. The custom was prevalent among the Indians and ancient Germans, and existed for many centuries in the Middle East.

1 SAMUEL

1:9 Seat of Judgment

Now Eli the priest was sitting on a chair by the doorpost *(sat upon a seat by a post, KJV)* of the Lord's temple.

In some parts of the ancient Middle East, a seat was placed in the courtyard where the master of the house sat and gave judgment on all domestic affairs. This seat was usually placed in some shady part of the court, against a wall or column. Thus in the text Eli "was sitting on a chair by the doorpost." David sat upon a seat by the wall (1 Samuel 20:25, KJV) These seats probably had no backs, and were therefore placed near the post or wall for support. Thus we are told that Eli fell backward from his seat at the gate and died (1 Samuel 4:18) The Assyrian monuments have many representations of such backless seats.

2:1 Horn

Then Hannah prayed and said: "My heart rejoices in the LORD; in the LORD my horn is lifted high.

The horn was a symbol of strength, and Hannah rejoiced that God had strengthened her that she might give birth to a son. Previously, Hannah's enemies had viewed her condescendingly and demeaned her because she was barren. But God had changed all that. He had given her strength and thus elevated her in privilege and honor. When the horn is spoken of as being depressed, it represents the loss of strength, privilege, and honor. See 1 Samuel 2:10, Job 16:15; Psalm 75:4-5; 89:17, 24; 92:10; 112:9.

In years past, the Druse women on Mount Lebanon wore a horn as part of their headdress. The horns were made of various materials according to the wealth of the owner: dough, pasteboard, pottery, tin, silver, and gold. They varied in length from six inches to two feet and a half, and were three or four inches in diameter at the base, tapering almost to a point. The veil is thrown over the horn, and from it flows gracefully down. When once put on, the horn was never taken off. It remained on the wearer's head by day and night, through sickness and health, even down to death.

 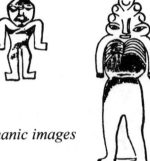

Talismanic images

Some writers have said that the Scripture passages referenced above all refer to this article of costume, and it is frequently spoken of as an illustration of them. It should be borne in mind, however, that some of the most judicious critics deny all such reference, there being no evidence that the horn was ever used by the Hebrews.

6:5 Talismanic Images

Make models of the tumors and of the rats that are destroying the country, and pay honor to Israel's god.

These were doubtless talismanic figures made according to some occult laws of astrology. Such talismans are very ancient. There were supposed to cure diseases and to ward off evils. One has theorized that these particular images originated in false views entertained by the Gentiles concerning the brazen serpent. His theory is that their astrologers, finding that among the Israelites the bite of serpents had been cured by the image of a serpent, concluded that all sorts of evils might be remedied if corresponding images were made under the proper astrological conditions. Whether this theory is correct or not, there is abundant evidence of the ancient prevalence of this superstition. Many still exist in some Middle East countries.

Talismans, generally of silver, were carried to the heathen temples for prayer or worship. These images represent as nearly as they could the diseases or special troubles under which the offerers suffered. It was believed that the gods would be favorable on seeing them, and give the sufferer the relief sought. Images of eyes, ears, mouth, nose, and hands were also hung in idolatrous temples. Some believe that "the blind and the lame," which were said to have the power to ward off David in 2 Samuel 5:6-8, were talismanic images set up in the fort by the Jebusites for their protection.

17:5 Helmets and Cuirasses (Breastplates)

He had a bronze *(brass, KJV)* helmet on his head and wore a coat of scale armor of bronze weighing five thousand shekels.

In the earliest times helmets were made of osier (willows) or rushes, and were in the form of beehives or skullcaps. The skins of the head of animals were sometimes used. Various other materials were employed at different times. The ancient Egyptian helmet was usually quilted linen cloth. It was thick and well padded, sometimes coming down to the shoulder to protect the back of the neck, and sometimes only a little below the ear. The cloth used was colored green, red, or black. The helmet had no crest, but the summit was often an obtuse point ornamented with two tassels. The Assyrian helmet was a cap of iron terminating above in a point, and sometimes furnished with back flaps that

Ancient helmets

were covered with metal scales to protect the neck. The Philistine helmet, as shown on ancient monuments, was of unique form. From the headband there arose curved lines, by which the outline of the helmet was hollowed on the sides and rounded on top. Goliath's helmet was doubtless of this shape, and, being made of bronze, must have presented a beautiful appearance. The form of the Hebrew helmets is unknown, but they probably did not vary widely from the Egyptian. As is seen in 1 Samuel 17:38 they were sometimes made of bronze. The helmet is also mentioned in 2 Chronicles 26:14; Jeremiah 46:4; Ezekiel 23:24, 27:10, and 38:5.

For protecting the body, the skins of beasts were probably the earliest protection in battle. Felt or quilted linen was later used. The ancient Egyptians had horizontal rows of metal plates well secured by bronze pins. The ancient Assyrians had scales of iron fastened on felt or linen. Iron rings closely locked together were likewise used by different nations. Scales made of small pieces of horn or hoof were also

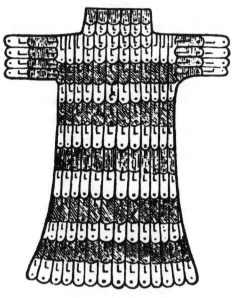

Egyptian cuirass

used. Sometimes a very serviceable armor was made of small plates of metal, each having a button and slit, fitting into the corresponding slit and button of the plate next to it.

It is believed that Ahab had on armor of this sort when he was slain, and that the "sections of his armor" (joints of the harness, KJV) through which the arrow entered him, were the groves or slits in the metallic plates, or the places between where they did not overlap (1 Kings 22:34, 2 Chronicles 18:33). Goliath's "coat of mail" in the KJV was scale armor

(Hebrew, *shiryon kaskassim*, armor of scales), as so translated in the NIV: "coat of scale armor." This kind of armor consisted of metallic scales rounded at the bottom and squared at the top, and sewed on linen or felt. The Philistine corselet covered the chest only. On the bas-relief at Nineveh are seen warriors with coats of scale armor that went to the knees or ankles.

In his book, *Discoveries in the Ruins of Nineveh and Babylon*, written in 1849, H. A. Layard reported discovering a number of the scales used for this armor in one of the ruined palaces. Each scale was of iron two to three inches long, rounded at one end and squared at the other, with a raised or embossed line in the center. Some were inlaid with copper. At a later period, the Assyrian armor was made of smaller scales, which were pointed and ornamented with raised figures, and the coat of mail reached no lower than the waist.

In several passages in the KJV *shiryon* is translated *habergeons* (coats of armor, NIV) (see 2 Chronicles 26:14 and Nehemiah 4:16). The *lorica* of the Romans and the *thorax* of the Greeks— translated *breastplate* in Ephesians 6:14 and 1 Thessalonians 5:8—were scale armor covering the chest and back.

17:6 GREAVES AND JAVELIN

On his legs he wore bronze *(brass, KJV)* **greaves, and a bronze javelin** *(target of brass, KJV)* **was slung on his back** *(between his shoulders, KJV).*

Greaves were leg armor that was worn below the knees. There are none shown on Egyptian monuments, but they are seen on the Assyrian sculptures. They were of leather, wood, or as in the case of Goliath, of bronze, and were bound by thongs around the calves and above the ankles. The word *kidon*, rendered *target* in the KJV, is translated *shield* (javelin, NIV) in 1 Samuel 17:45 and in Job 39:23 (lance, NIV). It's translated *spear* in Joshua 8:18, 26 (javelin, NIV), Job 41:29 (lance, NIV), and

Greave

Jeremiah 6:23. In Jeremiah 50;42, the KJV translates it *lance*, and the NIV translates it spears. It was probably a light javelin, which could easily be hurled at an enemy. Some believe it was decorated with a flag, much like the ones shown in period movies that have cavalrymen armed with lances. When not in actual use, the javelin was carried on the back, probably by means of a leather strap.

17:7 SPEAR AND LARGE SHIELD

His spear shaft was like a weaver's rod, and its iron point weighed six hundred shekels. His shield bearer went ahead of him.

The spear (Hebrew, *chanith*) was a heavier weapon than the javelin (Hebrew, *kidron*). (See 1 Samuel **17:6 Greaves and Javelin**.) The word is translated both *spear* and *javelin*. It was the chanith with which Saul endeavored to strike David (1 Samuel 18:10-11; 19:9-10), although the KJV translates the word as *javelin* in both cases. It was also the chanith that he aimed at Jonathan (1 Samuel 20:33). The heavy spear had at its

butt end a point by which it could be stuck in the ground. It was in this way that the position of Saul was marked while he lay sleeping in the camp at Hachilah, his spear being his standard (1 Samuel 26:7). The butt end of the spear

Egyptian large shield

was almost as formidable as the head. Often riders used it to strike backwards at pursuers, and it was with the butt end (hinder end, KJV) of the spear that Abner killed Asahel (2 Samuel 26:7). The size of Goliath's chanith is emphasized by the description of the staff and the head—the latter being of iron in contrast to the bronze head of his *kidon* and the bronze cuirass (see 1 Samuel **17:5 Helmets and Cuirasses (Breastplates)** and greaves.

The shield (Hebrew, *tsinnah*) in our text-verse was the largest kind of shield, and was designed

Assyrian large shield

to protect the whole body. This shield, as represented on Egyptian monuments, was about five feet high, with a pointed arch at the top and square on the bottom. The great shield of the Assyrians, as shown on their sculptures, was taller, oblong in shape, and sometimes had an inward curve at the top. The large shields were generally made of wicker work or of light wood covered with hides. They were held by a handle of wood or leather fixed to the inside of the shield. In Assyrian sculptures there are illustrations of warriors fighting while men in front of them held the large shields with the bottom resting on the ground, thus forming movable breastworks. The great shields of the Philistines seem to have been of circular shape.

The great beauty of Psalm 5:12, "For surely, O LORD, you bless the righteous; you surround them with your favor as with a shield," is that it is the *tsinnah* shield that is spoken of here, illustrating that God uses the great shield to protect His people.

17:39 Sword

David fastened on his sword over the tunic and tried walking around, because he was not used to them.

The sword was one of the earliest weapons in use. The Egyptian sword was short and straight, two and a half to three feet long, and double-edged. The handle was plain

Egyptian swords

and often recessed in the middle to provide a firm grip. The Hebrew sword probably resembled it.

17:40 STAFF, POUCH, AND SLING

Then he took his staff in his hand, chose five smooth stones from the stream, put them in the pouch *(scrip, KJV)* of his shepherd's bag and, with his sling in his hand, approached the Philistine.

The shepherd carried a *staff*, normally by holding it in the center. It was used as support in climbing hills, and to beat bushes and low brushwood in which the flock strayed, and where snakes and other reptiles might hide. Some of the staffs were curved at the upper end so that the shepherd could hook the neck or body of a sheep that had fallen down among rocks or into a hole and pull it out. Often the butt end of the staff was sharpened to a point so that it could be stuck into the ground, and used as a weapon to ward off wild animals. It was also used at times for correcting the sheep dogs and keeping them in subjection. Thus

Goliath said: "Am I a dog, that you come at me with sticks (staves, KJV)" (1 Samuel 17:43)? The shepherd's staff is mentioned in Genesis 32:10, Psalm 23:4,

Slinger

Micah 7:14, and many other places.

The KJV *scrip* was a leather pouch carried by a shoulder strap, and used by shepherds and travelers to carry provisions. It was usually made of the skin of a young goat, and was stripped off whole and tanned. First Samuel 17:40 is the only passage in the Old Testament where it is mentioned, but reference is made to it in several places in the New Testament:

Matthew 10:10; Mark 6:8; Luke 9:3, 10:4, 22:35-36.

The *sling* was made of leather, or plaited work of wool, rushes, hair, or sinews. The middle part, where the stone lay, was called the cup (Hebrew, *caph*) because of its cup-like depression. It was wider than the ends, but the sling gradually narrowed toward the ends so that it could be easily handled. In the Egyptian sling, which was probably the same as the Hebrew, there was a loop at one end that was placed over the thumb to hold the weapon secure when the stone was hurled by releasing the other end. The sling was used by shepherds to keep wild animals away from the flock, and also to keep the sheep from straying. Husbandmen (farmers) also used it to drive birds away from the grain fields, as did those who cared for vineyards. In war the sling was a formidable weapon in skillful hands.

The Egyptian slinger carried a bag of round stones in a pouch hanging from his shoulder, as David did. The Assyrians, however, according to their sculptures, had lying at their feet a heap of pebbles, which they picked up as they were needed.

In using the sling, the stone was put into the broad hollowed part (cup), the ends were grasped together in one hand, and then the sling was whirled around the head, or on one side, to give it impetus, and then one end of the sling was released as the cup moved in the direction of the target, which sent the stone flying on its way. Often the stone struck with sufficient force to penetrate a helmet or shield, or, in Goliath's case, with sufficient force to sink the stone into his forehead and knock him unconscious.

A weapon so peculiar in its formation and so great in its power was appropriately referred to as an illustration of swift and certain destruction. Thus Abigail said to David: "Even though someone is pursuing you to take your life, the life of my master will be bound securely in the bundle of the living by the LORD your God. But the lives of your enemies he will hurl away as from the pocket of a sling" (1 Samuel 25:29). Thus the Lord said to Jeremiah: "I will hurl (sling, KJV) out those who live in this land; I will bring distress on them" (Jeremiah 10:18). The figure in both these passages is drawn, not from the destructive power of the sling, but from the ease and rapidity with which, by a practiced hand, the stone was hurled from it.

The Benjamites were so skillful in the use of this weapon that among the Benjamite soldiers there were "seven hundred chosen men who were left-handed, each of whom could sling a stone at a hair and not miss" (Judges 20:16). The youthful David also showed great skill, since he hurled the pebble with such precision and force that it struck Goliath in the forehead and brought him to the ground (1 Samuel 17:49-50).

18:4 PRINCELY ROBES

Jonathan took off the robe he was wearing and gave it to David, along with his tunic, and even his sword, his bow and his belt (*girdle, KJV*).

It was considered a special mark of respect to be given by a prince some of the garments he has for his own wearing. The gift of a belt is a token of the greatest confidence and affection, and was highly prized. Joab expressed his intense desire for the death of Absalom by his willingness to give a "warrior's belt" (girdle, KJV) to the man who would kill him.

James Morier, in his book, *Second Journey through Persia, Armenia, and Asia Minor,* published in 1818, gave a particular instance of the estimation placed on the possession of garments that had once covered, and of weapons that had once adorned, a person of royalty. He wrote that when the treaty was made between Russia and Persia in 1814, the Persian plenipotentiary (diplomatic agent), who had been honored by various gifts of weapons and clothing from his sovereign, designated himself in the preamble of the treaty as "endowed with the special gifts of the Monarch, lord of the dagger set in jewels, of the sword adorned with gems, and of the shawl-coat already worn." It was in this way that the shepherd-warrior, David, was honored by Jonathan, the son of the king.

18:6 JOY IN VICTORY (*SHALISHIM*)

When the men were returning home after David

had killed the Philistine, the women came out from all the towns of Israel to meet King Saul with singing and dancing, with joyful songs and with tambourines and lutes *(with instruments of music, KJV).*

It was customary for the women to express their delight in victory by songs and music, and dancing in the presence of the conquerors (see Exodus 15:20 and Judges 11:34).

Precisely what is meant by the Hebrew word *shalishim,* which in the KJV is rendered "instruments of music" is not known. From the construction of the word there was evidently a triple arrangement of some sort in the formation of the *shalishim.* The margin of some Bibles has "three-stringed instruments." They may have been harps (or *lutes* as the NIV has it) of three strings, or of a triangular shape, which many authorities now agree is meant by *shalishim.* These instruments of percussion are said to have originated in Syria, and if so may have been known to the ancient Hebrews. They were well adapted for the ringing music of a military triumph.

18:7 RESPONSIVE SINGING

And the women answered one another as they played, and said, Saul hath slain his thousands, and David his ten thousands *(KJV).*

One part of the women probably sang, "Saul hath slain his thousands," and the others responded, "And David his ten thousand." Over four-hundred years before this, Mariam had led the women in the responsive chorus of victory on the occasion of the destruction of Pharaoh's army in the Red Sea, with the men and women alternating in the singing (Exodus 15:21). It is believed to have been an Egyptian custom. See also Ezra 3:11, Isaiah 6:3, Revelations 4:8-11 and 5:9-14.

19:10 FLEEING FROM THE DART

Saul tried to pin him to the wall with his spear *(javelin, KJV),* but David eluded him as Saul drove the spear into the wall. That night David made good his escape.

According to an ancient Asiatic custom, when a dart was

thrown at a freedman, and he escaped from it by flight, he was thereby absolved from all allegiance to his master. Thus Saul by his murderous fury gave complete liberty to David, whose subsequent acts of war against the king could not be considered rebellion. From that hour he was no longer a subject of King Saul.

19:24 NAKED, USE OF TERM

And he stripped off his clothes also, and prophesied before Samuel in like manner, and lay down naked all that day and all that night (KJV).

This does not mean absolutely without any clothing. A person was called naked whose outer garments were thrown aside, leaving nothing but the tunic and girdle (belt). Thus Isaiah was naked by simply removing his sackcloth mantle: "At the same time spake the LORD by Isaiah the son of Amoz, saying, Go and loose the sackcloth from off thy loins, and put off thy shoe from thy foot. And he did so, walking naked (stripped, NIV) and barefoot" (Isaiah 20:2, KJV). This is also

the meaning of "flee away naked (KJV)" in Amos 2:16. The young man who followed Jesus at the time of his arrest was undoubtedly "naked" in this same sense (Mark 14: 51-52). Peter was also "naked" in the same way at the time he cast himself into the sea to meet the Lord (John 21:7). Compare 2 Samuel 6:14, 20.

24:12 SPEAKER MENTIONS SELF FIRST

The LORD judge between me and thee, and the LORD avenge me of thee: but mine hand shall not be upon thee (KJV).

In polite society it has always been considered a lack, or ignorance, of etiquette for the speaker to mention himself first, no matter what the position, rank, or relationship of the other person. That this is true today can be seen from the NIV translator of this particular verse putting the speaker second: "May the LORD judge between you and me. And may the LORD avenge the wrongs you have done to me, but my hand will not touch you." Among ancient people in the Middle East, however, and even among many peoples today, it is customary for the speaker to name himself first.

From our text-verse it seems to have been considered perfectly respectful in the days of David, and we have instances more ancient still. When Ephron the Hittite was bargaining with Abraham for the sale of the cave of Machpelah, he said: "Listen to me, my lord; the land is worth four hundred shekels of silver, but what is that between me and you? Bury your dead" (Genesis 23:15). So also Sarai to her husband Abram: "the LORD judge between me and thee" (Genesis 16:5, KJV). So Laban said to Jacob: "The LORD watch between me and thee, when we are absent one from another" (Genesis 31:49, KJV).

25:1 Houses of the Dead

Now Samuel died, and all Israel assembled and mourned for him; and they buried him at his home in Ramah.

Some commentators assert that Saul was placed in a tomb erected in the house he occupied during his life, or in its court. Of this, however, there is no evidence. Long before Samuel's time the grave was spoken of as "the house (place, NIV) appointed for all living" (Job 30:23). So afterward Joab "was buried in his own house (on his own land, NIV) in the wilderness" (1 Kings 2:34). It is more probable that a tomb for the dead should be called a house than that a dwelling built for the living should be used as a tomb.

In 1824, a missionary, the Rev. W. Jowett, reported seeing on Mount Lebanon in Syria a number of small solid stone buildings that had neither doors nor windows. They were the "houses of the dead." Every time an interment took place it was necessary to open one of the walls. These were probably much like the small tombs that were built to house the dead during the 19th and early 20th century in this country, especially by the affluent. Many of them can still be seen in large cemeteries near major cities. The 733-acre, privately-owned cemetery near Cincinnati, Ohio, contains dozens of these structures, several in the form of small churches and temples.

26:11 CHIEFTAIN'S SPEAR AND CRUSE

But the LORD forbid that I should lay a hand on the Lord's anointed. Now get the spear and water jug *(cruse of water, KJV)* that are near his head, and let's go.

The spear here spoken of is the *chanith* described in the section 1 Samuel **17:7 Spear and Large Shield.** In a Middle East encampment the leader's tent was always recognized by a tall spear stuck in the ground in front of it; and the place where the leader reclined to rest when halting on a march was also designated in like manner. It's not known what was the precise shape of the cruse (Hebrew, *tsappachath*), or the material from which it was made. Some believe it to have been made of iron plates shaped like a shallow cup or bowl. Vessels used not many years ago in the Middle East for the purposes of a cruse or flask were globular in shape and made of blue porous clay. They were nine inches in diameter, with a neck three inches long. At the lower part was a small handle, and on the opposite side was a straight spout with an orifice about the size of a straw through which water was sucked. In the Bible the *tsappachath* is spoken of as a receptacle for oil (1 Kings 17:12), and also for water (see verse-text and 1 Kings 19:6).

The *cruse* mentioned in 1 Kings 14:3, and the one in 2 Kings 2:20, are different vessels from the cruse in this text, and the words themselves are different in the original.

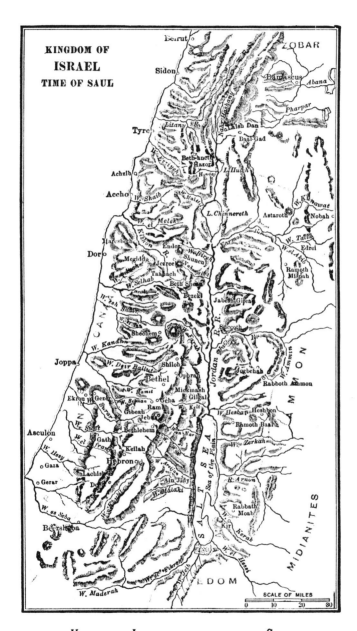

KINGDOM OF ISRAEL DURING THE TIME OF SAUL

2 SAMUEL

1:10 ARMLETS

"And I took the crown that was on his head and the band *(bracelet, KJV)* on his arm and have brought them here to my lord."

The Hebrew word *etsadah*, translated *bracelet* in the KJV, is more properly an anklet than a bracelet, but since it is here spoken of in our text-verse in connection with the arm it doubtless means an armlet; that is, an arm band. The word occurs also in Numbers 31:50, where it is associated with *tsamid* (bracelet), and is rendered *chains* in the KJV and *armlets* in the NIV. Saul's armlet is believed to have been a part of the insignia of his royalty. Egyptian monarchs are often illustrated on monuments wearing armlets and bracelets. The Persian kings often wore them, and they were common among the royalty in several Middle East countries not many years ago. Many of the bracelets and anklets were elaborately wrought and richly ornamented with jewels. From Song of Songs 8:6, it appears that the signet was sometimes placed in the armlet: "like a seal on your arm."

Egyptian armlets

3:27 RECESS IN GATEWAY

Now when Abner returned to Hebron, Joab took him aside into the gateway, as though to speak with him privately.

The expression "into the gateway," is literally *in the midst of the gate*, and probably refers to some dark corner in the vaulted gateway where two persons might retire and talk in private. To some such recess Joab invited Abner, supposedly for conversation, but in reality to kill him.

3:31 BEDS FOR BIERS

Then David said to Joab and all the people with him, "Tear your clothes and put on sackcloth and walk in mourning in front of Abner." King David himself walked behind the bier.

The Hebrew word *mittah*, translated *bier*, would be better rendered *bed*. Persons of distinction were sometimes carried to the grave on their beds. Josephus describes minutely the preparations that were made by Archelaus for the funeral of his father Herod. The body was placed on a gilded bed that was richly adorned with precious stones.

3:34 PRISONERS FETTERED

Your hands were not bound, your feet were not fettered.

By using this language, it is believed that David meant to distinguish Abner from those criminals who are carried to execution with their hands tied behind them, and from soldiers who are taken captive in war and have their feet fastened in fetters to prevent their running away.

4:6 STORING AND GRINDING GRAIN

They went into the inner part of the house as if to get some wheat.

It's been suggested that the pretense of these men that they were going into the house for wheat was made plausible by the fact that it was necessary to obtain grain in the afternoon in order to have it ready for grinding early the next morning, which was customarily done every day. All suspicion of their murderous intention was thus avoided. Ish-Bosheth was taking his usual daily nap after the noon meal (2 Samuel 4:5). They went toward the place where the grain was stored, and thus gained access to the apartment of the sleeping king and murdered him.

6:5 SISTRUM

David and the whole house of Israel were celebrating with all their might before the LORD, with songs and with harps, lyres, tambourines, sistrums *(cornets, KJV)* and cymbals.

This is the only place where the Hebrew word *menaanim* appears. The instrument it represents bore no resemblance to a cornet or to any other wind instrument. One person described it as "a musical instrument or rattle, which gave a tinkling sound when *shaken*." He believes this instrument was the ancient sistrum. Many authorities agree with this interpretation, but some reject it. The sistrum was used in the worship of the ancient Egyptians. It was "generally from eight to sixteen or eighteen inches in length, and consisted of bands of bronze or brass. It was sometimes inlaid with silver gilt, or otherwise ornamented, and was held

upright and shaken in a manner so that the bands separated and then struck against each other, creating the tinkling sound." The other instruments listed in our text-verse are described in other places.

10:4 BEARD CUT OFF

So Hanun seized David's men, shaved off half of each man's beard.

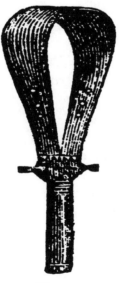

Sistrum

According to Middle East tradition no greater indignity could have been put upon them. The beard was considered a symbol of manhood, and, in some places, of freedom—slaves were compelled to shave their beards in token of servitude. By shaving half their beards, Hanun treated David's ambassadors with contempt and made them objects of ridicule. The beard was usually kept with care and neatness, and thus when David feigned madness in the presence of Achish, king of

Gath, he "let saliva run down his beard," which helped convince the beholders that he must have lost his senses (2 Samuel 21:13). It was considered so disgraceful to have a beard cut off, that

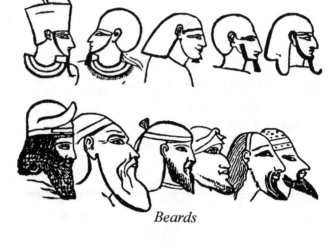

Beards

some ancient men preferred death to such a punishment.

Many years ago a writer named Niebuhr wrote a book titled *Description of Arabia*. In it he relates how in 1764, Kerim Kahn, one of three rebels who at the time desired to obtain dominion over Persia, sent ambassadors to Mir Mahenna, the prince of a little independent territory on the Persian Gulf, to demand a large tribute, and threatened to come to him with an army if he did not conduct himself as an obedient subject. Mahenna, however, treated the ambassadors with great contempt, which was especially marked by cutting off their beards. Upon hearing of this,

Kerim Kahy was so indignant that he sent a large army and subdued the territory and imprisoned Mir Mahenna.

11:1 Spring, Season for War

And it came to pass, after the year was expired *(spring, NIV)*, at the time when kings go forth to battle *(KJV)*.

"After the year was expired" is literally "at the return of the year"; that is, in the spring, as shown in the NIV. This was the time of the year for the commencement or renewal of military movements, the season of severe storms being over, and the ground starting to dry after the winter snows and rains.

11:2 WALKING ON THE ROOF

One evening David got up from his bed and walked around on the roof of the palace. From the roof he saw a woman bathing. The woman was very beautiful.

After he had taken his customary afternoon rest David walked on the flat roof of his palace. In the cool of the evening the roofs of the houses were often occupied by members of the household seeking refreshing air and exercise. In Daniel 4:29 there is an account of another king taking an evening walk: "At the end of twelve months he walked in the palace of the kingdom of Babylon" (KJV). Instead of walked *in* the palace, the marginal reading, in some Bibles, is *upon* the palace, as so shown in the NIV translation: "Twelve months later, as the king was walking on the roof of the royal palace of Babylon." It was on the roof that Nebuchadnezzar walked, and from there he had that view of the great city that lifted his heart with pride and made him forget God.

Some say that the bath in which Bathsheba was washing herself was probably in the courtyard of her house rather than on the roof as was customary. From the rooftop David would then be able to look down into the courtyard and see her. But then she might also have been exposed to being seen from the rooftops on any surrounding houses. So it is most likely that she was bathing on the roof of her house, and, for some reason not told to us, was not protected from being seen from the roof of the palace where David may have customarily walked in the evenings. See Deuteronomy **22:8 Parapet (Battlement, KJV).**

12:21 FASTING FOR BEREAVEMENT

His servants asked him, "Why are you acting this way? While the child was alive, you fasted and wept, but now that the child is dead, you get up and eat!"

What astonished the servants of David was that their master should act so contrary to old established customs of mourning in time of bereavement.

In 1636, in a book titled *Travels into Persia and the East Indies*, John Chardin wrote: The practice of the East is to leave a relation of the deceased person to weep and mourn, till on the third or fourth day at furthest the relatives and friends go to see him, cause him to eat, lead him to a bath, and cause him to put on new vestments, he having before thrown himself on the ground." In contrast, David changed his apparel and ate food as soon as he learned of the death of his new son.

15:30 COVERING THE HEAD

But David continued up the Mount of Olives, weeping as he went; his head was covered and he was barefoot. All the people with him covered their heads too and were weeping as they went up.

Covering the head, as well as uncovering the feet, was a token of great distress. It was probably done by drawing a fold of the outer garment over the head. When Haman mourned over his great discomfiture his head was covered: "Afterward Mordecai returned to the king's gate. But Haman rushed home, with his head covered in grief" (Esther 6:12). Jeremiah writes of the farmers (plowmen, KJV)

mourning in this way because of the severe drought: "The ground is cracked because there is no rain in the land; the farmers are dismayed and cover their heads" (Jeremiah 14:4).

15:32 DUST ON THE HEAD

Hushai the Arkite was there to meet him, his robe torn and dust *(coat rent, and earth, KJV)* on his head.

His torn robe signified mourning (see Genesis **37:34 Rending Garments and Wearing Sackcloth**), as did also the dust on his head. In a tombstone from Abydos, an ancient city of southern Egypt, there is an illustration of a funeral procession in which the mourners are showing their grief by throwing dust on their heads. There was an ancient tradition among the Egyptians that, in the infancy of their history as a people, their god Noum had taught their fathers that they were but clay or dust. The practice of putting dust on their heads is supposed to be symbolical of their origin from dust, and to convey the idea of their humility in view of that fact. We find frequent scriptural reference to the custom.

When the Israelites were defeated at Ai, Joshua and the elders "sprinkled dust on their heads" (Joshua 7:6). The Benjamite who brought Eli the news of the death of his sons came to Shiloh with "his clothes torn and dust on his head" (1 Samuel 4:12). The young Amalekite who brought to David the tidings of Saul's death came "with his clothes torn and with dust on his head" (2 Samuel 1:2) Tamar, when dishonored by brother Amnon, "Tamar put ashes on her head and tore the ornamented robe she was wearing" (2 Samuel 13:19). In the great feast that was held in Nehemiah's time in Jerusalem, the children of Israel had "dust on their heads" (Nehemiah 9:1). When Job's three friends mourned with him in troubles "they tore their robes and sprinkled dust on their heads" (Job 2:12. This shows the great antiquity of the practice.

Jeremiah, in lamenting over the desolations of Zion, says that the elders "have sprinkled dust on their heads and put on sackcloth" (Lamentations 2:10). Ezekiel, in predicting the destruction of Tyrian commerce,

says the sailors "will sprinkle dust on their heads and roll in ashes" (Ezekiel 27:30). And Revelations 18:19 says that when the merchants of the world see Babylon fall they "will throw dust on their heads."

16:13 Dirt Throwing

So David and his men continued along the road while Shimei was going along the hillside opposite him, cursing as he went and throwing stones at him and showering him with dirt.

Throwing dirt at a person was an Eastern way of expressing anger and contempt, perhaps much like today's Middle East way of throwing small rocks that have virtually no chance of harming anyone. Perhaps the intent is not to harm, but to express anger and contempt. In addition to the instance here given we find another in the history of Paul. The mob that he addressed in Jerusalem became agitated at his speech and sought to destroy him, declaring that he was not fit to live, and as evidence of their fury they were "flinging dust into the air" (Acts

22:23). We don't know exactly what the meaning is of this symbolic action. There may be, however, a connection between the custom and practice of people in trouble throwing dust on their own heads in token of grief. Throwing dust at others may be a symbolic gesture of wishing them so much trouble and grief that they will feel like covering themselves with dust as an expression of their misery.

17:18-19 Cistern in the Courtyard

But a young man saw them and told Absalom. So the two of them left quickly and went to the house of a man in Bahurim. He had a well in his courtyard, and they climbed down into it. His wife took a covering and spread it out over the opening of the well and scattered grain over it. No one knew anything about it.

The well (Hebrew, *beer*) spoken of here was not a living fountain, but simply a cistern or reservoir dug in the courtyard, as is still done in many places in the Middle East, and even in our country. Such cisterns sometimes became dry, and then made excellent hiding places for fugitives. The mouth of the cistern, which was normally level with the ground, could easily be covered by a mat or some other article, and with grain spread over this the cistern would be completely hidden.

18:24 Double Gates

While David was sitting between the inner and outer gates, the watchman went up to the roof of the gateway by the wall.

At the gateways of walled cities special care was taken to increase the strength of the wall and the power of resistance, since the most formidable attacks of the enemy would probably be made there. The ordinary thickness of the wall not being sufficient it was here increased, or, more properly, doubled by building another wall. Considerable space was included between the outer and the inner wall, and in each of these walls there was a gate. It was in that area that David sat "between the inner and outer gates."

18:26 WATCHMAN AND GATEKEEPER

Then the watchman saw another man running, and he called down to the gatekeeper (porter, KJV).

Even strong walls and double gates could not of themselves secure a city from an enemy. Men were therefore employed to watch day and night on the top of the walls, and especially at the gates. It was thus that the messengers from the army were seen long before they reached the place where David anxiously sat. In like manner the watchman (lookout, NIV) of Jezreel saw in the distance the company of Jehu driving furiously (2 Kings 9:17-20). So Isaiah in one of his sublime visions saw a lookout standing by his tower day and night (Isaiah 21:5-7). A figurative use of the watchman and his work is beautifully made in Isaiah 62:6; Ezekiel 33:2, 6-7; and Habakkuk 2:1.

It was the business of the gatekeeper (porter, KJV) to open and shut the gates at the proper time. In the incident in our text-verse the gatekeeper, being in a convenient position below, could receive the intelligence from the watchman above and communicate it to David. In 2 Kings 7:10 these men are called " the city gatekeepers." (The KJV refers to them as "the porter of the city," which is singular, but then says "and they told them," which is plural.) Gatekeepers are spoken of in connection with the rebuilding of the walls by Nehemiah (Nehemiah 7:1). In Solomon's Temple there were four thousand of them (1 Chronicles 23:5) who were divided into divisions (courses, KJV) (2 Chronicles 8:14) and had their posts assigned by lot (1 Chronicles 26:13).

18:33 ROOM OVER THE GATE

The king was shaken. He went up to the room (chamber, KJV) over the gateway and wept.

This room was on the second story, and was built over the area referred to in 2 Samuel **18:24 Double Gates**, and corresponded to its size. It was reached by the below area by a stairway, and David retired there that he might have greater privacy in his grief. It was on the roof above this, which was a higher point of observation than the ordinary height of the wall, that the watchman stood when he saw the messengers coming, referenced to in 2 Samuel **18:26 Watchman and Gatekeeper**.

19:4 LAMENTATIONS OVER THE DEAD

The king covered his face and cried aloud, "O my son Absalom! O Absalom, my son, my son!"

Though concealed from sight in the upper chamber, the lamentations of the bereaved king could easily be heard by his followers, for he "cried aloud (with a loud voice, KJV)." These loud exclamations are alluded to in several other places. At Jacob's funeral "they lamented loudly and bitterly" (Genesis 50:10). When Jephthah, after his vow, saw his daughter coming, he cried, "Oh! My daughter!" as if she were already dead (Judges 11:35). When the old prophet of Bethel buried in his own grave the disobedient prophet whom he had deceived to his death, he cried out, "Oh, my brother!" (1 Kings 13:30). Among the curses heaped on Jehoiakim the LORD decreed that: "They will not mourn for him: 'Alas, my brother! Alas, my sister!' They will not mourn for him: 'Alas,

my master! Alas, his splendor!'" (Jeremiah 22:18).

In E. W. Lane's book, *An Account of the Manners and Customs of Modern Egyptians*, written in 1842, he reported that there was still a similar custom in Egypt in those days, and that when the master of a house died, the wives, children, and servants cried out: "O my master!" "O my camel!" "O my lion!" "O camel of the house!" "O my glory!" "O my resource!" "O my misfortune!"

Rev. J. Roberts, in his book *Oriental Illustrations of the Sacred Scriptures*, written in 1844, gives a number of striking examples of Hindu lamentations over the dead that were still prevalent at that time. Among them were the expressions of grief uttered by a husband on the loss of his wife: "What, the apple of my eye gone! my swan, my parrot, my deer, my Lechimy! Her color was like gold; her gait was like the stately swan; her waist was like lighting; her teeth were like pearls; her eyes like the kiyal-fish (oval); her eyebrows like the bow; and her countenance like the full-blown lotus. Yes, she has gone, the mother of my children! No more welcome, no more smiles in the evening when I return. All the world to me is now as the place of burning. Get ready the wood for *my* pile. O my wife, my wife! listen to the voice of your husband."

A father also would say over the body of his son: "My son, my son! art thou gone? What! am I left in my old age? My lion, my arrow, my blood, my body, my soul, my third eye! Gone, gone, gone!"

19:18 FERRYBOAT

And there went over a ferry boat *(crossed at the ford, NIV)* to carry over the king's household, and to do what he thought good *(KJV)*.

This is the only passage in the KJV where a ferryboat is named, and some Bible translators think that a mere crossing of a ford is meant. The Hebrews could not have been ignorant of boats, however, since boats were used by the Egyptians, as is evident from illustrations on their monuments. The king's servants in our text-verse might have used rafts, or flat-bottomed boats, to carry his household over the river.

20:7 KERETHITES AND PELETHITES

So Joab's men and the Kerethites *(Cherethites, KJV)* and Pelethites and all the mighty warriors went out under the command of Abishai.

Exactly who the Kerethites and Pelethites were is not known, and commentators are equally divided in their opinions about them. Some say they were people who probably lived with the Philistines, or a bit south of them and so adopted Philistine names: "We made an invasion upon the south (Negev, NIV) of the Cherethites" (1 Samuel 30:14). They may have come from Crete. Two Samuel 8:18 indicates that David used them as his personal bodyguards. But many scholars don't believe that David would have employed foreign soldiers to guard him, so they say these may have been Israelites who lived for some time among the Philistines and so adopted foreign names. Whatever the case, in the Book of Ezekiel the LORD pronounced judgment upon them (Ezekiel 25:16), as He did in the Book of Zephaniah (Zephaniah 2:5), both of which seem to indicate that the Kerethites and Pelethites were Philistine soldiers.

20:9 TAKING HOLD OF BEARD

Joab said to Amasa, "How are you, my brother?" Then Joab took Amasa by the beard with his right hand to kiss him.

Taking hold of someone's beard and kissing his cheek was a customary Oriental greeting. By so doing, Joab showed the base treachery of his heart by coming to Amasa as a friend, and thus entirely concealing his murderous intent. He inquired about Amos's health, took hold of his beard with his right hand as if to kiss him, and then, while undoubtedly still holding it so Amasa could not pull back, plunged the dagger he held in his left hand into Amasa's belly. In Oriental culture, to touch the beard of another, except as an act of friendship and respect, was an insult.

22:6 CIRCLING NETS

The cords of the grave *(sorrows of hell, KJV)* coiled around me; the snares of death confronted me.

Cords is a better rendering than sorrows, and is more consistent with the figure of speech employed in the text. The allusion is to an ancient mode of hunting, that is still in use in some Middle East nations. A certain tract of land where wild animals are known to be is surrounded by a circle of nets, which is gradually contracted as the animals are driven in, until they are all brought to one common center, where escape is impossible because of the fence-like circle the contracted net has formed, and which now encompasses them. Similar reference is made in Psalm 18:5, 116:3; and Isaiah 51:20. Illustrations of this manner of hunting have been found on Egyptian and Assyrian monuments.

1 KINGS

1:40 Pipes or Flutes

And all the people went up after him, playing flutes *(piped with pipes, KJV)* and rejoicing greatly, so that the ground shook with the sound.

The pipe or flute was one of the most ancient, and one of the simplest, of instruments. It was originally merely a reed with holes bored in it at selected distances; from this it derived its Hebrew name *chalil*, which means *bored through*. As its use became more general it was made with greater care, and sometimes of other materials, such as brass or bronze, boxwood, animal horn, bone, or ivory. Sometimes a double pipe was used, one part being played with the right hand and the other with the left hand, and both sides of the pipe uniting at the mouthpiece. The pipe was used for times of merriment and joy. See 1 Samuel 10:5, Isaiah 5:12, and Luke 7:32. It also served to enliven journeys to the great feasts (Isaiah 30:29), even as music was used for several centuries in the Middle East to entertain companies of travelers. Sometimes, because of its soft wailing tones, the pipe was used at funerals (see Jeremiah 48:36 and Matthew 9:23, NIV).

1:50 Horns of the Altar

But Adonijah, in fear of Solomon, went and took hold of the horns of the altar.

Taking hold of the horns of the altar was a claim to protection, but it was not automatically guaranteed. In Exodus 21:12-14 the LORD said: "Anyone who strikes a man and kills him shall surely be put to death. However, if he does not do it intentionally, but God lets it happen, he is to flee to a place I will designate. If a man schemes and kills another man deliberately, take him away from my altar and put him to death." And in 1 Kings 2:28-29 this is recorded: " When the news reached Joab, who had conspired with Adonijah though not with Absalom, he fled to the tent of the LORD and took hold of the horns of the altar. King Solomon was told that Joab had fled to the tent of the LORD and was beside the altar. Then Solomon ordered Benaiah son of Jehoiada, 'Go, strike him down!'" Cities of refuge were also appointed by the LORD for a person who killed someone accidentally (Numbers 35:15-32).

2:10 Burial in Cities

Then David rested with his fathers and was buried in the City of David.

This was a rarity, for the normal custom was to bury the dead outside the cities. It was therefore a mark of high honor to the remains of the departed king that he was buried within the city, the stronghold of Zion, that was named after him. Here, also, Solomon was afterward buried (1 Kings 11:43). Ahaz was likewise buried in the city, though not in the tomb of the kings (2 Chronicles 28:27). His son Hezekiah was buried "on the hill where the tombs of David's descendants are," which is rendered in the KJV as: "in the chiefest of the sepulchres of the sons of David" (2 Chronicles 32:33). Manasseh, who succeeded him, and his son Amon, were both buried in Jerusalem, "in the garden of Uzza" (2 Kings 21:18, 26).

The location of the tomb (sepulcher, KJV) of David was known in apostolic times (Acts 2:29). The place of his tomb is still pointed out as being on the southern hill of Jerusalem, commonly called Mount Zion, under the Mosque of David. Some believe, however, that "the Tomb of David is several hundred yards east of the traditional locality."

5:9 Rafts

My men will haul them down from Lebanon to the sea, and I will float them in rafts by sea *(convey them by sea in floats, KJV)* to the place you specify.

The KJV "floats" are rafts that consist of a number of planks fastened together and launched upon the water. The practice is an ancient one, and it is said that the earliest boats were nothing more than mere rafts made in this way.

6:2 SOLOMON'S TEMPLE

The temple that King Solomon built for the LORD was sixty cubits long, twenty wide and thirty high.

The idea of the temple did not originate with Solomon, but with David, who was not permitted to carry out his intention of building a house for God because he was a warrior and had shed blood (1 Chronicles 28:2-3). The Spirit of God gave him a plan for the temple, as God had previously given Moses the plan for the tabernacle. This plan David gave to Solomon and directed him to erect the building (1 Chronicles 28:11-19).

Before his death David had provided materials in great abundance for the building of the temple on the summit of Mount Moriah (see 1 Chronicles 22:14; 29:4; 2 Chronicles 3:1), on the east of the city, in the area where Abraham had offered up Isaac (Genesis 22:1-14 , and where David had erected the altar on the threshing floor of Araunah the Jebusite (2 Samuel 24:21-25, 2 Chronicles 3:1).

In the beginning of his reign Solomon set about giving reality to the desire that had been so earnestly cherished by his father, and prepared additional materials for the building. From subterranean quarries at Jerusalem he obtained huge blocks of stone for the foundations and walls of the temple. These stones were prepared for their places in the building under the eye of Tyrian master-builders. He also entered into a compact with Hiram II, king of Tyre, for the supply of whatever else was needed for the work, particularly timber from the forests of Lebanon, which was brought in great rafts by the sea to Joppa, from where they were conveyed to Jerusalem (1 Kings 5).

Since the hill on which the temple was to be built did not have sufficient level space, a huge wall of solid masonry of great height, in some places more than 200 feet high, was raised across the south of the hill, and a similar wall on the eastern side, and in the spaces between were erected many arches and pillars, thus raising up the general surface to the required level. Solomon also provided for a sufficient water supply for the temple by hewing in the rocky hill vast cisterns, into which water was conveyed by channels

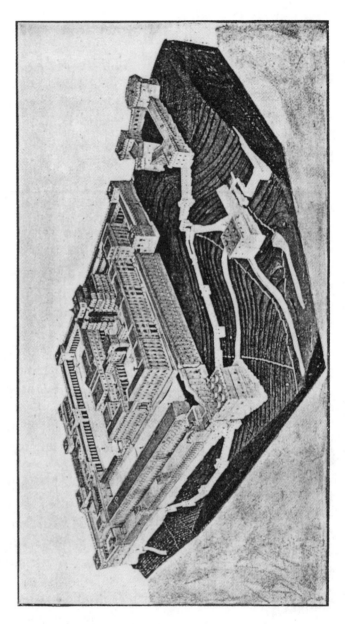

Solomon's Temple

from the pools near Bethlehem. One of these cisterns, the "great sea," could hold three-million gallons. The overflow was led off by a conduit to the Kidron Valley.

These preparatory undertakings took about three years, and then the process of erecting the great building began, under the direction of skilled Phoenician builders and workmen, in the fourth year of Solomon's reign, 480 years after the Exodus (see 1 Kings 6 and 2 Chronicles 3). Thousands of laborers and skilled artisans were employed in the work. Huge stones prepared in the quarries underneath the city (1 Kings 5:17, 18) were gradually placed on the massive walls, and closely fitted together without any mortar between, until the whole structure was completed. "In building the temple, only blocks dressed at the quarry were used, and no hammer, chisel or any other iron tool was heard at the temple site while it was being built" (1 Kings 6:7). As someone wrote: "Like some tall palm the noiseless fabric sprang."

The building was 60 cubits (90 feet) long, 20 cubits (30 feet) wide, and 30 cubits (45 feet) high. In the 1800s the engineers of the Palestine Exploration Fund, in their explorations around the temple area, discovered what is believed to have been the "chief corner stone" of the temple, "the most interesting stone in the world." It lies at the bottom of the south-eastern angle, and is 3 feet 8 inches high by 14 feet long. It rests on the solid rock at a depth of 79 feet 3 inches below the present surface. In examining the walls the engineers were "struck with admiration at the vastness of the blocks and the general excellence of the workmanship."

Finally, in the autumn of the eleventh year of his reign, seven and a half years after it had been begun, the temple was completed in all its architectural magnificence and beauty. For thirteen years there it stood, on the summit of Moriah, silent and unused. The reasons for this strange delay in its consecration are unknown. At the close of these thirteen years, preparations for the dedication of the temple were made on a scale of the greatest magnificence.

The priests brought the ark from the tent in which David had deposited it in the Most Holy Place in the temple (2 Chronicles 5:7). After the priests finished their work and left the Holy

Place: "All the Levites who were musicians—Asaph, Heman, Jeduthun and their sons and relatives—stood on the east side of the altar, dressed in fine linen and playing cymbals, harps and lyres. They were accompanied by 120 priests sounding trumpets. The trumpeters and singers joined in unison, as with one voice, to give praise and thanks to the LORD. Accompanied by trumpets, cymbals and other instruments, they raised their voices in praise to the LORD and sang: "He is good; his love endures forever." Then the temple of the LORD was filled with a cloud, and the priests could not perform their service because of the cloud, for the glory of the LORD filled the temple of God."

Then Solomon ascended a platform that had been erected for him, in the sight of all the people, and lifting up his hands to heaven poured out his heart to God in prayer (1 Kings 8; 2 Chronicles 6, 7).

The feast of dedication, which lasted seven days, followed by the feast of tabernacles, marked a new era in the history of Israel. On the eighth day of the feast of tabernacles, Solomon dismissed the vast assemblage of the people, who returned to their homes filled with joy and gladness. Someone has said: "Had Solomon done no other service beyond the building of the temple, he would still have influenced the religious life of his people down to the latest days. It was to them a perpetual reminder and visible symbol of God's presence and protection, a strong bulwark of all the sacred traditions of the law, a witness to duty, an impulse to historic study, an inspiration of sacred song."

The temple consisted of:

1. The oracle or most holy place (1 Kings 6:19; 8:6), called also the "inner house" (1 Kings 6:27), and the "holiest of all" (Hebrews 9:3). It was 20 cubits (35 feet) in length, breadth, and height. It was floored and wainscoted with cedar (1 Kings 6:16), and its walls and floor were overlaid with gold (1 Kings 6:20, 21, 30). There was a two-leafed door between it and the holy place overlaid with gold (2 Chronicles 4:22); also a veil of blue purple and crimson and fine linen (2 Chronicles 3:14; compare Exodus 26:33). It had no windows (1 Kings 8:12). Two gigantic cherubim made of olivewood and covered with gold

were in the oracle. They were ten cubits high, and their outstretched wings, touching each other at the tips, reached across the width of the room (1 Kings 6:23-28). They were in a standing position, and had their faces turned toward the veil (2 chronicles 3:1-13). The ark of the covenant was put in the oracle under the wings of the cherubim after the temple was finished (1 Kings 8:6). No doubt the original cherubim and the mercy seat accompanied the ark, although this is nowhere expressly stated. It may be inferred, however, from the fact that after the temple was built the LORD is represented, as in the days of the tabernacle, "dwelling between the cherubim." Compare 1 Samuel 4:4, 2 Samuel 6:2, Psalm 80:1, and 99:1 with 2 Kings 19:15 and Isaiah 37:16.

2. The holy place (q.v.), 1 Kings 8:8-10, called also the "greater house" (2 Chronicles 3:5) and the "temple" (1 Kings 6:17).

3. The porch or entrance before the temple on the east (1 Kings 6:3; 2 Chronicles 3:4; 29:7). In the porch stood the two pillars Jachin and Boaz, They were made of bronze and highly ornamented (1 Kings 7:21; 2

Kings 11:14; 23:3). It's not definitely stated that they were placed in the porch as a support to that part of the building, but this would seem probable, though some don't believe so.

4. The chambers, which were built about the temple on the southern, western, and northern sides (1 Kings 6:5-10). These formed a part of the building. Round about the building were:

a. The court of the priests (2 Chronicles 4:9), called the "inner court" (1 Kings 6:36). It contained the altar of burnt-offering (2 Chronicles 15:8), the Sea of cast bronze (2 Chronicles 4:2-5, 10), and ten lavers (1 Kings 7:38, 39).

b. The great court, which surrounded the whole temple (2 Chronicles 4:9). Here the people assembled to worship God (Jeremiah 19:14; 26:2).

This temple erected by Solomon was many times pillaged during the course of its history, (1 Kings 14:25, 26; 2 Kings 14:14; 2 Kings 16:8, 17, 18; 2 Kings 18:15, 16). Then it was pillaged and destroyed by Nebuchadnezzar (2 Kings 24:13; 2 Chronicles 36:7). He burned the temple, and carried all its treasures with him to Babylon (2 Kings 25:9-17; 2 Chronicles

36:19; Isaiah 64:11). These sacred vessels were at length, at the close of the Captivity, restored to the Jews by Cyrus (Ezra 1:7-11).

8:2 Month of Ethanim

All the men of Israel came together to King Solomon at the time of the festival in the month of Ethanim, the seventh month.

Ethanim was the seventh month of the sacred year, and the first of the civil year, and corresponded nearly with our month of October. The great day of atonement and the Feast of Tabernacles took place during this month. It is to this feast that reference is made in our text-verse.

8:22 Uplifted Hands in Prayer

Then Solomon stood before the altar of the LORD in front of the whole assembly of Israel, spread out his hands toward heaven.

This was an ancient custom in prayer, not only among the Hebrews, but among the heathen.

Many Mohammedans pray in this manner, as do those of other religions. The allusions to it in classic writing are frequent, and so also are references to in the Scriptures. See Exodus 9:29, 33; 2 Chronicles 6:12; Ezra 9:5; Job 11: 13; Psalm 28:2, 44:20, 68:31, 88:9, 134:2, 143:6; and Isaiah 1:15.

10:16 Large Shields of Gold

King Solomon made two hundred large shields of hammered gold; six hundred bekas *(six hundred shekels, KJV)* of gold went into each shield.

The shield here is similar to the one spoken of in 1 Samuel 17:7 (see 1 Samuel **17:7 Spear and Large Shield**). These great golden shields were probably made of wood, and covered with hammered plates of gold instead of leather.

10:17 Small Shields of Gold

He also made three hundred small shields of hammered gold, with three minas *(three pound, KJV)* of gold in each shield.

These shields were of a smaller size than those referred to in the sixteenth verse. The Hebrew word *magen* (shield) is in some places in the KJV rendered *buckler* (2 Samuel 22:31 and 2 Chronicles 23:9). Although the two words are interchanged by the KJV translators, there was an essential difference in the size and weight of the two objects represented by them. The *tsinnah* in 1 Kings 10:16 was for heavy troops, and was large enough to protect the entire person. The *magen* in 1 Kings 10:17 was a shield that only protected a part of the person, could be carried on the arm, and was used by light troops. See also 2 Chronicles 9:16.

10:18 SOLOMON'S THRONE

Then the king made a great throne inlaid with ivory and overlaid with fine gold.

The body of the throne was probably of wood, entirely covered with ivory and gold, both being visible and relieving each other. Judging from the description given of this throne it must have been one of extraordinary magnificence. It had, by the two arms, lions such as are represented on the monumental pictures of ancient

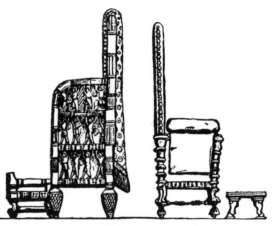

Thrones

Egyptian and Assyrian thrones. Six steps reached to the platform on which it was placed, and on either side of each step was an image of a standing lion. Thus the upward passage to the throne was guarded by twelve lions, six on either side. Oriental monarchs were always noted for the splendor of their thrones. Gold and precious stones of every kind, and wrought by the most elaborate workmanship in forms of rarest beauty, have been described by travelers in the past as dazzling the eye by the brilliancy of their appearance. Ancient thrones were often covered with diamonds, rubies, emeralds, and pearls of almost fabulous size, and designed to resemble birds, animals, trees, and vines with leaves and fruit. See also 2 Chronicles 9:17.

11:5 ASHTORETH AND MOLECH

He followed Ashtoreth the goddess of the Sidonians, and Molech *(Milcom, KJV)* the detestable god of the Ammonites.

Ashtoreth was the companion deity to Baal (see Judges **3:7 Baalim and the Groves**). Out text-verse and 2 Kings 23:13 are the only places where the word is used in the singular. In all other passages in the KJV it is Ashtaroth (the Ashtoreths, NIV), which is a term probably corresponding to Baalim, the plural of Baal. The two words are in several places coupled together. See Judges 10:6, 1 Samuel 7:4 and 12:10. Ashtoreth, or Astarte, was a goddess of the Sidonians, and also of the Philistines (1 Samuel 31:10).

Under different names Ashtoreth was worshiped in all the countries and colonies of the Syro-Arabian nations. As Baal is supposed to have represented the sun, so Astarte is thought to have represented the moon; though some take the two to stand for Jupiter and Venus. The worship of Astarte is very ancient, and was undoubtedly connected with impure rites. But little is known of the form of the goddess or the mode of worship. She is sometimes seen represented with the head and horns of a cow, and sometimes having a woman's head with horns. Genesis 14:5 speaks of the city *Ashteroth Karnaim*—that combination of words means *Ashtaroth of (the) double horns.* As the city was doubtless named because of the worship of Astarte, the word *Karnaim* is believed to refer to the horns of the goddess, either lunar or bovine, or both.

If "the Queen of Heaven" spoken of by Jeremiah was meant for Astarte, as many believe, we have a little light thrown on the mode of her worship. "Do you not see what they are doing in the towns of Judah and in the streets of Jerusalem? The children gather wood, the fathers light the fire, and the women knead the dough and make cakes of bread for the Queen of Heaven. They pour out drink offerings to other gods to provoke me to anger" (Jeremiah 7:17-18). See also Jeremiah 44:17-10. Here a whole family is represented as engaging in the worship of the goddess. They made cakes like her image and gave her drink offerings, and burned incense. The worship of Astarte is also referred to in Judges 2:13, and 1 Samuel 7:3 and 12:10. Molech is called Malcham and Milcom in the KJV (see Zephaniah 1:5, KJV, and Leviticus **18:12 Molech**).

14:3 CRACKNELS

Take ten loaves of bread with you, some cakes *(cracknels, KJV)* and a jar of honey, and go to him.

Cakes or cracknels (Hebrew *nikkuddim*) were some sort of thin hard biscuit carried by common people on their journeys. The name (from *nakad*, to mark with points) may indicate thin punctured biscuits, or biscuits that will easily crumble.

15:13 MONSTROUS IDOL

He even deposed his grandmother Maacah from her position as queen mother, because she had made a repulsive Asherah pole *(idol in a grove, KJV)*. Asa cut the pole down and burned it in the Kidron Valley.

The Hebrew word *miphletseth*, rendered "idol" in the KJV here and in the parallel passage in 2 Chronicles 15:16, has been defined as "horror, terror, monstrosity." From the mode of its destruction in our text-verse, the image was evidently made of wood. It's believed to have been an obscene figure, the worship of which shows the demoralizing influence of idolatry. Such figures were often worshiped among the ancient idolaters, and some are still worshiped in India.

17:10 STICKS FOR FUEL

So he went to Zarephath. When he came to the town gate, a widow was there gathering sticks.

There seems to have been a scarcity of fuel in Palestine. Twigs, branches, sticks of all kinds, and even thorns (Psalm 58:9), were carefully gathered for making fires, and the greatest economy was practiced in their use.

17:12 MEAL JAR

"As surely as the LORD your God lives," she replied, "I don't have any bread—only a handful of flour in a jar *(barrel, KJV)* and a little oil in a jug.

The Hebrew word *kad* does not mean what we understand to be a *barrel*, as so rendered in the KJV, but a vessel made of clay. For centuries it was customary in the Middle East to keep grain in earthen jars. The same sort of vessel that was used for flour (meal, KJV) by this widow was afterward used for water on the occasion of Elijah's sacrifice (1 Kings 18:33).

18:27 HABITS OF A HEATHEN GOD

At noon Elijah began to taunt them. "Shout louder!" he said. "Surely he is a god! Perhaps he is deep in thought, or busy, or traveling. Maybe he is sleeping and must be awakened."

In his three-volume book, *Origin of Pagan Idolatry*, written in 1816, Dr. G. S. Faber maintains the identity of Baal with the Hindu deity Jagan Nath, the "lord of the universe," who is represented by his followers as sometimes wrapped in profound meditation, sometimes sleeping, and sometimes taking long journeys. He says, "Elijah is not simply ridiculing the worship of the idolatrous priests; he is not taunting them, as it were, at random; but he is ridiculing their senseless adoration, based upon their own acknowledged principles."

18:28 LACERATIONS IN IDOL WORSHIP

So they shouted louder and slashed themselves with swords and spears, as was their custom, until their blood flowed.

It was customary for the heathen to make lacerations in

their flesh, not only as a mark of mourning for the dead (see Leviticus **19:28 Tattooing Forbidden**), but also as an act of idolatrous worship. This custom was not, however, of Egyptian origin, as were many of the customs practiced in Canaan. J. G. Wilkinson in his book, *Manners and Customs of the Ancient Egyptians*, published in 1841, says that the Egyptians beat themselves at the close of their sacrifices, as is shown of some of the illustrations in their tombs. He also says that the custom of cutting was from Syria. The same practice is still followed at the present time among idolaters of different nations. They will cut their flesh in various ways until they are streaming with blood. They consider that this voluntary blood shedding is meritorious and will help to wash away their sins. Even so, in cult Christianity practiced in such places as the Philippines and Haiti, some of the devotees will flagellate themselves, while others will have themselves nailed to crosses. All as acts of repentance toward a false god and false christ.

18:36 HOUR OF EVENING WORSHIP

And it came to pass at the time of the offering of the evening sacrifice, that Elijah the prophet came near *(KJV)*.

The precise time at which that sacrifice was offered is a matter of dispute. In Exodus 29:39, it is directed to be offered at twilight (even, KJV); literally, *between the two evenings*. The controversy turns on the meaning of this expression. Some believe the first evening to start at sunset, and the second evening at the time when the stars become visible. The two evenings must have been earlier than this in Elijah's time, since the events that took place after his sacrifice on this occasion required a longer period of daylight than can be found so late in the day (see 1 Kings 18:40-46). The tradition among the Jews is that the first evening was at the time the sun began to decline toward the west; that is, shortly after noon. The second evening was the time the sun set. The time of the evening sacrifice would thus be midway between noon and sunset, or from 2:30 P.M. to 3:30 P.M. This was about the time of its offering in the days of Christ.

18.41 Sound of Rain

And Elijah said to Ahab, "Go, eat and drink, for there is the sound of a heavy rain."

According to the Rev. J. Roberts (*Oriental Illustrations of the Sacred Scriptures*, 1844), in the Middle East it is as common to say sound of rain as with us to say appearance of rain, or more colloquially, "looks like rain." The expression, "sound of rain," sometimes refers to the thunder that precedes rain, and sometimes to a blowing sound in the clouds that shows the approach of rain.

18:46 Cloak, Tucking up, and Running Footmen

The power of the LORD came upon Elijah and, tucking his cloak into his belt *(girded up his loins, KJV)*, he ran ahead of Ahab all the way to Jezreel.

The belt (girdle, KJV) was one of the most useful articles of clothing, and frequently the most ornamented of all. With the long loose clothing that was worn it became a necessity to gather up

Running footmen

the clothing and tuck it into the belt, for it would have been difficult to walk and impossible to run without the clothing thus tightened and held up out of the way of the legs. So Elijah tucked "his cloak into his belt," in preparation for running (see also 2 Kings 4:29 and 9:1). Because freeing the legs, which contain some of the largest muscles in the body, gave the sense of increased strength, the word translated "gird" in the KJV is sometimes used figuratively to denote strength (see Job 40:7, Psalms 65:6 and 93:1).

In ancient days belts were of various sizes, and were made of different materials, from calico to cashmere. The rich used silk or linen, and sometimes decorated their belts with gold, silver, and precious stones. The poor had them of coarser materials, leather being very commonly used. Elijah's belt was of leather (2 Kings 1:8), and was that of John the Baptist (Matthew 3:4).

The Rev. William Graham (*The Jordan and the Rhine*, 1854) described the belt (girdle) as being put on in the following manner. "Your servant, or slave, having folded it in the right breadth, holds it at one end, while you take the other and lay it upon your side, and roll yourself round and round, as tight as possible, till you arrive at the servant, who remains immovable. If you have no servants, a hook or a branch of a tree will answer the same purpose." When running, the ends of the outer garment were tucked into the belt.

In the Middle East it was customary for many centuries to do honor to a king by running before his chariot; and the same honor was often conferred upon persons of less distinction. Dr. W. M. Thomson (*The Land and the Book*, 1863) wrote that when Mohammed Ali came to Jaffa some years before with a large army to quell the rebellion in Palestine, he had his quarters inside the city, while the camp was on the sand hills to the south. The officers in their travels from camp to headquarters "were preceded by runners, who always kept just ahead of the horses, no matter how furiously they were ridden; and in order to run with the greatest ease, they not only girded their loins very tightly, but also tucked up their loose garments under the girdle, least they should be incommoded (inconvenienced) by them."

Reference is also made to this custom in 1 Samuel 8:11, 2 Samuel 15:1, and 1 Kings 1:5.

19:4 Day's Journey

While he himself went a day's journey into the desert.

This is a very ancient method of estimating distances, and is still used in some parts of the Middle East. A "day's journey" varies, according to the circumstances and difficulty of traveling; it ranged from 18 to 30 miles. The ordinary day's journey of the Scriptures is probably not far from 20 miles. (See also Genesis 30:36 and 31:23; Exodus 5:3 and 8:27; Numbers 11:31; Deuteronomy 1:2; Kings 3:9; and Luke 2:44) The Sabbath day's walk (journey)" was a shorter distance—only about half a mile (2000 cubits).

19:13 Covering the Face

When Elijah heard it, he pulled his cloak over his face and went out and stood at the mouth of the cave.

Covering the face was a sign of reverence and fear in the presence of God. Thus Moses, when the Lord appeared to him in the burning bush, "hid his face, because he was afraid to look at God" (Exodus 3:6). So also the seraphim seen by Isaiah in his temple vision covered their faces with two of their wings in the presence of God's holiness and glory: "With two wings they covered their faces, with two they covered their feet, and with two they were flying. And they were calling to one another: "Holy, holy, holy is the LORD Almighty; the whole earth is full of his glory" (Isaiah 6:2).

19:19 Plowing

So Elijah went from there and found Elisha son of Shaphat. He was plowing with twelve yoke of oxen, and he himself was driving the twelfth pair.

The plow they used was a rude affair, far inferior to modern plows. It did not enter deep into the soil, and was of light simple constructions, sometimes made merely of the trunk of a young tree having two branches running in opposite directions. Most plows,

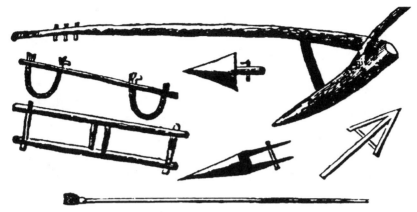

The plow and other agricultural instruments

however, were not quite so primitive in structure. Some of them had one handle and some two handles, and they were usually drawn by oxen. Often the plowman worked in company. In his book (*The Land and the Book,* 1860), Dr. W. M. Thompson reported seeing more than a dozen plows at work in the same field, each having its plowman and yoke of oxen, and all moving along in single file. Rev. Joseph Anderson (*Bible Light from Bible Lands,* 1856) makes a similar statement. So we can see how Elijah "was plowing with twelve yoke of oxen." He had not, as some have imagined, twelve-four ox yoked to a single plow, but there were twelve plows in a file, each having its own oxen and plowman, and he "was driving the twelfth pair"—that is, he had charge of the last plow in the file.

20:11 Military Belts

And the king of Israel answered and said, Tell him, Let not him that girdeth on his harness boast himself as he that putteth it off *(KJV).*

The girdle was a convenient place for carrying different weapons, namely the sword and the dagger. We are told in 1 Samuel 25:13 that David and his men girded on their swords. Similar allusions to this use of the girdle are made in Deuteronomy 1:41, Psalm 45:3,

Song of Songs 3:8, and Isaiah 8:9.

The military girdle was not, however, a mere sword-sash, but a strong belt that was designed to strengthen the body and at the same to cover such portions of the abdomen as might be unprotected by the cuirass. Some girdles, indeed, seem to have been a constituent part of the cuirass, intended to fasten it more firmly. The importance of the girdle as a piece of armor is seen in the fact that thorough preparation for the fight is called "girding on." Paul says: "Stand therefore, having your loins girt about with truth." The NIV has it: "Stand firm then, with the belt of truth buckled around your waist" (Ephesians 6:14).

Military girdles were made of stronger materials than those designed for common purposes. Leather, iron, and bronze were used in their construction, and, where rich ornament was required, silver and gold.

The proverbial saying in our text-verse means: "Tell the one who is about to begin a battle not to boast like the one who has already fought and won a battle."

20:16 PAVILIONS

They set out at noon while Ben-Hadad and the 32 kings allied with him were in their tents *(pavilions, KJV)* getting drunk.

The Hebrew word *cukkah*, rendered *pavilions* in the KJV, can also be rendered booths or tents. In Genesis 33:17, Job 27:18, and Jonah 4:5 the KJV renders it *booths*, and the NIV renders it *shelters, huts, shelter*. In Isaiah 1:8 the same word is rendered *hut* in the NIV and *lodge* in the KJV. There was nothing splendid about them, however, no matter what they're called. They were nothing but temporary structures of boughs or fabrics erected to keep off the heat, and even kings weren't beyond using them. In many remote areas in the Middle East such temporary shelters are still used by desert travelers today.

20:28 GODS FOR HILLS AND VALLEYS

The man of God came up and told the king of Israel, "This is what the LORD says: 'Because the Arameans *(Syrians, KJV)* think the

LORD is a god of the hills and not a god of the valleys, I will deliver this vast army into your hands, and you will know that I am the LORD.'"

There seems to be an allusion here to the opinion, prevalent among all heathen nations, that the different parts of the earth had different divinities. They had gods for the woods, the crops, the mountains, the seas, the rivers, the heavens, and for the lower regions of the earth. Apparently the Arameans thought that the God of the Israelites, Jehovah, was only the god of the hills and nowhere else. But the one true God soon proved to them that He ruled everywhere.

20:32 Token of Abasement

Wearing sackcloth around their waists and ropes around their heads, they went to the king of Israel.

This was a sign of deep abasement and submission. In ancient Persia it was a custom for persons desiring clemency from the sovereign to approach him with a sword suspended from the neck. The same practice was also been seen in Egypt. Rev. Thomas Harmer (*Observations on Various Passages of Scripture*, 1808), wrote that these servants of Ben-Hadad appeared before Ahab with ropes around their necks from which their swords hung. Others believe the ropes were halters; that is, a rope with a noose used for execution by hanging.

21:3 Sale of Patrimony

But Naboth replied, "The LORD forbid that I should give you the inheritance of my fathers."

The law of Moses would not permit the sale of a person's patrimony (an inheritance from a father or other ancestor), except in cases of extreme destitution. See Leviticus 25:23-25 and Numbers 36:7. In his book, *Oriental Illustrations of the Sacred Scriptures* (1844), the Rev. J. Roberts wrote an interesting description of a Middle East garden and of the high value placed on it by its owner, who had inherited it from his ancestors, and whose dearest associations in life are connected with it. "For him to part with it," Roberts wrote, "would be like parting with life itself."

21:8 SEALS

So she wrote letters in Ahab's name, placed his seal on them, and sent them to the elders and nobles who lived in Naboth's city with him.

The seal was of more importance than the signature, and was often used in the place of a signature. No document was valid without it. The ordinary way of using it was to cover the seal with an ink substance and press it on the paper. The seal was often connected with a ring and worn on the finger. (See Genesis **41:42 Signet Ring**)

Ancient seals have been found of various shapes—cylindrical, square, pyramidal, oval, and round. A common

style of seal among the ancient Egyptians was one made of stone, rounded on one side and flat on the other. The inscription for the seal was on the flat surface, and the round surface was skillfully wrought into the form of a scarabaeus or beetle. Since the beetle was worshiped by the Egyptians, whose example was followed by the Phoenicians, after whose deities Ahab had gone, some believe that Ahab's seal fits this description.

Seals that were not set in rings were perforated with a hole through which a cord passed. The seal was then hung from the neck. It's believed that Judah's seal was worn in this way: "He said, 'What pledge should I give you?' 'Your seal and its cord, and the staff in your hand,' she answered" (Genesis 38:18).

Many ancient seals were in the shape of a cylinder, and some

Egyptian signet rings

of these were set in a frame that enabled the seal to revolve as the impression was made. Some beautiful specimens of this kind of seal have been found among the ruins in Chaldea and Assyria.

Various figures were engraved on the seals. Some Hindu seals of fairly recent origin had the name of the owner on them, and often a sentence from the Koran. The ancient seals often had embossed symbolic figures and either hieroglyphic or cuneiform characters. The seals were made of brass, silver, gold, potter, and stone, either precious or common, and set in metal. The art of engraving stones is very ancient. See Exodus 28:11, 36, and 39:6.

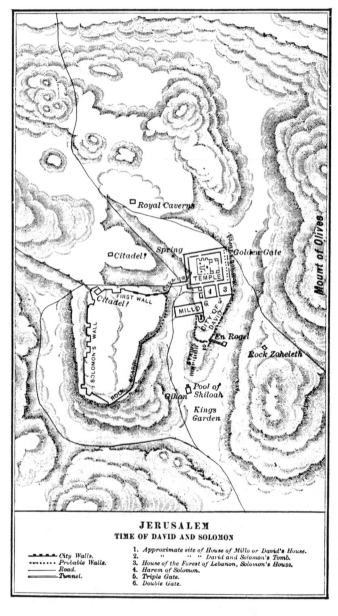

JERUSALEM
TIME OF DAVID AND SOLOMON

━━━ City Walls.	1. Approximate site of House of Millo or David's House.
•••••••• Probable Walls.	2. " " " David and Solomon's Tomb.
━━━ Road.	3. House of the Forest of Lebanon, Solomon's House.
━━━ Tunnel.	4. Harem of Solomon.
	5. Triple Gate.
	6. Double Gate.

JERUSALEM DURING THE TIME OF DAVID AND SOLOMON

2 KINGS

1:2 THE FLY GOD

Now Ahaziah had fallen through the lattice of his upper room in Samaria and injured himself. So he sent messengers, saying to them, "Go and consult Baal-Zebub, the god of Ekron, to see if I will recover from this injury."

Baal-Zebub is literally "the fly god," or Baal of (the) fly." Whether this name was given in honor or in contempt is not known. It may have been at first a name of contempt, but after, because of common use, lost its original significance. Some believe this god to have been of the medical idols of the Philistines, receiving its title from its imaginary influence over pestiferous insects, such as flies, that were said to infest Philistia. In Taylor's Calmet [unknown] there is a curious paste representing a head of Jupiter, and having the appearance of a huge fly.

In his book (*The Court of the Gentiles*, 1672), the Rev. Theophilus Gale wrote: "The Phoenicians styled their principal god Baal Same, 'the lord of heaven,' (in the Phoenician language). The Jews called him Baal-Zebub, 'lord of a fly.' Scaliger [unknown] supposes that the original name was Baal-Zebahim, 'lord of

The fly-god

sacrifices,' contracted, by way of contempt, to Baal-Zebub, 'lord of flies,' to mean he could not keep flies away from his sacrifices."

It is thought by some that *Beelzebul*, which means *dung-god*, is a contemptuous designation of this Philistine Baal. See Matthew 10:25 and 12:24, Mark 3:22, and Luke 11:15, 18, and 19. According to many the name Beelzebub, as so rendered in those verses should have been rendered Beelzebul, which is a name for Satan. The Jews, being fond of a play on words, may have intentionally altered the name of this god. Some, however, define Beelzebul to mean "the lord of the dwelling" and deny any connection between Beelzebul of the New Testament and Baal-Zebub of the Old Testament.

2:3 Schools of the Prophets

The company *(sons, KJV)* of the prophets at Bethel came out to Elisha.

The disciples of the prophets were called sons, as teachers are sometimes called father (2 Kings 2:12 and 6:21). These "sons of the prophets" (KJV), formed a particular order, whose mission seems to have been to assist the prophets in their duties, to minister to them, and in time to succeed them—just as Joshua was a minister to Moses, and eventually succeeded him: "And Moses rose up, and his minister Joshua" (Exodus 24:13). These prophets were not a monastic order, as some believe, nor were they merely theological students, though they probably studied the law and the history of God's people, together with sacred poetry and music.

The "schools of the prophets" in which these "sons" were trained are believed to have been founded by the prophet Samuel, thought their origin and history remain obscure. They were located not only in Bethel, as appears from our text-verse, but also in Rama (1 Samuel 19:19-20), in Jericho (2 Kings 2:5), in Gilgal (2 Kings 6:1, in Gibeah (1 Samuel 10:5-10, NIV) and undoubtedly in other places (2 Kings 6:1). Their members were numerous—a hundred are spoken of in Gilgal (2 Kings 4:43), and at least fifty in Jericho (2 Kings 4:38).

How long the schools of the prophets lasted is not definitely known. They seem to have flourished most in the time of

Samuel, Elijah, and Elisha. Fifty years after Elisha's death Amos prophesied, and according to his statement he had no training in a prophetic school; that is, he was not "a prophet's son." This would seem to indicate that the sons, or disciples, of the prophets were known in Amos's days, but is not sufficient proof that the schools still existed.

2:20 Bowl

"Bring me a new bowl (*cruse, KJV*)," he said, "and put salt in it." So they brought it to him.

The Hebrew word *tselochith*, translated *bowl* in the NIV and *cruse* in the KJV, is rendered *dish* in 2 Kings 21:13, *pan* in 2 Chronicles 35:13, and *bosom* in the KJV in Proverbs 19:24 and 26:15. It is believed to have been a flat metal dish.

3:11 Washing Hands

"Elisha son of Shaphat is here. He used to pour water on the hands of Elijah."

It is probable that eating utensils such as knives and spoons were not used to eat with, and so it was necessary the hands be washed at the end of each meal. Usually a pitcher and basin were used for this. The hands were held over the basin while a servant poured water on them. The water was caught so that it could be used for other purposes rather than being lost into the ground. The expression in the text-verse, "used to pour water on the hands" shows that Elisha performed the work of a servant

Mode of washing hands

for Elijah. He was Elijah's assistant as well as his disciple.

3:27 Human Sacrifices

Then he took his firstborn son, who was to succeed him as king, and offered him as a sacrifice on the city wall.

The offering of human sacrifices is an ancient custom, and was practiced at different times among many nations. The Rev. Samuel Burder (*Oriental Literature*, 1822) listed several nations who were known to have offered human sacrifices. Among these were the Ethiopians, Phoenicians, Scythians, Egyptians, Chinese, Persians, Indians, Gauls, Goths, Carthaginians, Britons, Arabians, and Romans. The victims were sacrificed in various ways: knifed, drowned, burned, buried alive. In some instances, as in the case in our text-verse, parents sacrificed their children. The idolatrous Israelites followed the example of their Phoenician neighbors in this respect (Jeremiah 19:5). Allusion is made to this custom in Micah 6:7. Quite a number of years ago it was said that an inscription discovered in Behistun was deciphered by a Professor Grotefend of Hanover, and found to contain an offer by Nebuchadnezzar to let his son be burned to death in order to ward off the affliction of Babylon.

4:1 Rights of Creditors

"But now his creditor is coming to take my two boys as his slaves."

If a person could not pay his debt, the Mosaic law gave his creditor the right to claim his services and that of his children until the year of Jubilee (Leviticus 25:39-41). Reference is made to this custom in Nehemiah 5:5-8, Job 24:9, and Isaiah 50:1.

There was a similar but severer law among other nations, who are believed to have derived the idea from the Israelites (Matthew 18:25).

4:2 Vessel for Oil

And she said, Thine handmaid hath not any thing in the house, save a pot of oil *(KJV).*

The Hebrew word *asuk* (*'acuwk*), which means *oil-flask* or *pot*, is believed to have been an earthen jar, deep and narrow, with a pointed bottom that was inserted into a stand of wood or stone, or stuck into the ground like the Roman and Egyptian *amphora*. Some believe the *asuk* had no handles, while the amphora had a handle on each side. *Amphorae* were used to contain water or carry oil, wine, or water. Though

Amphorae

usually of earthenware, they were sometimes made of metal. The *jar* (pitcher, KJV) referred to in Mark 14:13 and in Luke 22:10 is believed to have been an *amphora*.

4:10 PROPHET'S ROOM

"Let's make a small room (little chamber, KJV) on the roof (on the wall, KJV) and put in it a bed and a table, a chair and a lamp for him. Then he can stay there whenever he comes to us."

This room was probably much like the room referred to in 2 Samuel 18:33, "the room over the gateway" where David went to mourn for Absalom. It is rendered from the Hebrew word *aliyah*, which contains within it the meaning of *room* and *stair-way*. It was usually built upon the second story of a roof and accessible by a stairway. The room often had a window looking out over the street in front of the house, was well furnished, and kept as a room for the entertainment of honored guests. In the case of Elisha, the Shunammite and her husband built the room specially for his use. It was probably in such a room that Elijah stayed in Zarephath at the house of the widow (1 Kings 17:19, 23).

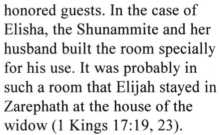

The KJV translates the first use of *aliyah* as loft and the second use as chamber, which gives the impression of a bare, desolate attic-type room, but that is far from the fact. In *The Land and the Book*, 1860, Dr. Thompson reported that the poorer houses he had seen had no *aliyah*, which led him to the conclusion "that this widow woman was not originally among the poorest classes, but that her extreme destitution was owing to the dreadful famine that then prevailed."

A room separated from the main part of the house makes an ideal place of rest for visitors, or for what was then called "the master of the house." Ahaziah was in an *aliyah* in his palace in Samaria when he fell through the latticework of the window and injured himself (2 Kings 1:2). Eglon, King of Moab, was in a room of this type in his summer palace when he was assassinated by Ehud (Judges 3:20). *Aliyah* is in this text rendered *summer palace or parlour*, but some marginal references read *a parlor of cooling*. Doubtless the latticed windows were so arranged as to keep the room as cool and comfortable as possible.

It was on the roof of an *aliyah* in the palace of Ahaz that the kings of Judah had erected altars for idolatrous worship (2 Kings 23:12). It was in an *aliyah* where Daniel lived and prayed three times daily to the one true God, even while in the midst of idolaters (Daniel 6:10). *Aliyoth* are also referred to in Jeremiah 22:13-14 and in Psalm 104:3, 13, where the word is beautifully used in a figurative sense.

In the New Testament the *aliyah* is referred to under the name "upper room." It was in such a place that the disciples gathered immediately after the ascension of the Savior (Acts 1:13). In a room of this kind the corpse of Tabitha or Dorcas was placed. Here the widows whom she had helped wept over her, and here Peter restored her to life (Acts 9:37, 39). In a similar place in the city of Troas, Paul once preached until midnight, and put a young man to sleep (Acts 20:7-9).

Some commentators believe that the "upper room" where Jesus ate the Passover with his disciples was a room of this description (Mark 14:15 and Luke 22:12). But the Greek word used for this room is not the same word used elsewhere for *aliyah*.

In our text-verse, the word rendered *chair* in the NIV and *stool* in the KJV seems to indicate something basic and even crude. In reality, however, the original Hebrew word *kisse* is used elsewhere to designate a throne. So the chair provided for the prophet in his room was probably the best that could be obtained.

Based upon the room built for Elisha, it has been the custom for many years in some Christian churches that a room be set aside in the pastor's home or in the home of one or more members of the congregation for the exclusive use of visiting Bible teachers and evangelists or other church dignitaries. The room is customarily designated "the prophet's room."

4:23 Times of Public Instruction

"Why go to him today?" he asked. "It's not the New Moon or the Sabbath."

The prophets probably assembled the people at the new moon and on the Sabbath for instruction and edification. The question of the husband of the Shunammite appears, therefore, to express astonishment that she would go to the prophet at a time that was neither new moon nor Sabbath. The prophet represents the greedy, sordid, men of his day as saying: "When will the New Moon be over that we may sell grain, and the Sabbath be ended that we may market wheat?" (Amos 8:5) They preferred their worldly business to the keeping of sacred days, or listening to the instructions of the men of God.

5:18 Rimmon

When my master enters the temple of Rimmon to bow down and he is leaning on my arm.

Rimmon is supposed to have been a prominent deity of the Syrians, perhaps even their principal deity in the time of Naaman. Traces of the names are found in Tabrimon, the father of Ben-Hadad, king of Syria (1 Kings 15:18), and in Zechariah 12:11—"On that day the weeping in Jerusalem will be great, like the weeping of Hadad Rimmon in the plain of Megiddo." He also appears in extrabiblical texts as Ramanu or Ramman, and is identified with Hadad, the god of thunder and storm, as shown in the Zechariah reference.

Apparently it was part of court etiquette that the king support himself by leaning on the arm of one of his chief officers, especially when he was bowing—it would not do for the king to fall on the floor in front of everyone. The king of Israel also had this custom (2 Kings 7:2, 17). The Jews have a tradition that two young women waited on Esther when she was queen of Persia, one to hold up her train, and the other for her to lean on.

6:25 CAB

A quarter of a cab of seed pods for five shekels.

The cab was a dry measure of uncertain quantity, but probably held about two quarts.

7:1 MARKET AT THE GATE

"About this time tomorrow, a seah of flour will sell for a shekel and two seahs of barley for a shekel at the gate of Samaria."

The vicinity of the gate was a convenient place for the sale of produce, since what was for sale would be exposed to the view of all passing in or out. Reference is made to this in Nehemiah 13:20-21. H. A. Layard (*Discoveries in the Ruins of Nineveh and Babylon*, 1853) wrote about the vaulted recesses in the gateways of Assyrian cities: "Frequently in the gates of cities, as at Mosul [since 1925 a city of northern

Iraq on the Tigris River north-northwest of Baghdad], these recesses are used as shops for the sale of wheat and barley, bread and grocery."

8:9 OSTENTATION IN GIVING PRESENTS

Hazael went to meet Elisha, taking with him as a gift forty camel-loads of all the finest wares of Damascus. He went in and stood before him.

There is no reason to believe, as some commentators do, that these camels were loaded with all that they could carry of "the finest wares of Damascus." It was merely Ben-Hadad's desire for an extravagant outward display that sent the forty camels. No doubt the royal present was really valuable, but the different articles of which it was composed were probably so distributed that each camel had but a small portion, and thus a caravan was brought into use. One who wrote long ago about such customs in the Middle East said: "Through ostentation [boastful showiness], they never fail to load upon four or five horses what might easily be carried by one; in like manner, as to the jewels, trinkets, and other things of value, they place in fifteen dishes what a single plate would very well hold."

Possibly the present that the children of Israel sent to Eglon, king of Moab, was accompanied with a similar parade, It is said of Ehud that after he "had presented the tribute, he sent on their way the men who had carried it" (Judges 3:18). This indicates that a number of men were used to carry the gift. It's said that in ancient Persia it was a custom that when a present was brought to a king, no person was allowed to carry more than one article, no matter how small it was.

10:8 ENEMIES BEHEADED

When the messenger arrived, he told Jehu, "They have brought the heads of the princes." Then Jehu ordered, "Put them in two piles at the entrance of the city gate until morning."

Beheading enemies is a very ancient custom. Thus David cut off the head of Goliath and carried it to Saul (1 Samuel 31:9). So also the Philistines cut off the head of Saul (1 Samuel 31:9). H. A. Layard (*Monuments of Nineveh*, 1853) found illustrations of scenes at Nineveh that well illustrated our text-verse. Heads of slain enemies are collected and brought to the king, or to the officer appointed to take account of their number. It was the ancient version of the Vietnam War's body count. In Morier's narrative of his *Second Journey through Persia* (1818), he related that prisoners have been known to be put to death in cold blood in order to increase the number of heads of the slain, which are deposited in heaps at the palace gate. Many such heaps, he said, were piled up in Persia. Sir William Ousely, who was in Persia in the early 1800s reported seeing some of these heaps on which skulls seemed to be stuck together in a mass of clay or mortar. Similar accounts were given by travelers to Persia in the mid-1800s.

10:22 PRIESTLY ROBES

And Jehu said to the keeper of the wardrobe, "Bring robes for all the ministers of Baal." So he brought out robes for them.

Like the priests of almost all nations, the priests of Baal had their particular sacred robes that they used only while officiating. They were made probably of white byssus [a fine-textured linen of ancient times], and were kept in a particular wardrobe of the temple under the care of a person appointed for that purpose.

11:2 STORAGE FOR BEDS

She put him and his nurse in a bedroom *(bedchamber, KJV)* to hide him from Athaliah; so he was not killed.

Literally, *in the chamber of beds*, which was a room, not for sleeping, but for storing beds, from where they could be brought out when needed. Thus their place of concealment was less likely to be discovered than if they had been hidden in a mere bedroom. See also 2 Chronicles 23:11.

11:12 CORONATION CEREMONIES

Jehoiada brought out the king's son and put the crown on him; he presented him with a copy of the covenant *(gave him the testimony, KJV)* and proclaimed him king. They anointed him, and the people clapped their hands and shouted, "Long live the king! *(God save the king, KJV)*"

Here we have the most important ceremonies connected with the coronation of a Hebrew king—see also 2 Chronicles 23:11.

1. The crown was put upon him. We have no definite knowledge of the shape of the crowns that were worn by the Hebrew kings. The original word used here is the same that is used to denote the diadem of the high priest, which was a plate of gold tied around the head with a ribbon (Exodus 39:30-31). Doubtless there were other forms of crowns, as other words for crown are used in various passages.

2. They gave him "a copy of the covenant." That is, they formally presented him a copy of the divine law as an indication that this was to be his guide in administering the government.

3. They anointed him. This was not done in every case of coronation, and from the

expression that they "proclaimed him king," which precedes the statement of his anointing, it's inferred that the essential parts of the coronation ceremony were those connected with the crown and the covenant. Thus indicating that the anointing of the founder of a dynasty was all that was necessary so long as the succession was unbroken in his family. There is also the possibility, of course, that the anointing was *after* the coronation because it was *the king* who was to be anointed and not the person prior to being king. Saul was thus anointed (1 Samuel 10:1), and so was David (2 Samuel 2:4). Solomon was likewise anointed (1 Kings 1:39), because there was a probability that his right to the throne would be disputed, and Joash, in our text-verse, was anointed for the same reason.

Anointing was a ceremony connected with coronation before the Israelites ever had a king, as is evident from Judges 9:8, 15. It was by divine command that the people of God adopted it (see 1 Samuel 9:16, 10:1, and Kings 1:34, 39). Because of the custom of anointing at a coronation, the king was called "the Lord's anointed" (see 1 Samuel 12:3, 5,

2 Samuel 1:14, 16, Psalm 2:2, and Habakkuk 3:13).

4. The people then clapped their hands and shouted "Long live the king!" This was part of the ceremony and denoted approval of the newly crowned sovereign. In a book written in 1801 (*Observations on Various Passages of Scripture*), the Rev. Thomas Harmer points out that the Hebrew word translated *hands* in our text-verse is actually singular and is more properly rendered *hand*. From this he suggests that a different sort of clapping may have been meant by this than what is ordinarily understood by clapping hands, where the palm of one hand is forcibly struck against the palm of the other hand. He refers to an ancient Middle-East custom of striking the fingers of one hand gently and rapidly upon the lips as a token of joy, and believes that the expression *clap the hand*, as distinctive from *clap the hands*, relates to some similar custom observed by the ancient Hebrews.

11:14 The King's Place

She looked and there was the king, standing by the pillar, as the custom was.

This place near the pillar was some prominent place that the king was in the habit of occupying in the temple. It's also referred to in 2 Kings 23:3. Second Chronicles 24:31 says that King Josiah "stood in his place" (KJV)—the NIV has it as, "stood by his pillar." The same word is used there that is rendered *pillar* in our text-verse. The place near the pillar is believed to have been an elevated stand or platform, and some commentators believe it was identical with the bronze platform (brazen scaffold, KJV) that Solomon built in the center of the temple court (see 2 Chronicles 6:13 and 23:13). Why the king's *place* was built near a pillar is not known— perhaps it had something to do with support of the platform or protection.

Assyrian and Egyptian quivers and bows

13:15 Bow and Arrows

Elisha said, "Get a bow and some arrows," and he did so.

1. The bow is a very ancient weapon, and it's mentioned early in the Bible. Ishmael became an archer (Genesis 21:20). Isaac sent Esau to get venison by means of a bow (Genesis 27:3). It also came into early use as a weapon of war (Genesis 48:22). Bows were made of various materials: wood, horn, and even ivory were used. Sometimes the wood and horn were united in the bow, the wood being backed with horn. Metallic bows were also used (see job 20:24 and Psalm 18:34). Bows were of various shapes. The Egyptian bow—a round piece of wood from five feet to

five and a half feet long—was either nearly straight, with a slight curve at each end, or else showed a deep curve in the center when unstrung.

Assyrian bows were sometimes curved and sometimes angular. They were shorter than the Egyptian bows. The strings of ancient bows were of leather thongs, horse hair, hide, or catgut. Various methods were used for bending the bow: the hand, the knee, or the foot being used. It was probably most usually bent by the aid of the foot, since the Hebrew word *darak*, the word commonly used in speaking of bending the bow, literally means to *tread*.

2. The arrows were made of reed or wood and tipped with metal or horn. There were sometimes feathered, though not always. Psalm 38:2 may indicate that they were sometimes barbed, and so were difficult to remove once they had pierced a person.

13:17 Way of Declaring War

"Open the east window," he said, and he opened it. "Shoot!" Elisha said, and he shot. "The Lord's arrow of victory, the arrow of victory over Aram!" Elisha declared.

This was similar to an ancient way of declaring war, and is often referred to in ancient and classical writings. A herald would go to the border of an enemy's territory, and after performing certain ceremonies, would cry with a loud voice: "I wage war against you," or similar words. At the same time, he would give reasons for the war—hoping someone on the other side was near enough to hear him. Possibly all this would be done near an enemy's encampment to be certain they heard the herald and saw what he was doing. After declaring war vocally, he would shoot an arrow or hurl a spear into the country to be invaded. This was considered sufficient warning of warlike intentions. Thirty days were allowed for peaceable settlement. If no such settle was reached during that time, hostilities began on day thirty-one.

13:21 Hebrew Way of Burial

Once while some Israelites were burying a man, suddenly they saw a band of raiders; so they threw the man's body into Elisha's tomb. When the body touched Elisha's bones, the man came to life and stood up on his feet.

To understand this text fully, it's necessary to remember that the Israelites did not bury their dead in coffins, as is common with most Western countries today. The Egyptians sometimes used coffins (see Genesis **50:26 Joseph's Coffin**), but the Israelites, who brought many other customs out of Egyptian with them, did not adopt this particular one. They wrapped their dead in linen cloths and laid them in a tombs. It was in this manner that the man in our text-verse was about to be buried when his friends saw the Moabites. Seeing that they could not reach the grave prepared for him without being seen by the enemy, they quickly rolled away the stone from Elisha's sepulcher, which was nearby, and put the corpse in there. As there was no coffin for either body, the body of the newly dead could easily touch the bones of the buried prophet.

17:30-31 Succoth Benoth—Heathen Gods

The men from Babylon made Succoth Benoth, the men from Cuthah made Nergal, and the men from Hamath made Ashima; the Avvites made Nibhaz and Tartak, and the Sepharvites burned their children in the fire as sacrifices to Adrammelech and Anammelech, the gods of Sepharvaim.

1. The precise meaning of *Succoth Benoth* is not known. Its literal meaning is "booths of the daughters," and is believed to be not the name of a god but of places where women abandoned themselves to impure rites connected with the worship of Babylonian deities. One writer believes it's possible that the word represents the Chaldee goddess Zir-banit, worshiped at Babylon and called queen of the place. Another suggested that based upon verse 29, "perhaps verse 30 should read *Succoth Benoth, the booths in high places*, consecrated to idols."

2. *Nergal* was a well-known Assyrian deity. The word signifies *great man* or *hero*. He is called by various names on several monuments: *the great brother, the storm ruler, the god of battles, the god of the chase.* The last is his principal title, and he seems to have been the chief patron of hunting, which has led some to believe that he represented the deified hero *Nimrod*. The name of Nergal often appears on Assyrian seals and cylinders, and his symbol was a man-lion, or human-headed lion with eagle's wings. Astronomically, Nergal corresponds to Mars.

3. *Ashima* was a god of the people of Hamath. The majority of Jewish writers assert that this deity was worshiped under the form of a goat without wool; others say the form of a lamb. The goat is found among sacred animals on Babylonian monuments. This would make Ashima correspond to the Egyptian Mendes and the Greek Pan. It's also believed by some commentators that Ashima was the same as the Phoenician god Esmun, the Phoenician Esclapius, to whom were also attributed the characteristics of Pan.

4. *Nibhaz* was a god of the Avvites, but nothing is known with certainty of the peculiarities of the *deity* or the shape of the idol. Some Hebrew interpreters say that the idol was in the form of a man with the head of a dog. The Egyptians worshiped the dog and, according to some commentators, their god Anubis was represented by a man with a dog's head, though some say it's the head of a jackal. The family relation of the two animals is, however, sufficiently near for the purposes of idolatry.

5. *Tartak* was another Avite deity. Some Jewish writers believe the idol to have been in the form of an ass, but others assert that this is mere conjuncture, and that the name, which they render "hero of darkness," has reference to some planet of supposed malign influence, such as Mars or Saturn.

6. *Adrammelech* was a god of the Sepharvites, and is believed to be identical to Molech (see Leviticus **18:21 Molech**). One commentator identified Adrammelech with the Chaldean god *San* or *Sansi*.

7. *Anammelech* was also a god of the Sepharvites. No satisfactory etymology of the

name has been found. Some believe this deity to be represented by the Arabian constellation Cepheus, containing the shepherd and the sheep. Some authorities give the idol the figure of a horse, others that of a pheasant or a quail. Human sacrifices were offered to this god as well as to Adrammelech.

18:11 DEPORTATION

The king of Assyria deported Israel to Assyria and settled them in Halah, in Gozan on the Habor River and in towns of the Medes.

The practice of deporting all the inhabitants of a city or of a section of country was used by the Assyrians from almost the beginning of their history, and is frequently referred to and illustrated on their monuments. G. Rawlinson (*The History of Herodotus*, 1858-60) wrote: "In the most flourishing period of their dominion—the reigns of Sargon, Sennacherib, and Esar-Haddon—it [deportation] prevailed most widely, and was carried to the greatest extent. Chaldean were transported into Armenia; Jews and Israelites into Assyria and Media; Arabians, Babylonians, Lusianians, and Persians into Palestine—the most distant portions of the empire changed inhabitants, and no sooner did a people become troublesome from its patriotism and love of independence than it was weakened by dispersion, and its spirit subdued by a severance of all its social associations."

Tiglath Pileser carried a large number of captives to Assyria twenty years before the captivity referred to in our text-verse (see 2 Kings 15:29). Eight years after this, Sennacherib took "the fortified cities of Judah" (2 Kings 18:13). An account of this event is given on one of the Assyrian monuments. The king claims to have carried away over two-hundred-thousand of the inhabitants. More than a hundred years after this, Nebuchadnezzar, king of Babylon, invaded Judea, and by several distinct deportations carried people into captivity. See 2 Kings 24:14 and 25:11, 2 Chronicles 36:20, and Jeremiah 52:28-30.

18:34-35 CAPTIVE GODS

Where are the gods of Hamath and Arpad? Where are the gods of Sepharvaim,

Hena and Ivvah? Have they rescued Samaria from my hand? Who of all the gods of these countries has been able to save his land from me? How then can the LORD deliver Jerusalem from my hand?"

The Assyrian monuments give evidence of a custom that illustrates the haughty language of this verse. It was the practice of Assyrian conquerors to take the idols that they found in the temples of the people whom they subdued and carry them to Assyria, and put them in Assyrian temples as captive gods. Thus Sennacherib spoke to the Israelites by his ambassador and informed them that the Assyrian deity was so powerful that no other god could cope with him. The gods of all other people against whom the Assyrians had fought had been captured, and it was foolish for the Israelites to expect their God to save them.

19:37 Nisroch

One day, while he was worshiping in the temple of his god Nisroch.

Nisroch was an idol of Nineveh. There have been various conjectures about him. Some Jewish historians said that it was made out of one of the planks of Noah's ark. Others believed it to be an image of the dove that Noah sent out from the ark. Some have thought it represented the planet Saturn, and some the constellation of the eagle. Others have suggested Nisroch to be a representation of Asshur, the deified patriarch and head of the Assyrian pantheon.

These various opinions show the obscurity connected with this god. The etymology of the word, Nisroch, which occurs only here and in Isaiah 37:38 is uncertain. Some philologists think that Nisroch is not a correct reading, while others believe the word to mean the *great eagle*. This bird was held in veneration by the ancient Persians, and was also worshiped by the Arabians before the time of Mohammed. From the frequent appearance on the Assyrian sculptures of a human figure with the head of an eagle or a hawk, H. A. Layard (*Monuments of Nineveh*, 1823) conjectured that this was the representation of Nisroch, and this has so often been asserted that many imagine that whenever there is a picture of one of these hawk-headed figures they see a picture of Nisroch. Rawlinson (*The History of Herodotus*, 1858-60), however, asserts the contrary, and says that the hawk-headed figure is more like a subordinate character, an attendant genius, than a god. No name of any god has yet been discovered on the monuments that bears any resemblance to Nisroch.

20:18 HEZEKIAH'S TREASURES

Hezekiah received the messengers and showed them all that was in his storehouses—the silver, the gold, the spices and the fine oil—his armory and everything found among his treasures.

Hezekiah was not displaying the wealth, which God had given him, for the glory of the LORD, but for his own vanity. It was an exhibition of arrogance on his part, and it resulted in the LORD rebuking him (verses 17-18), and eventually brought the downfall of Judah.

23:11 HORSES USED FOR IDOLATRY

He removed from the entrance to the temple of the LORD the horses that the kings of Judah had dedicated to the sun. They were in the court near the room of an official named Nathan-Melech. Josiah then burned the chariots dedicated to the sun.

Reference is made here to a peculiar form of worship. Among the Persians, horses were considered sacred to the sun. When the king of Persia sacrificed he offered a white horse to the sun. When the people sacrificed to the sun, they mounted their horses in the early morning and rode toward the rising sun as if to salute it, and then sacrificed their horses to it,

The kings of Judah had evidently heard of this custom and imitated it. Some commentators, however, doubt that they actually slew the animals but rather rode out in the early morning to see the sun rise and adore it. Some also believe that the horses in our text-verse were not real, but merely statues made of wood, stone, or metal, that stood at the entrance of the temple. The "chariots dedicated to the sun" in the latter part of our text-verse seems, however, to indicate that living animals were intended, and that they were harnessed to these chariots. Whether they were really sacrificed or not, they were kept and used for idolatrous purposes, and therefore became proper subjects of Josiah's confiscation.

23:17 TOMBSTONES

The king asked, "What is that tombstone *(title, KJV)* I see?" The men of the city said, "It marks the tomb *(sepulchre, KJV)* of the man of God who came from Judah and pronounced against the altar of Bethel the very things you have done to it."

This refers to the custom of marking the graves of the dead by some distinguishing sign. The word here rendered *title* in the KJV is that same that in Ezekiel 34:15 is rendered *sign* in the KJV and *marker* in the NIV. It means a pillar set up to designate a grave, and served the twofold purpose of a tablet for an epitaph and of a sign to warn all passersby lest they should become ceremonially unclean by touching the grave. The absence of any such sign is what is referred to in Luke 11:44—"Woe to you, because you are like unmarked graves, which men walk over without knowing it."

25:7 PRISONERS BLINDED— SHACKLES

They killed the sons of Zedekiah before his eyes. Then they put out his eyes, bound him with bronze shackles *(fetters, KJV)* and took him to Babylon.

1. Blinding was a common punishment (see Judges 16:21 and 1 Samuel 11:2). In Persia, during

Blinding a prisoner

the time of the younger Cyrus, men deprived of their sight for crimes were a common spectacle along the highway. This penalty was inflicted by the Persians for many centuries on princes who were declared to have forfeited their rights to the throne. John Chardin (*Travels into Persia and the East Indies*, 1636) reported that one method of blinding still practiced was by holding a red-hot copper plate close to the eyes. This, however, did not always produce total blindness, and sometimes the point of a spear or dagger was thrust into the eye. The Babylonians and the Assyrians, as well as the Persians, made use of this same cruel punishment. Frequent representations of it are found on ancient sculptures. The illustration with this text represents part of a scene from a marble slab discovered at Khorsabad in Iraq. (Modern Khorsabad was ancient Dur Sharrukin, the location of the palace of the Assyrian king Sargon II, which was discovered in 1843 by Paul-Émile Botta.) The Assyrian king has several prisoners brought before him to be blinded. In his left hand he holds a cord that is tied to a hook in the prisoner's lips. In his right hand is a spear that he thrusts into the prisoner's eyes—the cord prevents the prisoner from backing away from the spear.

2. Shackles (fetters, KJV) were of various shapes and materials. Those that were put on Zedekiah were made of bronze (brass, KJV) or copper, so also were those with which Samson was fastened (see Judges **16:21 Grinding, a Punishment**). In a British museum there is a pair of bronze shackles brought from Nineveh that weigh eight pounds and eleven ounces, and are sixteen and a half inches long. These probably resemble the shackles put on Zedekiah. Said Samuel Sharpe (*Texts from the Holy Bible Explained by the Help of Ancient Monuments*, 1869): "The rings which inclose the ankles are thinner than the other part, so that they could be hammered smaller after the feet had been passed through them. One of these rings has been broken, and when whole the fetters may have weighed about nine pounds."

Bronze shackles from Nineveh

1 CHRONICLES

2:34-35 Marriage of Servant to Master's Daughter

Sheshan had no sons—only daughters. He had an Egyptian servant named Jarha. Sheshan gave his daughter in marriage to his servant Jarha, and she bore him Attai.

According to Mosaic law, daughters were not to marry outside their own tribe. This was commanded in order to keep the inheritance of each tribe to itself (see Numbers 36). In our verse-text, Sheshan, who had no sons, gives his daughter in marriage to an Egyptian servant. Although this was contrary to the laws of Moses, it seems to have been a custom long practiced in the Middle East. The Rev. Thomas Harmer (*Observations on Various Passages of Scripture*, 1808) quotes from a letter sent to him by a writer named Maillet. In the letter Maillet tells of one Hassan, who had been a slave to Kamel, the "Kiaia of the Asaphs of Cairo; that is, colonel of four or five thousand men who go under that name." Says Maillet: "Kamel, according to the custom of the country, gave Hassan one of his daughters in marriage, and left him at his death one part of the great riches he had amassed together in the course of a long and prosperous life. Hassan also succeeded his master in his office."

25:5 Horn

All these were sons of Heman the king's seer. They were given him through the promises of God to exalt him *(to lift up the horn, KJV).*

This verse may refer to blowing an actual horn or to the fact that Heman's sons helped him. The KJV translators choose it to mean an actual horn, the NIV translators choose it to mean to help or exalt Heman.

Some of the earliest wind instruments were no doubt made of the horns of animals, and when afterward metals were used in their manufacture they retained more or less of the original shape, and continued to be called by the original name. The difference between the *keren*, horn, and the *shophar*, trumpet or cornet, is supposed to have been principally in the shape, the latter having less of a curved shape than the former (see Psalm 98:6). The *keren* is mentioned as a musical instrument in Joshua 6:5 and in Daniel 3:5, 7, 10, and 15. In the verses in Daniel, it's translated *cornet* in the KJV and *horn* in the NIV.

2 CHRONICLES

8:5 Fortified Cities

He rebuilt Upper Beth Horon and Lower Beth Horon as fortified cities, with walls and with gates and bars.

1. Fortifications are as ancient as cities. Indeed, some writers assert that the difference between ancient cities and villages was nothing more than the difference between walled and unwalled towns. The Egyptian and Assyrian sculptures contain representations of fortified cities with walls of squared stone or squared timber on the summit of scraped rocks. Some of the fortified cities of the Scriptures are thought to have been protected by stockades of wood. Sometimes there was more than one wall to a fortified city. It was thus with Jerusalem (see 2 Kings 25:4 and 2 Chronicles 32:15). The gates were strongly protected with bolts or bars of bronze or iron. Sometimes there was built at some central point within the city a citadel or stronghold that might resist attack even after the walls were destroyed.

2. To *build* a city often meant not to give a new town a location, and to erect the houses, but to build walls around a town already inhabited. It was thus that Solomon built the two Beth Horons mentioned in our text-verse. Thus Rehoboam built the cities named in 2 Chronicles 11:5-10. So Jeroboam built Shechem and Penuel (1 Kings 12:25), and Heil built Jericho (1 Kings 16:34), a city that had been inhabited long before (Judges 1:16 and 3:13).

Walls and towers from Babylonian coins

16:14 CREMATION

They buried him in the tomb that he had cut out for himself in the City of David. They laid him on a bier covered with spices and various blended perfumes, and they made a huge fire *(very great burning, KJV)* in his honor.

There is a division of opinion among commentators concerning the meaning of the last clause in this verse. Some of the best authorities believe that the huge fire was the burning of the odoriferous substances that were brought together. They understand that a large quantity of these substances was collected and placed in the sepulcher of Asa, and that after these were burned the body of the dead king was laid upon the perfumed ashes, as on a bed. This is also referred to in the promise that was made to Zedekiah concerning his burial (Jeremiah 34:5). It is likewise thought to have been this that was denied to Jehoram, on the occasion of his death, because of his wickedness (2 Chronicles 21:19).

On the other hand, it's asserted that burning spices and perfumes in this way for the dead does not find a parallel in the customs of any nation ancient or modern, and that these various passages refer to the burning of the body together with the spices on a funeral pyre. Jahn (*Biblical Archaeology*, 1866) says, "The ancient Hebrews considered burning the body a matter of very great reproach, and rarely did except when they wished, together with the greatest punishment, to inflict the greatest ignominy" (Genesis 38:24). Jahn considers the burning of Saul and his sons (1 Samuel 31:12) an exceptional instance, designed by their friends to prevent any further indignities from the Philistines.

The sentiment in reference to the burning of bodies afterward underwent a change. A hundred and forty years after Saul's death the body of Asa was burned, and the event is spoken of by the historian not as a new thing, as a custom already established. Over a century later we find the same customs referred to (Amos 6:10). In time the revolution of sentiment became so complete that while burning was considered the most distinguished honor, *not* to be burned was regarded the most signal disgrace, as in the case of Jehoram already mentioned.

Another change of sentiment eventually took place. After the captivity the Israelites conceived a great hatred toward this rite, and the Talmudists endeavored to explain the passages respecting it as referring to the burning of the aromatic substances alone.

In his book, *Oriental Illustrations of the Sacred Scriptures* (1844), Roberts takes substantially the same view as above, and gives a detailed account of the Hindu method of cremation that he saw in the Middle East in the early 1800s. The Hindus, he said, burn the bodies of nearly all their illustrious dead, and it is considered disgraceful not to have the ceremony performed. They first wash the corpse with water mingled with fragrant oils and scented waters. The body is then placed on a bed, or on a chariot covered with crimson cloth, and is carried on men's shoulders to the place of burning. The funeral pyre is seldom more than five feet high, and when prepared for a great man is made of sandal and other aromatic woods, to which are added sweet odors and spices. The body is then placed on the pyre. The son or nearest relative has his head shaved. Then the son takes a torch and, turning his head away from the pile, sets fire to it,

and returns home. Those who remain to see the corpse consumed throw clarified butter and oils on the fire to hasten the combustion.

25:12 EXECUTED BY BEING THROWN FROM A CLIFF

The army of Judah also captured ten thousand men alive, took them to the top of a cliff and threw them down so that all were dashed to pieces.

This was a very ancient punishment, practiced among different nations. In Greece, according to the Delphian law, those who were guilty of sacrilege were punished in this manner. The Romans also inflicted the same punishment for various offenses. Among the Turks and the Persians a similar method of capital punishment was adopted. One commentator has suggested that the way of Jezebel's death is an illustration of this custom (2 Kings 9:23). See also Matthew **26:39 Cup of Suffering**.

26:10 Towers

He also built towers in the desert.

The duties of shepherds often led them into wild districts where their lives were in danger from wandering bandits. Hence it became necessary to erect towers into which they might retire for safety from the attacks of large forces, and from which they could drive off the marauders. The reason assigned for building the towers by Uzziah is the same as that given for digging the wells: "because he had much livestock in the foothills and in the plain." See also 2 Chronicles 27:4. A beautiful figurative use is made of this custom in Psalm 61:3, and in Proverbs 18:10. Towers were also built in vineyards.

26:15 War Machines

In Jerusalem he made machines designed by skillful men for use on the towers and on the corner defenses to shoot arrows and hurl large stones.

The invention of these war machines marks an era in warfare, since by their use the power of an army was greatly increased whether for attack or defense. They were simply machine bows and slings, which, by the application of mechanical

Towers in the desert

principles, were made to propel heavier projectiles than the smaller weapons that were held by hand. We have here perhaps the origin of the *ballista* and *catapulta* that afterward became so famous in Roman warfare. The Romans used the word *ballista* to designate an engine used to hurl stones and *catapulta* for one that shot arrows and darts (spears), although the larger catapults mounted a single long arm, which hurled stones and other objects. Nearly all catapults employed in ancient and medieval artillery operated by a sudden release of tension on wooden beams or twisted cords of horsehair, gut, sinew, or other fibers. Historians speak of three sizes of *ballista*, which were graded according to the weight of the stones they propelled, namely: a half hundred weight, a whole hundred weight, and three hundred weight. Occasionally, there were some used that threw stones as light as two pounds. Several balls of limestone that were found in excavations in Jerusalem in 1869 are believed to have been used as missiles and hurled from a ballista. Catapults were named according to the length of the darts (spears) or arrows that could be shot from it.

36:4 CHANGING NAME

The king of Egypt made Eliakim, a brother of Jehoahaz, king over Judah and Jerusalem and changed Eliakim's name to Jehoiakim.

It was long a custom among ancient Middle East people to change their names on the occurrence of some great event in life. It was in accordance with the divine command at the time of the renewal of the covenant that the name of Abram was changed to Abraham (Genesis 17:5 and Nehemiah 9:7) and that of Sarai to Sarah (Genesis 17:15). Jacob's name was changed to Israel in commemoration of his prevailing prayer (Genesis 32:28 and 35:10). The king of Egypt changed the name of Joseph to Zaphnath-Paaneah because of his ability to reveal secrets (Genesis 41:45). Another king of Egypt subsequently changed the name of Eliakim, the son of Josiah, to Jehoiakim when he made him king of Judah, as told in our text-verse and 2 Kings 23:34. When the king of Babylon made Mattaniah king he changed his name to Zedekiah (Esther 2:7).

When Nebuchadnezzar wished to have a few of the

young Israelite prisoners taught in the Chaldean language and customs, he changed their names from Daniel, Hananiah, Mishael, and Azariah, to Belteshazzar, Shadrach, Meshach, and Abednego (Daniel 1:6-7). This was done to make them more Babylonian. Daniel means "God is judge," and Belteshazzar means "May Bel protect his life." Hananiah means "Yahweh is gracious," and Shadrach possibly means "command of Aku" (the moon god). Mishael means "Who is what God is?" and Meshach may mean "Who is what Aku is?" Azariah means "Whom Yahweh helps," and Abednego means "servant of Nebo." In each case the Hebrew name contained a name for the true God (either *el* or *iah*, an abbreviation for *Yahweh*), and the Babylonian name contained the name of a heathen god.

The effect it can have when a ruler changes his name is well illustrated in Sir John Chardin's *Travels in Persia*. He states that the first years of King Sefi's reign were unhappy because of wars and famine in many of the Persian provinces. So he was persuaded by his counselors to change his name as a means of changing the tide of fortune. They argued that there must be some hidden power of evil in the name Sefi. He was, therefore, crowned anew in 1666 under the name of Solyman III. All seals, coins, and other public symbols that had on them the name of Sefi were destroyed. It was as if the king had died and a successor had taken his place on the throne. Whether changing the king's name had any positive effect or not on the country is not said.

EZRA

2:43 Nethinim

The temple servants
(Nethinim, KJV).

These were men who assisted the Levites in performing the meanest offices connected with the temple service. Part of them lived in Jerusalem, and part were distributed among the Levitical cities. Some commentators believe they were Canaanites reduced to servitude (Joshua 9:21-27), and captives taken in war who were set apart to this service, and thus called nethinim, which means *the given, the devoted.* They were held in low esteem by the Israelites, occupying a social position even lower than the *mamzer*: illegitimate offspring. They are mentioned several times in the books of Ezra and Nehemiah.

2:69 Persian Daric

According to their ability they gave to the treasury for this work 61,000 drachmas *(drams, KJV)* of gold, 5,000 minas of silver.

The *drachmas* referred to here and in chapter 8:27 and in Nehemiah 7:71-72 is the Persian *daric.* They were thick, gold, coins. On one side was the figure of a king with a bow and javelin, or bow and dagger, and on the other an irregular oblong depression. A daric was equivalent to four days' wages. It was probably introduced by Darius I (522-486 B.C.), and was possibly the earliest coined money used by the Jews who became acquainted with it during the Exile.

Persian daric

6:3-4 Temple of Zerubbabel

In the first year of King Cyrus, the king issued a decree concerning the temple of God in Jerusalem: Let the temple be rebuilt as a place to present sacrifices, and let its foundations be laid. It is to be ninety feet high and ninety feet wide, with three courses of large stones and one of timbers.

This temple, sometimes called the second temple, and sometimes the temple of Zerubbabel, was built on the site of the first, or Solomon's temple. Unlike Solomon's temple, there is no specific description given of it. The second temple was larger than the first. The row of stones are believed to refer to three stories of chambers, such as were attached to Solomon's temple, and on these was placed an additional story of wood. The temple of Zerubbabel, though of greater size than that of Solomon, was inferior to it in magnificence. According to some Jewish authorities its altar of burned-offering was of stone instead of bronze, and it had but one table of consecrated bread (showbread, KJV) and but one lamp stand (candlestick, KJV). It's also said that the sanctuary was entirely empty, except that in the place of the ark of the covenant a stone was set three fingers high. On this the high priest placed the censer and sprinkled the blood of atonement. Some believe, however, that a new ark was made and set in the sanctuary. Jewish historians list five important features that were lacking in the second temple: 1. The Ark of the Covenant; 2. The Sacred Fire; 3. The Shekinah (visible manifestation of God's presence); 4. The Holy Spirit; 5. The answer by Urim and Thummim. Some commentators, however, consider these distinctions to be a bit fanciful.

6:15 Adar

The temple was completed on the third day of the month Adar, in the sixth year of the reign of King Darius.

Adar was the twelfth month, the closing month of the year, and corresponds very closely to our month of March. According to Haggai's date of the resumption of building, "on the twenty-fourth day of the sixth month in the second year of King Darius" (Haggai 1:15), and Ezra's date of the completion in our text-verse, the time required for reconstruction was four years, five months, and ten days. It has been estimated that by our modern calendar that the Temple was completed on March 12, 515 B.C.

NEHEMIAH

1:1 KISLEV (CHISLEU) AND HEBREW CALENDAR

The words of Nehemiah son of Hacaliah: In the month of Kislev *(Chisleu, KJV)* in the twentieth year.

Kislev corresponds very closely to our month of December. The *twentieth year* undoubtedly refers to the reign of Artaxerxes I (464-424 B.C.) According to verse 12:23, Nehemiah's time frame, which begins here, ends with the high priesthood of "Johanan son of Eliashib." The Elephantine papyri, which were discovered in 1907, identify Johanan as high priest just prior to the reign of Artaxerxes II.

Correlating the Hebrew religious calendar with our Western calendar, the corresponding months are as follows:

Nisan (Abib) = March-April
Iyyar (Ziv) = April-May
Sivan = May-June
Tammuz = June-July
Ab = July-August
Elul = August-September
Tishri (Ethanim) = September-October
Marchesvan (Bul) = October-November
Kislev = November-December
Tebeth = December-January
Shebat = January-February
Adar = February-March

1:11 ROYAL CUPBEARER

I was cupbearer to the king.

The office of royal cupbearer is of high antiquity, and was a place of great honor in the Persian court. The cupbearer, being in the daily presence of the king, and seeing him at his seasons of relaxation from care, had many opportunities to ingratiate himself into the goodwill of the monarch, and thus could obtain many favors

The royal cup-bearer

that were denied others. Cupbearers were generally eunuchs, and are often illustrated on Assyrian monuments. In these illustrations they hold the cup in the left hand, and in the right hand a fly-flap made of split palm leaves. A long, richly embroidered and fringed, napkin is carried over the left shoulder for the king to wipe his lips with. Among the Medes and Persians the cupbearer would taste the wine before serving the king, so the king could tell if it

was poisoned without running any personal risk. To do so, the cupbearer would pour the wine from its container into the cup, and then pour some from the cup into the palm of his left hand and drink it. Pharaoh had cupbearers to attend him (Genesis 40:2), and so did Solomon (1 Kings 10:5 and 2 Chronicles 9:4).

5:13 SHAKING THE LAP

I also shook out the folds of my robe *(shook my lap, KJV)* and said, "In this way may God shake out of his house and possessions every man who does not keep this promise. So may such a man be shaken out and emptied!" At this the whole assembly said, "Amen," and praised the LORD.

This was a gesture that symbolized complete rejection of any who might violate this agreement. It was not an uncommon action, and was used to symbolize many things. Samuel Burder (*Oriental Customs*, 1822) wrote that when the Roman ambassadors proposed the choice of peace or war to the Carthaginians, they made use of a similar ceremony. "When the Roman ambassadors entered the senate of Carthage they had their togas gathered up in their bosoms. They said, 'We carry here peace and war; you may have which you will.' The senate answered, 'You may give which you please.' They then shook their togas and said, 'We bring you war.' To which all the senate answered, 'We cheerfully accept it.'"

In a similar way Nehemiah told the usurers of his time that if they failed to keep the covenant of restitution that they had made they would be completely exterminated.

6:5 LETTERS

Then, the fifth time, Sanballat sent his aide to me with the same message, and in his hand was an unsealed (open, KJV) letter.

1. The first mention made of a letter in the Scriptures is the one David sent to Joab (2 Samuel 11:14). Jezebel wrote letters in the name of Ahab (1 Kings 21:8). The king of Syria wrote a letter to the king of Israel (2 Kings 5:5-7). And Jehu wrote letters (2 Kings 10:1). As time progresses in the Bible, letters are mentioned more frequently.

What material these letters were written on is not known. Possibly they were written on palm leaves, or on papyrus paper, which was used by the ancient Egyptians and may have been learned by their neighboring nations.

2. When letters were sent to persons of distinction, they were normally rolled up in a scroll and sealed with clay or wax. See Isaiah 8:16 and 29:11; Daniel 12:4, 9; and Revelation 5:4, 9, 10:4, and 22:10. (For methods of sealing see 1 Kings **21:8 Seals**.) Among other things, such as privacy, sealing a letter was considered a mark of respect, and a recognition of the rank or position of the person to whom it was sent. When sent to inferiors, or to persons whom the writers wished to treat with contempt, the letters were left unsealed. Since our text-verse places special emphasis on the fact that the letter Nehemiah received from Sanballat was unsealed, it's possible that Sanballat saw him as a person of inferior position and wanted to indicate that.

6:15 ELUL

So the wall was completed on the twenty-fifth of Elul, in fifty-two days.

Elul corresponds to August-September. To finish repairing the wall in 52 days was a tremendous accomplishment, and one that even their enemies recognized was due to the power of God, as shown in verse 16: "When all our enemies heard about this, all the surrounding nations were afraid and lost their self-confidence, because they realized that this work had been done with the help of our God."

8:10 SENDING PORTIONS

Nehemiah said, "Go and enjoy choice food and sweet drinks, and send some to those who have nothing prepared."

This has generally been interpreted to mean that the needs of the poor were to be supplied. As one commentator has stated: "Nehemiah characteristically admonished the people to send portions to the poor who were unable to prepare anything themselves, so that they, too, could find joy." But in *Observations on Various Passages of Scripture* (1808), Thomas Harmer says it refers to the custom of sending portions of a feast to those who could not come to it, especially to the relatives of those who gave the feast, and to those in a state of mourning who, in their grief, could make no preparation. In Esther 9:19 it's said that among the ceremonies of the feast of Purim there was to be a day for "giving presents (sending portions, KJV) to each other." In the twenty-second verse of the same chapter some of the ways of celebrating the feast of Purim are recorded, and it says that the rural Jews "observe the days as days of feasting and joy and giving presents of food (sending portions, KJV) to one another and gifts to the poor." From this verse it's obvious that "giving presents of food" is not the same as giving "gifts to the poor."

This latter custom, however, may be different than the one referred to in Nehemiah, and may mean that these pious Israelites expressed their joy by a mutual exchange of the good things provided for the feast. This custom is alluded to in Revelation 11:10, where the enemies of the "two witnesses" are represented as gloating over their death: "The inhabitants of the earth will gloat (rejoice, KJV) over them and will celebrate by sending each other gifts, because these two prophets had tormented those who live on the earth."

13:25 WOOD FOR THE SACRIFICES

"We—the priests, the Levites and the people—have cast lots to determine when each of our families is to bring to the house of our God at set times each year a contribution of wood *(wood offering, KJV)* to burn on the altar of the LORD our God, as it is written in the Law.

The work of supplying the wood necessary for the altar fires was a part of the task assigned to the Nethinim (see Ezra **2:43 Nethinim**). On the occasion of the captivity the Nethinim were scattered and their organization broken up. Though some returned to Jerusalem, they were probably not as numerous as before. It

became necessary, therefore, for all classes of people to attend the work of gathering wood, and the time when they did this was regulated by lot. This work is what is called a "wood offering" in the KJV rendering of our text-verse and in chapter 13:31. There is no further mention of it in the Scriptures, but some Jewish writers give additional accounts of how the work was done. Different families had different times of the year assigned to them for their share of the work. This was the origin of a great festival that was known by the name of the Feast of Wood-Carrying and was celebrated annually on a certain day in Ab (July-August). This was the last day of the year on which wood could be cut for this purpose, and all the people without distinction of tribe or grade brought wood to the temple on that day. The festival was joyously kept, and no fasting or mourning was permitted.

13:25 TEARING OUT HAIR

I rebuked them and called curses down on them. I beat some of the men and pulled out their hair.

13:25 Tearing Out Hair

This is equivalent to what we term "tearing the hair out by the roots." It was sometimes a self-inflicted suffering as a token of mourning (Ezra 9:3), sometimes an act of wanton persecution (Isaiah 50:6), and sometimes punishment, as represented in our text-verse. It's said that the ancient Athenians punished adulterers by tearing the hair from the scalp and then covering the head with hot ashes. Israel continued to intermarry with the pagans nations even after they made a covenant to remain a separate people (Nehemiah 10). Nehemiah himself had dictated the words of the oath and had the people repeat the penalty of God's curse falling on them if they intermarried with the heathen. He drove "one of the sons of Joiada" away from him because his marriage to a pagan woman "defiled the priesthood (Nehemiah 13:28-29) and violated the covenant between God and the Levites. The seriousness of what they had done is demonstrated in Nehemiah's severity.

ESTHER

1:8 Drinking Customs

And the drinking was according to the law; none did compel: for so the king had appointed to all the officers of his house, that they should do according to every man's pleasure *(KJV)*.

Revelers of all nations seem to have had their peculiar drinking customs that were as binding as laws. Among the Egyptians, wine was offered before dinner commenced, and the guests also drank during the meal. Among the Greeks, each guest was obliged to keep the round or leave the company. "Drink or be gone," was the proverb. At the Roman feasts, a master of the feast was chosen by throwing dice. He prescribed rules to the company, which all were obliged to follow.

One commentator suggests that the above text-verse means that though it was the custom to compel men to drink whether they wanted to or not, on this occasion the king directed that each guest be left to his own discretion, and that no one was obliged to drink according to the custom. Leaving out the word *was*, which the KJV translators supplied, and rendering the Hebrew word *dath* as *custom* rather than *law*, as in our text-verse, and slightly changing the punctuation, the verse translates: "The drinking according to custom, none did compel." Thus no one would incur the king's displeasure who violated the customary rules of drinking.

The NIV translates the verse as: "By the king's command each guest was allowed to drink in his own way, for the king instructed all the wine stewards to serve each man what he wished." No normal custom of drinking is shown, but is, nevertheless, alluded to by the fact that the king issued a command to allow each guest to drink in his own way. The command was obviously intended to change the customary way of drinking.

1:9 Feasts for the Women

Queen Vashti also gave a banquet *(feast, KJV)* for the women in the royal palace of King Xerxes.

The women did not have banquets in the same room with the men. This separation of the sexes is an ancient custom that was observed at this time at the court of Persia, although one commentator, speaking of the custom, says that "Babylon and Persia must, however, be looked upon as exceptions, where the ladies were not excluded from the festivals of the men (Daniel 5:2), and if we may believe the testimony of ancient authors, at Babylon they were not noted for their modesty on such occasions."

As far as Babylon is concerned the remark is correct, and it serves to illustrate the relaxation of manners that showed itself among the dissolute Babylonians. It's not true, however, in reference to Persia, as is plainly seen by the indignation of Vashti when her drunken husband sent for her to come and display her beauty before the revelers. Her womanly spirit was aroused and she refused (Esther 1:12).

1:10 Chamberlains

On the seventh day, when King Xerxes was in high spirits from wine, he commanded the seven eunuchs *(chamberlains, KJV)* who served him—Mehuman, Biztha, Harbona, Bigtha, Abagtha, Zethar and Carcas.

The Hebrew word *sarisim* is variously rendered in the KJV as *chamberlains, officers*, and *eunuchs*. They were emasculated men who had charge of the harems of monarchs, and who were also employed by them in various offices about the court. They often became the confidential advisers of the monarch, and were frequently men of great influence, and sometimes had high military office. This was especially the case in Persia, where they acquired great political power, and filled positions of great prominence. So much sometimes, that they engaged in conspiracy against the life of the king, as illustrated in Esther 2:21. In that verse the word translated *officers* in the NIV and *chamberlains* in the KJV is the Hebrew word *sarisim*, as used in verse 1:10.

The Hebrew monarchs had such men in their courts. See 1 Samuel 8:15; 1 Kings 22:9; 2 Kings 8:6, 9:32, 23:11, and 25:19; 1 Chronicles 28:1; Jeremiah 29:2, 34:19, 38:7, and 52:25.

Though it was the barbarous custom of ancient Middle East sovereigns to mutilate many of their young prisoners in the manner here indicated, there is no evidence that the Hebrew kings ever did this. The eunuchs employed by them are believed to have been imported. It's thought by many commentators, however, that Daniel and his companions were made eunuchs by the king of Babylon in fulfillment of the prediction contained in 2 Kings 20:17-18 and Isaiah 39:7.

2:16 TEBETH

She was taken to King Xerxes in the royal residence in the tenth month, the month of Tebeth, in the seventh year of his reign.

The time of this occurring fits extrabiblical information about Xerxes' reign. Approximately four years passed between the time the king deposed of Vashti and chose Esther as his new queen. During that time (483-479 B.C.), he was engaged in an unsuccessful campaign against Greece. *Tebeth* corresponds to January-February in our calendar.

2:17 PERSIAN QUEEN

Now the king was attracted to Esther more than to any of the other women, and she won his favor and approval more than any of the other virgins. So he set a royal crown on her head and made her queen instead of Vashti.

One of the wives of the Persian monarchs always occupied a higher position than the others, and she alone was given the title of queen. Rawlinson (*Five Ancient Monarchies*, 1871) wrote, "The chief wife or queen-consort was privileged to wear a royal tiara or crown. She was the acknowledged head of the female apartments of *Gynaeceum*, and the concubines recognized her position by bowing before her. On great occasions, the king would entertain the men in one part of the palace, and she would entertain the women in her part of the palace. She had a large revenue assigned to her, not so much by the decree of her husband as by established law or custom. Her clothing was the best the palace could afford, and she was able to indulge freely any love she might have for ornaments and jewelry."

This was the elevated position, filled by Vashti, and after her downfall by Esther.

4:1 ASHES

When Mordecai learned of all that had been done, he tore his clothes, put on sackcloth and ashes, and went out into the city, wailing loudly and bitterly.

In the Scriptures, ashes are often related to sacrifices, mourning, and fasting. The ashes were not some special kind, but came from the ashes of normal fires, and were normally dumped outside the city in a place designated for them. Humiliation and grief were often shown by putting ashes on the head, such as Tamar did (see Genesis **37:34 Rending Garments and Wearing Sackcloth**), or by sitting in them as Job did: "Then Job took a piece of broken pottery and scraped himself with it as he sat among the ashes" (Job 2:9).

Sackcloth, fasting, dirt or dust, rending of clothes, and ashes vividly demonstrated the person's emotions. At times of great anguish in prayer, the person often combined fasting with sackcloth and ashes, as Daniel did: "So I turned to the Lord God and pleaded with him in prayer and petition, in fasting, and in sackcloth and ashes" (Daniel 9:3). In Jeremiah 6:26 and Ezekiel 27:30 the Scriptures speak of rolling in ashes.

Ashes that remained from the burning of a sacrifice were sometimes kept and used in rituals of purification: "A man who is clean shall gather up the ashes of the heifer and put them in a ceremonially clean place outside the camp. They shall be kept by the Israelite community for use in the water of cleansing; it is for purification from sin" (Numbers 19:9).

Ashes are also used at times to express the results of divine destruction: "By your many sins and dishonest trade you have desecrated your sanctuaries. So I made a fire come out from you, and it consumed you, and I reduced you to ashes on the ground in the sight of all who were watching" (Ezekiel 28:18). Using ashes to express grief or repentance continued into New Testament times.

In Hebrews 9:13-14, external purification by blood and ashes is compared to internal cleansing by the blood of Christ: "The blood of goats and bulls and the ashes of a heifer sprinkled on those who are ceremonially unclean sanctify them so that they are outwardly clean. How much more, then, will the blood of Christ, who through the eternal Spirit offered himself unblemished to God, cleanse our consciences from acts that lead to death, so that we may serve the living God!"

Peter wrote that God's condemning of Sodom and Gomorrah and burning them to ashes represents what will happen to the ungodly (see 2 Peter 2:6).

4:11 ETIQUETTE OF PERSIAN COURT

"All the king's officials and the people of the royal provinces know that for any man or woman who approaches the king in the inner court without being summoned the king has but one law: that he be put to death. The only exception to this is for the king to extend the gold scepter to him and spare his life."

Etiquette in the Persian court was very strict. Except for the "seven nobles" (see Esther 1:4), no one could approach the king unless they were summoned by him. The punishment for entering without being summoned was death, the same punishment given for murder or rebellion. The intruder was instantly put to death by the court attendants unless the king extended his golden scepter to the person to show approval, or at least acceptance, of the act. It was well understood, therefore, that whoever so appeared before the king risked his life. The fact that Ahasuerus extended his scepter to Esther when she entered the court uninvited shows the influence she had gained with him. See Esther 5:2 and 8:4.

5:12 Feasting with the King

"And that's not all," Haman added. "I'm the only person Queen Esther invited to accompany the king to the banquet she gave."

It was a rare privilege for a subject, however high his station, to be permitted to banquet with the king. Occasionally, however, this was allowed, and Haman had reason to feel highly honored at the invitation he received from the queen with the king's permission, which was always required. It should be understood, however, that no equality was meant by this invitation to feast with royalty, and the honored guest was so seated as to remind him of his inferior position in relation to the king. Rawlinson reported on an invitation he had to a Persian court in the early 1800s: "The monarch reclined on a couch with golden feet, and sipped the rich wine of Helbon; the guests drank an inferior beverage, seated on the floor." On some very special occasions the rigidity of this custom was relaxed. At those times the king would preside openly at a banquet where large numbers of dignitaries were assembled, and royal couches and royal wine were provided for them all. Such a banquet is alluded to in Esther 1:3.

6:8 Royal Honors Given to Subjects

"Have them bring a royal robe the king has worn and a horse the king has ridden, one with a royal crest placed on its head."

To be given a royal robe previously worn by the king was a sign of great honor and the king's favor. Herodotus, the fifth century B.C. Greek historian, who is known as "the Father of History," and who wrote chiefly about the Persian Wars, stated that the kings of Persia had horses of remarkable beauty and of peculiar breed that were brought from Armenia. To ride a horse that the king had ridden was almost as great an honor as to sit upon his throne; almost, but not quite.

Because of the sentence structure and choice of words in the KJV rendering of our text-verse: "and the horse that the king rideth upon, and the crown royal which is set upon his head," some believe that the crown royal was set upon the head of Mordecai, but that is unlikely. Assyrian reliefs depict the practice of setting crown-like headdresses on horses, so it's more likely that the royal crest—or royal crown—was headdress that was put upon the horse, thereby denoting that the rider was on a horse that the king rode.

once considered himself to have been insulted by an inappropriate joke that one of his favorites had foolishly related in his presence. At the end of the story, the king abruptly got up and left the place, and the favorite immediately knew that his fate was sealed. He went home in dismay, and in a few hours the king's guards came for his head.

7:7 SIGN OF ROYAL DISPLEASURE

The king got up in a rage, left his wine and went out into the palace garden. But Haman, realizing that the king had already decided his fate, stayed behind to beg Queen Esther for his life.

The king getting up in an observable rage and abruptly leaving the room was enough for Haman to know that he was going to be condemned to death. This was apparently a Persian custom to denote royal displeasure and vengeance. There is a story told about a similar incident that took place in the court of Schah Sefi in the 17th century (see 2 Chronicles **36:4 Change of Name**). King Sefi

7:8 FACE COVERED

As soon as the word left the king's mouth, they covered Haman's face.

The precise purpose of covering the face of a condemned man is not known, though it has been conjectured that it was intended to signify that the person was no longer worthy to look on the face of the king. Obviously, however, many other meanings could be tied to it. The custom was observed in other nations as well as among the Persians.

9:26 FEAST OF PURIM

(Therefore these days were called Purim, from the word pur.)

Pur is a Persian word signifying a part, and from there denoting a lot. With the Hebrew plural ending it becomes *purim*: *lots*. This is the name by which the feast is known, which is kept to commemorate the deliverance of the Jews from the plot of Haman. It's called the Feast of Lots because Haman, being very superstitious, cast the lot in order to determine the most favorable time for carrying out his plot against the Jews (Esther 3:7). Some commentators believe the name was given in irony, to indicate the contempt in which the Jews held Haman and his divination.

There's a tradition that the introduction of the Feast of Lots met with some opposition, though afterward it was celebrated by most Jews. The day before the feast is kept as a solemn fast. On the day of the feast the people assemble in the synagogue, where the book of Esther is read amid hand clapping and feet stamping. These are intended to show contempt for Haman and joy for the deliverance of the Jews. After leaving the synagogue there are great feasts at home.

JOB

1:3 Pastoral Wealth

He owned seven thousand sheep, three thousand camels, five hundred yoke of oxen and five hundred donkeys, and had a large number of servants. He was the greatest man among all the people of the East.

Among pastoral and nomadic people it was natural to estimate wealth by the number of animals owned, and by the number of servants. Abram was very rich in cattle, sheep, camels, and donkeys, in silver and gold, and had many servants (see Genesis 13:2 and 24:35). Lot had so many flocks and herds that the land could not support both his and Abram's (Genesis 13:5).

5:5 Grain and Thorns

The hungry consume his harvest, taking it even from among thorns, and the thirsty pant after his wealth.

This may refer to a thief who takes all the grain, even that which is growing among the thorns, or more likely it refers to an ancient custom in the Middle East, which Thomson mentions in *The Land and the Book* (1860). "The farmers, after they have threshed out the grain, frequently lay it aside in the chaff in some private place near the floor, and cover it up with thorn bushes to keep it from being carried away or eaten by animals. Robbers who found and seized this would literally take it from among the thorns."

6:4 Poisoned Arrows

The arrows of the Almighty are in me, my spirit drinks in their poison.

Without doubt this refers to the practice, among barbarous nations of all times, of dipping the points of arrows into a poisonous substance for the purpose of ensuring the death of the person who is pierced in any way by the arrow tip. In the days of the Romans, this was sometimes done with the points of daggers.

9:25 PRIMITIVE POSTMEN

"My days are swifter than a runner *(post, KJV)*; they fly away without a glimpse of joy."

In ancient times, and even not many years ago in some undeveloped countries, swift runners were used to carry important messages from one place to another. Kings kept a number of these men in their service as a part of the royal household. When Hezekiah sent invitations to the solemn Passover that he was going to hold at Jerusalem, it's recorded that "At the king's command, couriers (posts, KJV) went throughout Israel and Judah with letters from the king and from his officials." (2 Chronicles 30:6). In the time of Jeremiah there seems to have been a regular postal service established, for in prophesying

the destruction of Babylon he writes: "One courier follows another and messenger follows messenger to announce to the king of Babylon that his entire city is captured." (Jeremiah 51:31). Said one commentator about this passage: "The famous courier system of the Babylonians would announce the destruction."

The Persians also made use of swift messengers. The order commanding the murder of all the Jews in the empire was sent by this means (Esther 3:13-15). The order that counteracted this proclamation was sent by "couriers, riding the royal horses (mules and camels, KJV), raced out, spurred on by the king's command" Obviously the horses were faster and had more endurance than the runners, although it was said that some of the ancient couriers could outrun and outlast a horse.

While there may have been no systematic communication of this type in Job's day, yet it's probable from our text-verse that fast runners were employed when needed. The patriarch compares the swiftness of his day to a runner; most likely a runner carrying news. This would have been the swiftest way of communication with which he was familiar, and his days went swifter still.

12:6 ROBBERS

The tents of marauders are undisturbed, and those who provoke God are secure— those who carry their god in their hands.

(The KJV rendering of this verse reads: "The tabernacles of robbers prosper, and they that provoke God are secure; into whose hand God bringeth abundantly." But most commentators agree that the last phrase could, and more likely should, read, "who bring their god in their hands." That is, the god of robbers is the weapon in their hands.)

Marauding bands have been common from early periods of history in every nation in the world, and oftentimes it appears to law-abiding people that the robbers fare better than they do. But such is never the case. Ultimately, prison or a violent death awaits each of them. In ancient days, and even today in some Middle East nations, their punishment often included physical mutilation, such as having their hands cut off.

During biblical times, whole tribes, and in some instances whole nations, adopted robbery as a means of livelihood. The Sabeans, who were nomadic Bedouins living in the area of Uz and to the south, stole Job's oxen and donkeys, and the "Chaldeans formed three raiding parties and swept down on your camels and carried them off" (Job 1:15-17). (These Chaldeans were another regional group of nomadic marauders. They were not the later Chaldeans, who lived in, and for a time ruled, Babylon during the 7th and 6th centuries B.C.)

The Shechemites "set men on the hilltops to ambush and rob everyone who passed by" (Judges 9:25). The robbery Jesus told about in His parable of the Good Samaritan (Luke 10:30) was based on actual robberies that frequently took place in those days. Unfortunately, we have almost returned to those times, since there are few places today that individuals can travel and be completely safe from robbery or physical harm from marauders.

15:26 BOSSES

He runneth upon him, even on his neck, upon the thick bosses of his bucklers *(KJV)*.

(The NIV renders this verse as: "defiantly charging against him with a thick, strong shield.")

The boss was the external convex part of the round shield, its thickest and strongest portion. There were some shields whose shape was wholly convex, the center being an elevated point, as may be seen in the illustration, which represents an Assyrian convex shield.

There were also convex ornaments that were placed on the outside of shields, adding strength as well as beauty. Layard (*Nineveh and its Remains*, 1849) found circular bronze shields at Nimroud (or Nimrud). Each shield had an iron handle fastened

Convex shield

by six nails, with the heads of the nails forming bosses on the outside of the shield.

15:28 FRAIL HOUSES

He will inhabit ruined towns and houses where no one lives, houses crumbling to rubble.

Many of the rude huts in the ancient Middle East were made of small stones or built of mud. The roof was made by covering the beams with brushwood, and this in turn with soil, such as mud or clay. The rain would soak into the soil, and weight settling on the brush and beams would gradually break them down unless the occupant was industrious and continually made repairs. Ecclesiastes 10:18 says: "If a man is lazy, the rafters sag; if his hands are idle, the house leaks." When the roof broke down, the walls easily gave way, and the whole house soon became a heap of rubble. This was true not only of rude mud huts, but of large edifices like temples and palaces that were built of sun-dried brick, as the ruins of Babylon and Nineveh mutely and amply testify.

18:5-6 Light and Darkness as Symbols

"The lamp *(light, KJV)* of the wicked is snuffed out; the flame *(spark, KJV)* of his fire stops burning. The light *(candle, KJV)* in his tent becomes dark; the lamp beside him goes out."

In every society throughout the centuries, light has had the sense of good, and dark the sense of evil. From childhood to adulthood many people welcome the light and dread, even fear, the darkness. Light is friendly, darkness is not. In many ancient homes, even as in the rooms of some children today, a light was kept burning all night. In the Bible, light is used to symbolize good and to symbolize prosperity, and the extinguishing, or lack, of it to symbolize evil and to symbolize calamity.

Thus Job speaks of those days when he was prosperous as being when God's lamp shone upon his head, and when by His light he walked through darkness (Job 29:3). David says, "You, O LORD, keep my lamp burning; my God turns my darkness into light" (Psalm 18:28). Then when great affliction comes upon Job, we find him saying: "Yet how often is the lamp of the wicked snuffed out" (Job 21:17)? Solomon says: "If a man curses his father or mother, his lamp will be snuffed out in pitch darkness" (Proverbs 20:20); "for the evil man has no future hope, and the lamp of the wicked will be snuffed out" (Proverbs 24:20).

On two occasions Jesus speaks of the punishment of the wicked as their being "thrown outside, into the darkness" (Matthew 8:12 and 22:13). Both ideas of light symbolizing blessing and darkness symbolizing cursing are joined in Proverbs 13:9—"The light of the righteous shines brightly, but the lamp of the wicked is snuffed out."

19:6 NET USED IN COMBAT

Then know that God has wronged me and drawn his net around me.

Because of the many possible translations of the Hebrew word that is rendered *drawn* in the NIV and *compassed* in the KJV, some commentators see in our text-verse a reference to an ancient method of fighting that was practiced by the Persians, Goths, and Romans. Among the Romans one of the gladiators would have, perhaps, a sword and shield, while the other would have, perhaps, a trident (a long three-pronged weapon) and net. The latter would try to throw his net over the head of his adversary. If he succeeded, he immediately drew the net around his neck with a noose that was attached to it, pulled him to the ground, and killed him with the trident. If he failed to throw the net over his adversary's head, however, he was in considerable danger while he tried to set his net for another throw, or to retrieve it in case it had pulled from his hands.

If Job knew of this manner of fighting in his day, he represents himself in our text-verse as having engaged in a contest with God and being defeated, and now is entangled in the net and completely at God's mercy.

19:23-24 SCROLLS - TABLETS - MONUMENTS

"Oh, that my words were recorded, that they were written on a scroll *(book, KJV)*, that they were inscribed *(graven, KJV)* with an iron tool *(pen, KJV)* on lead, or engraved *(lead, KJV)* in rock forever!

Three different substances for the preservation of records are referred to here:

1. *Scrolls*. These were made of linen or cotton cloth, skins, or the leaves of the papyrus. It's from the last word that we get our word *paper*. The inner bark of trees was also sometimes used. The Latin word for *bark* is *liber*, and this word came to signify a *book*, and is related in Latin to our word *library*. When made of cloth or skins the book was made up in the form of a roll.

2. *Lead tablets*. These are of high antiquity. In Rome in 1699, a traveler (Montfaucon) bought a very old book made entirely of

lead. It was about four inches long and three wide, and had a cover and six leaves or sheets. The hinges and nails were also made of lead. The volume contained Egyptian gnostic figures and inscriptions in Greek, and Etruscan characters.

In a temple in the Carian city of Cnidus, erected in honor of Hades and Persephone, about the fourth century before Christ, the women were in the habit of depositing thin sheets of lead on which were written the names of people they hated, together with their alleged misdeeds. They also inscribed on the lead tablets imprecations against those who had injured them. Many of these tablets were discovered in 1858 when excavations were made in the ruins of the temple.

It's not certain, however, that in our text-verse Job refers to leaden tablets or leaves on which inscriptions were made. He may have been referring to the custom of first cutting letters in stone and then filling them up with molten lead. There are indications that some of the incised letters in Assyrian monuments were filled with metal.

3. *Stone monuments*. The law was originally written on tables of stone "with the finger of God" (Exodus 31:18). The second set of tables were written by Moses by divine command (Exodus 34:4, 28). Joshua copied the law on the stone altar at Mount Ebal (Joshua 8:32). This method of recording important truths and events was common in ancient times. In our text-verse Job desires that his sentiments should be so engraved, that generations to come might read the record.

The stone records of ancient Oriental nations are all illustrations of the custom that Job evidently had in mind. Many of these bear on Scripture facts and history, confirming and supplementing the sacred record. One of the most remarkable, in some respects, is the famous Moabite stone, which created intense excitement among Bible scholars and antiquarians when it was discovered in 1868. The Moabite stone is a slab of black basalt, dating from 9th century B.C., which bears ancient Semitic inscription describing victory of Mesha, Moabite king, over the Israelites. Unfortunately, negotiations for its purchase by the French led to quarrels among the Arabs and it was broken into pieces. Fragments of it are now in the Louvre Museum in Paris.

24:16 Houses of Clay

In the dark, men break into houses *(dig through, KJV)*, but by day they shut themselves in; they want nothing to do with the light.

The KJV rendering refers to houses built of clay. There were several varieties. Some had a framework of branches thickly daubed with mud. Others had walls made of layers of mud placed one on top of the other, each drying before the next was put on. And others were made of sun-dried bricks. This style of building is very ancient and was common in the Middle East for many centuries. A thief could easily break into a house of this type by digging or chopping a hole through the wall.

Houses like these are referred to by Eliphaz in Job 4:19 where he speaks of "houses of clay, whose foundations are in the dust, who are crushed more readily than a moth!" In Ezekiel 12:5 the prophet is commanded to "dig through the wall" as a figurative example. The Savior also refers to this type of house when he speaks of thieves breaking through (KJV) to steal (Matthew 6:19). The frailty of the walls of such houses is also probably referred to in Psalm 62:3, and especially in Isaiah

Ancient oil-presses

30:13: "this sin will become for you like a high wall, cracked and bulging, that collapses suddenly, in an instant."

29:6 STONE OIL PRESSES

The rock poured out for me streams of olive oil.

Some think the reference here is to the fact that the olive tree sometimes grows in very rocky soil, but allusion is more probably made to stone oil-presses, from which the oil flowed like a river. See also

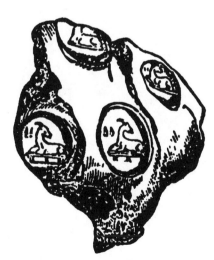

Impressions of seals

Ezekiel 32:14. Moses speaks of "oil from the flinty crag" (Deuteronomy 32:13).

38:14 IMPRESSIONS OF SEALS

The earth takes shape like clay under a seal.

The bricks of Egypt, Babylonia, and Assyria bear marks that have evidently been made with a seal. Egyptian wine jars and mummy pits were sometimes sealed with clay. In Assyria, public documents were found that were made of clay and that had letters stamped in them and marks of official sealing. For centuries in the Middle East doors of granaries and treasure rooms were sealed with clay so that it was impossible to enter without first breaking the seal, thus not even the least amount of anything could be stolen without it being known. The sepulcher of Christ was probably sealed in this way (see Matthew **27:66 Sealing the Tomb**). Clay was used in preference to wax because the former hardens with heat and the latter melts. The illustration represents a lump of clay from Assyria that had several impressions of seals on it. (See 1 Kings **21:8 Seals**.)

41:7 FISHING SPEARS

Can you fill his hide with harpoons or his head with fishing spears?

This is an allusion to an instrument resembling the *bident* or two-forked fish spear used by the Egyptians and frequently depicted on monuments. This spear was a slender rod some ten or twelve feet long, and doubly feathered at the end like a modern arrow. It had two sharp points about two feet in length that were used to impale the fish. The fisherman pushed along the Nile in a flat-bottomed boat among the papyrus reeds and lotus plants, and on spotting a fish drove the weapon with his right hand, steadying it in the curve of his left hand.

PSALMS

1:8 Irrigation of Gardens

He is like a tree planted by streams *(rivers, KJV)* of water, which yields its fruit in season and whose leaf does not wither. Whatever he does prospers.

Several commentators call attention to the fact that the Hebrew words *palge-mayim*, here rendered *streams of water* by the NIV and *rivers of water* by the KJV, literally means *divisions of waters*, and most likely refers to the favorite mode of irrigation in some ancient Middle-East countries. Canals were dug in every direction, and through these the water was carried to all the vegetation. Egypt was once covered with these canals, and in this way the waters of the Nile were carried to every part of the valley through which the river ran. Some gardens were so arranged that water was conveyed around every plot and even to every tree. Allusion is probably made to this custom in Ezekiel 31:3-4 where Assyria is spoken of as a cedar: "The waters nourished it, deep springs made it grow tall; their streams flowed all around its base and sent their channels to all the trees of the field." We don't know that this ancient custom existed as early as the time of Job, but Job 38:25 seems to indicate it: "Who cuts a channel for the torrents of rain, and a path for the thunderstorm, to water a land where no man lives, a desert with no one in it, to satisfy a desolate wasteland and make it sprout with grass?"

Solomon says in Proverbs 21:1— "The king's heart is in the hand of the LORD; he directs it like a watercourse wherever he pleases." The figure of speech used here is an allusion to the eastern method of irrigation in which several canals were dug from one stream, enabling the farmer to direct a stream as he pleased by a simple action. In Ecclesiastes 2:5-6 he says: "I made gardens and parks and planted all kinds of fruit trees in them. I made reservoirs to water groves of flourishing trees." For way of raising water, see Deuteronomy **11:10 Watering with the Foot**. See also Isaiah 1:30, 58:11; Jeremiah 17:8 and 31:12.

Several methods were adopted for conveying the water from a river to the canals that ran through the gardens. Sometimes the water was raised from the river to the canal by means of a *shadoof*, or well-sweep, which was a horizontal pole that was hung on a perpendicular one, and that had a bucket on one end and a balance of stones on the other.

2:12 KISSING, AN ACT OF HOMAGE

Kiss the Son, lest he be angry and you be destroyed in your way, for his wrath can flare up in a moment.

"Kiss the Son" means "do homage to the Son"—the kiss is a sign of homage and submission. When Samuel anointed Saul he kissed the newly-made king. This act of homage was a recognition of his royalty (1 Samuel 10:1). In this way the Psalmist desires all men to recognize the royalty of the Son.

On the negative side, kissing was also an act of worship among idolaters (see 1 Kings 19:18, Job 31:27, and Hosea 13:2).

In a book written about 150 years ago, the writers told of an incident that took place near Petra, an ancient ruined city of Edom in what is now southwest Jordan: "One day about mid-afternoon, a great cavalcade entered our camp from the southward. There were many mounted Arabs with lances, and we observed that there were some among the horsemen who wore richer turbans, and of more gaudy colors, than is usual among Bedouins or peasants. As the procession advanced, several of Abou Raschid's Arabs went out and led the horses of the chiefs by the bridles into the camp. The whole procession alighted at the tent of our chief, and kissed his turban. This was a signal of pacification. Peace was immediately proclaimed throughout the camp, and notice was given that all of the men bearing arms who had come from a distance, many of whom had joined us that very morning, were to return to their respective homes."

In a large branch of Christianity today, the rings of certain church leaders are kissed by the ordinary saints as a sign of homage and submission especially the rings of the bishops, cardinals, and the pope.

TWENTY-THIRD PSALM (KJV)

The best known of the Psalms of the Old Testament, often read at funerals as a profession of faith in God's temporal and eternal protection:

The Lord is my shepherd; I shall not want.
He maketh me to lie down in green pastures;
He leadeth me beside the still waters.
He restoreth my soul;
He leadeth me in the paths of righteousness for his name's sake.
Yea, though I walk through the valley of the shadow of death, I will fear no evil;
For thou art with me;
Thy rod and thy staff, they comfort me.
Thou preparest a table for me in the presence of mine enemies;
Thou anointest my head with oil; my cup runneth over.
Surely goodness and mercy shall follow me all the days of my life:
And I will dwell in the house of the Lord for ever.

23:5 ANOINTING GUESTS

You anoint my head with oil; my cup overflows.

Anointing was an ancient custom practiced by the Egyptians and afterward by the Greeks and Romans and other nations. Olive oil was used, either pure or mixed with fragrant and costly spices, often brought from a long distance. (See note at Matthew **26:7 Alabaster - Tables**) Anointing was done not only as a part of the ceremony in connection with the coronation of kings (see 2 Kings **11:12 Coronation Ceremonies**) and at the installation of the High Priest (Psalm 133:2), but also as an act of courtesy and hospitality toward a guest. Thus Jesus accuses Simon of lacking hospitality in neglecting to anoint His head when Simon invited Him to eat with him (Luke 7:46).

There are illustrations on Egyptian monuments showing guests having their heads anointed. Oil was used for other parts of the body as well as for the head, and at home as well as when visiting. Biblical references are numerous: Deuteronomy 28:40, Ruth 3:3, Psalm 92:10 and 104:15, Ecclesiastes 9:8, Micah 6:15, Matthew 6:17, and many others. The neglect of anointing was considered a sign of mourning (see Samuel 14:2 and Daniel 10:3). Conversely, an anointed face was a sign of joy, and so we read of being anointed with the "oil of joy (gladness, KJV)" (Psalm 45:7 and Hebrews 1:9). In our text-verse, the Psalmist represents himself as an honored guest of the LORD, who prepares a table for him, hospitably anoints him, and pours out for him such an abundance that his cup overflows.

Anointing a guest

In a book published in the early 1800s, *Oriental Customs*, a Captain Wilson wrote about an experience he had that was like that spoken of by the Psalmist: "I once had this ceremony performed on me in the house of a great and rich Indian, in the presence of a large company. The gentleman of the house poured upon my hands and arms a delightful odoriferous perfume, put a golden cup into my hands, and poured wine into it until it ran over. Assuring me at the same time that it was a great pleasure to him to receive me, and that I should find a rich supply of my needs in his house."

24:7 Lifting up Ancient Doors

Lift up your heads, O you gates; be lifted up, you ancient doors, that the King of glory may come in. Who is this King of glory? The LORD strong and mighty, the LORD mighty in battle. Lift up your heads, O you gates; lift them up, you ancient doors, that the King of glory may come in. Who is he, this King of glory? The LORD Almighty— he is the King of glory. *Selah*

In this prophetic passage, reference is made to gates and doors that open vertically rather than horizontally as is commonly done. This would then be a fortification type of gate, one that could be lowered quickly, literally dropped, when necessary. This type of gate was called *cataracta*, because of the force and noise with which it fell. It was, as said, used in the fortification of cities, and corresponds to the more recent *porticullis*, which was a grating of iron or wooden bars or slats, suspended in the gateway of a fortified place and lowered to block passage. The *cataracta* was believed to have been known in David's time. During his time the "King of glory" was represented by the ark being brought in a triumphal procession to the sanctuary.

The fivefold use of "King of glory" in our text-verse passage, and this King's identification as the "Lord of hosts," leads many commentators to believe that this passage is messianic (compare Joshua 5:14-6:2). As such, these verses speak prophetically of the ascension of Christ after His victory over sin and death and of His coming reign as King over all the earth.

24:7 SYMBOLICAL HAND-WASHING

I wash my hands in innocence, and go about *(compass, KJV)* your altar, O LORD.

There were several occasions on which the Jews washed their hands in connection with religious rites. The Psalmist may have had one of these in mind when he wrote the text. See also Psalm 73:13.

1. There was the washing required of the priests in the service of the tabernacle and temple. The brazen laver was made for this purpose (see Exodus **40:7 Laver**). It's said that it was customary for the priests to wash their hands and then bind the sacrifice to the horns of the altar and march around it. Thus David wrote: "So I will go about your altar, O LORD."

2. The Jews also washed their hands before engaging in

prayer. Some commentators believe Paul is referring to this custom in the expression "holy hands" in 1 Timothy 2:8.

3. There were certain ceremonies that were to be observed in cases of murder when the murderer was unknown. The elders of the city nearest to where the body was found were directed to break a heifer's neck, and "Then all the elders of the town nearest the body shall wash their hands over the heifer whose neck was broken in the valley, and they shall declare: "Our hands did not shed this blood, nor did our eyes see it done" (Deuteronomy 21:6-7). This was considered a most solemn affirmation on their part that all in their city were innocent of the murder. In the time of Jesus, Pilate, though a Gentile, had probably lived long enough among the Jews to understand this custom, and is, therefore, believed to refer to it when, because of the demand of the people that Barabbas be freed and Jesus be crucified, "he took water and washed his hands in front of the crowd. 'I am innocent of this man's blood,' he said. 'It is your responsibility! (see ye to it, KJV)'" (Matthew 27:24).

Since David desires in our text-verse to symbolize inward purity by outward washing, any one of these customs may serve for illustration.

33:2 PSALTERY

Praise the LORD with harp: sing unto him with the psaltery and an instrument of ten strings *(KJV)*.

These two instruments, the "psaltery" and "an instrument of ten strings," as so rendered in the KJV, are thought to be the same, the latter expression being used to explain the "psaltery" (see also Psalms 42:3 and 144:9). Thus the NIV renders our text-verse as: "Praise the LORD with the harp; make music to him on the ten-stringed lyre." The shape of the *nebel*, or psaltery, is unknown. Some believe it was shaped like an inverted triangle, closed on all sides. From the name, others believe it was shaped like a leather bottle—the Hebrew word *nebel* contains this meaning, also. Still others believe it was shaped something like a modern guitar, and that it resembled that instrument in its overall styling.

The Jewish historian, Josephus, says: "The psaltery had

Assyrian triangular lyre

twelve musical notes, and was played upon by the fingers." These twelve "notes" are believed to have been represented by twelve strings, whereas our text-verse speaks of only ten. It may be that the number differed in different varieties of the instrument. If we assume these varieties to have been designated by the number of strings, we may find the reason for the explanatory clause in our text-verse—the Psalmist was referring to the psaltery that had "ten strings." Whatever their number, the strings were stretched over a wooden frame (see 1 Samuel 6:5 {KJV}, and 1 Kings 10:12).

When the *nebel* was invented and when it came into use among the Hebrews is unknown. It's first mentioned in connection with the inauguration of King Saul. When the company of young prophets met him, shortly after Samuel had anointed him, one of the instruments on which they played was a *nebel* (1 Samuel 10:5). The *nebel* was used in Divine worship (see 2 Samuel 6:5; 1 Chronicles 13:8, 15:16, 16:5, and 25:1; and Amos 5:23). It was also used on festive occasions (see Isaiah 5:12 and 14:11; and Amos 6:5—in these passages the KJV renders *nebel* as *viol*). From what is written in 1 Chronicles 13:8, 15:16, and Amos 5:23, it appears that the *nebel* was at times used to accompany singing.

35:13-14 Posture of Face in Prayer

But as for me, when they were sick, my clothing was sackcloth: I humbled my soul with fasting; and my prayer returned into mine own bosom. I behaved myself as though he had been my friend or brother: I bowed down heavily, as one that mourneth for his mother.

Some commentators believe that in verse 13 the psalmist is

referring to an Oriental custom of praying with the head inclined forward until the face is almost hidden in the bosom of the outer garment. Others, and perhaps most, believe that it means that the Psalmist's prayers had gone unanswered. The NIV renders the verse in this manner; note also the changes made in the punctuation, so that verse 13 continues in verse 14: "Yet when they were ill, I put on sackcloth and humbled myself with fasting. When my prayers returned to me unanswered, I went about mourning as though for my friend or brother. I bowed my head in grief as though weeping for my mother."

40:6 PIERCING THE EAR

Sacrifice and offering you did not desire, but my ears you have pierced *(mine ears hast thou opened, KJV)*; burnt offerings and sin offerings you did not require.

The Psalmist uses the expression about his ears to denote that he is a servant of God, ready to do his will, as he further declares in verse eight. He seems to have in mind the ceremony by which a Hebrew servant, if desiring to stay with his master, might be bound to him for life: "if the servant declares, 'I love my master and my wife and children and do not want to go free,' then his master must take him before the judges. He shall take him to the door or the doorpost and pierce his ear with an awl. Then he will be his servant for life" (Exodus 21:5-6, see also Deuteronomy 15:16-17). This custom was observed not only by the Jews but also by many other ancient nations.

This psalm is definitely messianic. Verses from the psalm are quoted in Hebrews 10:5-7, where they are quoted as being from Christ. This passage is used by the writer of Hebrews to magnify the obedience of the Son that led to His death on the Cross. (See Philippians 2:5-8.)

41:9 BETRAYAL BY FRIEND

Even my close friend, whom I trusted, he who shared my bread, has lifted up his heel against me.

To betray a friend who trusted you was considered a great act of evil. Today not much is thought of it, and betrayal by trusted friends or family members, or by someone who was given private information, is commonplace. Today Judas would not be given 30 pieces of silver, he would be given a book contract and hundreds-of-thousands of dollars for interviews and pictures.

Our text-verse is made messianic by Jesus' referral to it in John 13:18. He quoted the verse as He prophesied His betrayal at the hands of Judas Iscariot, and this is obviously the Scripture that Peter refers to in his statement in Acts 1:16. Like Judas, Ahithophel the Gilonite, who was once David's trusted counselor and the close friend who's referred to in our text-verse, eventually hung himself (2 Samuel 17:23), and thereby became a pre-shadow of Judas.

Hyssop

51:7 HYSSOP

Cleanse me with hyssop, and I will be clean; wash me, and I will be whiter than snow.

Hyssop, a small leafy shrub, was directed to be used in ceremonial purification. It was used in connection with Passover (Exodus 12:22), the cleansing of lepers (Leviticus 14:4, 6, 49, 51, and 51), and the sacrifice of the red heifer (Numbers 19:6, 18). Hebrews 9:19 says that hyssop was used to sprinkle blood on the scroll (book, KJV) containing the law and on the people, although hyssop is not mentioned in Exodus 24 where the actual sprinkling is recorded. Today the aromatic leaves of the hyssop plant are used in perfumery and as a condiment, but this may not be the same plant referred to in the Bible, since that is actually an unidentified plant.

56:8 TEARS RECORDED

Record my lament; list my tears on your scroll—are they not in your record *(book, KJV)*?

This is one of the many figures of speech used in the Scriptures. Many of the writers, especially David and Isaiah, were highly poetic and expressive in their writing. Here David is using a figure of speech to implore God to take notice of the reason for each of his teardrops and the sorrows associated with them. "Your record" is undoubtedly similar to God's "scroll of remembrance" as spoken of in Malachi 3:16.

58:4-5 SERPENT CHARMING

Their venom is like the venom of a snake *(serpent, KJV)* , like that of a cobra that has stopped its ears *(deaf adder, KJV)*, that will not heed the tune of the charmer, however skillful the enchanter may be.

Apparently serpent charming, as sometimes pictured in the movies, on television, or in books, is a very ancient art. We've probably all been fascinated by pictures of a deadly cobra balancing on its body while a charmer played a tune on a flute of some type. This same art of charming a poisonous snake is obviously what the Psalmist is referring to in our text-verse. Besides this Scripture, reference is made to snake charming in several other passages. Solomon refers to in Ecclesiastes 10:11— "If a snake bites before it is charmed, there is no profit for the charmer." In a prophecy of Jeremiah, there is allusion to the same practice: "See, I will send venomous snakes among you, vipers that cannot be charmed, and they will bite you," declares the LORD." The prophecy is that the Babylonians would be like poisonous snakes to bite Judah, and there would be no deliverance from their venom.

58:9 THORNS FOR FUEL

Before your pots can feel the heat of the thorns—whether they be green or dry—the wicked will be swept away.

A great variety of thorny shrubs and plants abound in the Middle East. These were gathered for fuel. Some of them make a quick, hot, fire that is kindled easily and soon expires. The idea conveyed in our text-verse is that of quick destruction. The wicked will be destroyed quicker than the heat from a fire of thorns can reach the cooking vessels.

A similar figure of speech is used in one of Isaiah's prophecies: "The peoples will be burned as if to lime; like cut thorn bushes they will be set ablaze" (Isaiah 33:12). It has been thought from this verse that thorns may have been used in lime-kilns.

Allusion to the use of thorns for fuel is also made in 2 Samuel 23:6-7; Psalm 118:12; Ecclesiastes 7:6; Isaiah 9:18 and 10:17; and Nahum 1:10. (See 1 Kings **17:10 Sticks for Fuel**, and Matthew 6:30.)

79:2 UNBURIED BODIES

They have given the dead bodies of your servants as food to the birds of the air, the flesh of your saints to the beasts of the earth.

To be deprived of burial was considered by the Jews one of the greatest dishonors that could be inflicted on a human being. In this they shared the common feeling of civilized man. We find a number of scriptural references to this sentiment. The Psalmist, lamenting the desolation he beheld, wrote: "our bones have been scattered at the mouth of the grave" (Psalm 141:7). Solomon speaks of it as a great disgrace if a man "does not receive proper burial (have no burial, KJV)" (Ecclesiastes 6:3). The LORD said of Jehoiakim, king of Judah: "his body will be thrown out and exposed to the heat by day and the frost by night" (Jeremiah 36:30). In our text-verse, the bodies are spoken of not only as unburied, but as further dishonored by being eaten by birds and beasts. This was one of the curses pronounced by Moses for disobedience to the Divine law (Deuteronomy 28:26). It was a threat mutually exchanged between David and Goliath (1 Samuel 17:44-46). The prophet Jeremiah has several references to this dishonorable treatment of the bodies of the dead (Jeremiah 7:33, 16:4, 19:7, and 24:20).

In connection with this subject, it may not be amiss to state that a reverse of this belief was held by the Magi (members of the Zoroastrian priestly caste of the Medes and Persians), who exposed the bodies of their dead so that they *would* be eaten by birds. Their religious theory being that any other method of disposing of a corpse would pollute at least one of the four elements: earth, air, fire, or water. Thus if living beings devoured the dead, the pollution would be prevented.

About two-hundred years ago, the Guebres, or Fire-worshipers, the descendants of the ancient Persians, followed the same practice and even had apparatus prepared for the purpose. A traveler to their area wrote: "Round towers of considerable height, without either door or window, are constructed by the Guebres, having at the top a number of iron bars, which slope inwards. The towers are mounted by means of ladders, and the bodies are placed crossways upon the bars. The vultures and crows which hover about the towers soon strip the flesh from the bones, and the bones then fall through the bars to the bottom of the tower. The Zend-Avesta (the entire body of sacred writings of the Zoroastrian religion) contains particular directions for the construction of such towers, which are called *dakhmas*, or 'towers of silence.'"

88:4 THE PIT

I am counted among those who go down to the pit.

There are several Hebrew words that are rendered *pit*. In our text-verse the Hebrew word translated *pit* signifies an abyss or deep hole like a dungeon. Solomon represents those who are trying to entice the innocent youth into ways of wickedness as saying: "let's swallow them alive, like the grave, and whole, like those who go down to the pit" (Proverbs 1:12). In this verse, *pit* has the same significance, but *grave* signifies *Sheol*; that is, Hades or the world of the dead. In Hezekiah's song of thanksgiving for his recovery from sickness, he says: "For the grave cannot praise you, death cannot sing your praise; those who go down to the pit cannot hope for your faithfulness" (Isaiah 38:18). In this verse, also, *pit* signifies a deep abyss or dungeon, while *death* signifies Sheol. Sometimes the KJV renders the word meaning Sheol as *pit*, while the NIV renders it as *death* (see Job 17:16). In other places the word rendered *pit* means exactly that or *destruction* (see Psalm 28:1).

91:3 BIRD SNARES

Surely he will save you from the fowler's snare and from the deadly pestilence.

Several different words are used in the Hebrew to denote various snares that were employed in fowling. The Hebrew word *pach*, which is used in out text-verse, denoted a spring, or trap-net. In a book written in 1856 the writer describes one such net used by the Egyptians as being: "in two parts, which, when set, were spread out upon the ground, and slightly fastened with a stick (trap-stick), so that as soon as a bird or animal touched the stick, the parts flew up and enclosed the bird in the net or caught the foot of the animal." The word *mokesh* is also used to denote a snare of the same type, thought it is sometimes used to signify a circle of nets for capturing animals (see 2 Samuel **22:6 Circling Nets**).

Snares that were spread on the ground and caught the bird by

Ancient Egyptian snares

the feet, or, loosing a spring, encircled it with a net, are often referred to by biblical writers as illustrative of the dangers that beset people. See Job 18:8-10, where several varieties seem to be named. The same is true of Psalm 140:4. See also Psalm 124:7, 141:9, and 142:3; Proverbs 7:23 and 22:5; Hosea 9:8, and Amos 3:5.

98:6 TRUMPETS

With trumpets and the blast of the ram's horn (cornet, KJV)—shout for joy before the LORD, the King.

1. *Chatsotserah*, rendered *trumpet*, was a long, straight, and slender wind instrument, such as Moses was commanded to furnish for the service of the Israelites (Numbers 10:2). Hebrew historian Josephus gives this description of it: "In length it was little less than a cubit. It was composed of a narrow tube, somewhat thicker than a flute, but with so much breadth as was sufficient for admission of the breath of a man's mouth; it ended in the form of a bell, like common trumpets."

The *chatsotserah* was used for notifying the people of the different feasts, for signaling the change of camp, and for sounding alarms in time of war (see Numbers 10:1-10 and Hosea 5:8). It was at first used in sacrificial rites only on special occasions, but in the time of David and Solomon its use for such purposes was much extended.

2. It's impossible to give an accurate description of the *shophar*, here in our text-verse and in other passages in the KJV rendered *cornet*, but often translated *trumpet*. The NIV renders it *ram's horn*. The KJV translators rendered it *trumpet* except when, as in our verse-text, they were compelled to make a distinction between it and *chatsotserah*, which they invariably render *trumpet* (See 1 Chronicles 15:28, 2 Chronicles 15:14, and Hosea 5:8), and so they translate *shophar* as *cornet*. In those passages the NIV prefers to translate it as simply *horn*. In Exodus 19:16, Leviticus 25:9, Job 39:25, Joel 2:1, and Amos 2:2, *shophar* is translated *trumpet*.

Authorities differ as to the *shophar's* shape, some believing it to have been straight, while others contend that it was slightly bent like a horn. The latter opinion seems the more probably from the fact that the horn (*keren*) in Joshua 6:5 is elsewhere throughout that chapter spoken of as a *shophar*, or trumpet. From its name, which means bright or clear, the shophar is thought to have had a clear, shrill, sound. It was used for announcing the beginning of the year of jubilee, and for other ceremonial purposes, such as calling the people to important proclamations, declaration of war, and for demonstrations of joy. See Leviticus 25:9, Judges 3:27, 1 Samuel 13:3, 2 Chronicles 15:24, and Isaiah 18:3.

119:83 SHRIVELED AND USELESS BOTTLES

Though I am like a wineskin in the smoke, I do not forget your decrees.

Bottles made of animal skin were often hung in tents and other places where they were subject to the deteriorating action of the smoke from cook and camp fires. In some cases, skins of wine were deliberately hung in the smoke to give the wine a peculiar favor. When skin bottles were long exposed to smoke, they became black, hard, and shriveled—good for nothing. That is the sense of the figure of speech in our text-verse.

123:2 WATCHFUL SERVANTS

As the eyes of slaves look to the hand of their master, as the eyes of a maid look to the hand of her mistress, so our eyes look to the LORD our God, till he shows us his mercy.

Servants were not always spoken to when their master wanted something. The wishes of the master were made known by signs, so it became necessary for the servants to watch the hand of the master to ascertain when they are wanted and what is required to them. Clapping of the hands may be used to summon them, and a silent motion of the hand may be all that is used to signal the master's wish. Servants were trained to watch for these signs and to obey them. This custom is undoubtedly alluded to in our text-verse, but there is a stronger force suggested in its special application that should be noted. One commentator paraphrased the passage this way: "As a slave, ordered by a master or mistress to be chastised for a fault, turns his or her imploring eyes to that superior, till the motion of the hand appears that puts an end to the bitterness that is felt, so our eyes are put up to Thee, our God, till Thy hand shall give the signal for putting an end to our sorrows."

129:6 GRASS ON HOUSETOPS

May they be like grass on the roof, which withers before it can grow.

Because of the mud and clay that was often used to build houses in the East, grass would sometimes sprout on the flat plastered roofs of the houses. Roof grass is used as an emblem of speedy destruction, because the grass was weak and would soon wither away under the scorching rays of the sun (see also 2 Kings 19:26 and Isaiah 37:27).

141:5 STRIKING THE HEAD

Let a righteous man strike me—it is a kindness; let him rebuke me—it is oil on my head. My head will not refuse it.

Oil was often used for medicine, both for humans and animals. It was poured on the heads of sheep to kill mites and other parasites, and to protect their thinly-haired heads from the hot sun. Applied to the skin, olive oil had a softening and soothing effect, and could be used for cleansing; it is often used as an ingredient in soap today.

Another ancient Eastern custom was to chastise children, servants, and slaves by striking them on the crown of the head. Some would even beat their slaves on the head with their knuckles. It is said that the ancient Hindus had a figure of speech similar to that used in our text-verse: "Let a holy man smite my head! and what of that? it is an excellent oil." or "My master has been beating my head, but it has been good oil for me." David uses such a figure of speech to denote that he welcomes reproof from the godly lest he be tempted to compromise with evil.

144:12 CARYATIDES

Then our sons in their youth will be like well-nurtured plants, and our daughters will be like pillars *(corner stones, KJV)* carved to adorn a palace.

Some commentators feel that reference is being made here to the *caryatides* or columns representing female figures. These were common in Egyptian architecture, and their appearance was doubtless familiar to the Hebrews. The psalmist wishes the fair daughters of the land to be like pillars that were beautifully sculptured to adorn a palace, thus combining strength with beauty. He desires that they be noted not merely for their loveliness, but also for their moral usefulness, holding up the social fabric as pillars hold up a temple. As one commentator has put it: "This picture of peace and prosperity involved vigorous sons, dependable daughters . . . and God's presence."

150:5 ORGANS

Praise him with tambourine and dancing, praise him with the strings and flute *(organs, KJV)*.

The Hebrew word *uwgab*, rendered organ in the KJV and flute in the NIV, represents one of the most ancient instruments, supposedly invented by Jubal (see Genesis **4:20-21 Use of the Term "Father"**). From Job 21:12 and 30:31, it appears to have been used on festive occasions. In our verse-text it is spoken of as appropriate for use in the worship of God.

Various opinions have been expressed as to the character of this instrument. Some very old authorities believe that the *uwgab* resembled the bagpipe. They say it consisted of two pipes fastened in a leather bag, one above and the other below. Through the upper pipe, which had a mouthpiece, the bag was filled with air, while the lower pipe had holes that were closed or opened with the fingers much like a flute. Air was forced through this bottom pipe by pressure on the bag.

Most authorities, however, identify the *uwgab* with the *syrinx* or *panpipe*, which is undoubtedly a very ancient instrument, and is generally conceded to be the germ of the modern pipe organ. One commentator says that the *syrinx* was the instrument that was meant by the KJV translators when they used the word *organ*, thus relieving them from the charge of obscurity, since that word has changed its meaning since the 17th century. The American Heritage Dictionary defines *panpipe* as: "A primitive wind instrument consisting of a series of pipes or reeds of graduated length bound together, played by blowing across the top open ends. Often used in the plural. Also called mouth organ, Pandean pipe, *syrinx*."

The syrinx or panpipe was used by the Arcadian and other Grecian shepherds, who believed that it was invented by Pan, their tutelary (guardian or protector) god, who they imagined they sometimes heard playing on it on Mount Maenalus. In Greek mythology, Pan was the god of woods, fields, and flocks, and had a human torso and head, and goat's legs, horns, beard, and ears. The syrinx was made of cane, reed, or hemlock. In an old book, the writer described the panpipe this way: "In general, seven hollow stems of these plants were fitted together by means of wax, having been previously cut to the proper length, and adjusted as to form an octave; but sometimes nine were admitted,

giving an equal number of notes. Another refinement in the construction of this instrument, which, however, was rarely practiced, was to arrange the pipes in a curve so as to fit the form of the lip, instead of arranging them in a plane." In the 1800s the instrument was still in use in some parts of what is now called the Middle East.

150:5 Cymbals

Praise him with the clash of *(loud, KJV)* cymbals, praise him with resounding *(high sounding, KJV)* cymbals.

Eunuch playing the cymbals

The ancient cymbals resembled those in use today, consisting of two circular concave plates of brass, or other metal, and producing a clanging sound by being struck against each other.

Two kinds of cymbals are thought to be mentioned in our text-verse, as rendered in the KJV. The *loud cymbals* are believed to correspond to the castanets that are used in Spanish and Latin music. Two of these small cymbals were held in each hand. The *high sounding* cymbals are believed to have been the larger kind that are used today in military bands and symphony orchestras. They were often used in military bands in ancient times, and were also used by the Hebrews in Divine worship as an accompaniment to a chorus of singers (1 Chronicles 15:16 and 25:6, 2 Chronicles 5:13). Paul refers to this instrument in 1 Corinthians 13:1—"If I speak in the tongues of men and of angels, but have not love, I am only a resounding gong or a clanging cymbal."

PROVERBS

9:2 Mɪxᴇᴅ Wɪɴᴇ

She has prepared her meat and mixed *(mingled, KJV)* her wine; she has also set her table.

There is a variety of opinion about what *mixed wine* means. One commentator believes that it means old wine that was drawn from jars where it had become turbid and strong by being mixed with the sediment that normally settled during fermentation (lees). Mixed wine would then mean old or strong wine, and the announcement in our verse-text that she has *mixed her wine* would mean that she has opened the wine for use, because the meal was ready.

Another commentator believes the mixed wine to be strong wine, but made so by mixing in foreign substances. He stated: "Whereas the Greeks and Latins by *mixed wine* always understood wine diluted and lowered with water, the Hebrews, on the contrary, generally meant by the expression that it was wine made stronger and more inebriating by the addition of higher and more powerful ingredients, such as honey, spices, myrrh, mandragora, opiates, and other strong drugs. Or wine inspissated by boiling it down to two thirds or one half its normal quantity."

Still another commentator says that in most, if not all, cases where mixed wine is spoken of, it means wine mingled with water, and he quotes Isaiah 1:22 as an illustration: "Your silver has become dross, your choice wine is diluted with water." But in that verse Isaiah is not speaking of wine that is ordinarily drunk at feasts, but of wine that is deteriorated in quality because of being mixed with water, or as another commentator put it: "adulterated, spoiled by mixing water with it." Through Isaiah, God is saying that His people had become debased, they were like wine mixed with water.

The other passages that speak of mixed wine certainly seem to refer to a drink that is strengthened rather than weakened by that with which it is mixed (see Psalm 75:8, Proverbs 23:30, Song of Songs 8:2, and Isaiah 5:22).

11:21 SHAKING HANDS

Though hand join in hand *(Be sure of this, NIV)*, **the wicked shall not be unpunished (KJV)**

Literally, *hand to hand*, which is an allusion to shaking, or striking, hands to confirm a matter. There is in some Scriptures the sense of a covenant being confirmed (see Ezra 10:19 and Ezekiel 17:18). A more solemn form of expressing faithfulness, amounting, indeed, to an oath is seen in the uplifted hand (see Genesis **14:22 Uplifted Hand**, and Ezekiel 21:14).

Joining, or striking, hands was frequently practiced as a method of pledging security, and is thus referred to in Job 17:3, and Proverbs 6:1, 17:18, and 22:26.

17:19 HIGH GATES

He who loves a quarrel loves sin; he who builds a high gate invites destruction.

In certain areas houses were subject to invasion by marauding bands on horses at any time, and a high gate, or gateway, allowed them to ride into the court area with their horses. To prevent this, gateways were built low enough to make it difficult for a horse and rider to enter. Some went to extremes and built the gateways so low that it was difficult for a person on foot to enter without bending over. Travelers of many years ago reported seeing gateways as low as three feet. In contrast, in Persia a lofty gateway was a sign of royalty, which some of the lesser citizens, out of vanity, imitated as far as they dared. One traveler reported: "The house in which I dwelt in Jerusalem had an arch, or gateway, a few yards from the door, which was so low that a person on horseback could not pass under it. It was evidently built for the sake of security."

The meaning to the text is that he who has a high gate to his house invites the robber by a show of prosperity and by allowing easy entrance. He thus invites destruction.

18:18 THE LOT

Casting the lot settles disputes and keeps strong opponents apart.

Using a lot to settle disputed questions is very ancient, and was practiced by most nations. It was used in almost all the varied affairs of life. Magistrates and priests were appointed by it, and the land of conquered enemies was distributed by it. Casting lots by mixing small stones in a container and then taking one out, or casting lots by some other method, was a popular form of divination used by both pagans and the Hebrew.

For the Hebrews its use was sanctioned by divine authority. The scapegoat was selected by lot (Leviticus 16:8). The inheritances of the tribes in the Promised Land were determined by lot (Numbers 34:13 and Joshua 14:2). The lot was subsequently used on many occasions; here are only a few. The men who attacked Gibeah were selected by lot (Judges 20:9). By lot Jonathan was detected as the violator of Saul's command concerning fasting during the fight with the Philistines (1 Samuel 14:41-42). The positions of the gatekeepers (porters, KJV) in the temple were decided by lot (1 Chronicles 26:13). When Jonah was on the ship and a fierce storm came up, the heathen sailors cast lots to determine who was causing their trouble (Jonah 1:7). See also Joshua 18:6 and Nehemiah 10:34.

In the New Testament we have reference to this same practice. The Roman soldiers divided the garments of Jesus by lot (Matthew 27:35 and Mark 15:24). And by this method Matthias was chosen to fill the place of Judas (Acts 1:23-26).

The Scriptures don't tell us how the lots were cast. One commentator wrote about a method he saw many years ago in the Middle East—several people were involved in the lots: "Little counters of wood, or some other light material, were put into a jar with a neck so narrow that only one could come out a time. After the jar had been filled with water and the contents shaken, the lots were determined by the order in which the bits of wood, representing the several parties, came out with the water. In other cases the pieces of wood were put into a wide, open, jar and drawn out by hand. At other times they were cast somewhat in the manner of dice."

In Church history, one notable user of lots was John Wesley, who often cast lots to decide what God wanted him or someone else to do. In a letter George Whitefield wrote to John Wesley, he twice mentions Wesley's practice of casting lots during their disagreement on the doctrine of election:

"When you were at Bristol, I think you received a letter from a private hand, charging you with not preaching the gospel, because you did not preach election. Upon this you drew a lot: the answer was 'preach and print.' I have not questioned, as I do now, whether in so doing, you did not tempt the Lord. A due exercise of religious prudence, without a lot, would have directed you in this matter. Besides, I never heard that you enquired of God, whether or not election was a gospel doctrine?" . . .

"The morning I sailed from Deal for Gibraltar, you arrived from Georgia [in America]. Instead of giving me an opportunity to converse with you, though the ship was not far off the shore; you drew a lot, and immediately set forwards to London. You left a letter behind you, in which were words to this effect: 'When I saw God, by the wind which was carrying you out, brought me in, I asked counsel of God. His answer you have enclosed.' This was a piece of paper, in which were written these words. 'Let him return to London.'

When I received this, I was somewhat surprised. Here was a good man telling he had cast a lot, and that God would have me return to London. On the other hand, I knew my call was to Georgia, and that I had taken leave of London . . ."

21:9 Living on the Roof

Better to live on a corner of the roof than share a house with a quarrelsome wife *(brawling woman, KJV)*.

It was customary to build arbors or booths on the flat roofs of houses, for the purpose of resting from the heat of the day during the summer, and as places to sleep in the cool air at night. Some believe that Saul slept in a place of this sort, though he may have slept on the open roof (see 1 Samuel 9:25-26). These temporary structures served an excellent purpose during the hot season of the year; most were not intended as permanent structures, and were completely unsuitable for the cold, rainy, season. Yet in the estimation of the writer of this proverb, it's better to live in a cheerless spot like this than in a comfortable house that has a quarrelsome wife in it. No external conveniences can replace the desire and need for internal peace.

25:13 REFRESHING SNOW

Like the coolness of snow at harvest time is a trustworthy messenger to those who send him; he refreshes the spirit of his masters.

Without question this verse doesn't refer to snow in the summer time of harvest, for that would be undesirable, but rather to either cold ice water from the mountain snow, or a cool mountain breeze. The Lebanon Mountains run for approximately 100 miles and rise to an elevation of 10,131 feet. Consequently they normally have snow at their highest elevations, and since much of the snow melts during the summer heat, the waters running down from it into various streams are ice cold. In the same way, winds blowing across the mountain tops and down into the valleys would bring refreshing coolness with them.

26:14 DOOR HINGES

As a door turns on its hinges, so a sluggard turns on his bed.

Most of the door hinges consisted of pivots inserted into sockets both above and below. Regardless of the type of hinges used, the proverb is quite clear: A lazy person is as attached to his bed as a door is to its hinges.

26:25 NUMBER SEVEN

Though his speech is charming, do not believe him, for seven abominations fill his heart.

Hinges

The number seven is used frequently in Scripture, and expresses the idea of completeness or fullness. This text represents the hypocrite as having a heart completely filled with abominations. The Scripture passages where the word seven is used are too numerous to be quoted here. They are scattered all through the Bible, especially in the prophetical books, with the Book of Revelation making the most frequent symbolic use of the word: 55 times in 31 verses. Why the number seven is used to symbolize completeness has as many explanations as there are commentators.

27:22 MORTARS

Though you grind *(bray, KJV)* a fool in a mortar, grinding him like grain *(wheat, KJV)* with a pestle, you will not remove his folly from him.

A *mortar* is a vessel in which substances are crushed or ground with a pestle; a *pestle* is a club-shaped, hand-held tool for grinding or mashing substances in a mortar. Mortars and pestles were used for grinding grain for many centuries, and in some areas in the Middle East they are still used today. Mortars were made of metal, earthenware, wood, or stone, with stone being the most common material. The pestle was usually about five feet long. Sometimes two people would work a mortar at the same time, striking alternately with their pestles. The Israelites used the mortar for crushing the manna they gathered (Numbers 11:8). There is no evidence of punishment being inflicted on anyone in the manner expressed in our text-verse, so it is undoubtedly simply a figure of speech that is used to show that no manner of punishment can remove a fool's folly from him.

Egyptian mortar

ECCLESIASTES

1:2 "Vanity of vanities, all is vanity."

Vanity of vanities, saith the Preacher, vanity of vanities; all is vanity *(KJV)*.

The major theme of Ecclesiastes is the pointlessness of human activity. Like Job, however, the author insists that God's laws must be kept, whether keeping them results in happiness or sorrow. The expression still endures today to point out to many the meaningless of life without God. In this light, the NIV renders this verse as, "Meaningless! Meaningless!" says the Teacher. "Utterly meaningless! Everything is meaningless."

1:5 "The sun also rises."

The sun also ariseth, and the sun goeth down, and hasteth to his place where he arose *(KJV)*.

Ernest Hemingway made the expression, *The Sun Also Rises*, famous when he used it as the title for his first novel, which was published in 1926. The story tells of young people in postwar Paris and their search for values in a world that in many ways has lost its meaning. In this novel that first made his name known, Hemingway captured the disillusionment and cynicism of what Gertrude Stein labeled "the lost generation," referring to those Americans who wandered about Europe after World War I.

1:9 "Nothing new under the sun."

What has been will be again, what has been done will be done again; there is nothing new under the sun.

The author of Ecclesiastes complains frequently in the book

about the monotony of life. His phrase "nothing new under the sun" has come down through the centuries to express that sense of sameness in all that happens.

3:2 "A TIME TO BE BORN AND A TIME TO DIE."

A time to be born and a time to die, a time to plant and a time to uproot.

This expression is still in use today, and still means what the writer was expressing; that is, there is a right moment for all things.

9:8 WHITE CLOTHING

Always be clothed in white, and always anoint your head with oil.

In any area with strong sunlight, white clothing is preferred because white reflects the sunlight and so decreases the heating effect of it. In addition, white garments in the East were symbols of purity, and so were worn on certain special occasions. The symbols and custom were adopted by the West and is reflected especially in the wedding ceremony. The oil was symbolic of joy. Together they signified purity and the joy of festive occasions.

In the Bible there are several references to white garments symbolizing purity, righteousness, or holiness. In Daniel 7:9, the clothing worn by the "Ancient of Days . . . was as white as snow." When Jesus was transfigured, "his clothes became as white as the light" (Matthew 17:2). The angels appeared in white robes when they appeared to the soldiers guarding Jesus' tomb and when the women went to the tomb after He had risen (Matthew 28:3, Mark 16:5, Luke 24:4, and John 20:12), and also when Christ ascended into heaven (Acts 1:10). In the ages to come, the redeemed will be clothed in white (Revelation 7:13 and 19:14).

11:1 "CAST YOUR BREAD UPON THE WATERS."

Cast your bread upon the waters, for after many days you will find it again.

The exact meaning of this expression or where it originated

is unknown. Yet it is a saying that has endured since it was written in the Book of Ecclesiastes, and for centuries has continually called on people, both religious and secular, to act with faith that the benefit of their good deeds will not be lost to them.

SONG OF SONGS

1:5 Tents

Dark am I, yet lovely, O daughters of Jerusalem, dark like the tents of Kedar, like the tent curtains of Solomon.

Tents were among the early habitations of man, though not the earliest, since they apparently were not introduced until the time of Jabal, who was in the seventh generation from Adam (see Genesis 4:20). The first tents were doubtless made of skins, though afterwards, when the process of weaving became known, they were made of cloth of camel's hair, or goat's hair, spun by women. The latter is the material most commonly used by the Arabs, and since the goats were usually black, or a very dark brown, the tents had the same appearance. It was thus in the days of Solomon with the tents made the descendants of the Ishmaelitish Kedar. "Kedar," which means "powerful" in Arabic and "black" in Hebrew, designates the descendants of Ishmael in North Arabia. Individually the tents were not very attractive, but when arranged in the form of a circular encampment, with the animals enclosed by the circle of tents, and usually the leader's tent in the center, they presented a picturesque picture. Balaam was impressed with the beauty of such a scene when he saw the vast encampment of the Israelites and exclaimed: "How beautiful (comely, KJV) are your tents, O Jacob, your dwelling places (thy tabernacles, KJV), O Israel" (Numbers 24:5)!

If ancient tents were made like tents used for centuries by the Arabs, then the tents were usually of various sizes, according to the number in the family or the wealth of the owner. The number of poles to a tent varied from one to nine. Some tents were circular in shape, some square, and others oblong. The covering was spread over the poles, which were fastened into the ground. The edges of the cover had loops made of leather or some other strong material, and to them were fastened the cords of the tent,

Tents

which were sometimes stretched out tight and fastened to the ground by means of iron or wooden pins, or else were fastened to upright posts, on which a curtain was hung around the tent, forming the walls, which could be removed whenever desired without disturbing the rest of the tent. Other cords reached from the top of the tent to the ground, where they were fastened with tent pegs (pins, KJV), thus steadying the entire structure. It was one of these tent pegs that Jael drove with a mallet into the head of Sisera (Judges 4:21). The mallet and tent peg were easily accessible, since pitching a tent was the woman's job.

The tent erected and its cords stretched out are often figuratively spoken of in the Scriptures. Isaiah speaks of God as the one Who "stretches out the heavens like a canopy, and spreads them out like a tent to live in" (Isaiah 40:22). In speaking of the glorious prosperity of the Church and the need of enlargement he says: "Enlarge the place of your tent, stretch your tent curtains wide, do not hold back; lengthen your cords, strengthen your stakes" (Isaiah 54:2). See also Isaiah 33:20.

It's strenuous work to pitch a tent properly, especially a large one, and requires the united effort of willing hands. Hence the pathetic language of Jeremiah in mourning over the desolation of God's people: "My tent is destroyed; all its ropes are snapped. My sons are gone from me and are no more; no one is left now to pitch my tent or to set up my shelter" (Jeremiah 10:20).

The large tents, still assuming they were made like Arab tents, had nine poles, placed in three rows, covering sometimes a space twenty to twenty-five feet long, ten feet wide, and eight to ten feet high in the middle, with the sides sloping. Such tents often had a curtain hung on the middle row of poles, dividing the tent into two parts, one for the men and one for the women. The poles that held up the tent and divided it into sections were further made useful by having hooks driven into them from which were suspended clothes, baskets, saddles, weapons, and various other articles of daily use.

These tents were rapidly taken down and moved from place to place, so that where there was a large encampment today there would be nothing tomorrow but wilderness. Isaiah says: "Like a shepherd's tent my house has been pulled down and taken from me" (Isaiah 38:12). The facility with which tents were taken down and the frailty of their material are beautifully alluded to by Paul in 2 Corinthians 5:1. See also 2 Peter 1:13-14.

In recent centuries tents of cotton, linen, or silk were used in the East for traveling or for holiday purposes. They were of a variety of colors and sometimes quite magnificent. Travelers to that region in the 18th and 19th centuries told of the splendor of state tents that were made for the comfort of Oriental monarchs. Silver, gold, precious stones, silk, velvet, camel's hair cloth, and brocades were all combined to make these structures splendid and costly. The personal tent of Tamerlane, the Mongolian conqueror who led his nomadic hordes from their capital at Samarkand in central Asia to overrun vast areas of Persia, Turkey, Russia, and India, and who lived from 1336-1405, was said to have had poles of solid silver inlaid with gold, curtains of velvet, and ropes of silk. The outside of the personal tent of Nadir Shah, the monarch of Persia, was of fine scarlet broadcloth with a lining of violet-colored satin. On this lining, embroideries in pearls, diamonds, rubies, emeralds, amethysts, and other precious stones were used to illustrate birds, animals, trees, and flowers.

No description is given of Solomon's state tents, as mentioned in our text-verse. But it's probable that Solomon, the luxurious king who spared no expense to gratify his taste, had tents of a magnificence that was commensurate with his royal grandeur. Nebuchadnezzar, the king of Babylon, had a royal canopy (pavilion, KJV), which was undoubtedly a state tent, but no description is given of it (Jeremiah 43:10).

1:7 RESTING SHEEP AT MIDDAY

Tell me, you whom I love, where you graze your flock and where you rest your sheep at midday (noon, KJV).

During the heat of the midday the shepherds customarily led their flocks to some cool and shady spot, where they would recline and rest until late afternoon while the sheep also rested or ate what was available.

1:10 JEWELS AND NECKLACES

Your cheeks are beautiful with earrings *(comely with rows of jewels, KJV)* , your neck with strings of jewels *(chains of gold, KJV).*

Although the NIV uses *earrings* where the KJV uses *row of jewels*, it was a centuries-old fashion in the East for a woman to wear a cord of gold around her forehead, and on that cord hang precious stones of various sorts, which hung down over her checks. Thus she would, indeed, have cheeks that were "comely with rows of jewels."

Neck chains or necklaces were made of gold or other metal, or consisted of strings of pearls, corals, or precious stones. They were sometimes made of solid gold-pieces shaped like a half moon. This is probably what is

3:9-10 ROYAL LITTER

King Solomon made for himself the carriage *(chariot, KJV)*; he made it of wood from Lebanon. Its posts *(pillars, KJV)* he made of silver, its base of gold. Its seat was upholstered with purple, its interior lovingly inlaid by the daughters of Jerusalem.

Assyrian and Egyptian neck chains

referred to in Isaiah 3:18—In that day the Lord will snatch away their finery: the bangles and headbands and crescent necklaces (round tires like the moon, KJV)." These necklaces hung low upon the breast, and were worn both by men and women (see Proverbs 1:9). This was the custom among the Egyptians as well as the Hebrews. Joseph had a gold chain put around his neck by Pharaoh (Genesis 41:42). The Medes, Persians, Babylonians, and other ancient nations, followed the same custom (see Daniel 5:7, 16, and 29). Neck chains or necklaces are also referred to in Song of Songs 4:9 and Ezekiel 16:11.

The Hebrew word *appiryone* that is translated *carriage* or *chariot* refers to a *palanquin*, which is a covered litter that was carried on poles on the shoulders of two or four men, and was formerly used in eastern Asia—it dates far back in antiquity. The same vehicle is referred to by the Hebrew word *tsab* that is translated *wagons* by the NIV and *litters* by the KJV in Isaiah 46:20. The palanquin was made of a light framework of wood covered with cloth. If covered overhead, it normally had a lattice door or window on each side. Two strong poles were fastened to it, which was borne on the shoulders of two or four men. Sometimes, depending on its structure, it was harnessed to horses or camels, one at each end.

Ancient Egyptian litter or palanquin

Litters were often of great magnificence, especially if they belonged to royalty. The woodwork would be richly carved and ornamented with gold, silver, or precious stones. The canopy would be made of silk, satin, or brocade and ornamented with jewels. The palanquin was ordinarily shaped like a couch, and was made so that the traveler could stretch out full length if desired.

Watchmen were not only stationed on the walls of a city to guard against the approach of an enemy (see 2 Samuel **18:26 Watchman and Gatekeeper**), some of them were assigned to patrol the city streets to keep it safe from strangers and wayward citizens (see Psalm 127:1 and Song of Songs 3:3). This is much as it has become today, where almost no city is safe in any nation unless policemen guard its streets at night.

5:7 CITY WATCHMEN

The watchmen found me as they made their rounds in the city. They beat me, they bruised me; they took away my cloak, those watchmen of the walls!

ISAIAH

1:6 Treatment of Wounds

Wounds and welts and open sores, not cleansed *(not been closed, KJV)* or bandaged or soothed with oil.

The Hebrew word *zoor* that is translated *cleansed* in the NIV and *closed* in the KJV means *to press together*. The Hebrews had only a little knowledge of surgery, less than the Egyptians, who were quite competent in some areas. The Hebrews seldom used internal remedies, but trusted mainly in outward applications. Our text-verse in the KJV rendering illustrates the treatment of wounds: they were closed; that is, the lips of the wound were pressed together and bound so that natural sealing of the parts might take place. Dr. John Kitto, writing in 1866, described a typical Eastern treatment of wounds that was current in his day: "There was, and is, no sewing up of wounds in the East; and hence the edges, healing without being perfectly united, make the scar of a wound more conspicuous and disfiguring than with us. The only attempt to produce cohesion is by 'binding up' the wound after the edges have been, as far as possible, 'closed' by simple pressure."

1:8 Shelter in a Vineyard

The Daughter of Zion is left like a shelter in a vineyard, like a hut in a field of melons, like a city under siege.

Since the vineyards and other fields did not always have fences, it was necessary to have someone watch them, especially while the produce were ripening, in order to keep away all predators, whether man, animal, or bird. These "men guarding the field" (keepers of the field, KJV) are referred to in Jeremiah 4:17 and are still used in some Middle East areas today. During the ripening season they watched day and night through all sorts of weather, and so needed some protection from excessive heat, dew, or storms. This protection was provided by temporary huts that were made of closely twined branches and leaves, or of pieces of matting thrown over a rude framework of poles. There is an allusion to such a frail structure in Job 27:18 and in Isaiah 24:20. When the crop was harvested and the field deserted for the season, the temporary hut would often crumble and fall to the ground, leaving a scene of utter desolation and loneliness. It was to such a scene that Isaiah compared the "Daughter of Zion" in our text-verse.

2:4 Plowshares and Pruning Hooks

They will beat their swords into plowshares and their spears into pruning hooks.

In the passage in Joel the expression is reversed: "Beat your plowshares into swords." Commentators are divided as to the meaning of the Hebrew word *ayth*, variously rendering it *plowshares*, *spades*, *hoes*, or *mattocks*. The word refers to instruments capable of stirring up the soil in some way, and since they are capable of being beaten into swords, they would have to be of a nature as to be readily converted by hammering them into shape. It's believed that plowshares were the cutting blade of a plow, which somewhat resembled a short sword, and so might easily have been beaten into one. Conversely, a sword could be readily converted into a plow's cutting blade.

A *pruning hook* today is a long pole with a curved saw blade and usually a clipping mechanism on one end, used especially for pruning small trees. Undoubtedly ancient pruning hooks did not have clipping mechanism, and so probably consisted of a cutting device like a saw or curved knife attached to a long or short pole. See also Joel 3:10 and Micah 4:8.

3:16 Ornaments on Ankles

"The women of Zion are haughty, walking along with outstretched necks, flirting with their eyes, tripping along with mincing steps, with ornaments jingling on their ankles *(tinkling with their feet, KJV)*."

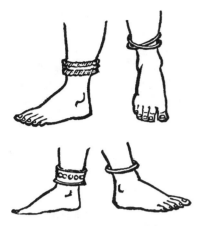

Ancient Egyptian anklets

them, which struck like small clappers. One commentator suggests that it may have been in some such way that the wife of Jeroboam announced her presence: "when Ahijah heard the sound of her feet" (1 Kings 14:6, KJV). The NIV, however, renders that portion of the verse as "the sound of her footsteps," which would mean that it was not the tinkling of anklets that Jeroboam heard.

The ringing or tinkling sound may have been made by striking one anklet upon another, or by bells or other small ornaments attached to the anklets. These anklets were of gold, silver, or iron, according to the taste and means of the wearer, and are still worn by many women in the Middle East, and even some in Western countries who consider anklets fashionable. Some of the anklets were quite heavy and special pains were taken to strike them together, in order to make a jingle. When the anklets were hollow, as often was the case, the sharp sound was increased. In times past, travelers in Egypt and India reported that some of the anklets had small round bells attached to them, and these bells sometimes had little pebbles in

3:18 HEADBANDS AND CRESCENT NECKLACES

In that day the Lord will snatch away their finery: the bangles and headbands and crescent necklaces *(cauls, and round tires like the moon, KJV).*

What is meant by the Hebrew word *shebisim* or *shaw-beece,* which is rendered *headbands* in the NIV and *cauls* in the KJV, is not certain. Strong's dictionary says that the word means *to interweave; a netting for the hair.* Hair nets were anciently worn, as can be seen on Egyptian and Assyrian monuments and from specimens that have been

collected by
museums. A
few
commentators
think that
reference is
made in our
text-verse to
the manner of
dressing the
hair, arranging

Assyrian headbands

it into tresses, and attaching to it
golden ornaments and small
coins, or so braiding it as to
resemble checker-work.

Crescent necklaces, Hebrew
saharonim, were metallic moon-
shaped ornaments hung around
the neck. Similar ornaments
were sometimes hung about the
necks of camels. (See Judges
8:21 Ornaments on Camels.)

3:19 Jewelry and Veils

The earrings *(chains,
KJV)* and bracelets and veils
(mufflers, KJV).

1. *Netiphoth* were probably
pendants, or earrings (See
Genesis **24:22 Earrings, KJV.**)

2. *Sheroth* were probably
bracelets made of gold wire, and
wreathed or woven.

3. *Realoth* were thin veils.
The Hebrew name was given to

them because of their fluttering
motion.

3:26 Sitting on the Ground

The gates of Zion will
lament and mourn; destitute,
she will sit on the ground.

Sitting on the ground was a
position that denoted deep
distress. When Job's friends
came to sympathize with him:
"they sat on the ground with
him for seven days and seven
nights. No one said a word to
him, because they saw how
great his suffering was" (Job
2:13). When the Jew were in
captivity, it's said: "By the
rivers of Babylon we sat and
wept when we remembered
Zion" (Psalm 137:1). Jeremiah
writes about the same custom in
Lamentations 2:10 and 3:28.
The same idea is represented in

a more intensified form in the expressions "roll in ashes" (Jeremiah 6:26) and "roll in the dust" (Micah 1:10).

Most of the Roman coins that were struck in commemoration of the capture of Jerusalem have on one side the figure of a woman sitting on the ground, usually, but not always, sitting in the shade of a palm tree. She generally has one hand to her head, which rests upon it inclining forward, and the other hand hanging over one knee, thus presenting a picture of great grief. On some coins, her hands were tied behind her back. These coins were issued during the reigns of Vespasian, who fought against the Jews in Judea and was Emperor of Rome from A.D. 69 to A. D. 79; Titus, destroyed Jerusalem in A.D. 70 and was Emperor of Rome from A.D. 79 to A.D. 81; Domitian, who was a cruel persecutor of Christians and Emperor of Rome from A.D. 81 to A.D. 96. Some of the coins were struck in Judea and some in Rome. They were of gold, silver, and brass, and give an apt illustration of the custom referred to in our text-verse.

15:2 Shaved Head a Sign of Mourning

Every head is shaved and every beard cut off.

To shave the head or cut off the beard was a sign of mourning, and sometimes humiliation, among the Hebrews and many other nations. See Ezra 9:3; Job 1:20; Isaiah 22:12; Jeremiah 7:29, 16:6, 41:5, 47:5, and 48:37; and Micah 1:16.

16:10 Singing at Work

Joy and gladness are taken away from the orchards; no one sings or shouts in the vineyards; no one treads out wine at the presses, for I have put an end to the shouting.

It was common among the Egyptians to sing at their work. The Hebrews did the same, and were especially jubilant at the time of grape harvesting. They gathered the grapes with acclamations of joy and carried them to the winepress. There they alleviated the labor of treading the grapes with music, singing, and joyous shouts. References are made to the joyful character of the work of harvesting a grape crop in Judges 9:27, Jeremiah 25:30 and 48:33.

18:2 Papyrus Boats

Which sends envoys by sea in papyrus *(bulrushes, KJV)* boats over the water.

The papyrus was used on the Nile for making boats. Sometimes bundles of the plant were rudely bound together in the form of a raft. At other times the leaves were plaited like a basket and then coated with bitumen and tar after the boat was constructed. See Exodus **2:3 Moses' Ark.** Similar boats were used on the Euphrates and Tigris rivers. The boats were circular in shape, and sometimes covered with leather instead of bitumen.

Another style of vessel was also used on the Nile. The leaves of the papyrus or the palm were spread as a floor over rafts made of earthen jars that were tied together by the handles. These jars were made in Upper Egypt and floated down stream by the potters, who sold their wares and walked back to their homes.

On the Euphrates and Tigris the floats were made of inflated skins covered with a flooring of leaves and branches made into wicker work, and having a raised bulwark (side) of the same. These vessels were called *kelleks*, and were of various sizes, from the

Assyrian skinboat

little family boat resting on three or four inflated skins, to great rafts forty feet or more long and proportionately wide. The large ones floated on several hundred inflated skins, and carried an assorted cargo of merchandise and passengers. When the cargo reached its destination the wood frame was sold for fuel, and the skins were carried back by land to be reformed into another vessel. Boats of this description have been used from early historic times, and are referred to by the Greek historian Herodotus and other ancient writers.

19:8 EGYPTIAN FISHING

The fishermen will groan and lament, all who cast hooks *(angle, KJV)* into the Nile; those who throw *(spread, KJV)* nets on the water will pine away.

Reference is made in this "oracle concerning Egypt" (verse 1) to the Egyptian fisheries. The Egyptians consumed enormous quantities of fish, which they obtained from the teeming waters of the Nile, and of the canals that irrigated the land. So important was the traffic in fish that at one time the royal profits from Lake Moeris amounted to a talent of silver a day, which today would probably be close to five-million dollars a year. (Lake Moeris was an ancient lake that was fed by the Nile and once occupied a large area of the al-Fayyum depression in Egypt—it is now represented by the much smaller Lake Qarun.) Large quantities of fish were salted, and many were simply dried in the sun.

Two methods of Egyptian fishing are mentioned in our text-verse:

1. *Chekkah* is rendered *hooks* by the NIV and *angle* by the KJV, which renders it *hook* in Job 41:1. Angling was a favorite pastime with all ranks of Egyptians. Their hooks were of bronze, and were baited with worms or insects. Sometimes a short pole was used and sometimes the fisherman held the line in his hand, much as today.

2. *Mikmoreth* was a *dragnet* and is so rendered by the NIV in Habakkuk 1:15-16, where it is rendered *drag* by the KJV. It was of a lengthened form, having floats along one edge and weights along the other, with a rope at each end. It

corresponded to a modern-day seine (a large fishing net made to hang vertically in the water by weights at the lower edge and floats at the top), and was sometimes cast by hand, the men wading out with it and dragging it back to the shore, bringing the fish with it. At other times a boat was used, the net being cast overboard as the boat was rowed along. Egyptian monuments have a number of illustrations of fishing by nets as well as with hooks.

21:5 OILING SHIELDS

They set the tables, they spread the rugs, they eat, they drink! Get up, you officers, oil *(anoint, KJV)* the shields!

Shields were made of two or more thicknesses of bull hide stretched over a wooden frame, and sometimes strengthened with metallic rims and ornamented in various places with pieces of metal. An occasional rubbing with oil was necessary to keep the leather from drying and cracking, and was often done just prior to a battle. So to "oil the shields" was equivalent to a preparation for battle.

22:6 QUIVERS AND SHIELD CASES

Elam takes up the quiver, with her charioteers and horses; Kir uncovers the shield.

The quivers were commonly carried on an archers back, with the top near the right shoulder so that the arrows could be conveniently drawn, much as is seen today. The quiver usually had two rings, one near the top and the other near the bottom. To these were fastened a strap that the archer slipped over his left arm and head. Occasionally the quiver was thrust through one of the belts that crossed the chest, or was attached to the waist by a belt. In chariots the quivers were attached to the sides of the vehicle. Quivers were probably of wood or leather, and were often highly ornamented (see 2 Kings **13:15 Bows and Arrows**).

When not in use, shields were kept in cases or covers, probably made of leather, to preserve them from drying out and from dust. "Uncover the shield" would be equivalent to a preparation for battle, and has the same meaning as "oil the shields" in verse 22:6.

22:22 KEY ON SHOULDER

I will place on his shoulder the key to the house of David; what he opens no one can shut, and what he shuts no one can open.

The key figuratively depicts the responsibility of a position and the power to make decisions in that position—i.e, to open and close doors. So to place the key on someone's shoulder denotes giving that person the power and responsibility of a certain position. In our text-verse, Shebna, the treasurer of Hezekiah, is warned that Eliakim will carry "the key to the house of David." This is a figurative way of expressing what was already said in the 21st verse: "I will . . . hand your authority over to him."

The idea contained in both these passages is expressed in Isaiah 9:6, where it is said of the Messiah: "the government will be on his shoulders." The word keys is used figuratively again when Jesus says to Peter: "I will give you the keys of the kingdom of heaven; whatever you bind on earth will be bound in heaven, and whatever you loose on earth will be loosed in heaven" (Matthew 16:19).

Matthew 16:18 has caused considerable controversy, but verse 19 has been even more fiercely debated. Nothing in either verse, however, suggests the possibility that Peter or any of the apostles were given authority to forgive sins. The words *bind* and *loose* are rabbinic terms meaning *to forbid* and *to permit*. *Keys* were the symbol of knowledge or the fruit of the scribal or teaching office. This is clearly shown in Luke 11:52

Keys carried on the shoulder

where Jesus says to the lawyers, "Woe to you experts in the law, because you have taken away the key to knowledge." Peter and the apostles were given the "keys of the kingdom"; that is, the gospel of Christ that would loose those who received it and bind those who did not.

The use of those keys—knowledge of the gospel—would build the church. Peter did precisely this at Pentecost (Acts 2:14), at Samaria (Acts 8:14), and for Cornelius the Gentile (Acts 10). Phillip did it at Samaria (Acts 8:5), and Paul did it throughout all of Asia (Acts 19:10). To say that only Peter had the keys to heaven would give the power of salvation to Peter and not to the gospel: "the gospel, . . . is the power of God for the salvation of everyone who believes: first for the Jew, then for the Gentile" (Romans 1:16).

The expressions "will be bound in heaven" and "will be loosed in heaven," as rendered in Matthew 16:19, are examples in Greek of the periphrastic future perfect passive construction and should, therefore, be translated "will have been bound already" and "will have been loosed already" in heaven. In other words, Peter's pronouncement of "binding" or "loosing" is dependent upon what

heaven has already willed, rather than earth's giving direction to heaven. It's illogical and unscriptural to think that heaven is subject to earth and must follow what it directs; earth is always subject to heaven, and only that which heaven has already willed can be done on earth.

For some reason, perhaps lack of courage or bondage to tradition by other Bible translators, only the *New American Standard Bible* renders Matthew 16:19 correctly: "I will give you the keys of the kingdom of heaven; and whatever you bind on earth shall have been bound in heaven, and whatever you loose on earth shall have been loosed in heaven." See Revelation 1:18 and 3:7 for Who truly has the keys.

22:23 WOODEN PEGS

I will drive him like a peg into a firm place; he will be a seat of honor for the house of his father.

The reference here is not to tent pegs that are driven into the ground to hold the tent cords, but to wooden pegs that are driven into the wall to hold clothing and various other items. Eliakim would be as such a peg, but if the people trusted him wholly they would be disappointed, for even the peg in the firm place would eventually be sheared off, and all that hung on it would fall (Isaiah 22:25).

24:13 GRAPE GLEANING

So will it be on the earth and among the nations, as when an olive tree is beaten, or as when gleanings are left after the grape harvest.

The Hebrews were directed not to pick their grapes closely, but to leave a few for the poor. See Leviticus 19:10 and Deuteronomy 24:21. This merciful provision is referred to by Gideon when he says: "Aren't the gleanings of Ephraim's grapes better than the full grape harvest of Abiezer" (Judges 8:2)?

24:22 RESERVED FOR DAY OF TRIUMPH

They will be herded together like prisoners bound in a dungeon; they will be shut up in prison and be punished after many days.

One commentator suggests that there is a reference in this verse to "the custom of kings, who used to confine the chief commanders of their enemies whom they had taken prisoners and reserve them for some extraordinary day of triumph, and then bring them out for public punishment."

25:6 WINES ON THE LEES

A feast of wines on the lees, of fat things full of marrow, of wines on the lees well refined (KJV).

This refers to wines that were kept long in kegs and had the dregs mixed with them, and were therefore old and strong. They were refined or filtered by being strained through a cloth sieve, thus separating the liquor from the lees. Most of their old wine was turbid and required straining before it was fit to drink. The NIV renders this passage as: "a banquet of aged wine—the best of meats and the finest of wines." This rendering presents the thought that the wine was not simply old but deliberately aged until it reached its peak of flavor.

28:27-28 Threshing

Caraway is not threshed with a sledge, nor is a cartwheel rolled over cummin; caraway is beaten out with a rod, and cummin with a stick. Grain must be ground to make bread; so one does not go on threshing it forever. Though he drives the wheels of his threshing cart over it, his horses do not grind it.

The KJV renders the verses this way: "For the fitches are not threshed with a threshing instrument, neither is a cart wheel turned about upon the cummin; but the fitches are beaten out with a staff, and the cummin with a rod. Bread corn is bruised; because he will not ever be threshing it, nor break it with the wheel of his cart, nor bruise it with his horsemen."

Three different methods of threshing are mentioned:

1. With a rod and stick. This was for the small delicate seeds, such as caraway and cummin (or preferred spelling: cumin). They were also used for grain when only a small quantity was to be threshed , or when it was necessary to conceal the operation from an enemy. It was doubtless in this manner that Ruth, when she was in the field of Boaz, "beat out" (KJV) at

Threshing with a sled

evening what she had gleaned during the day (Ruth 2:17). It was probably in the same way that Gideon was "threshing wheat in a winepress to keep it from the Midianites" (Judges 6:11). With a rod or stick he could beat out a little at a time, and conceal it in the tub of the winepress from the hostile Midianites.

2. The Hebrew word *charuwts* is rendered *sledge* by the NIV and *threshing instrument* by the KJV. It can also mean *threshing-sledge*. This was probably a machine in some respects resembling a stone-sledge that was used many years ago by American farmers. One writer describes one that he saw in Beirut, Lebanon, in the mid-1800s: "The frame was composed of thick pieces of plank, turned up in front like our stone-sledge, and perforated with holes underneath for holding the teeth. The teeth consisted of sharp basaltic rock about three inches long, and almost as strong as iron. This machine was drawn over the grain by horses or oxen, and served, together with the trampling of the feet of the animals, to beat out the kernels and cut up the straw preparatory to winnowing." Sometimes the teeth were made of iron.

3. The Hebrew word *agalah*, translated *cartwheel* or *cart*, means *a wheeled vehicle*. It's believed to be the same as the *mowrag*, threshing sledge, in 2 Samuel 24:22, 1 Chronicles 21:23, and Isaiah 41:15, although some commentators say the *mowrag* and the *charuwts* are the same. Some years ago there was what seemed to be a similar instrument in Egypt known as the *mowrej*. It consisted of three or four heavy rollers of wood, iron, or stone, roughly made and joined together in a square frame, which was in the form of a sledge or drag. The rollers were said to be somewhat like large, modern, barrels. They were parallel to each other and had many square-pointed spikes projecting from them. It was used in the same way as the *charuwts*. The driver sat on the machine to increase the weight on the rollers. This instrument or one like it is probably referred to in Proverbs 20:26 where it says: "A wise king winnows out the wicked; he drives the threshing wheel over them."

(Commentators don't agree as to the difference between the *charuwts*, the *agalah*, and the *mowrag*. We have, however, tried as much as possible to harmonize the conflicting opinions.)

Isaiah 37:29 Prisoners Bridled

Because you rage against me and because your insolence has reached my ears, I will put my hook in your nose and my bit in your mouth, and I will make you return by the way you came.

The Assyrians often led their captives by ropes attached to hooks in their noses. In 1843, Botta, Paul-Emile French consul and archaeologist, made a momentous discovery of the palace of the Assyrian king Sargon II at Dur Sharrukin (modern Khorsabad), Iraq. Among sculptures discovered in later diggings on the site, were some depicting prisoners who had iron rings thrust through their lower lips. Cords were attached to these rings so that they could be led or held with ease. See 2 Kings **25:7 Prisoners Blinded—Shackles.** See also 2 Kings 19:28, and Ezekiel 29:4 and 38:8.

40:3-4 Preparing the Way of the King

A voice of one calling: "In the desert prepare the way for the LORD ; make straight in the wilderness a highway for our God. Every valley shall be raised up, every mountain and hill made low; the rough ground shall become level, the rugged places a plain.

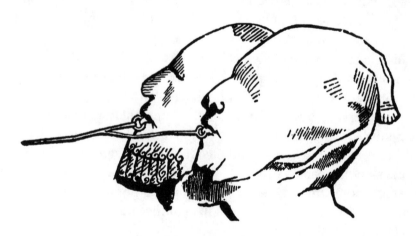

Male prisoners bridled

It's been the custom for centuries for Eastern monarchs who are traveling through their domain to send men before them to prepare their way by removing stones (see Isaiah 62:10), leveling rough places, filling up hollows, cleaning up trash and litter, and generally making the road pleasant and easy for the distinguished travelers and their guests. One of the stories told about the semilegendary Queen Sammu-ramat (Semiramis of Greek legend, and mother of king Adad-nirari III, who reigned from 810 to 783), is that on one of her journeys she came to a rough, mountainous, region, and ordered the hills leveled and the hollows filled, which was done at enormous cost. Her object was not only to shorten her way, but to leave to posterity a lasting monument to herself. Since her time there have been other instances of similar character, but none involving so much labor and expense.

In Matthew 3:3, Mark 1:3, Luke 3:4, and John 1:23, this passage is applied to John the Baptist who, as a herald, preceded the Messiah to announce His coming and prepare the way for Him (see Malachi 3:1).

42:3 LAMP WICKS

A bruised reed he will not break, and a smoldering wick *(flax, KJV)* he will not snuff out.

Lamp wicks were made of linen, and the allusion is to a wick that is burning with feeble flame from lack of oil and is about to expire. The ease with which the flame of such a wick can be put out is referred to in Isaiah 43:17—"they lay there, never to rise again, extinguished, snuffed out like a wick." The Hebrew word *pishtah* that the KJV renders as *tow* in this verse is the same word that it renders as *flax* in our text-verse.

44:10 MAKING IDOLS

Who shapes a god and casts *(molten, KJV)* an idol, which can profit him nothing?

The term cast or molten, as it is in the KJV, doesn't mean that the entire idol was cast of solid metal. They may have been made that way sometimes, especially small ones, but usually the metallic part of idols was a thin plating of metal on a wood frame. (See Exodus **32:4 Metallic Idols**), Thus the carpenter and the goldsmith worked together. See Isaiah 40:19 and 41:7, and Jeremiah 10:3-4.

The work of the carpenter was to take a rude log and form it into an image ready to receive the metallic plates. This is aptly described in Isaiah 44:13—"The carpenter measures with a line and makes an outline with a marker; he roughs it out with chisels and marks it with compasses. He shapes it in the form of man, of man in all his glory, that it may dwell in a shrine." In a book titled, *Travels in Egypt*, written in the early 1800s, the writer described an idol that he saw: "On one of the columns of the portico of Tentyra [the modern town of Dandarah, on the west bank of the Nile in Upper Egypt, is built on the ancient site of Ta-ynt-netert (She of Divine Pillar), or *Tentyra*]. It was covered with stucco and painted. The stucco being partly scaled off, gave me the opportunity of discovering *lines traced* as if with *red chalk*. Curiosity prompted me to take away the whole of the stucco, and I found the form of the figure sketched, with corrections

of the outline. It was separated into twenty-two parts, with the separation of the thighs being in the middle of the whole height of the figure, and the head comprising rather less than a seventh part."

It was some such plan, probably, that idols were made in the time of Isaiah. Once made, the wood image could be worshiped as it was, or it could be covered with plaster or metal. Sometimes, however, the metallic outside did not always cover wood, but was filled with clay, as were some of those made in India in recent centuries.

46:1 NEBO

Bel bows down, Nebo stoops low; their idols are borne by beasts of burden.

When used as a proper name, *Bel* refers to *Marduk*, the supreme deity of Babylon. Like the Hebrew "Baal," "Bel" is the generic name for any god. Babylonian mythology presents him as the spokesman of the gods and the son of Marduk. Even as there were many Baals, so there were many Bels, many ancient nations having their own, slightly different from that of other nations.

Nebo comes from the same root as the Hebrew word for prophet. His non-Hebrew name was Nabu. He was considered to be the god of learning and a major god in the Assyro-Babylonian pantheon. He was patron of the art of writing and a god of vegetation. Nebo's symbols were the clay tablet and the stylus, the instruments deemed proper to him who inscribed the fates assigned to men by the gods.

Nebo—statue in British Museum

The worship of Nebo is denounced in our text-verse, and he and Bel are presented as so powerless that they must be carried on the backs of beasts of burden, thus figuratively denoting that they are useless and a burden to the people.

The popularity of Nebo can be seen in the combination of his name with the names of ancient kings: for example, *Nebu*chadnezzar, *Nebu*zaradan, *Nebu*hashban, *Nabo*nedus, *Nabo*nassar, *Nabu*rianus, *Nabo*nabus, *Nabo*polassar. Several statues of Nebo were found at Nimrud, an ancient city of Assyria south of present-day Mosul, Iraq. In 1862 a block of black basalt was found that had on it an inscription of six hundred and twenty lines, divided into ten columns. In this inscription reference is made by the author, King Nebuchadnezzar, to Nebo, about whom he says: "Nebo, the guardian of the hosts of heaven and earth, has committed to me the scepter of justice to govern men."

The expressions "bows down" and "stoops low" evidently refer to the downfall of these idols and the system of idolatry that they symbolized. According to the prophecy this was to be accomplished by Persian power. Although the Persians worshiped the sun, moon, earth, etc., images of gods were unknown to them. Herodotus, the Greek historian, says of them: "They have no images of the gods, no temples no altars, and consider the use of them a sign of folly." Thus it was in perfect agreement with their own customs that the Persians destroyed the graven images of other nations. In Isaiah 45:1, the work of destruction is assigned to the Persian monarch Cyprus.

47:13 ASTROLOGERS

Let your astrologers come forward, those stargazers who make predictions month by month, let them save you from what is coming upon you.

Efforts to foretell future events by watching the motions of the heavenly bodies are very ancient. The ancient Babylonians and Chaldeans were especially celebrated for their attempts in this direction (see Daniel 2:2). In Chaldea the astrologers formed a particular caste, in which the knowledge acquired was transmitted from father to son.

They taught that the universe was eternal, that a divine providence ruled over it, and that the movements of the heavenly bodies were directed according to the council of the gods. Their long observations had made them more competent than other men to calculate the movements and influence of the stars. From the rising and setting of the planets, their orbits and color, they predicted storms, heat, rain, comets, eclipses, and earthquakes. And from the varied appearances of the heavens they foretold events that not only affected lands and nations, but also brought happiness or unhappiness to kings and common people.

To assist them in making calculations from the stars, the astrologers divided the heavens, visible and invisible, into twelve equal parts, six above the horizon and six below. These they called *houses*, and the various subjects that affect the happiness of human beings, such as fortune, marriage, life, death, religion, etc., were distributed among them. From the position of the stars in these houses the calculations were made.

But in the passages before and after our text-verse, God says that all their predictions and so-called abilities to determine human destiny and successful activities are useless: "Surely they are like stubble; the fire will burn them up. They cannot even save themselves from the power of the flame." The blind leading the blind.

57:6 STONE WORSHIP

The idols among the smooth stones of the ravines are your portion; they, they are your lot. Yes, to them you have poured out drink offerings and offered grain offerings.

Worship of stone pillars is an ancient practice, and one to which many nations and peoples were devoted. Some commentators have said that when Jacob anointed the stone at Bethel he was practicing stone worship, but there is no direct scriptural evidence of that, and God never rebuked him for doing so. Worship of stones is referred to in Deuteronomy 7:5 and 12:3, and in many passages where the word *images* is used. (In those passages, the KJV says: "break down their images," but the NIV renders it: "smash their sacred stones.") It's probable also that the allusion to the rock of the heathens in Deuteronomy 32:33 and 37 is a reference to the same kind of idolatry. The "image, which fell from heaven" (Acts 19:35) that was worshiped by the Ephesians is undoubtedly another instance of stone worship.

The ancient custom was to anoint stones that were worshiped, and to present offerings to them. One ancient writer said of a superstitious person: "a worshiper of every shining stone." Arnobius the Elder, an early 4th century Christian convert who defended Christianity by demonstrating to the pagans their own inconsistencies, wrote that when he was a pagan he never saw an oiled stone without addressing it and praying to it.

60:11 OPEN GATES

Your gates will always stand open, they will never be shut, day or night.

The gates of walled cities were shut at sundown, or shortly thereafter, but always before dark. Travelers nearing cities would hurry as they saw the shadows lengthening so that they would reach the city before the gates closed. If they did not make it in time they were exposed to whatever came along, robbers or storms. Isaiah speaks of the coming Church of Christ as always having her gates open. This was in marked contrast to the custom that the people of his time were used to. Surely they must have wondered what city the prophet was writing about.

A similar illustration is given by the apostle John in his beautiful description of New Jerusalem: "On no day will its gates ever be shut, for there will be no night there" (Revelation 21:25). Endless day, endless shelter, endless entrance into the never-ending city of God.

JEREMIAH

2:37 Hands on the Head

You will also leave that place with your hands on your head, for the LORD has rejected those you trust; you will not be helped by them.

Hands on the head

This is a way of expressing great grief, and is thought by some commentators to signify that the heavy hand of God's affliction is pressing on the mourner. This was one of the tokens of mourning adopted by Tamar after the cruel maltreatment she received from Amnon: "She put her hand on her head and went away, weeping aloud as she went" (2 Samuel 13:19). An excavated Egyptian sculpture showed mourners at a funeral with their hands on their heads. This was a common way of expressing grief in Egypt. Said one commentator about a similar custom in a Middle East nation: "When people were in great distress, they put their hands on their head, the fingers being clasped on the top of the crown. Should a man who is plunged into despair meet a friend, he would immediately put his hands on his head to illustrate his circumstances. When a person heard of the death of a relation or friend he forthwith clasped his hands and placed them on his head. When young boys were punished at school they would run home with their hands on their heads."

6:29 BELLOWS

The bellows blow fiercely to burn away the lead with fire.

Ancient bellows consisted of a leather bag in a wooden frame, with a long mouthpiece of reed tipped with metal to preserve it from the heat of the fire. The operator stood with a bellows under each foot. In each hand, attached to the instrument under the foot, was a cord by which he

Egyptian bellows

lifted the top side of the bag of skin when it was emptied of air by the pressure of his foot.

8:22 "IS THERE NO BALM IN GILEAD?"

Is there no balm in Gilead? Is there no physician there? Why then is there no healing for the wound of my people?

Balm is a soothing, healing, or comforting agent or quality. "Balm in Gilead" refers to various resins used for healing and was available only a few miles away in Gilead, which was famous for the healing properties

The Balm of Gilead

of the fragrant ointments made from its balsam plants and trees. The expression was used to mean that God's help was near, but the people had refused it. Today the expression is sometimes used to mean there appears to be no healing or comforting to be found anywhere. It's an expression of near hopelessness and despair.

9:17-18 HIRED MOURNERS

This is what the LORD Almighty says: "Consider now! Call for the wailing women to come; send for the most skillful of them. Let them come quickly and wail over us till our eyes overflow with tears and water streams from our eyelids.

For long centuries it was the custom in the East to not only mourn the lost of a loved one with great lamentations, but, if the family could afford it, to also hire professional mourners. They would range from a few to a great number, depending on the family's finances. Each group of mourners would try to outdo other similar groups in their display of agonized bereavement. They would tear their clothes and throw ashes and dirt upon themselves, sing in a sort of chorus mingled with shrill screams and loud wailing, and distort their bodies in various ways to show the uncontrollable depth of their anguish. Swaying back and forth in a kind of melancholy dance to the thrumming music of tambourines, they would recount the virtues of the deceased, calling him or her by terms of tenderest endearment, and plaintively ask of him why he left his family and friends. With wonderful ingenuity these hired mourners would seek to make a genuine lamentation among the visitors who came to the funeral, pointing out those among them who had also suffered the lost of a loved one and the agony and suffering they felt, thus eliciting cries of true grief from those who are sorrowing.

It is to this custom that Jeremiah alludes in our text-verse, and also in the verse 20: "Teach your daughters how to wail; teach one another a lament." Hired mourners were present at the burial of good king Josiah (2 Chronicles

35:25), and Solomon refers to such mourners in Ecclesiastes 12:5—"mourners go about the streets." Amos also speaks of them: "There will be wailing in all the streets and cries of anguish in every public square. The farmers will be summoned to weep and the mourners to wail (Amos 5:16). Hired mourners were present with their instruments, which were specially designed for the mournful song of funeral dirges, at the house of Jairus after the death of his daughter (Matthew 9:23 and Mark 5:38).

Egyptian potter

18:3 POTTER

So I went down to the potter's house, and I saw him working at the wheel.

The potter's art has been practiced from very ancient times. Egyptian monuments show that it was known in Egypt before the Hebrews moved into that country. Some expositors have inferred from Psalm 81:6 that the Israelites were used in pottery as well as brick making while they were in bondage: He says, "I removed the burden from their shoulders; their hands were set free from the basket (pots, KJV)." Other expositors, and interpreters, give to the Hebrew word *duwd* the meaning of *basket*, as shown in the NIV, and thus make it refer to the baskets that the brick makers used to carry clay.

The clay was first trodden with the feet by the potter (Isaiah 41:25), and when it was the proper consistency he put it on the wheels. There were usually two stone wheels, one above the other, like a pair of millstones. The softened clay was put upon the upper wheel and fashioned by the potter's hands. On some of the devices the lower stone was immovable, and the upper revolved on an axis that was turned by the potter by means of a treadle and sometimes by an attendant. On other devices the lower stone was larger and was turned by the potter's feet; as it turned it rotated the upper wheel where the clay was worked. In later times the wheels were made of wood, which made them lighter and easier to turn.

31:19 STRIKING THE THIGH

After I strayed, I repented; after I came to understand, I beat my breast *(thigh, KJV)*.

Although the NIV renders the Hebrew word *yarek* as *breast*, it has no such meaning in *Strong's Exhaustive Concordance*. There it states that the word is from an unused root meaning *to be soft; the thigh* (from its fleshy softness), and by euphemism to mean *the generative parts*; that is, the sexual organs, as it is so used in other Scriptures.

Striking the thigh was a method the Jews used to express deep sorrow in time of mourning. Ezekiel was commanded to act in a similar manner as a significant way of expressing the sorrow that was to come on rebellious Israel (Ezekiel 21:12). For many

centuries the Greeks and Persians had a similar custom, as did many parts of the East.

34:18 CUTTING THE COVENANT

I will treat like the calf they cut in two *(twain, KJV)* and then walked between its pieces.

This method of making a covenant dates back to the first covenant recorded in the Bible, the one between God and Abraham (Genesis 15:10). The two contracting parties killed an animal, cut the body in two, and passed between the parts. Some commentators believe that the design was to symbolize a curse that if the covenant should be broken, the same fate would befall the party who violated it as befell the animal. But normally the curses of the covenant were spoken and not symbolized. Other commentators think that the design was intended to symbolize that as the divided parts belonged to one animal, so the parties making the covenant were of one mind and heart regarding the covenant.

This way of making a covenant is referred to in the Hebrew word used to express making a covenant. The Hebrew word *karath* rendered *make* by most translations (see Genesis 31:44) actually means *cut*, and if so rendered would make clear that most of the covenants in the Old Testament were blood covenants.

46:22 Heavy Axes

They will come against her with axes, like men who cut down trees.

The Hebrew word *qardom*, here translated axes, was given to an axe that seems to have been used especially to cut down trees, and is believed to have had a heavier head that was especially designed for that purpose. It's also mentioned in Judges 9:48, 1 Samuel 13:20, and Psalm 74:5.

46:25 Ammon

The LORD Almighty, the God of Israel, says: "I am about to bring punishment on Amon god of Thebes *(multitude of No, KJV)*, on Pharaoh, on Egypt and her gods and her kings, and on those who rely on Pharaoh.

Most commentators now agree that the Hebrew word *amon*, rendered in the KJV as *multitude*, is a proper name and should be left untranslated. The original is *amon minno*; that is, *Amon of No*. By No is undoubtedly meant the celebrated Egyptian city of Thebes, which was situated on both sides of the Nile, and was noted for its hundred gates of bronze, and its numerous and splendid temples, obelisks, and statues. Amon was the name of an Egyptian deity, and probably of a Libyan and

Amon

Ethiopian god, whose worship had its seat in Thebes, where there was a shrine dedicated to it.

For this reason the names of the city and the god were joined. This is so in our text-verse and in Nahum 3:8. In that verse the NIV renders *No Amon* as *Thebes* and the KJV renders it as *populous No*. The name *No Amon* in Egyptian meant *City of (the god) Amun*. The ancient Egyptians also called the city *Waset*, but the Greeks called it Thebes. The Greeks likened this god to Zeus, and the Romans called him *Jupiter Ammon* or *Hammon*. He appears to have been a personification of the sun, and is thought by some to have corresponded to Baal of the Phoenicians.

At one time it was believed that Amon was represented by the figure of a man with a ram's head, but this is no longer in vogue. In 1837, J. G. Wilkinson wrote in his book, *Manners and Customs of the Ancient Egyptians*, "The figure of *Amun* was that of a man, with a head-dress surmounted by two long feathers; the color of his body was light blue, like the Indian *Vishnoo*, as if to indicate his peculiarly exalted and heavenly nature. But he was not figured with the head or under the form of a ram as the Greeks and Romans supposed."

50:15 Sign of Submission

She surrenders *(hath given her hand, KJV)*, her towers fall, her walls are torn down.

As rendered in the KJV this is an expression denoting submission or surrender, and perhaps has relation to the custom of giving the hand in pledge of a covenant. There are several Scriptures where the expression is alluded to or used. Lamentations 5:6—"We have given the hand (submitted, NIV) to the Egyptians, and to the Assyrians, to be satisfied with bread" (KJV). See also 1 Chronicles 29:24 and 2 Chronicles 30:8. In the latter, "yield yourselves unto the LORD," as so rendered in the KJV, is literally *give the hand to Jehovah*.

60:20 Battle Axes

"You are my war club *(battle axes, KJV)*, my weapon for battle— with you I shatter nations, with you I destroy kingdoms."

The Hebrew word *mappets*, rendered war club in the NIV and

battle axes in the KJV, is said by one commentator to be "a mallet, a maul, a battle ax," and he makes it identical with *mephiyts*, which in Proverbs 25:18 is rendered *maul* by the KJV and *club* by the NIV. But others believe that a heavy bladed instrument, fit for violent battle, is meant. The Egyptian battle-ax was from two to two and a half feet long, with a single blade that was secured to the handle by bronze pins; the handle at that point was wrapped with a leather cord to keep the wood from splitting. A soldier on a march either held the axe in his hand, or hung it on his back with the blade down. The blade on some was shaped like a half circle, often divided at the back into two smaller segments whose points were fastened to the handle by pins. The blade was made of either bronze or steel. Another kind of battle-axe was about three feet in length, and had a large metal ball at the end, to which the blade was fixed. Either of these weapons was terrible because of the combination of weight and sharpness. See note at Deuteronomy **19:5 Axes.**

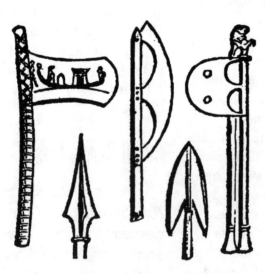

Egyptian battle axes

many places in Africa, prisoners, both Christian and secular, were often hung by their hands as punishment, while others were left that way to die. In some areas that is still being done.

LAMENTATIONS

5:12 Hung by the Hands

Princes have been hung up by their hands; elders are shown no respect.

Whether this hanging by the hands took place before or after execution is not known. One noted commentator says after the execution as a means of adding indignity to the person. Others say that hanging prisoners by the hands was either a form of torture or an extended means of execution. Such things are not unknown even in our day. It was customary for the communists to so treat persecuted Christians in the former Soviet Union, for North Koreans to so treat prisoners during the Korean War, and for the North Vietnamese to so do during the Vietnam War. During the turbulent years in

EZEKIEL

2:9-10 WRITING ON BOTH SIDES

In it was a scroll *(roll of a book, KJV)*, which he unrolled before me. On both sides of it were written words of lament and mourning and woe.

Scrolls were usually written on only one side—rarely both sides. The scroll given to Ezekiel, however, was written on both sides, thus indicating the extensiveness of the troubles that were to come upon the children of Israel. Something like this is meant in Revelation 5:1.

4:1 RECORDS ON POTTERY

"Now, son of man, take a clay tablet *(tile, KJV)*, put it in front of you and draw the city of Jerusalem on it."

Assyrian and Babylonian records were kept not only on sculptured slabs of stone, but also on pottery. There were so-called cylinders, some barrel-shaped, and some hexagonal or octagonal. They were made of very fine, thin, and strong terra-cotta, and were hollow. They were from a foot and a half to three feet high, and were closely covered with cuneiform writing, which was often in such small characters as to require the aid of a magnifying glass to decipher it. These cylinders were placed at the corners of the temples, where many of them were discovered during archeological excavations. They were written in columns, and usually contained histories of the monarchs who reigned when the temples were built.

In addition to these, clay tablets of various sizes were used, from nine inches by six to one inch by one and a half. These were entirely covered with writing and pictorial representations. It was on such a tile that Ezekiel was directed to make a drawing of Jerusalem. The characters were put into the clay when it was in a soft, moist state, sometimes by a stamp, but usually by a sharp edged bronze *style* about a foot long, which was used like a modern pen to trace each character by hand. After the drawings were completed the clay was baked, and so perfect was the entire production that some of the tablets have lasted for over three thousand years.

The tablets often varied in color, perhaps from being left in the kiln for different lengths of time, or because coloring was added to the clay. Among those found there have been some that were bright brown, pale yellow, pink, red, and some nearly black. Usually the cylinders are a pale yellow and the tablets a light red or pink, which may have been properties of the clay that was used. Some of the tablets are unglazed and others are coated with a hard white enamel.

4:2 Ramps, Siege Works, Rams

Then lay siege to it: Erect siege works against it *(build a fort, KJV)*, build a ramp up to it *(cast a mount against it, KJV)*, set up camps against it and put battering rams around it.

Several important operations in ancient sieges are here mentioned:

1. The ramp was an inclined plane that the besiegers of a castle or a walled town built up to the walls so that they could bring their war machines closer and work at a better angle. The ramp was made of all sorts of materials:

Assault on a city—artificial mount

Battering rams

earth, timber, bricks, and stones, with the sides usually being walled up with brick or stone and the inclined top made of layers of brick or stone or rows of timber, thus forming a strong road for the machines. Some of these machines are described in 2 Chronicles **26:15 War Machines**. Ramps were used by the Assyrians, Babylonians, Egyptians, Jews, and Greeks, and the KJV often refers to them in the Old Testament under the name of *banks, bulwarks,* or *mounts.* The NIV refers to them as siege *ramps* or just plain *ramps.* See Deuteronomy 20:20; 2 Samuel 20:15; 2 Kings 19:32; Isaiah 37:33; Jeremiah 6:6 and 33:4; and Ezekiel 17:17.

2. The Hebrew word *dayeq,* rendered *forts* by the KJV and *siege works* by the NIV, were undoubtedly much like trenches and watch towers of modern times. At the area of the attack, dirt would be piled high to protect the soldiers while they prepared attacks, and towers would be erected for the purpose of watching the enemy and harassing them. If arrows were used, they would often be shot from such towers because of the advantage of height. See also 2 Kings 25:1, Jeremiah 53:4, Ezekiel 17:17, 21:22, and 26:8.

3. The battering ram is believed to have been first used by the Phoenicians. It consisted of a heavy beam of wood strengthened with iron plates, and terminating in an iron head made like that of a ram or a spear point. Suspended from wooden framework by ropes or chains, the beam was swung back and forth by the soldiers, thus slamming it continually into

the wall until a breach was made. The Assyrian armies were abundantly supplied with similar engines of war, though they were made somewhat differently. It's to these that Ezekiel refers in our text-verse. See also Ezekiel 21:22 and 26:9—in the latter verse the KJV refers to them as engines of war.

8:16 POSTURE IN HEATHEN WORSHIP

With their backs toward the temple of the LORD and their faces toward the east, they were bowing down to the sun in the east.

This showed that they were sun worshipers. Worship of the stars and planets was highly developed in Babylon. The 25 men Ezekiel saw were probably priests or Levites who were worshiping Shamash, the Babylonian sun-god, at the very entrance of the temple. They had turned their backs on the inner part of the temple of the living God and were standing in the entrance, looking toward the East, and worshiping false gods.

9:2 INKHORN

With them was a man clothed in linen who had a writing kit *(writer's inkhorn, KJV)* **at his side.**

If like inkhorns of recent antiquity, the writing kit or inkhorn consisted of two parts, a receptacle for the pens and a box for the ink. Sometimes it was made of ebony or some other hard wood, but generally of metal: bronze, copper, or silver; often highly polished and of exquisite workmanship. It was about nine or ten inches long, one and a half or two inches wide, and about half an inch deep. The hollow shaft contained pens of reed and a penknife and had a lid. The inkhorn was usually carried in the belt or suspended by cords.

Inkhorn

21:14 STRIKING HANDS TOGETHER

"So then, son of man, prophesy and strike *(smite, KJV)* your hands together."

Several different emotions seem to have been represented by striking the hands together.

1. It was sometimes a sign of *contempt*. Of the wicked rich man Job said: "It (Men, KJV) claps its hands in derision and hisses him out of his place." Jeremiah represents Jerusalem as so desolate that all those passing by clap their hands at her (Jeremiah 2:15).

2. It was sometimes a sign of *anger* or *judgment*. When Balaam blessed Israel instead of cursing them, "Then Balak's anger burned against Balaam. He struck his hands together" (Numbers 24:10). So when the LORD saw the wickedness of Israel, his anger and judgment are expressed in these words: "I will surely strike my hands together at the unjust gain you have made and at the blood you have shed in your midst" (Ezekiel 22:13).

3. It was sometimes a sign of *sorrow*. The LORD commanded Ezekiel to strike his hands together in sorrow for the idolatry of Israel (Ezekiel 6:11).

4. It was sometimes a sign of *triumph*. In this manner the Ammonites rejoiced over fallen Israel. God said: "you have clapped your hands and stamped your feet, rejoicing with all the malice of your heart against the land of Israel" (Ezekiel 25:6). In this verse, clapping the hands is associated with stamping the feet, as it was in the previous verse.

23:12 ASSYRIAN GARMENTS

She too lusted after the Assyrians—governors and commanders, warriors in full dress *(clothed most gloriously, KJV)*, mounted horsemen, all handsome young men.

The Assyrians were famous for their rich and costly clothing. The expression *Assyrian garments* became synonymous with elegant and expensive clothing. One commentator wrote: "The robes of the Assyrians were generally ample and flowing, but differed in form from those of the Egyptians and the Persians. They consisted of tunics or robes varying in length, in mantles of diverse shapes, of long-fringed scarves and of embroidered belts. Ornaments were scattered with profusion over these outer garments, some of which appear to have been emblematic of certain dignities or employments." Figures sculptured on Assyrian marbles attest to the truth of this description.

Assyrian fringed dress

valuable articles that belonged to the temple. See 1 Chronicles 9:26, 2 Chronicles 31:11, and Nehemiah 10:38.

DANIEL

1:2 TEMPLE TREASURES

These he carried off to the temple of his god in Babylonia and put in the treasure house of his god.

It was customary in every heathen temple to have a particular place for storing sacred jewels and other valuables that were supposed to be the special property of the idol that was worshiped. When Nebuchadnezzar brought from Jerusalem the sacred vessels of the temple, he placed them in the temple of Belus at Babylon, side by side with the costly ornaments and utensils that were appropriated for idolatrous worship. In the temple at Jerusalem there were also rooms specially set apart for the reception of tithes and storage of

1:5 BABYLONIAN MANNER OF LIVING

The king assigned them a daily amount of food and wine from the king's table.

This would have been a luxurious manner of living for these Hebrew boys, quite in contrast to what they had been accustomed to, and to the extremely plain diet that Daniel requested for himself and his companions. The Babylonian kings and nobles were noted for their high living. Their tables were loaded with wheat breads, meats in great variety and luscious fruits. The usual beverage was wine of the best varieties, and most of them were fond of drinking to excess. The ancient Persian kings followed the custom of the Babylonian monarchs, and fed their attendants from their own tables.

2:5 PUNISHMENT OF CRIMINALS

I will have you cut into pieces and your houses turned into piles of rubble.

Cutting into pieces was a punishment common to many ancient nations. It was known to the Hebrews, and was inflicted by the prophet Samuel upon Agag, king of the Amalekites (1 Samuel 15:32).

According to Babylonian customs, the house in which the criminal lived was usually destroyed, and the land upon which his house stood was cursed forever and could never be used again. The custom was also known to the Persians—see the decree of Darius in Ezra 6:11. It was likewise practiced in Athens in later years. There were many spots in the midst of that populous city that were kept perpetually vacant because of a decree similar to that referred to in the text.

At the present time in Sudan, a Muslim nation, the houses of Christians are habitually marked for destruction. "More than 1.2 million Christians—men, women, and children—living in the capital city of Khartoum have had their homes destroyed by the Muslim government—since 1992, 250,000 homes have been bulldozed" (*The New Foxes Book of Martyrs*, 1997).

3:6 BURNING ALIVE

"Whoever does not fall down and worship will immediately be thrown into a blazing furnace."

Burning alive was an ancient punishment among the Babylonians, and possibly among other nations. Jeremiah mentions two false prophets who were put to death in this manner (Jeremiah 29:22).

In recent years in Africa, many of the black Africans who worked for the apartheid white government and treated their own people cruelly were punished by being burned alive. In most cases a car tire would be put around the victim's neck, and he would then be dowsed with gasoline and set on fire.

6:10 TIME OF PRAYER

He went home to his upstairs room where the windows opened toward Jerusalem. Three times a day

Burning alive

he got down on his knees and prayed, giving thanks to his God, just as he had done before.

First note that Daniel did not look toward the sun as the sun worshiper did (see note at Ezekiel **8:16 Posture in Heathen Worship**), but toward Jerusalem where the temple of the LORD stood. This seems to have been a custom among the Jews when they were away from the Holy City (see 1 Kings 8:44, 48; 2 Chronicles 6:34; Psalm 5:7, 28:2, and 138:2; and Jonah 2:4).

There was no law in Israel as to when prayers were to be said. The morning and evening sacrifice would naturally be suggested to the mind of a pious Jew as suitable times for prayer. To this might easily be added a time midway. This appears to have been the case with David, who said: "Evening, morning and noon I cry out in distress, and he hears my voice" (Psalm 55:17). The order in which these three seasons are named by the psalmist seems to indicate the origin of the custom as just suggested. In our text-verse Daniel is said to have prayed three times a day. From Daniel 9:21, it appears that one of these

times of prayers was at the time of the evening sacrifice. Compare Acts 2:15, 3:1, and 10:9.

6:15 COURT ETIQUETTE AND IRREVERSIBLE EDICTS

"Remember, O king, that according to the law of the Medes and Persians no decree or edict that the king issues can be changed."

First note that in our text-verse the expression "Medes and Persians" is used, the Medes being named first because Darius was a Mede. In Esther 1:19, however, the expression is "Persians and Medes," Persians being named first because Ahasuerus was a Persian.

The strict etiquette of the Persian court obliged the king never to revoke an order once given, however much he might regret it, because in so doing he would contradict himself, and, according to Persian notions, the law could not contradict itself.

A curious instance of the unchangeable character of the Medo-Persian law is seen in the fact that after Ahasuerus had issued the order directing the cruel slaughter of the Jews (Esther 3:13), he would not reverse it even at the urgent request of his queen (Esther 8:5). Instead, he issued another edict in which he granted the Jews permission to "to assemble and protect themselves; to destroy, kill and annihilate any armed force of any nationality or province that might attack them and their women and children (Esther 8:11). Thus the first irreversible edict was completely neutralized by another just as irreversible as itself, and so the king continued to act his part as a character but little short of divinity—infallible, immutable, wholly free from the weakness of repentance, and wiser than all men.

AMOS

2:8 Idolatrous Customs

They lie down beside every altar on garments taken in pledge. In the house of their god they drink wine taken as fines.

The text-verse refers to the unjust habits and the idolatrous practices of the backslidden Israelites, especially of those in authority. They took money that they had exacted by the imposition of fines and with it purchased wine that they drank in pagan temples. In addition, they took from the poor as a pledge for debts their outer garments, which were their covering through the night as well as during the day. Instead of returning these at sundown as required by the law (Deuteronomy 24:12—see note at Deuteronomy **24:10-13 Debtors Protected**), they kept them all night and slept upon them in the pagan temples. Their sleeping there may be a result of their idolatrous feasts, or the custom that was sometimes practiced among the pagans of sleeping near the altars of their gods so that they might communicate with them while they slept.

9:9 Sieve

I will shake the house of Israel among all the nations as grain *(corn, KJV)* is shaken in a sieve.

Part of the process of winnowing grain consisted in using a sieve. As it was shaken, the dirt and other impurities that clung to the grain during the threshing process were separated from it. In addition to this verse, reference is figuratively made to the sieve in Isaiah 3:28 and Luke 22:31. See note on Ruth **3:2 Time for Winnowing.**

NAHUM

1:10 Ninevite Conviviality

They will be entangled among thorns *(folden together as thorns, KJV)* and drunk from their wine *(drunken as drunkards, KJV).*

The prophet here refers to the drinking customs of the Ninevites. Their monuments give ample illustration of their habits. Wrote one commentator about the picture presented by the scenes on the monuments: "In the banquet scenes of the sculptures it is drinking, and not eating, that is presented. Attendants dip the wine cups into a huge bowl or vase, which stands on the ground and reaches as high as a man's chest, and carry them full of liquor to the guests, who straightway start carousing. Every guest holds in his right hand a wine cup of the most elegant shape, the lower part modeled into the form of a lion's head, from

Assyrian drinking scene

which the cup itself rises in a graceful curve. They all raise their cups to a level with their heads, and looks as if they were pledging each other or else one and all drinking the same toast."

2:3 Assyrian Warriors

The shields of his soldiers are red; the warriors are clad in scarlet. The metal on the chariots flashes *(with flaming torches, KJV)* on the day they are made ready; the spears of pine are brandished *(fir trees shall be terribly shaken, KJV)*.

This is a vivid description of ancient Assyrian warriors and their battle equipment.

Various commentators have various opinions as to what each expression in this verse means. One states: "The Medes and Babylonians made their shields red by painting them or overlaying them with copper (see Ezekiel 23:14); their tunics were scarlet; their chariots flashed with steel because they attached scythes at right angles to the axles. They also used cypress spears." Another commentator wrote about the KJV rendering: "In the phrase 'flaming torches,' the Hebrew is not clear. It appears to be a reference to the chariots, or the weapons on them, flashing brightly in the sun."

Fighting equipment of ancient warriors were often made a bright blood-red color. This was intended to not only frighten their enemies by its flashing appearance in the sun, but also to conceal the blood of their own wounds, which might inspire their enemies with new courage and hope.

Assyrian war chariot of the early period

HABAKKUK

1:16 Worship of Weapons

Therefore he sacrifices to his net and burns incense to his dragnet.

These fishing implements are used figuratively to represent the weapons of war that the Chaldeans intended to use to overcome the Jews. It was customary among the ancient nations to offer sacrifices to their weapons. The Scythians offered sacrifices to a sword that was set up as a symbol of Mars. Referring to this, Herodotus, the Greek historian, wrote: "Yearly sacrifices of cattle and of horses are made to it, and more victims are offered thus than to all the rest of their gods."

3:9 Uncovering the Bow

You uncovered your bow *(Thy bow was made quite naked, KJV)*, you called for many arrows.

The bow was usually kept in a case made of leather or some other protective material. To uncover it meant to take it out of its case to use it. The expression signifies preparation for battle, and has the same meaning as uncover the shield. See note on Isaiah **22:6 Quivers and Shield Cases.**

ZECHARIAH

14:20 Bells for the Horses

On that day HOLY TO THE LORD *(HOLINESS UNTO THE LORD, KJV)* will be inscribed on the bells of the horses.

It was quite common among ancient nations to have bells hung around the necks of horses, both for ornament and to accustom warhorses to noise. Some commentators believe that the Hebrew word *metslloth*, rendered bells, were not bells as we know them, but small pieces of metal resembling cymbals, which made a tinkling noise by striking against each other as the horses moved. Others prefer bells as we know them.

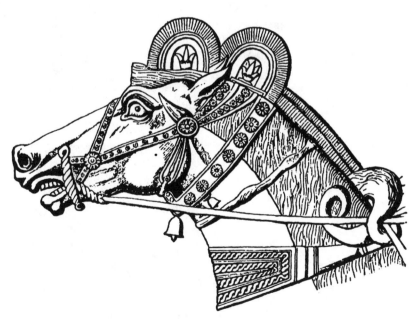

Head of chariot horse with collar and bell attached

JERUSALEM

MATTHEW

1:18 PLEDGES OF MARRIAGE

"Mary was pledged to be married to Joseph."

An espousal or betrothal is the act of engagement for marriage, a formal agreement that may take the form of a verbal promise or a written contract between two individuals. The betrothal is an ancient custom dating from biblical times when marriages were arranged by a parent or guardian. It was considered the beginning of marriage, and since it was legally binding, the pledge could not be broken except by a bill of divorce. This is the reason why Joseph is referred to as the husband of Mary in verse 19 of the first chapter of Matthew.

The presentation of gifts often accompanied or signified a marriage contract. When Abraham's servant received the consent of Rebekah's father and brother to make her the wife of his master's son, he presented valuable gifts to Rebekah (see Genesis 24:53).

In societies where arranged marriages still exist, the families concerned must negotiate dowries, future living arrangements, and other important matters before marriage can be arranged. Espousals were often made very early in life, though marriage did not take place until the bride reached twelve years of age or had experienced her first menstrual cycle. Infant betrothal or marriage, still prevalent in places such as India and Melanesia, is a result of concern for family, caste, and property alliances. During the Middle Ages, arranged betrothals were used to strengthen royal dynasties, establish diplomatic alliances, and increase estates and fortunes. Even when the age was suitable, the marriage was not consummated for some time after the betrothal. The bride remained at her father's or guardian's home until the time of the marriage.

In most societies today, marriage is entered into through a contractual procedure, generally with some sort of religious sanction. In Western societies the contract of marriage is regarded as a religious sacrament, and it is indissoluble only in the Roman visits, lead to the final wedding ceremony and give publicity to the claims of the partners on one another. The new bonds between the married couple are frequently represented, as in the U.S. and many other countries, by an exchange of rings or the joining of hands. Finally, the

The marriage in Cana of Galilee

Catholic and Eastern Orthodox churches. Most marriages are preceded by a betrothal period, during which various ritual acts, such as exchanges of gifts and interest of the community is expressed in many ways, through feasting and dancing, and, in Christian communities, through the publishing of banns, the presence of witnesses, and the official sealing of marriage documents.

Arranged marriages, which had been the accepted form of marriage almost everywhere throughout history, eventually ceased to predominate in Western societies, although they continued to persist as the norm in aristocratic society to the mid-20th century.

2:1 MAGI

After Jesus was born in Bethlehem in Judea, during the time of King Herod, Magi from the east came to Jerusalem.

These wise men, or more properly named, *magi*, belonged to a large and influential order of men. Though the origin of Magism is somewhat obscure, it's thought to have had its beginning among either the Chaldeans or the Assyrians; more probably among the former. Starting in Chaldea, it naturally made its way to Assyria, Media, and the adjoining countries. From Media, it was brought into Persia, where it exerted a powerful influence in modifying the ancient religious faith of the people. Some profess to trace the Magian doctrines to Abraham.

There are several references in the Old Testament to the Magi.

Chaldean diviner

In Jeremiah 39:3, 13, Nergal-sharezer is said to have been the *Rab-mag*, or chief of the Magi. His name is supposed to be recorded in the Babylonian inscriptions, where mention is made of Nergal-shar-uzur, who is styled Rabu-emga or Rab-mag. The *chakamim*, or "wise men," referred to in Jeremiah 1:35 were probably Magi.

In Daniel's time the Magi were prominent in Babylon: "So the king summoned the magicians, enchanters, sorcerers and astrologers to tell him what he had dreamed" (Daniel 2:2). "Then the king commanded to call the magicians, and the astrologers, and the sorcerers, and the Chaldeans, for to show the king his dreams" (KJV). "The secret which the king hath demanded cannot the wise men, the astrologers, the magicians, the soothsayers, show unto the king" (Daniel 2:27, KJV). Magicians, astrologers, sorcerers, Chaldeans, and soothsayers are mentioned in the second chapter of Daniel. Some writers think that five distinct classes of Magi are here referred to. It is difficult, however, to specify the difference between them.

"There is a man in your kingdom who has the spirit of the holy gods in him. In the time of your father he was found to have insight and intelligence and wisdom like that of the gods. King Nebuchadnezzar your father—your father the king, I say—appointed him chief of the magicians, enchanters, astrologers and diviners" (Daniel 5:11). "Then the king placed Daniel in a high position and lavished many gifts on him. He made him ruler over the entire province of Babylon and placed

him in charge of all its wise men" (Daniel 2:48). "Finally, Daniel came into my presence and I told him the dream. (He is called Belteshazzar, after the name of my god, and the spirit of the holy gods is in him.) I said, 'Belteshazzar, chief of the magicians, I know that the spirit of the holy gods is in you, and no mystery is too difficult for you' " (Daniel 4:8-9). These verses seem to indicate that Daniel himself was made a member of the Magian order, and its chief; but the expressions used may only mean that the king regarded Daniel as superior to all the magicians in his dominion, and as having authority over them. In any case, it's doubtful that Daniel embraced any theological notions of the Magi that were in opposition to Hebrew orthodoxy.

The Magians were a priestly caste, and the office was hereditary. They uttered prophesies, explained omens, interpreted dreams, and practiced *rhabdomancy* or divination by rods: "They consult a wooden idol and are answered by a stick of wood" (Hosea 4:12). Their notion of the peculiar sanctity of the elements led to a singular mode of disposing of the bodies of the dead: "They have given the dead bodies of your servants as food to the birds of the air, the flesh of your saints to the beasts of the earth" (Psalms 79:2).

In Persia, they became a powerful body under the guide of Zoroaster, known in ancient Persia as Zarathustra, and were divided into three classes: *Herbeds,* or disciples; *Mobeds,* or masters; and *Destur-mobeds,* or perfect masters. Later, the term Magi became more extended in its meaning. As the Magi were men of learning, devoting special attention to astronomy and the natural sciences, eventually all men celebrated for learning were called Magi, whether belonging to the priestly order or not. So as the Magi joined to the pursuits of science the arts of soothsayer, in process of time mere conjurers who had no scientific knowledge were called Magi. Simon Magus (Acts 8:9) and Bar-Jesus or Elymas (Acts 13:6, 8) were men of this sort. The Magi who came to visit the infant Savior were no doubt of the better class. The idea, however, that they were kings and three in number is mere imagination, and impossible to prove. They were evidently skilled in astronomical knowledge, and were earnest seekers after the newborn king.

Where they came from is disputed. Various writers have suggested that they were Babylonians, Arabians, Persians, Bactrius, Parthians, or even Brahmins from India. Matthew says they were from "the east," which is a geographical term of elastic meaning.

3:4 CAMEL'S HAIR GARMENTS - LOCUSTS AS FOOD

John's clothes were made of camel's hair, and he had a leather belt around his waist. His food was locusts and wild honey.

1. The rough camel-hair garment seems to have been characteristic of a prophet: "On that day every prophet will be ashamed of his prophetic vision. He will not put on a prophet's garment of hair in order to deceive" (Zechariah 13:4). John the Baptist's garment was made of camel's hair by which he was distinguished from royalty who wore soft raiment. This was also the case with Elijah (2 Kings 1:8), who is called "a hairy man," from his wearing such raiment. "This is one of the most

Locust

admirable materials for clothing; it keeps out the heat, cold, and rain." The "sackcloth" so often alluded to was probably made of camel's hair. The camel's flesh was not to be eaten, as it was ranked among unclean animals (Leviticus 11:4; Deuteronomy 14:7).

2. Locusts and grasshoppers are perhaps the best-known insects of the Bible. This group was so prolific that the Bible contains approximately a dozen words that describe them. The numerous words may indicate different species or even different stages of development. Disagreement exists as to the translation of many instances of the words. Thus the different species cannot be identified positively from the Hebrew words. In the New Testament, locusts are mentioned as forming part of the food of John the Baptist (see also Mark 1:6). By the Mosaic law they were reckoned "clean," so that he could lawfully eat them. Permission is given for its consumption in Leviticus 11:22. Locusts are prepared as food in various ways. Sometimes they are pounded, and then mixed with flour and water, and baked into cakes; "sometimes boiled, roasted, or stewed in butter, and then eaten." They were eaten in a preserved state by the ancient Assyrians. One form of the locust, indicated by the Hebrew word *arbeh,* has been called the migratory locust, or desert locust.

It is remembered as the locust of the plague (Exodus 10:4-5). Not only was the *arbeh* destructive; it was also edible. The *solam* is called "the bald locust" in Leviticus 11:22 (KJV) and was also allowed for food. *Akris* is the New Testament word for locust.

3:11 CARRYING SANDALS

"But after me will come one who is more powerful than I, whose sandals I am not fit to carry."

Carrying the master's sandals was considered the most menial duty that could be performed. Upon entering a house, the sandals were removed by a servant who took care of them

and brought them again when needed. If the master desired to walk barefoot, the servant removed his sandals and carried them. John felt himself unworthy to do for Christ even the meanest work of a servant.

3:12 WINNOWING GRAIN

"His winnowing fork is in his hand, and he will clear his threshing floor, gathering his wheat into the barn and burning up the chaff with unquenchable fire."

Winnowing is a step in the processing of grain whereby the grain is separated from the inedible parts. The stalks are thrown into the air with a wooden shovel or a wooden fork

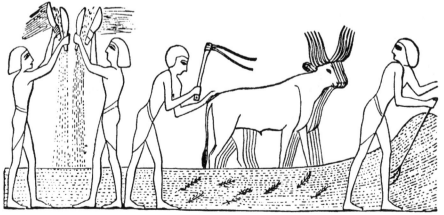

Threshing and winnowing

having two or three prongs and a handle three or four feet long (this is the "fan" mentioned in a number of Scriptures: Ruth 3:3; Isaiah 30:24; Jeremiah 4:11,12). The wind blows away the chaff and the straw, letting the heavier pure grain fall back to the ground. As a rule this was done in the evening or during the night, when the west wind from the sea was blowing, which was a moderate breeze and fitted for the purpose. The north wind was too strong, and the east wind came in gusts. John the Baptist used winnowing as an analogy of God's judgment, when the Lord would separate the sinful from the righteous. The scattering of the chaff by the wind after fanning is frequently alluded to figuratively in the Old Testament (see Job 21:18; Psalms 1:4; Isaiah 29:5; 41:16; Daniel 2:35; Hosea 13:3).

4:5 PINNACLE OF THE TEMPLE

Then the devil taketh him up into the holy city, and setteth him on a pinnacle *(highest point, NIV)* of the temple *(KJV)*. (See Luke 4:9.)

A pinnacle is by definition a little wing. This is commonly supposed to have been the summit of the royal gallery built by Herod within the area of the temple buildings on the edge of the Kidron Valley. On the southern side of the temple court was a range of porches or cloisters forming three arcades. At the southeastern corner the roof of this cloister was some 300 feet above the Kidron Valley. The pinnacle, some parapet or wing-like projection, was above this roof, and hence at a great height, probably 350 feet or more above the valley.

Josephus, the Jewish historian, says of it: "This cloister deserves to be mentioned better than any other under the sun; for, while the valley was very deep, and its bottom could not be seen if you looked from above into the depth, this farther vastly high elevation of the cloister stood upon that height, insomuch that if anyone looked down from the top of the battlements, or down both those altitudes, he would be giddy, while his sight could not reach to such an immense depth."

4:23 SYNAGOGUE

Jesus went throughout Galilee, teaching in their synagogues, preaching the good news of the kingdom.

The synagogue was the local meeting place and assembly of the Jewish people during New Testament times. Some Jewish traditions say that the synagogue was begun by Moses, but the Old Testament does not support this claim. While the origin of synagogues is unknown, it may well be supposed that buildings or tents for the accommodation of worshipers may have existed in the land from an early time, and thus the system of synagogues would be gradually developed. Psalm 74:8, written late in Old Testament times, seems to refer to local places of worship destroyed when the Temple was destroyed.

The synagogue, as we find it in the New Testament, had its roots in the time after Solomon's Temple was destroyed and many of the people were carried into Exile. Local worship and instruction became necessary. Even after many of the Jews returned to Jerusalem and rebuilt the Temple, places of local worship continued. By the time of Jesus these places and assemblies were called synagogues. There were no fixed proportions in the building, as

The interior of a synagogue

there were in the tabernacle and in the Temple. Usually it was built upon the highest ground available and, if possible, the top was erected above the roofs of surrounding buildings. Where this could not be done, a tall pole was placed on the summit in order to make the building conspicuous. Synagogues were often built without roofs and were so constructed that the worshipers faced Jerusalem. The form and internal arrangements of the synagogue would greatly depend on the wealth of the Jews who erected it, and on the place where it was built, but all synagogues had certain commonalities: the arrangements for the women's place in a separate gallery or behind a partition of latticework; the desk in the center, where the reader, like Ezra in ancient days, from his "high wooden platform . . . instructed the people in the Law . . . [and] read from the Book of the Law of God, making it clear and giving the meaning so that the people could understand what was being read" (Nehemiah 8:4, 8); the carefully closed ark on the side of the building nearest to Jerusalem, for the preservation of the rolls or manuscripts of the law; the seats all round the

building; and the "chief seats" (Matthew 23:6, KJV) that were appropriated by the "ruler" or "rulers" of the synagogue.

The leading object of the synagogue was not worship, but instruction. The Temple was "the house of prayer" (Matthew 21:13)—the synagogue was not referred to by that name. Reading and expounding the law was done in the synagogue and, though a liturgical service was connected with these, it was not its main function.

The priests had no official standing or privileges in the synagogue, though they were always honored when present. They were the hereditary officials of the Temple, but the officers of the synagogue were elected either by the congregation or by the council.

The leader of the congregation might ask any suitable person to address the assembly. Persons who were known as learned men, or as expounders of religious faith, were allowed to speak. Hence, in the text and parallel passages we find Christ publicly speaking in the synagogue (see Matthew 13:54; Mark 6:2; Luke 4:15, 16-22; John 18:20). The Apostles also addressed the people in the synagogues during their missionary journeys (see Acts 13:5, 15; 14:1; 17:10, 11, 17; 18:19).

5:1 THE SERMON ON THE MOUNT

Now when he saw the crowds, he went up on a mountainside and sat down. His disciples came to him, and he began to teach them.

What is commonly called "the sermon on the mount" is the first sermon of Jesus. It's a central expression of his teachings regarding the new age he has come to proclaim. It incorporates all the basic tenets of the New Covenant Christianity that was to be instituted when He shed His blood on the Cross at Cavalry. Like much in the New Testament, the Sermon on the Mount is familiar throughout the Western worlds, especially the Beatitudes.

5:3-12 BEATITUDES

"Blessed are the poor in spirit, for theirs is the kingdom of heaven. Blessed are those who mourn, for they will be comforted.

Blessed are the meek, for they will inherit the earth. Blessed are those who hunger and thirst for righteousness, for they will be filled. Blessed are the merciful, for they will be shown mercy. Blessed are the pure in heart, for they will see God. Blessed are the peacemakers, for they will be called sons of God. Blessed are those who are persecuted because of righteousness, for theirs is the kingdom of heaven. Blessed are you when people insult you, persecute you and falsely say all kinds of evil against you because of me. Rejoice and be glad, because great is your reward in heaven, for in the same way they persecuted the prophets who were before you."

Eight sayings of Jesus at the beginning of the Sermon on the Mount. The opening word is from the Latin *beatus*, meaning "blessed," and each of the Beatitudes begins with the word *blessed*.

The Sermon on the Mount

5:13 "SALT OF THE EARTH."

"You are the salt of the earth. But if the salt loses its saltiness *(savour, KJV)*, how can it be made salty again? It is no longer good for anything, except to be thrown out and trampled by men."

Salt was used to season food (Job 6:6), and mixed with the fodder of cattle (Isaiah 30:24). All meat-offerings were seasoned with salt (Leviticus 2:13). To eat salt with someone was to partake of his or her hospitality, to derive subsistence from him; and hence he who did so was bound to look after his host's interests. Ezra 4:14 reads: "We have maintenance from the king's palace" (KJV), or "We share the salt of the palace" (NRSV).

A "covenant of salt" (Numbers 18:19; 2 Chronicles 13:5) was a covenant of perpetual obligation. Newborn children were rubbed with salt (Ezekiel 16:4). In our text-verse, disciples are likened unto salt, with reference to its cleansing and preserving uses. A number of years ago, Sir Lyon Playfair, a biblical writer, argued on scientific grounds that under the generic name of "salt" in certain passages, the substance mentioned is actually petroleum or its residue asphalt. Thus in Genesis 19:26 it would read "pillar of asphalt;" and in Matthew 5:13, instead of "salt," "petroleum," which loses its essence by exposure, as salt does not, and becomes asphalt, from which pavements were made.

Someone who is referred to as the "salt of the earth" has a basic, fundamental goodness; the phrase can be used to describe any good person.

5:18 JOT AND TITTLE

"For verily I say unto you, Till heaven and earth pass, one jot or one tittle shall in no wise pass from the law, till all be fulfilled" *(KJV)*.

There may be allusion here to the great care taken by the copyists of the law to secure accuracy even to the smallest letters, or curves, or points of letters. *Jot* refers to the *"yodh,"* the smallest letter in the Hebrew alphabet. *Tittle* is an "apex" or "little horn," and refers to the horn-like points that are seen on Hebrew letters.

5:22 RACA

"But I tell you that anyone who is angry with his brother will be subject to judgment. Again, anyone who says to his brother, 'Raca,' is answerable to the Sanhedrin. But anyone who says, 'You fool!' will be in danger of the fire of hell."

Raca is a word of reproach meaning "empty" or "ignorant," that the Hebrew writers borrowed from the Aramaic language. Jesus uses it here as a strong term of derision, second only to "fool." He placed it in the context of anger and strongly condemned one who would use it of another person.

The Jewish teachers had heretofore taught that nothing except actual murder was forbidden by the sixth commandment. Thus they explained away its spiritual meaning. Christ showed the full meaning of this commandment; according to which we must be judged hereafter, and therefore ought to be ruled now. All rash anger is heart murder. Our "brother" here indicates any person, status notwithstanding, for we are all made of one blood. "Raca," is a scornful word, and is evidence of pride: "Thou fool," is a spiteful word, and denotes hatred. Malicious slanders and censures are lethal poison.

5:25 AGREEING WITH AN ADVERSARY

"Agree with thine adversary quickly, whiles thou art in the way with him; lest at any time the adversary deliver thee to the judge, and the judge deliver thee to the officer, and thou be cast into prison" *(KJV)*.

According to Roman law, if a person had a quarrel that he could not settle privately, he had the right to order his adversary to accompany him to the praetor. If he refused, the prosecutor took someone present to witness by saying, "May I take you to witness?" If the person consented, he offered the tip of his ear, which the prosecutor touched; a form that was observed toward witnesses in some other legal ceremonies among the Romans. Then the plaintiff might drag the defendant to court by force in any way, even by the neck (see Matthew 28:28), but worthless persons such as thieves and robbers might be dragged before the judge without the formality of calling a witness. If on the way to the judge the difficulty was settled, no further legal steps were taken.

Jesus refers to this custom in the text. When the accused is thus legally seized by the accuser, he is urged to make up his quarrel while on the way to the judge, so that no further legal process should be necessary.

5:33-37 OATHS

"Again, you have heard that it was said to the people long ago, 'Do not break your oath, but keep the oaths you have made to the Lord.' But I tell you, Do not swear at all: either by heaven, for it is God's throne; or by the earth, for it is his footstool; or by Jerusalem, for it is the city of the Great King. And do not swear by your head, for you cannot make even one hair white or black. Simply let your 'Yes' be 'Yes,' and your 'No,' 'No'; anything beyond this comes from the evil one."

Most do not consider that solemn oaths in a court of justice, or on other proper occasions, are wrong, provided they are taken with due reverence. Others, however, such as Quakers, take this verse in its most literal sense and will not swear any type of oath. But all oaths taken without necessity, or in common conversation, must be sinful, as well as all those expressions that are appeals to God, though persons think thereby to evade the guilt of swearing. Evil men and women are not bound by oaths, the godly have no need of them.

5:38 "AN EYE FOR AN EYE."

"You have heard that it was said, "Eye for eye, and tooth for tooth.""

This is the principle of justice that requires punishment equal in kind to the offense (not greater than the offense, as was frequently given in ancient times). Thus, if someone puts out another person's eye, one of the offender's eyes should be put out. The principle is stated in the Book of Exodus as "Thou shalt give life for life, eye for eye, tooth for tooth, hand for hand, foot for foot." This saying is often quoted today by those who wish to extract equal revenge for something done against them.

5:39 "Turn the other cheek."

"But I tell you, Do not resist an evil person. If someone strikes you on the right cheek, turn to him the other also."

This means to accept injuries and not to seek revenge. Or, in other words, swallow your pride and walk away, and thus avoid a confrontation that could result in permanent injury or death to someone; to say nothing, in this day, of ensuing lawsuits.

5:41 "Go the extra mile."

"If someone forces you to go one mile, go with him two miles."

The reference here is to an ancient Persian custom. The Persians introduced the use of regular couriers to carry letters or news. The king's courier had absolute command of all help that was necessary in the performance of his task. He could press horses into service, and compel the owners to accompany him if he desired. To refuse compliance with his demands was an unpardonable offense against the king. There was also a practice in Roman-occupied territory that any Roman soldier could require a citizen to carry his equipment, cloak, or other burdens for one mile. This may have been the practice that the Lord was specifically referring to when He instructs His followers to unselfishly "go the extra mile" as testimony to the generosity of the Christian spirit. The expression has come to mean to help someone beyond what is required or expected of you.

6:2 Alms and Trumpets

"Therefore when thou doest thine alms, do not sound a trumpet before thee" (KJV).

Some have thought from these words that it was customary to sound a trumpet before an alms-giver. However this might have been in the streets, it was not permitted in the synagogues, as it would disturb the services there. There is no evidence however, that any such custom was ever practiced. The words are therefore to be understood in the figurative sense. The Lord warns against hypocrisy and outward show in religious duties. All deeds must be done from an inward principle, that the doer may be approved of God, not praised of men. When the doer takes least notice of his or her good deeds, God takes most notice of them. To "sound one's own trumpet" today is to flaunt one's own good works or accomplishments.

6:7 REPETITIVE PRAYERS

"But when ye pray, use not vain repetitions, as the heathen do: for they think that they shall be heard for their much speaking" *(KJV).*

Some of the rabbis in the Lord's time taught that oft-repeated prayers were of certain efficacy. This type of praying was an imitation of the heathens of the time who were noted for repetitive prayer. When Elijah challenged the worshipers of Baal, they called on their god "from morning even unto noon, saying, O Baal, hear us" (2 Kings 18:26, KJV). When Paul excited the rage of Demetrius, who in turn aroused the mob at Ephesus, the angry crowd "all with one voice about the space of two hours cried out, 'Great is Diana of the Ephesians'" (Acts 19:34). It would seem that the further people become removed from true spiritual worship, the greater estimate they put on oft-repeated forms.

6:9 "THE LORD'S PRAYER"

"This, then, is how you should pray: 'Our Father in heaven, hallowed be your name, your kingdom come, your will be done on earth as it is in heaven. Give us today our daily bread. Forgive us our debts, as we also have forgiven our debtors. And lead us not into temptation, but deliver us from the evil one.'"

All Christian prayer is based on the Lord's Prayer, but its spirit is also guided by that of His prayer in Gethsemane and of the prayer recorded in John 17. The Lord's Prayer is the comprehensive type of the simplest and most universal prayer. Three forms of the Lord's Prayer exist in early Christian literature—two in the New Testament (see Matthew 6:9-13; Luke 11:2-4) and the other in the *Didache* 8:2, a non-canonical Christian writing of the early second-century from northern Syria. Their similarities and differences may be seen if the three forms are set side-by-side. Matthew and Luke used the Lord's Prayer in different ways in their Gospels. In Matthew the prayer appears in the Sermon on the Mount where Jesus spoke about a righteousness that exceeds that of the scribes and Pharisees (5:20). It is located in a section that warns against practicing one's piety before men in order to be seen by them (6:1-18). Almsgiving, praying, and fasting are for God's eyes and ears. When praying one should not make a public display (6:5-6) nor heap up empty phrases, thinking that one will be heard for many words (6:7). Prayer should be private and brief. The Lord's Prayer serves as an example of how to pray briefly. It is seen as a substitute for the wrong kind of prayer.

In Luke the prayer comes in the midst of Jesus' journey to Jerusalem (9:51-19:46). In His behavior Jesus is an example of one who prays. His prayer life caused one of His disciples to ask for instruction in prayer, as John the Baptist had given his disciples. What follows (11:2-13) is a teaching on prayer in which the disciples are told what to pray for (11:2-4) and why to pray (11:5-13). Here the Lord's Prayer is a model of what to pray for. To pray in this way is a distinguishing mark of Jesus' disciples. The Lord's Prayer seems to be Jesus' synopsis of various Jewish prayers of the time. The first two sentences: "Hallowed be thy name; thy kingdom come," echo the language of the Jewish prayer, the *Kaddish*. It begins: "Magnified and hallowed be his great name in the world . . . And may He establish His kingdom in your lifetime and in your days . . . quickly and soon." The third, "Your will be done," is similar to a prayer of Rabbi Eliezer (about A.D. 100): "Do Thy will in heaven above and give peace to those who fear Thee below" (Babylonian Talmud, *Berakoth*).

The petitions in the Lord's prayer also echo ancient Jewish prayers. The first, "Give us our bread," is akin to the first benediction of grace at mealtime. "Blessed art thou, O Lord our God, king of the universe, who feedest the whole world with thy goodness . . . ; thou givest food to all flesh. . . . Through thy goodness food hath never failed us: O may it not fail us for ever and ever."

The second, "Forgive us," echoes the Eighteen Benedictions, 6: "Forgive us, our Father, for we have sinned against thee; blot out our transgressions from before thine eyes. Blessed art thou, O Lord, who forgivest much." The accompanying phrase, "as we also have forgiven," reflects the Jewish teaching found in Sirach 28:2: "Forgive the wrong of your neighbor, and then your sins will be forgiven when you pray."

The third petition, "Lead us not into temptation," is similar to a petition in the Jewish Morning and Evening Prayers. "Cause me to go not into the hands of sin, and not into the hands of transgression, and not into the hands of temptation, and "not into the hand of dishonor."

The final words, "Hallowed be thy name," "Thy kingdom come," and "Thy will be done in earth, as it is in heaven,"

constitute a prayer for the final victory of God over the devil, sin, and death. It is possible that they were also understood by the early Christians to be a petition for God's rule in their lives in the here and now.

The Lord's Prayer has become the most famous prayer in the Western world since it was put to music about two centuries ago. It's a rare person who hasn't heard the prayer sung or recited or doesn't know it by heart.

6:16-18 FASTING

"When you fast, do not look somber as the hypocrites do, for they disfigure their faces to show men they are fasting. I tell you the truth, they have received their reward in full. But when you fast, put oil on your head and wash your face, so that it will not be obvious to men that you are fasting, but only to your Father, who is unseen; and your Father, who sees what is done in secret, will reward you."

Fasting is the laying aside of food for a period of time when the believer is seeking to know God in a deeper experience. It is to be done as an act before God in the privacy of one's own pursuit of God (Exodus 34:28; 1 Samuel 7:6; 1 Kings 19:8). The sole fast required by the law of Moses was that of the Great Day of Atonement in Leviticus 23:26-32. It is called "the fast" in Acts 27:9. The only other mention of a periodical fast in the Old Testament is in Zechariah 7:1-7; 8:19. During their captivity, the Jews observed four annual fasts: *the fast of the fourth month*, kept on the seventeenth day of Tammuz, the anniversary of the capture of Jerusalem by the Chaldeans; to commemorate also the incident recorded Exodus 32:19; *the fast of the fifth month*, kept on the ninth of Ab (Numbers. 14:27), to commemorate the burning of the city and temple (Jeremiah 52:12, 13); *the fast of the seventh month*, kept on the third of Tisri (2 Kings 25), the anniversary of the murder of Gedaliah (Jeremiah 41:1, 2); *the fast of the tenth month* (Jeremiah 52:4; Ezekiel 33:21; 2 Kings 25:1), to commemorate the beginning of the siege of the holy city by Nebuchadnezzar. There was, in addition to these, the fast appointed by Esther (Esther 4:16). Public national fasts on account of sin or to supplicate divine favor were sometimes held (1 Samuel 7:6, 2 Chronicles 20:3; Jeremiah 36:6-10; Nehemiah 9:1), as were local fasts (Judges 20:26; 1 Samuel 31:13; 2 Samuel 1:12; 1 Kings 21:9-12; Ezra 8:21-23; Jonah 3:5-9).

There are many instances of occasional fasting by individuals (1 Samuel 1:7; 20:34; 2 Samuel 3:35; 12:16; 1 Kings 21:27; Ezra 10:6; Nehemiah 1:4; Daniel 10:2, 3). Moses fasted forty days (Exodus 24:18; 34:28), as did Elijah (1 Kings 19:8). Jesus fasted forty days in the wilderness (Matthew 4:2). Apparently the practice of fasting was lamentably abused (Isaiah 58:4; Jeremiah 14:12; Zechariah 7:5). Jesus rebuked the Pharisees for their hypocritical pretenses in fasting. The early Church often fasted in seeking God's will for leadership in the local church (Acts 13:2). When the early Church wanted to know the mind of God, there was a time of prayer and fasting. Jesus Himself appointed no specific fast. The early Christians, however, observed the ordinary fasts according to the law of their fathers (Acts 13:3; 14:23; 2 Corinthians 6:5).

6:24 "No man can serve two masters."

"No one can serve two masters."

One's loyalties must be undivided. You cannot serve money and God at the same time, neither can you serve two people at the same time, not even yourself and someone else.

6:30 Grass as Fuel

"The grass of the field, which is here today and tomorrow is thrown into the fire."

Almost every kind of combustible matter was used for fuel, such as the withered stalks of herbs (or grass); wood (Isaiah 44:14-16); charcoal (Jeremiah 36:22; John 18:18); shrubs (Psalms 120:4); thorn bushes (Ecclesiastes 7:6; Nahum 1:10); weeds (Matthew 13:40); vines (Ezekiel 15:4, 6); branch trimmings (John 15:6); animal or even human dung (Ezekiel 4:12); and the bloodstained clothing of fallen warriors (Isaiah 9:5). Oil was used as a fuel for lamps (Matthew 25:3). Coal was not known to the Hebrews. Fuel is also frequently used figuratively as a symbol of total destruction (Isaiah 9:19; Ezekiel 15:6; 21:32).

For Jesus, God's extravagant love shown in clothing grass destined to be burned as fuel with beautiful flowers illustrated His even greater care for human beings.

7:1 "Judge not, or you too will be judged."

"Do not judge, or you too will be judged."

The teaching implies that since all people are sinners, no one is worthy to condemn another. It also means that to the degree that you judge other people, other people—and God—will judge you.

7:6 Dogs

"Do not give dogs what is sacred."

The word "dog" is often used to signify contempt or the inferiority of a person or item. To "go to the dogs" is to go to ruin; degenerate. Dogs were not generally domesticated in biblical times except for use as hunters. Prairie dogs, coyotes, hyenas, wolves, and others of the family *Canidae,* are carnivorous mammals and when not domesticated, will feed on carrion. See also Exodus 22:31; 1 Kings 21:23; Psalms 22:16;22:20; 59:14; 68:23; Jeremiah 15:3; Matthew 15:26-27; Mark 7:27-28; Luke 16:21; Philippians 3:2; and Revelation 22:15.

7:6 "Do not cast your pearls before swine."

"Neither cast ye your pearls before swine" *(KJV).*

Generally, to cast pearls before swine is to share something of value (pearls) with those who will not appreciate it. Pigs, swine, or the wild boar, which is common among the marshes of the Jordan valley (Psalms 80:13), were regarded as the most unclean and the most abhorred of all animals (Leviticus 11:7; Isaiah 65:4; 66:3, 17; Luke 15:15, 16).

7:7 "Ask and it will be given to you."

"Ask and it will be given to you; seek and you will find; knock and the door will be opened to you."

This passage suggests that God will give whatever is needed to those who have the faith to ask for it. It also suggests that once you have asked, you should seek it in faith that God is giving it, and when you believe you have found it, knock and see if that is the door God is opening for you.

7:9 Giving Stones for Bread

"Which of you, if his son asks for bread, will give him a stone?"

The point of this question is apparent when it is remembered that the loaves of bread in ancient times often resembled round, flat stones since they were not baked in oblong pans as common store-bought bread is today. A similar allusion is used in the narrative of the Lord's temptation, where the devil suggests that Jesus change the stones into bread (Matthew 4:3; Luke 4:3). Even today some Bedouin women bake their bread by inverting shallow pans over a fire and then baking the bread on the bottom of the pan in large, flat, cakes.

7:12 "The Golden Rule"

"So in everything, do to others what you would have them do to you, for this sums up the Law and the Prophets."

The Mosaic Law contains a parallel commandment: "Whatever is hurtful to you, do not do to any other person." "Do unto others" is a central ethical teaching of Jesus. "The Golden Rule" is another one of those teachings of Jesus that has gained fame throughout the Western world, and there are few who haven't heard it or don't know what it means.

7:15 "Wolves in sheep's clothing"

"Watch out for false prophets. They come to you in sheep's clothing, but

Scribes

419

inwardly they are ferocious wolves."

An image for false prophets, adapted from words of Jesus in the Sermon on the Mount. Now used figuratively to describe anyone who disguises a ruthless nature or evil intent by an outward show of innocence.

7:16 "BY THEIR FRUIT YOU WILL KNOW THEM."

"By their fruit you will recognize them. Do people pick grapes from thornbushes, or figs from thistles?"

It suggests that we are able to distinguish between false and genuine prophets by the things they do and not by what they say. A colloquial modification of this saying is: "Actions speak louder than words."

7:29 SCRIBES

For he taught them as one having authority, and not as the scribes. (See also Mark 1:22.)

In ancient times the scribes were merely officers whose duties included writing of various kinds; but, on the return of the Jews from Babylonian captivity, the *sopherim*, as the scribes were called, were organized by Ezra into a distinct body. Among other duties, they copied the Pentateuch, the Phylacteries, and the Mezuzoth. So great was their care in copying that they counted and compared all the letters to be sure that none were left out that belonged to the text, or none inserted wrongly. On stated occasions they read the law in the synagogues. They also lectured to their disciples. Because of the knowledge they obtained through their work, they became natural interpreters of God's law as well as copyists.

The lawyers (Matthew 22:35; Luke 7:30; 11:45; 14:3) and the doctors of the law (Luke 2:46; 5:17; Acts 5:34) were substantially the same as the scribes. Efforts have been made to show that different classes of duties were assigned to lawyers, doctors, and scribes, but without any measurably different results. It may be, as some believe, that the doctors were a higher grade than the ordinary scribes. The scribes were all carefully educated for their work from early life, and at an appropriate age—some say thirty-years-old—they were admitted to office through a solemn ceremony.

The scribes were not only copyists of the law, they were also keepers of the oral traditional comments and additions to the law. Gradually accumulating with the progress of time, these were numerous, and were regarded by many as of equal value with the law itself. To this Jesus alludes in Mark 7:5-13. Paul represents himself as having been, before his conversion, "exceedingly zealous of the traditions" of his fathers (Galatians 1:14). The scribes also adopted forced interpretations of the law, endeavoring to find a special meaning in every word, syllable, and letter. Thus the Savior charges them: "Woe to you experts in the law, because you have taken away the key to knowledge. You yourselves have not entered, and you have hindered those who were entering" (Luke 11:52).

At the time of Christ the people were increasingly dependent on the scribes for a knowledge of their Scriptures. The language of the Jews was passing into the Aramaic dialect, and the majority of the people, being unable to understand their own sacred books, were obliged to accept the interpretation that the scribes put upon them. Hence their astonishment, as indicated in our text-verse, at the peculiar style of teaching adopted by Jesus, and especially illustrated in His Sermon on the Mount. The scribes repeated traditions, but Jesus spoke with authority: "I tell you." The scribes had little sympathy with the masses, but Jesus mingled with the people, explaining to them in a simple, practical way the requirements of religion.

8:2 LEPER, LEPROSY

A man with leprosy came and knelt before him and said, "Lord, if you are willing, you can make me clean."

Leprosy is a generic term applied to a variety of skin disorders from psoriasis to true leprosy. Its symptoms ranged from white patches on the skin to running sores to the loss of digits on the fingers and toes. For the Hebrews it was a dreaded disease that rendered its victims ceremonially unclean—that is, unfit to worship God (Leviticus 13:3). Anyone who came in contact with a leper was also considered unclean. Lepers

Jesus healing a leper

were therefore isolated from the rest of the community. Jesus did not consider this distinction between clean and unclean valid. A person's outward condition did not make one unclean. What proceeds from the heart determines one's standing before God (Mark 7:1-23; Acts 10:9-16). Therefore, Jesus did not hesitate to touch lepers (Mark 1:40-45) and even commanded His disciples to cleanse lepers (Matthew 10:8).

9:6 PALSY - THE BED

Then saith he to the sick of the palsy *(to the paralytic,*

NIV), "Arise, take up thy bed, and go unto thine house" *(KJV)*.

1. Palsy as used in the KJV is a shorter form of *paralysis*. Many paralyzed persons were healed of their affliction by the Lord (Matthew 4:24; 8:5-13; 9:2-7; Mark 2:3-11; Luke 7:2-10; John 5:5-7) and by the apostles (Acts 8:7; 9:33, 34).

2. Greek, *kline*; a couch (for sleep, sickness, sitting, or eating); bed, table. The "bed" was often simply a mat or blanket that could be carried in the hands. The Hebrew word *er'es* denotes a canopied bed, or a bed

Rolling up the bed

paralytic was told to take up his bed and go home. All he had to do was roll up his blanket and depart. A similar incident took place at the pool of Bethesda (John 5: 8, 9, 11, 12). On such simple "beds" the sick were easily carried (Matthew 9:2; Mark 2:3-4; Luke 5:18; Acts 5:15).

with curtains (Deuteronomy 3:11; Psalms 132:3).

In the New Testament it was sometimes a litter with a coverlet as in our text-verse (also Luke 5:18; Acts 5:15). The Jewish bedstead (frame supporting the bed) was frequently merely the divan or platform along the sides of the house, sometimes a very slight portable frame, sometimes only a mat or one or more quilts. Sleeping in the open air was not uncommon—the sleeper simply wrapped himself in his outer garment (Exodus 22:26, 27; Deuteronomy 24:12, 13).

In our text-verse the healed

9:10 PUBLICANS

And it came to pass, as Jesus sat at meat in the house, behold, many publicans and sinners came and sat down with him and his disciples.

Publicans is from the Greek word, *telones*; collector of public revenue; tax collector. One who farmed the taxes (e.g.,

Pharisees and publicans praying

Zacchaeus, Luke 19:2) to be levied from a town or district, and thus undertook to pay to the supreme government a certain amount. In order to collect the taxes, the publicans employed subordinates (Luke 5:27; 15:1; 18:10), who, for their own profit, were often guilty of extortion and embezzlement. In New Testament times these taxes were paid to the Romans, and hence were regarded by the Jews as a heavy burden. Tax collectors were frequently Jews and were hated and usually spoken of scornfully. Jesus was accused of being a "friend of publicans and sinners" (Luke 7:34).

9:15 Use of the Term Children

And Jesus said unto them, Can the children of the

bridechamber mourn, as long as the bridegroom is with them *(KJV)*? (See also Mark 2:19; Luke 5:34.)

The "children of the bridechamber" were the friends and acquaintances who participated in the marriage festivities. The expression "child" or "children," like that of "father," is a form of speech designed to show some relation between the person to whom it is applied and certain qualities existing in that person, or certain circumstances connected with him—these qualities or circumstances being the result of that relation. Thus people who are brought together on occasion of a marriage feast are called the "children of the bridechamber."

When any passion or influence, good or bad, controls a person, they are said to be the children of that passion or influence. Thus we have "children of wickedness" (2 Samuel 7:10); "children of pride" (Job 41:34); "children of the kingdom," and "children of the wicked one" (Matthew 13:38); "children of this world, " and "children of light" (Luke 16:8); "children of disobedience" (Ephesians 2:2, Colossians 3:6);

and "children of wrath" (Ephesians 2:3). Similar use is made of the words "son" and "daughter." We have "sons of Belial" (Judges 19:22); "sons of the mighty" (Psalms 89:6); "sons of thunder" (Mark 3:17); "son of consolation" (Acts 4:36); "sons of perdition" (2 Thessalonians 2:3); "daughter of Belial" (1 Samuel 1:16); "daughters of music" (Ecclesiastes 12:4); "daughters of troops" (Micah 5:1).

9:17 SKIN BOTTLES

"Neither do men pour new wine into old wineskins. If they do, the skins will burst, the wine will run out and the wineskins will be ruined. No, they pour new wine into new wineskins, and both are preserved."

Ancient skin bottles

The use of bottles made from the skins of animals is very ancient. Water or wine bottles were frequently made from animal skins (Joshua 9:4, 13; Judges 4:19; 1 Samuel 1:24; 10:3; 2 Samuel 16:1; Nehemiah 5:18; Job 32:19; Psalms 119:83; Mark 2:22; Luke 5:37). Such leather vessels are still popular among the Bedouin for their durability, portability, and accessibility since they are mostly pastoral nomads and animal herding is their main occupation.

The skins of goats were commonly taken for this purpose, and were usually fashioned to retain the figure of the animal. In preparing the bottle, the head and feet of the animal were cut off and the skin stripped whole from the body. The neck of the animal often made the neck of the bottle; in other cases one of the forelegs was used as an aperture through which the liquid was poured out. The thighs served as the handles, and by attaching straps to them the bottle could be fastened to the saddle or slung over the shoulder of the traveler. For a large party, and for long journeys across the desert, the skins of camels or of oxen were used. Two of these, when filled with water, made a good load for a camel. They were coated with grease to prevent leakage and evaporation.

The "bottle" that Hagar carried into the wilderness, and from which she gave Ishmael drink, was probably a kidskin. (Genesis 21:14.) A similar scene is represented in the engraving shown here from an ancient Assyrian sculpture. Skin bottles were also used for milk (Judges 4:19) and for wine (1 Samuel 16:20).

In our text-verse and its

Woman giving drink to a child from a skin bottle

parallels, allusion is made to this use of skins. When the skin is green, it stretches with the fermentation of the liquid and retains its integrity. But when it becomes old and dry, the fermentation of the new wine soon causes the skin to burst. This expression is still used today to mean that it is often difficult, if not impossible, to put new things into old ways.

9:20 Fringe, Hem, or Edge of His Cloak

Just then a woman who had been subject to bleeding for twelve years came up behind him and touched the edge of his cloak. (See also Luke 8:44.)

Greek *kraspedon*; a margin, i.e., a fringe or tassel, border, hem. According to the Mosaic law every Jew was obliged to wear a fringe or tassel at each of the four corners of the outer garment, one thread of each tassel to be blue. These tassels were to be to them a perpetual reminder of the law of God, and of their duty to keep it. (See Numbers 15:38, 39; Deuteronomy 22:12.) This was

the "hem" that the woman touched, perhaps supposing there was some peculiar virtue in it. So also the people of Gennesaret brought their sick to Christ for a similar purpose (Mark 6:53-56). The Pharisees prided themselves greatly on these tassels. They considered them as marks of special sanctity in the wearers, and therefore sought to enlarge their size (Matthew 23:5).

10:4 Shaking Dust off the Feet

"If anyone will not welcome you or listen to your words, shake the dust off your feet when you leave that home or town." (See also Mark 6:11; Luke 9:5.)

For Jews to shake dust off their feet was a sign that Gentile territory was unclean. In the New Testament this action indicates that those who have rejected the gospel have made themselves as Gentiles and must face the judgment of God. (See also Acts 13:51) *To sprinkle dust on the head* was a sign of mourning (Joshua 7:6), and *to sit in dust* denotes extreme affliction (Isaiah 47:1). "Dust" is used to denote the grave (Job 7:21). *To lick the dust* is a sign of abject submission (Psalms 72:9); and *to throw dust at someone* is a sign of abhorrence (2 Samuel 16:13; Acts 22:23). *To bite the dust* is to suffer a defeat. It became a common expression through its use in American movies about the early west.

10:9 Belts

"Do not take along any gold or silver or copper in your belts *(purses, KJV)*" (See also Mark 6:8; Luke 10:4.)

Greek *zone*, (dzo'-nay); a belt; a pocket: girdle, purse. In your belts is, literally, in your

girdles. It is quite common to this day to use the folds of the girdle as a pouch, or pocket for keeping money. Money is also sometimes carried in a bag, which is put in the belt. This is referred to in the parallel passage to our text-verse in Luke, where the word rendered "purse" signifies a bag. A person referred to as a "moneybags" is a rich, often extravagant, person.

10:10 Sandals

"Take no bag for the journey, or extra tunic, or sandals." *(See also Luke 10:4.)*

Greek *hupodema*, (hoop-od'-ay-mah); something bound under the feet, i.e. a shoe or sandal. In our Lord's time there were, besides sandals, other coverings for the feet more nearly approaching our idea of a shoe. Some of these covered the entire foot, while in others the toes were left bare, as represented in the engraving. Ancient shoes are well known from paintings, sculptures, and carved reliefs, and several well-preserved ones have

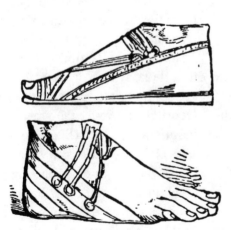

Sandals

Ancient shoes

wearing of sandals with multilayered leather soles nailed together, as this was the shoe worn by Roman soldiers, who needed such shoes for marching long distances.

10:10 "WORTH ONE'S SALT"

"For the worker is worth his keep *(meat, KJV)*."

Greek *trophe*, (trof-'ay); nourishment, rations (wages), food, meat. Worth one's salary or wages. From the Roman custom of paying soldiers with salt. Today the saying denotes that workers should be paid what they're worth.

10:16 SNAKES AND DOVES

"I am sending you out like sheep among wolves. Therefore be as shrewd as snakes and as innocent as doves."

been found. The shoe was considered the humblest article of clothing and could be bought cheaply.

Two types of shoes existed: slippers of soft leather and the more popular sandals with a hard leather sole. Thongs secured the sandal across the insole and between the toes. Although shoes could be bought at a low price, they were often repaired by the poor. Shoes were removed at the doorway of the tent or house, or during a period of mourning. Shoes were also removed as evidence of humility in the presence of kings. The removal of the guest's sandals was the job of the lowliest servant who was also required to wash the dusty and soiled feet of the visitor. During New Testament times, Jewish practice forbade the

Because the disciples of Christ are hated and persecuted and their ruin is sought, they need the serpent's wisdom. The word serpent or snake is used symbolically of a deadly, subtle,

Snake

Dove

malicious enemy. (See Luke 10:19.) Yet Christ's followers are to be as harmless as doves—to neither hurt anyone, nor bear anyone ill will. In the political world today, a *dove* is a person who advocates peace, conciliation, or negotiation in preference to confrontation or armed conflict.

10:17 COUNCILS

"Be on your guard against men; they will hand you over to the local councils." (See also Mark 13:9.)

Greek *sunedrion*, (soon-ed'-ree-on); a joint session, i.e. specifically the Jewish Sanhedrin; a subordinate tribunal or council. The Jewish councils were the Sanhedrin, or supreme council of the nation. Subordinate to the Sanhedrin were smaller tribunals in the cities of Palestine. In the time of Christ the functions of the Sanhedrin were limited (John 16:2; 2 Corinthians 11:24).

In ecclesiastical history the word is used to denote an assembly of pastors or bishops for the discussion and regulation of church affairs. The first of these councils was that of the apostles and elders at Jerusalem, of which we have a detailed account in Acts 15.

10:17 FLOGGING

"And flog you in their synagogues"

Greek *mastigoo*, (mas-tig-o'-o); to flog or scourge. The discipline of the synagogue was severe. This is a harsh form of corporal punishment involving whipping and beating, and usually was done with the victim tied to a post or bench and administered by a servant of the synagogue (if for religious reasons), or by a slave or soldier. John 19:1 uses this word for the beating given Jesus before His crucifixion. Matthew and Mark use a word meaning "flog" (a lesser punishment), while Luke says that Pilate offered to have Jesus "chastise[d]" (23:16), which was a still lighter punishment. The number of blows was set in Deuteronomy 25:3 at forty, but later reduced to thirty-nine, or forty minus one. There were to be thirteen stokes on the chest and twenty-six on the back. Often the victim died from the beating, usually because of the type of whip that was used—some of them were embedded with metal and sharp objects so that they cut deeply into the flesh.

Jewish scholars listed 168 faults to be punished by scourging, in fact, all punishable faults to which the law had not annexed the penalty of death. Paul was thus beaten five distinct times (2 Corinthians 11:24). Scourging in synagogues is also referred to in Matthew 23:34. Paul had believers flogged in his days as a persecutor of the Church (Acts 22:19-20). See also Matthew 27:26; Mark 15:15; John 19:1.

10:27 PUBLIC PROCLAMATIONS

"What I tell you in the dark, speak in the daylight; what is whispered in your ear, proclaim from the roofs."

In the contrast expressed between hearing privately and proclaiming publicly, there may also be reference to the mode of instruction in the schools of the rabbis. The commentator Lightfoot expresses this opinion: "The doctor whispered, out of the chair, into the ear of the interpreter, and he, with a loud voice, repeated to the whole school that which was spoken in the ear."

The reference to the housetops may be an allusion to the custom of sounding the synagogue trumpet from the roof to usher in the Sabbath.

10:29 SPARROWS - FARTHINGS

"Are not two sparrows sold for a farthing" *(KJV)*?

1. Greek *strouthion*, (stroo-thee'-on); diminutive of

Assarion

strouthos, (a sparrow); a little sparrow. Sparrows are mentioned among the offerings made by

Sparrows

poor. Two sparrows were sold for a farthing, and five for two farthings (Luke 12:6). The Hebrew word thus rendered is *tsippor*, which properly denotes the whole family of small birds that feed on grain (Leviticus 14:4; Psalms 84:3; 102:7).

2. Greek *assarion*, (as-sar'-ee-on); of Latin origin; an *assarius* or a Roman coin equal to a tenth of a *denarius* or *drachma*. A coin formerly used in Great Britain worth one fourth of a penny.

11:16-17 GAMES OF CHILDREN

"To what can I compare this generation? They are like children sitting in the marketplaces and calling out to others: 'We played the flute for you, and you did not dance; we sang a dirge, and you did not mourn.'" (See also Luke 7:31-32.)

Christ here reflects on the scribes and Pharisees who were

proud and conceited. He compares their behavior to children at play, who being out of temper without reason, quarrel with all the attempts of their friends to please them, or to get them to join in their play. Thus it was that the people would receive neither Jesus nor John, and, like perverse children, they refused to be satisfied with any proposition made to them.

11:29-30 Yoke

"Take my yoke upon you and learn from me, for I am gentle and humble in heart, and you will find rest for your souls. For my yoke is easy and my burden is light."

A yoke was a wooden frame placed on the backs of oxen to make them pull in tandem. The simple yokes consisted of a bar with two loops either of rope or wood that went around the animals' necks. More elaborate yokes had shafts connected to the middle with which the animals pulled plows or other implements. Often the burden the ox had to bear was so heavy that it would cause them to stumble and fall under it, but Jesus promised that the burden of His followers would never be that heavy.

Cart with yoke on oxen

12:1 FREE GRAIN FOR THE HUNGRY

At that time Jesus went through the grainfields on the Sabbath. His disciples were hungry and began to pick some heads of grain and eat them. (See also Mark 2:23; Luke 6:1.)

It was perfectly lawful for persons when hungry to help themselves to as much of their neighbor's growing grain as they wished for food. The law of God allowed it (Deuteronomy 23:25).

12:25 "A HOUSE DIVIDED AGAINST ITSELF CANNOT STAND."

Jesus knew their thoughts and said to them, "Every kingdom divided against itself will be ruined, and every city or household divided against itself will not stand."

In a speech made at the Illinois Republican convention in 1858, Abraham Lincoln noted that conflict between North and South over slavery was intensifying. He asserted that the conflict would not stop until a crisis was reached and passed, for, quoting our text-verse, Lincoln said, "A house divided against itself cannot stand." He continued: "I believe this government cannot endure permanently half slave and half free. I do not expect the Union to be dissolved—I do not expect the house to fall—but I do expect it will cease to be divided. It will become all one thing, or all the other."

12:30 "HE THAT IS NOT WITH ME IS AGAINST ME."

"He who is not with me is against me."

A teaching of Jesus that suggests that indifference to His message is the same as active opposition to it. It has the same meaning today to denote that if you are not for a person, then you are, by the very nature of your decision, against him. This is one of those fundamental principles that has no gray area, although we often try to give it one to place ourselves in a better light.

Jesus in the grainfields

13:25 WICKEDNESS AT NIGHT

"But while everyone was sleeping, his enemy came and sowed weeds among the wheat, and went away."

In his book, *Oriental Illustrations of the Sacred Scriptures* (1844), J. Roberts states that this nocturnal evil occurs in this way: A man wishing to do his enemy an injury, watches for the time when he has finished plowing his field, and in the night he goes into the field and scatters *pandinellu*, or "pig-paddy." Says Roberts: "This being of rapid growth springs up before good seed, and scatters itself before the other can be reaped, so that the poor owner of the field will be some years before he can rid the soil of the troublesome weed. But there is another noisome plant that these wretches cast into the ground of those whom they hate: it is called *perum-pirandi*, and is more destructive to vegetation than any other plant."

13:33 LEAVEN

"The kingdom of heaven is like yeast *(leaven, KJV)*." (See also Luke 13:21.)

Leaven is an agent that causes batter or dough to rise. Leaven often symbolized a corruptive influence. In the New Testament, leaven is a symbol of any evil influence that, if allowed to remain, can corrupt the body of believers. Jesus warned His disciples against the leaven of the Pharisees, their teaching and hypocrisy (Matthew 16:5-12; Luke 12:1). Paul urged the Corinthians to remove wickedness from their midst and become fresh dough, unleavened loaves of sincerity and truth (1 Corinthians 5:6-13). In our text-verse, Jesus used leaven to illustrate the pervasive growth of the kingdom of God. He also used it in other places to illustrate the invasive influence of the corrupt doctrines of the Pharisees, and warned His disciples against it. Figuratively, leaven has much the same meaning today—it's defined as an element, influence, or agent that works subtly to lighten, enliven, or modify a whole.

13:44 HIDDEN TREASURE

"The kingdom of heaven is like treasure hidden in a field."

The possession of wealth often becomes a source of great perplexity because of its insecurity. Before the days of banks and secure deposit boxes, every man's ingenuity was taxed to devise some plan of concealment, or to find some place where money, jewels, and other valuables might remain free from molestation or suspicion. Sometimes their treasures were hidden in secret closets in the house, or in storage vaults under the house. Sometimes they were buried in a field in a spot unknown to all save the owner. Sometimes the owner went away and died before the time of his intended return, and his secret died with him. Times of war and pestilence carried off great numbers who left treasures concealed no one knows where. No doubt but that there are, even to this day, deposits of immense value buried and unfound in different parts of the world.

These facts illustrate the text. A man who discovers the place where treasure is hid keeps the discovery to himself, buys the field, and the treasure is his own. Other references of a similar character are made in different parts of the Bible, showing how ancient and how widespread is the custom of concealing treasures. It was thus that Achan hid the spoils of war in the earth in the middle of his tent (Joshua 7:21).

Job represents men who are weary of life, longing for death with the eagerness of treasure-seekers. They "dig for it more than hid treasures." They "rejoice exceedingly and are glad, when they find the grave" (Job 3:21-22). Solomon, perhaps, alludes to this custom when he speaks of those who search after wisdom "as for hid treasures" (Proverbs 2:4) though the reference may be, as some think, to mining operations. He may also refer to it when he says that "the abundance of the rich will not suffer him to sleep" (Ecclesiastes 5:12).

The more treasure one had the more care he had to take to conceal it, and the fear of discovery would naturally create sleeplessness. God's promise to Cyrus is a further illustration: "I will give thee the treasures of darkness, and hidden riches of secret places" (Isaiah 45:3). In the parable of the talents, the servant who had but one talent buried it in the earth (Matthew 25:18).

13:45-46 "A PEARL OF GREAT PRICE."

"Again, the kingdom of heaven is like unto a merchant man, seeking goodly pearls: Who, when he had found one pearl of great price, went and sold all that he had, and bought it."

A phrase from one of the parables of Jesus: He compares the journey to heaven to a search for fine pearls conducted by a merchant, "who, when he had found one pearl of great price, went and sold all that he had, and bought it." The expression has come to mean anything that is extremely valuable, and is worth almost anything to obtain.

13:47 FISHING NETS

"Once again, the kingdom of heaven is like a net that was let down into the lake and caught all kinds of fish."

The precise form of the fishing nets used by the Hebrews is not known; nor do we know the exact difference between the meanings attached to the several words that are translated "net." A kind of net commonly used resembled the modern *seine*—a large fishing net made to hang vertically in the water by weights at the lower edge and floats at the top. It is a net of this sort that is referred to here. Some suppose that in John 21:6, there is also an allusion to this kind of net, but others think that a net for deep-sea fishing is there meant; a net so arranged as to enclose the fish in deep water. Such a net seems to be intended in Luke 5:4, where the command is given, "Launch out into the deep, and let down your nets for a draught" (KJV).

14:6-7 FOOLISH AND COSTLY PROMISES

"On Herod's birthday the daughter of Herodias danced for them and pleased Herod so much that he promised with an oath to give her whatever she asked." (See also Mark 6:23.)

It was common for public dancers at festivals in great houses to ask for rewards from the company. An instance is recorded by *Thevenot*, in his

The miraculous catch of fish

Travels in Persia, written in the early 1800s, that reminds us of this extravagant promise of Herod. Shah Abbas was on one occasion so pleased with the performances of a dancing woman that he gave her the fairest khan (a *caravansary*—an inn built around a large court for accommodating caravans at night) in all Ispahan, one which yielded large revenues to the royal treasury. He was drunk at the time, and, when he became sober, repented of his rash generosity, and compelled the girl to accept instead a sum of money far below the value of the khan.

14:19 Giving Thanks at Meals

Taking the five loaves and the two fish and looking up to heaven, he gave thanks and broke the loaves. (See also Mark 6:41; Luke 9:16; John 6:11.)

It was customary among the Jews to give thanks to God at the commencement of every meal. The usual form was, "Blessed be thou, O Lord our God, the King of the world, who produced bread out of the earth." they also had a similar blessing for the wine, "Blessed art Thou, O Lord, the King of the world, who created the fruit of the vine." These, or similar blessings, were used at the celebration of the Passover.

Paul, referring to this blessing, calls the wine used in the Lord's supper, "the cup of blessing" (1 Corinthians 10:16). The expression "bless the sacrifice" in 1 Samuel 9:13, is also an allusion to the custom of asking a blessing before eating, the reference being to those parts of the peace-offering that were eaten by the offerer and his friends (Leviticus 7:11).

In compliance with the ancient Jewish custom, the Savior, before feeding the five thousand, blessed God for the gift bestowed. At another time, when four thousand were fed, "he took the seven loaves and the fish, and when he had given thanks, he broke them" (Matthew 15:36; also Mark 8: 6-7).

14:20 Baskets

The disciples picked up twelve basketfuls of broken pieces that were left over. (See also Mark 6:43; Luke 9:17; John 6:18.)

Feeding the five thousand

Greek, *kophinos,* (kof'-ee-nos); a (small) basket. The baskets used in biblical times resemble very much those that are represented on the monuments of Egypt. The baskets here referred to were probably the ordinary traveling baskets that the Jews took with them on a journey. They carried their provisions in them, so that they might not be polluted by eating the food of the Gentiles. It is also said that they carried hay in them, which they slept on at night. Thus they were able to separate themselves from the Gentiles in food and lodging. This will account for the contemptuous description that Juvenal, the Roman satirist (60?-140?), gave of the Jews, when he said that their household goods consisted of a basket and hay.

In the corresponding miracle in Matthew 15:37, where four

thousand are fed, a different kind of basket was employed. In this verse the Greek word *spuris* (spoo-rece') is used, which is defined as a woven hamper or lunch-receptacle. (See also Mark 8:8, 19, 20.)

15:3 TRADITION

Jesus replied, "And why do you break the command of God for the sake of your tradition?" (See also Mark 7:9.)

Tradition refers to any kind of teaching, written or spoken, handed down from generation to generation. In Mark 7:3, 9, 13, and Colossians 2:8, this word refers to the arbitrary interpretations of the Jews. The commentator Lightfoot gives a number of curious illustrations from the old Talmudic writers, showing the value that they set on traditions: "The words of the scribes are lovely, above the words of the law; for the words of the law are weighty and light, but the words of the scribes are all weighty. The words of the elders are weightier than the words of the prophets."

16:19 BINDING AND LOOSING

"I will give you the keys of the kingdom of heaven; whatever you bind on earth will be bound in heaven, and whatever you loose on earth will be loosed in heaven."

"Bind" in this verse is translated from the Greek word *deo*, (deh'-o), which means also to be in bonds; knit, tie, wind. "Loose" here referred to is from the Greek word *luo*, which also means to break (up), destroy, dissolve, (un-) loose, melt, put off.

Lightfoot gives a large number of citations from rabbinical authorities to show the common usage in the Jewish schools of the words "bind" and "loose," and also the meaning of these figurative terms. According to Lightfoot, bind means to forbid, while loose means to allow. Another commentator, Rosenmuller, says: "Binding and loosing—that is, prohibiting and permitting—were, in the Aramaic language that Jesus used, a customary expression to denote the highest authority. See Isaiah **22:22 Keys on Shoulder.**

17:24 TEMPLE TAX

"Doesn't your teacher pay the temple tax?"

A tax for the support of the temple service that every Jew was expected to pay. It was founded by Moses in connection with the tabernacle service (Exodus 30:13). It's also referred to in 2 Kings 12:4; 2 Chronicles 24:6, 9.

18:6 MILLSTONE AND DROWNING

"But if anyone causes one of these little ones who believe in me to sin, it would be better for him to have a large millstone hung around his neck and to be drowned in the depths of the sea." (See also Mark 9:42; Luke 17:2.)

1. A millstone was a cylindrical stone used in a mill for grinding grain. The millstone was normally from eighteen inches to two feet across, and might easily be hung around the neck of a person to be drowned. Some commentators, however, are of the opinion that by the "ass-millstone," as the original in both Matthew and Mark may be rendered, is meant a stone larger than that used in ordinary mills—one so large as to require brute power to turn it. Such a stone would sink a body to the depths of the sea beyond the possibility of recovery.

2. There is no evidence that the mode of punishment named in our text-verse was ever practiced by the Jews. It was in use, however, by the ancient Syrians, Romans, Macedonians, and Greeks. It was inflicted on the worst class of criminals, especially on parricides (one who murders his or her mother, father, or near relative), and those guilty of sacrilege.

18:34 TORMENTORS

"In anger his master turned him over to the jailers *(tormentors, KJV)* to be tortured, until he should pay back all he owed."

The "tormentors" are the jailers, who were allowed to scourge and torture the poor debtors in their care in order to get money from them for the creditors, or else to excite the compassion of friends and thereby obtain the amount of the debt from them. Trench states in

Notes on the Parables: "In early times of Rome there were certain legal tortures, in the shape, at least, of a chain weighing fifteen pounds, and a pittance of food barely sufficient to sustain life, which the creditor was allow to apply to the debtor for the purpose of bringing him to terms; and no doubt they often did not stop there."

19:13 BENEDICTIONS ON CHILDREN

Then little children were brought to Jesus for him to place his hands on them and pray for them. (See also Mark 10:13; Luke 18:15.)

It was common among the Jews to bring their children to men noted for piety, to have their blessings and their prayers. On the first anniversary of the birth of a child, it was usual to take him or her to the synagogue to be blessed by the rabbi.

The laying-on of hands when in prayer was also a customary form when invoking the divine blessing. Thus Israel, when his eyes were dim with age, laid his hands on the heads of Ephraim and Manasseh, and blessed them and prayed for them (Genesis 48:14), and thus Jesus "took them up in his arms, put his hands upon them, and blessed them" (Mark 10:16).

Matthew Henry's Concise Commentary regarding this practice states: "It is well when we come to Christ ourselves, and bring our children. Little children may be brought to Christ as needing, and being capable of receiving blessings from him, and having an interest in his intercession. We can but beg a blessing for them: Christ only can command the blessing. It is well for us, that Christ has more love and tenderness in him than the best of his disciples have. And let us learn of him not to discountenance any willing, well-meaning souls, in their seeking after Christ, though they are but weak. Those who are given to Christ, as part of his purchase, he will in no wise cast out. Therefore he takes it ill of all who forbid, and try to shut out those whom he has received. And all Christians should bring their children to the Savior that he may bless them with spiritual blessings."

Christ blessing children

19:24 EYE OF A NEEDLE

"Again I tell you, it is easier for a camel to go through the eye of a needle than for a rich man to enter the kingdom of God." (See also Mark 10:25; Luke 18:25.)

There is believed to be here a reference to a proverbial form of expression common in the Jewish schools, when one desired to express the idea of great difficulty or of impossibility. Lightfoot gives several quotations from the rabbis, where the difficulty is represented by the image of an elephant going through the eye of a needle.

Some writers, however, think that there is an allusion in our text-verse, not only to a proverbial form of speech, but also to a fact. They refer to the low, narrow entrance to houses in ancient times, and to the difficulty a camel would experience in entering, though even a camel might enter if his load were removed and he kneeled down, which may be considered a hint to rich men who would enter the kingdom of heaven.

Rev. J.G. Wood writes in *Bible Animals*, "In Oriental [ed. note: this term was used widely in years past to describe most of the Asian continent, now commonly referred to as the Middle East] cities there are in the large gates small and very low apertures, called metaphorically, 'needles-eyes.' These entrances are too narrow for a camel to pass through them in an ordinary manner, or even if loaded. When a laden camel has to pass through one of these entrances it kneels down, its load is removed, and then it shuffles through on its knees. A traveler to Cairo, Lady Duff Gordon, wrote to me saying, 'Yesterday I saw a camel go through the eye of a needle, namely, the low-arched door of an enclosure. He must kneel, and bow his head to creep through; and thus the rich man must humble himself.'"

It has been said that the purpose of the "eye of the needle" gate was so that merchandise could not be brought into Jerusalem on the Sabbath day, although the pack animals and the merchants could come in for protection, but only through this restrictive gate.

20:2 DENARIUS

"He agreed to pay them a denarius for the day and sent them into his vineyard."

The *denarius* is an ancient Roman silver coin. It was equivalent to ten *asses* (\'a-sez)—an *as* being a bronze coin of the ancient Roman republic. This coin represented a typical

reigning Caesar. (See Matthew 22:19-21; Mark 12:15-17.)

The "ten pieces of silver" mentioned in Luke 15:8 are supposed to have been ten *denarii*; and so are the "fifty-thousand pieces of silver" mentioned in Acts 29:19, though authorities vary in opinion.

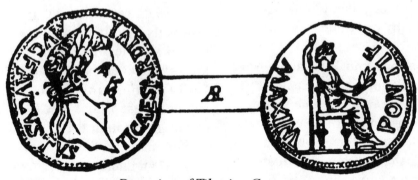

Denarius of Tiberius Caesar

day's wage for an ordinary laborer (Matthew 20:2). The KJV translates it "penny." This unit of Roman currency is the most frequently mentioned coin in the New Testament. Under the Republic, the denarius had on one side the head of Hercules, Apollo, Mars, Janus, or Jupiter. Under the Empire it bore the title and effigies of the

20:3 MARKETPLACE

"About the third hour he went out and saw others standing in the marketplace doing nothing."

The place for trading was often at the gates of walled cities. Here, also, laborers went to seek employment, and employers went to seek laborers. In *Second Journey through Persia* (1818), Morier says, "The most conspicuous building in Hamadan is the Mesjid Jumah, a large mosque now falling into decay, and before it a *maidan*, or square, which serves as a marketplace. Here we observed every morning, before the sun rose, that a numerous body of peasants collected with spades in their hands, waiting, as they informed us, to be hired for the day to work in the surrounding fields."

20:8 Daily Payment of Laborers

"When evening came, the owner of the vineyard said to his foreman, 'Call the workers and pay them their wages.'"

This was according to Mosaic law. It was instituted to protect the laborer from any employer who might wish to keep back his wages. (Leviticus 19:13; Deuteronomy 24:14-15.)

20:21 Post of Honor

"Grant that one of these two sons of mine may sit at your right and the other at your left in your kingdom." (See also Mark 10:37.)

It was evidently the intention of this ambitious mother to have positions of the greatest honor for her two sons. The right hand is usually considered the spot of the highest honor. See 1 Kings 2:19; Psalms 14:9; 80:17; 110:1; Mark 14:62; 16:19; Luke 20:42; 22:69; Acts 2:34; 7:55-56; Romans 8:34; Ephesians 1:20; Colossians 3:1; Hebrews 1:3, 13; 8:1; 10:12; 12:2; 1 Peter 3:22.

As an apparent exception to this usage, Sir John Chardin states in *Coronation of Solyman III* (1665), that among the Persians the left hand of the king is esteemed the most honorable. In biblical times, although the right hand was often considered more honorable than the left, yet a position on either hand near the king was considered a post of great honor. The Jewish historian Josephus represents Saul at supper with Jonathan his son on his right hand, and Abner, the captain of his host, on his left. In the Sanhedrin, the vice-president sat on the right hand of the president, and the referee, who was the officer next in rank, sat on the left. See note on Matthew **26:59 Sanhedrin.**

21:8 Branches Strewn

A very large crowd spread their cloaks on the road, while others cut branches from the trees and spread them on the road. (See Mark 10:37.)

It was usual to strew flowers and branches and to spread carpets and garments in the pathway of conquerors and great princes, and of others to whom it was intended to show particular honor and respect. In a similar way Jehu was recognized as king in 2 Kings 9:13.

In modern times we see this custom carried on in the wedding ceremony when the brides path is strewn with flower petals as a sign of honor. Important, powerful, or famous people are often honored with a red carpet spread in their walkway during a ceremony. To give someone "the

Jesus triumphal entry into Jerusalem

red carpet treatment" is to treat them particularly well.

21:12 TEMPLE MARKET

Jesus entered the temple area and drove out all who were buying and selling there. He overturned the tables of the money changers and the benches of those selling doves. (See Mark 11:15; Luke 19:45.)

In John 2:14 is an account of a similar occurrence that took place during the first year of Christ's ministry.

The temple market is supposed to have been established after the captivity, when many came from foreign lands to Jerusalem. Lightfoot says: "There was always a constant market in the temple in that place, which was called 'the shops' where, every day, was sold wine, salt, oil, and other requisites to sacrifices; as also oxen and sheep in the spacious Court of the Gentiles."

The moneychangers made a business of accommodating those who did not have the Jewish half-shekel for the annual temple tax (see Matthew **17:24 Temple Tax**). Everyone, rich and poor, was expected to pay the half-shekel for himself during the month of Adar. Thus it sometimes became necessary to change a shekel into two halves, or to exchange foreign money for the Jewish half-shekel. The men who followed this business made their living by charging a percentage for the exchange, and carried on their traffic within the temple area.

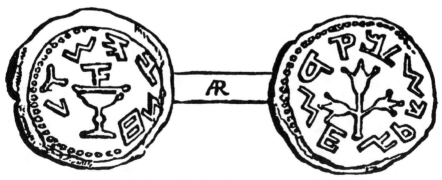

Half-shekel ascribed to Simon Maccabeus

21:16 "Out of the mouths of babes."

"Yea; have ye never read, Out of the mouth of babes and sucklings thou hast perfected praise" *(KJV)*?

Jesus refers here to Psalms 8:2: "Out of the mouth of babes and sucklings hast thou ordained strength because of thine enemies, that thou mightest still the enemy and the avenger" (KJV).

This phrase has come to mean that the innocent can speak nothing but the truth.

21:33 Vineyards - Fences - Wine-presses - Watchtowers

"There was a landowner who planted a vineyard. He put a wall around it, dug a winepress in it and built a watchtower."(See also Mark 12:1; Luke 20:9.)

Wine making has always been a major industry in Syria-Palestine. Sinuhe, the Middle Kingdom Egyptian official of the 12th dynasty (1938-1756 BC) who fled Egypt to settle in Syria, described the land as having "more wine than water."

Egyptian wine-press

452

Vine

1. There appears to have been several ways of planting vineyards in Palestine. Sometimes the vines were planted in rows and trained on stakes. In 1856, Dr. Robinson described the celebrated vineyards of Hebron as arranged in this manner: The vines "are planted in rows eight or ten feet apart in each direction. The stock is suffered to grow up large to the height of six or eight feet, and is there fastened in a sloping position to a strong stake, and the shoots suffered to grow and extend from one plant to another, forming a line of festoons. Sometimes two rows are made to slant toward each other, and thus form by their shoots a sort of arch. These shoots are pruned away in Autumn." The vines were sometimes planted on the side of a terraced hill. The old branches were permitted to trail along the ground, while the fruit-bearing shoots were propped with forked sticks.

An ancient mode of planting vineyards was by training the vines over heaps of stones. During a trip in the mid-1800s, E. H. Palmer discovered large numbers of these stone-heaps while traveling through the Negeb, or south country of Palestine. Near the ruins of El-'Aujeh he found stone-heaps.

"The black flint-covered hill-slopes which surrounded the fort are covered with long, regular rows of stones, which have been carefully swept together and piled into numberless little black heaps. These at first considerably puzzled us, as they were evidently artificially made, and intended for some agricultural purpose; but we could not conceive what plants had been grown on such dry and barren ground. Here again Arab tradition came to our aid, and the name *teleilat-el-'anab*, (grape-mounds) solved the difficulty. These sunny slopes, if well tended, with such supplies of water and agricultural appliances as the inhabitants of El-'Aujeh must have possessed, would have been admirably adapted to the growth of grapes, and the black flinty surface would radiate the solar heat, while these little mounds would allow the vines to trail along them, and would still keep the clusters off the ground." He said that these "grape-mounds" formed one of the most striking characteristics of the Negeb, and that some of the hillsides and the valley were covered with them for miles.

2. The vineyards were sometimes fenced with walls of stone (Numbers 22:24; Proverbs 24:31), and sometimes with a hedge of thorny plants (Psalms 80:12), and again with stone walls and hedges combined. The last method is probably referred to in Isaiah 5:5, where hedge and wall are both spoken of. In his Easter journey in 1697, Henry Maundrell saw another sort of wall that surrounded the gardens of Damascus: "The garden walls are of a very singular structure," he wrote. "They are built of great pieces of earth made in the fashion of brick, and hardened in the sun. In their dimensions they are two yards long each and somewhat more than one broad, and a yard thick. Two rows of these placed edgeways, one upon another, make a cheap, expeditious, and, in this dry country, a durable wall."

3. The winepress consisted of two parts—the receptacle for the grapes, and the vat for the liquor. Either part, by itself, is sometimes called the press. In Old Testament times the presses for making wine were usually cut or hewed out of rock (Isaiah 5:2) and were connected by channels to lower rock-cut vats where the juice was allowed to collect and ferment. The juice was squeezed from the grapes by treading over

them with the feet (Job 24:11; Amos 9:13).

After the juice had fermented, it was collected into jars or wineskins (Matthew 9:17). At ancient Gibeon, archaeologists discovered a major wine-producing installation dating from about 700 B.C. In addition to the presses and fermentation tanks, 63 rock-cut cellars were found with a storage capacity of 25,000 gallons of wine. In these cellars the wine could be kept at a constant cool temperature of 65 degrees Fahrenheit. By the New Testament period, both beam presses and presses with mosaic pavements were in use.

The harvesting and treading of the grapes was a time of celebration (Isaiah 16:10; Jeremiah 48:33; Deuteronomy 16:13-15). Abundance of wine is used in the Bible as a metaphor for God's salvation and blessing (Proverbs 3:10; Joel 3:18; Amos 9:13). The pressure by the feet on the grapes naturally spattered the red juice over the upper garments. Thus we read of Judah in the prophecy of the dying Jacob: "He washed his garments in wine, and his clothes in the blood of grapes" (Genesis 49:11). The question is also asked in Isaiah, "Why are your garments

red, like those of one treading the winepress?" (Isaiah 63:2). In Isaiah 63:3 we read, "I have trodden the winepress alone; from the nations no one was with me. I trampled them in my anger and trod them down in my wrath; their blood spattered my garments, and I stained all my clothing." God's judgment is portrayed in these passages as the treading of the winepress (see also Revelation 14:19-20).

4. The tower was designed as a place of temporary dwelling for the guard, who watched over the vineyard while the fruit was ripening. It was his job to keep away thieves and wild beasts. The tower was also sometimes used as a temporary abode by the owner during the vintage season. Many towers were frail structures, lasting only the one season; others were more durable, being made of stone. There were circular or square in shape, and varied in height from fifteen feet to fifty. In a garden near Beirut, Maundrell saw an unfinished tower that had been built to the height of sixty feet with walls twelve feet thick.

The towers could also be used during times of war to watch enemy movements in the distance. Similar towers were built in open country for use by shepherds (see 2 Chronicles **26:10 Towers**). The vineyard, the hedge, the winepress, and the tower are also referred to in Isaiah 5:1-2.

22:3 DOUBLE INVITATIONS

"He sent his servants to those who had been invited to the banquet to tell them to come."

This double invitation was customary among the wealthy in giving entertainments. The invitation was given some time in advance, as it is still done in modern times, and when the feast is ready, a servant was dispatched with an announcement of the fact. Esther invited Ahasuerus and Haman to a feast, and when it was ready, the king's chamberlains were sent to notify Haman (Esther 5:8; 6:14). The custom also finds illustration in the parable of the banquet in Luke 14:16-17: "A certain man was preparing a great banquet and invited many guests. At the time of the banquet he sent his servant to tell those who had been invited, 'Come, for everything is now ready.'" Here the two invitations are distinctly marked. Of additional interest in this parable is the fact that the second invitation was given only to those who had accepted the first.

22:11 WEDDING CLOTHES

But when the king came in to see the guests, he noticed a man there who was not wearing wedding clothes.

The surprise shown by the king at finding one of the guests without a suitable garment, when it could not be expected that people who had thus been suddenly called, and from poorer classes too, would furnish themselves with festive apparel, is an indication that the bounty of the king had provided a supply for the guests from his own wardrobe. The beauty of the parable, as well as its deep spiritual significance, is more clearly seen in the fact that beggars are represented as clothed in garments of royalty. Although there is no direct evidence to show that it was customary to furnish wedding guests with robes, the intimation is clearly made in the parable.

Historically, there have been other accounts of such kingly generosity. Extensive wardrobes were a show of wealth

Garments were often given as presents. It was a special mark of honor to receive one that had been used by the giver, and kings sometimes showed their munificence by presenting them. (See Genesis **45:22 Changes of Raiment**; 1 Samuel **18:4 Princely Robes**; Esther **6:8 Royal Honors Given to Subjects**.)

22: 14 "MANY ARE CALLED, BUT FEW ARE CHOSEN."

"For many are called, but few are chosen" *(KJV)*.

More plainly, salvation is difficult to attain, and though many are called to it, few are willing to give up their temporal flesh-life for the sake of their eternal soul-life. The saying is applied in many ways today to denote that many are given opportunities but few fulfill the requirements or demands of the opportunities.

22:15 PHARISEES

Then the Pharisees went out and laid plans to trap him in his words.

The Pharisees were a politico-religious party among the Jews. Their origin is obscure, but it's believed that the beginning of the party dates from a time after the Babylonian Captivity (a term applied to the period between the deportation of the Jews from Palestine to Babylon by the Babylonian king Nebuchadnezzar II and their release in 538 B.C. by the Persian king, Cyrus).

A Pharisee is, literally, one who is separated. It is thought that the name was given because these people separated themselves from all Levitical impurity. They were doubtless a pure people in the beginning, their design being to preserve the law from violation, and the Jewish people from contamination. As their influence increased, and political power came into their hands, they lost much of their original simplicity. In the time of Christ, they were numerous and influential, and occupied the chief offices among the Jews. They were divided into

A Pharisee

two schools: the School of Hillel and the School of Shammai.

The Pharisees were especially distinguished for belief in an oral law of Moses, as well as a written law. This oral law was supposed to be supplementary to the written law, and, with various comments added from time to time, had been handed down by tradition. The Pharisees had great veneration for this traditional code and for the traditional interpretations. They placed them in authority on a level with the written law, and sometimes even above it. (See Matthew **15:3 Tradition.**)

As a body they were not chargeable with immorality in life. On the contrary, there were many zealous and conscientious men among them, and many things that they taught were worthy of being observed as Jesus himself admitted (Matthew 23:3). These teachings were from the law, but when they attempted to make their traditions valid, Jesus denounced them. The great error of the most of them consisted in substituting human tradition for divine law, and in observing mere external forms. Many of those were burdensome and immature, and did not seek for inward purity of heart, which would have been accompanied by corresponding blamelessness in life.

It was but natural that such teachers should be bitterly opposed to Christ, and that He should vehemently denounce them and warn the people against them. They endeavored in various ways to "trap him in his words."

22:16 HERODIANS

They sent their disciples to him along with the Herodians.

The Herodians were more a political than religious party. They were Jews who attached themselves to the political fortunes of the Herodian family, hoping thereby to promote the interests of the Jewish people. They were loose in observing Jewish rituals, and though in this respect they were the opposite of the Pharisees, they easily fell in with them in efforts to ruin Jesus. (See Mark 3:6; 12:13.) Some suppose, comparing Matthew 26:6 with Mark 8:15, that the Herodians were all Sadducees; that they belonged to what is known as the Boethusian branch of that body.

22:21 "RENDER UNTO CAESAR THE THINGS WHICH ARE CAESAR'S, AND UNTO GOD THE THINGS THAT ARE GOD'S."

Then he said to them, "Give to Caesar what is Caesar's, and to God what is God's."

This was Jesus' response when His enemies tried to trap Him by asking whether it was right for the Jews, whose nation had been taken over by the Roman Empire, to pay tribute to the Roman emperor. He took a Roman coin that would be used to pay the tribute, and asked whose picture was on it. His questioners answered, "Caesar's." The reply of Jesus implied that in using Roman coins, the Jews accepted the rule of the Romans, and so the Roman government had the right to tax them, as long as the Jews were not compromising their religious duties.

In modern usage the phrase is often interpreted as, "Keep politics separate from certain other fields, such as religion." Or to say it another way: "Give to worldly authorities the things that belong to them, and to God what belongs to Him."

22:23 SADDUCEES

That same day the Sadducees, who say there is no resurrection, came to him with a question.

The origination of the Sadducees as a party among the Jews is unknown. It is generally believed that they had their origin about the same time as the Pharisees. The derivation of the name is also a matter of dispute. Some derive it from the Hebrew *tsedek, or* "righteousness," and suppose that the name was given them because of their piety. Others say that the Sadducees were organized by Zadoc, a scholar of Antigonus Socho, president of the Sanhedrin, and a disciple of Simon the Just. This

particular Zadoc died in 263 B.C. Others seek a derivation with Zadok the priest, who lived in the time of David (1 Kings 1:32).

The vital difference between the Pharisees and the Sadducees was in their opinion of the Law. The Sadducees rejected the traditional interpretations of the Law, to which the Pharisees attached great importance. Unlike the Pharisees, they did not believe in the oral law as a supplement to the written law, but took the Hebrew Scriptures, with the authoritative explanations that were developed over the course of time, as the only rule of faith and practice. They accepted those traditional explanations of the Law that could be deduced from the Scriptures, but rejected all that the Pharisees, without authority, had added. In some respects, they were more rigid interpreters of the Law than the Pharisees.

Also, the Sadducees accepted only the five books of Moses: Genesis, Exodus, Leviticus, Numbers, and Deuteronomy. For this reason they did not believe in the resurrection or in angels, for they said they could not find either in those books. One day they came to Jesus with a question about the law of the kinsman-redeemer, hoping to trap Him in

His doctrine of the resurrection, and He answered them out of the books of Moses and spoke of both angels and the resurrection (Matthew 22:23-32).

The Sadducees were not so numerous as the Pharisees, nor were their doctrines so acceptable to the people. They were an ancient, priestly aristocracy, having considerable wealth and great political power. In Acts 5:17 and 4:6, it's inferred that many of the kindred of the high priest at that time, as well as the high priest, were of the Sadduccean party, and that probably the priestly families in general belonged to them. They were too cold and austere in their manners to make many converts, and disappeared from history after the destruction of Jerusalem in A.D. 70.

22: 37-40 Greatest Commandment

Jesus replied, "Love the Lord your God with all your heart and with all your soul and with all your mind. This is the first and greatest commandment. And the second is like it: Love your neighbor as yourself. All the Law and the Prophets hang on these two commandments."

The love of God is the first and great commandment, and the sum of all the commands of the Law. Our love of God must be sincere, not in word and tongue only. All the powers of the soul and spirit must be engaged for Him, and carried out toward Him.

To love our neighbor as we love ourselves, is the second great commandment. There is a self-love that is corrupt, and the root of great sin, but there is a self-love that is the rule of the greatest duty: we must have a due concern for the welfare of our own souls and bodies—and we must love our neighbor as truly and sincerely as we love ourselves. In many cases we must also deny ourselves for the good of others.

23:3 "Practice what you preach."

The King James says it this way: "All therefore whatsoever they [the Pharisees] bid you observe, that observe and do; but do not ye after their works: for they say, and do not."

Or, more easily spoken, "Do yourself what you advise others to do." This has become a common expression today.

23:5 Phylacteries

"They make their phylacteries wide."

Greek *phulakteria*; defenses or protections. Called *tephillin*, or prayers, by most Jews. Phylacteries consisted of strips of parchment on which were inscribed these four texts: Exodus 13:1-10; Exodus 13:11-16; Deuteronomy 6:4-9; and

significance. This case was fastened by straps to the forehead, just between the eyes. The "wide phylacteries" spoken of by Jesus in our text-verse refers to the enlarging of the case so as to make it conspicuous.

Another form of the phylactery consisted of two rolls of parchment, on which the same texts were written, enclosed in a case of black calfskin. This was worn on the left arm near the elbow, to which it was bound by a thong. It was called the "*Tephillah* on the arm."

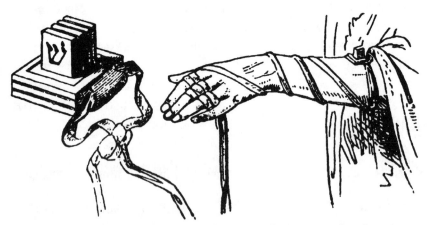

Phylacteries for the head and arm

Deuteronomy 11:18-21. These were enclosed in a square leather case, on one side of which was inscribed the Hebrew letter *shin*, to which the rabbis attached some

23:6 Places of Honor

"They love the place of honor at banquets and the

most important seats in the synagogues." (See also Mark 12:39; Luke 11:43; 20:46.)

These were seats that were prepared for the elders of the synagogue and the doctors of the law. They were also called "Moses' seat" in the 2nd verse of Matthew 23. They were placed in front of the ark of the covenant, which contained the Law, in the uppermost part of the synagogue at the "Jerusalem end" (see Matthew **4:23 Synagogue**). Luke calls them the "uppermost seats." Those who occupied them sat with their faces to the people. These seats were considered positions of great honor, and were eagerly sought by the ambitious scribes and Pharisees. It's probable that James refers to this custom of honor in the Jewish synagogue when he speaks of "a good place" where the rich man is invited to sit in the Christian "assembly" (James 2:2-3).

23:7 RABBI

"They love to be greeted in the marketplaces and to have men call them 'Rabbi.'"

Rabbi means "my master," and is applied to teachers and others of exalted or revered positions. During the New Testament period, the term rabbi came to be more narrowly applied to one learned in the law of Moses, without signifying an official office, although it was often used in place of *teacher*.

In the New Testament, rabbi, or an alternate form, *rabboni*, is used only in three of the gospels—our text-verse; John 1:49; 3:2,26; 4:31; 6:25; 9:2; 11:8; 20:16; Mark 9:5; 11:21; 14:45.

Luke never used the term rabbi, but the word *epistata*, the equivalent of "schoolmaster," a term more meaningful to his predominantly Greek readers (Luke 17:13). Jesus disciples were forbidden to call each other "rabbi," for "you have only one Master and you are all brothers" (Matthew 23:8).

23:27 WHITEWASHED TOMBS

"You are like whitewashed tombs, which look beautiful on the outside but on the inside are full of dead men's bones and everything unclean."

The tombs were whitened with lime, so that they could be easily distinguished, and thus prevent the Jews from being ceremonially defiled by approaching them. (Note the peculiar effect of limestone coffins in the note at Genesis **50:26 Joseph's Coffin,** especially with reference to Jesus' expression about dead men's bones.)

23:29 Decorated Tombs

"You build tombs for the prophets and decorate the graves of the righteous."

As is common even today in many countries and to many nationalities, the Jews' tombs or grave sites are ornamented in various ways. Much like the decorated monuments that you can find in almost every large cemetery in this country.

24:1 Herod's Temple

Jesus left the temple and was walking away when his disciples came up to him to call his attention to its buildings. (See also Mark 13:1; Luke 21:5.)

What is commonly known as Herod's temple was a restoration or reconstruction of the temple of Zerubbabel, which was taken down piece by piece and this temple gradually substituted for it. It was, however, larger and more splendid than the temple of Zerubbabel—its courts occupied more ground than those that surrounded that old temple, and far exceeded them in magnificence.

According to the Talmud, the entire temple area was five hundred cubits square (about 750 feet). Around the edge of this square and against the massive stone wall that enclosed it, cloisters were built, their cedar roofs being supported by rows of Corinthian columns of solid marble. The cloisters on the north, west, and east sides were alike in height and width, the columns that upheld the roof being twenty-five cubits high (about 37.5 feet), and the halls themselves thirty cubits wide (about 45 feet).

The colonnade on the east was called Solomon's Porch, and is mentioned in John 10:23; Acts 3:11; 5:12. The cloisters on the south formed an immense building known as the *Stoa Basilica,* or King's Porch. It was much wider than the cloisters on the other sides, and consisted of a nave (central part) and two aisles. This immense building, with its high nave, its broad aisles, and its marble column, presented a grand appearance. The Jewish historian Josephus says: "Its fineness, to such as had not seen it, was incredible; and to such as had seen it, was greatly amazing." The southeastern corner of this building is supposed to have been the "pinnacle of the temple" where the devil took Jesus in the Temptation (see Matthew **4:5 Pinnacle of the Temple**). In these cloisters the Levites resided. Here the doctors of the law met to hear and answer questions (Luke 2:46). They were favorite places of resort for religionists of different sorts to discuss various points of doctrine. Jesus often spoke to the people from here. After His death, His followers met here (Acts 2:46).

North of the center of the large area enclosed by these cloisters stood the sacred enclosure of the temple. Its boundaries extended nearer to the cloisters on the west than to Solomon's Porch on the east. The space surrounding this enclosure was the Court of the Gentiles, and was open to all. It was paved with various-colored stones. It was here that the cattle-dealers and moneychangers desecrated the house of God. (See Matthew **21:12 Temple Market.**) This was called the Outer Court, the Lower court, and, by the rabbis usually, the "Mountain of the Lord's House."

The enclosure of the temple proper was on a terrace about six cubits higher than the Court of the Gentiles. It was approached by steps, and was surrounded by a wall three cubits high (about 4.5 feet). This wall was designed to shut off the Gentiles, and there were pillars erected in the wall at certain distances with inscriptions in Latin, Greek, and Hebrew, warning all Gentiles to come no further under penalty of death. The Jews, on one occasion, accused Paul of having brought Greeks up the steps, and into the sacred enclosure, in violation of the standing order (Acts 21:28). It is believed that Paul refers to this wall of separation when he says: "For he himself is our peace, who has made the two one and has destroyed the barrier, the dividing wall of hostility" (Ephesians 2:14). At the top of the terrace, and going entirely around it, was a platform ten cubits wide (about 18 feet) extending to another wall.

In the eastern side of the latter wall was a gate of elegant workmanship, forty cubits wide (about 60 feet), and supposed to have been the "Gate Beautiful" mentioned in Acts 3:2,10. It was sometimes called the "Gate Susan" because it had a representation of the town of Susa sculptured in relief on it. Though there were gates on the north and south sides, this was the grand entrance to the Court of the Women, which was the general place of public worship at the time of the sacrifices. It received its name, not because it was exclusively appropriated by women, but because the women were not permitted to go beyond it. There were smaller courts in the four corners of this court, and on the north, east, and west sides were galleries supported by columns. In front of these columns were distributed the eleven treasure chests of the temple, in addition to the two at the "Gate Beautiful," for the half-shekel tax. It was into one of these that the widow threw her two mites (Mark 12:41-42; Luke 21:1-2). It was near these treasure chests that the incidents recorded in John 8:20 took place.

West of the Court of the Women, separated from it by a wall, and on a terrace higher still, was the Court of the Israelites. This was a narrow hall completely surrounding the Court of the Priests, and had cloisters on all sides supported by beautiful columns. The rooms of these cloisters were devoted to various purposes connected with the service of the temple. This court was entered from the Court of the Women by a flight of semicircular steps and through the Gate of Nicanor. The session room of the Sanhedrin was in the southeast corner of the Court of the Israelites.

On a terrace fifteen steps higher, and separated from the court of the Israelites by a low stone balustrade, was the Court of the Priests. In the eastern part of this was the great altar of burnt-offering, directly west of which arose the Great Temple itself. The building was of white marble, and some of the foundation stones were immense. It was divided into two parts, forming the Holy Place and the Most Holy Place, the two being separated by the veil (see

Matthew **27:51 Veil of the Temple**). The internal arrangements of these two sacred places were probably like those of the temple of Zerubbabel (see Ezra **6:3-4 Temple of Zerubbabel**). Above these were rooms used for various purposes, and on the sides were three stories of chambers. In the front part of the building was the porch, which projected a short distance beyond the building, north and south, forming a sideways T shape.

A striking feature in the general appearance of the temple and its various courts is the series of terraces; the different courts rising one above the other, until the temple itself was reached on a platform that was highest of all. The structure—the paved courts, the beautiful columns, the white marble cloisters, the gateways, which in themselves were high and massive buildings, and, crowning all, the white temple standing high above the rest, its front walls ornamented with thick plates of gold—produced an effect that was magnificent beyond description. (See Luke **21:5 Ornaments of the Temple**.)

24:41 HAND MILL

"Two women will be grinding with a hand mill." (See also Luke 17:35.)

The hand mill was commonly two circular stones used to grind grain. Usually, it was worked by two women. One woman fed the grain at the center, and the other guided the products into little piles. The grain to be ground was fed into the central hole in the upper stone and it gradually worked down between the stones. As the grain was reduced to flour, it flew out from between the stones onto a cloth or skin placed underneath the mill. To make fine flour, it was reground and sifted. The stone was made of basalt and was about a foot and a half in diameter and two to four inches thick.

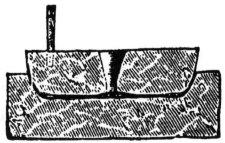

Section of Eastern hand-mill

It was forbidden to take millstones as a pledge because they were so important to sustaining life (Deuteronomy 24:6). In Revelation 18:21, the millstone was cast into the sea as a symbol of absolute destruction. (See Judges **16:21 Grinding, a Punishment**.)

25:1 MARRIAGE PROCESSION

"At that time the kingdom of heaven will be like ten virgins who took their lamps and went out to meet the bridegroom."

On the occasion of a marriage, the bridegroom, attended by his friends, went to the house of his bride, and brought her with her friends in joyful procession to his own house.

In pre-Mosaic times, when the proposals were accepted and the marriage price given, the bridegroom could come at once and take away his bride to his own house (Genesis 24:63-67). But in general the marriage was celebrated by a feast in the house of the bride's parents, to which all friends were invited (Genesis 29:22, 27); and, on the day of the marriage, the bride, concealed under a thick veil, was conducted to her future husband's home.

25:3-4 LAMPS - LANTERNS - TORCHES

"The foolish ones took their lamps but did not take any oil with them. The wise, however, took oil in jars along with their lamps."

Lamps are mentioned often in the Bible but seldom described. Archaeological excavations have provided numerous examples of these lighting implements used in ancient times, dating from before Abraham to after Christ.

Lamps of the Old Testament period were made exclusively of pottery and were an open-bowl design with a pinched spout to support the wick. Wicks were

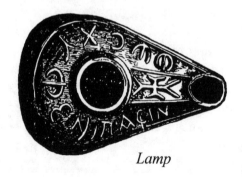

Lamp

made generally of twisted flax. Though the lamps almost exclusively burned olive oil, in later times oil from nuts, fish, and other sources were used.

Lanterns were commonly made of waxed linen, or even of paper, stretched over rings of wire, and having a top and bottom of tinned copper. When folded, the candle projects above the tops of the folds, so that the lantern may, in the house, serve the purpose of a candlestick.

Torches were also used for outdoor lighting. Torches were a portable light produced by the flame of a stick of resinous wood or of a flammable material wound about the end of a stick of wood.

Torches

25:10 CLOSED DOOR

"**The bridegroom arrived. The virgins who were ready went in with him to the wedding banquet. And the door was shut.**"

At all formal banquets, the invited guests presented their tablets or cards to a servant stationed at the entrance, whose job it was to keep out the uninvited. When the company were assembled, the "master of the house" shut the door, and thereafter the servant was instructed not to allow anyone to enter, no matter how insistent they were. This illustrates not only our text-verse, but also Luke 13:24-25.

25: 15 TALENTS

"To one he gave five talents of money, to another two talents, and to another one talent, each according to his ability."

A talent was a variable unit of weight and money used in ancient Greece, Rome, and the Middle East. In Hebrew weights it was equivalent to three-thousand shekels.

25:32-33 SHEEP AND GOATS

"All the nations will be gathered before him, and he will separate the people one from another as a shepherd separates the sheep from the goats. He will put the sheep on his right and the goats on his left."

Sheep and goats grazed in the same pasture, but it was necessary to separate the herds because male goats were often hostile toward the sheep. Thus Jesus seeks to illustrate the truth that though righteous and wicked are now together, there will come a time of separation.

Regarding the position in which the animals are placed, some think there is also a reference here to a custom in the Sanhedrin of putting the acquitted prisoners on the right of the president, and those who were convicted on his left.

Goat

Alabaster boxes

26:7 ALABASTER - TABLES

A woman came to him with an alabaster jar of very expensive perfume, which she poured on his head as he was reclining at the table. (See Mark 14:3; Luke 7:36-38; John 12:3.)

1. A stone found near Alabastron in Egypt, from which boxes were produced. The name was soon used for all perfume vessels, of whatever material they were formed. This stone resembles marble, but is softer in its texture, and hence very easily wrought into boxes. Mark 14:5 says that this box of ointment was worth more than 300 denarii (see Matthew **20:2 Denarius**).

2. Tables during biblical times were banqueting-couches or benches on which the Jews reclined when at meals. This custom, along with the use of raised tables like ours, was introduced among the Jews after their captivity in Babylon. Before this they had, properly speaking, no table but rather ate from a

skin or piece of leather spread out on the carpeted floor.

Among the Romans, three beds were generally used in the dining room, and thus combined were called *triclinium*. They were arranged around the sides of a square (also sometimes referred to as triclinium) in the center of the dining room. The tables were in front of and within easy reach of the guests, and the left side was open to allow servants room to move about.

Alabaster jars

The frames on which the couches were placed were sometimes made of costly wood and highly ornamented. The beds themselves were stuffed with straw, hay, leaves, woolly plants, seaweed, wool, and among the wealthy, feathers and swans' down. Cushions and pillows were placed on the beds so that the guests might rest the left arm at the elbow, and eat with the right

Reclining at meals

hand. Some authorities, however, state that when the guests began eating they lay on their stomachs, and afterward reclined on their left side.

The front of the bed was somewhat higher than the table, and as the triclinium was on an inclined plane, the feet of the guests lay toward the floor.

The Romans allowed 3 guests to each bed, making nine in all. It was the rule of Varro (Marcus Terentius: 116-27 B.C., Roman scholar and encyclopedist who reputedly produced more than 600 volumes, covering nearly every field of knowledge), that the "number of guests ought not to be less than that of the Graces [three sister goddesses], nor to exceed that of the Muses [nine daughters of Mnemosyne and Zeus]." The Greeks went beyond this number, as did the Jews.

Reclining at table is also referred to in Matthew 9:10; 26:20; Mark 14:18; 16:14; John 12:2.

26:15 THIRTY PIECES OF SILVER

"So they counted out for him thirty silver coins."

It is difficult to determine what coins are meant here. Numismatic authorities suggest that the thirty *arguria* mentioned here and in Matthew 28: 3,5, 6, 9, were not *denarii,* as many commentators suppose, but *shekels*, and that shekels must also be understood in the parallel passage of Zechariah 11:12-13. There seems to have been three kinds of shekel used in Israel: (1) a temple shekel of about ten grams (.351 ounces), which depreciated to about 9.8 grams (.345 ounces); (2) the common shekel of about 11.7 grams (.408 ounces), which depreciated to about 11.4 grams (.401 ounces); and (3) the heavy ("royal"?) shekel of about thirteen grams (.457 ounces). Thirty shekels of silver was the price of blood when a slave was accidentally killed (Exodus 21:32). As there were probably no current shekels during Jesus' time, it is supposed that the *tetradrachms* of the Greek cities of Syria were the coins that composed the thirty pieces of silver paid to Judas. These tetradrachms have the same weight as the shekels of Simon Maccabaeus, and the *stater* found by Peter in the fish was a specimen of them. (Compare Zechariah 11:13.)

26:17 Passover Guests

"Where do you want us to make preparations for you to eat the Passover?" (See Mark 14:12; Luke 22:9.)

The Israelites who came to Jerusalem to celebrate the Passover were received by the inhabitants as brothers, and apartments were gratuitously furnished them where they might eat the feast. In return the guests gave their hosts the skins of the paschal lambs and the vessels they had used in the ceremonies. According to this custom, the disciples, wishing to make arrangements for the Passover, inquired of the Lord if He had any special house where He desired to go.

26:19 Passover Preparations

So the disciples did as Jesus had directed them and prepared the Passover. (See Mark 14:16; Luke 22:13.)

In the afternoon, the two disciples, Peter and John, went to the temple with the paschal lamb. There the lamb was killed, with the nearest priest catching the blood in a gold or silver bowl, passing it to the next in the row of priests until it reached the priest nearest the altar, who instantly sprinkled it on the altar's base. The lamb was then flayed and the entrails removed to be burnt on the altar with incense. At dark the lamb was roasted. They likewise provided bread, wine, bitter herbs, and sauce. See Exodus **23:15 Passover (Feast of Unleavened Bread).**

26:20 Last Supper

When evening came, Jesus was reclining at the table with the Twelve. (See Mark 14:17; Luke 22:14.)

This was the traditional Passover meal that Jesus ate with the Apostles the night before His death. At this supper Jesus blessed bread and broke it, telling the disciples, "Take, eat; this is My body." He then passed a cup of wine to them, saying, "This is My blood." Jesus' words refer to the crucifixion He was about to suffer to atone for mankind's sins. He told the Apostles, "This do in remembrance of Me." The

The Last Supper

actions of Jesus at the Last Supper are the basis for the Christian sacrament of Holy Communion, or the Eucharist, in which the faithful partake of bread and wine. Although called the "Last Supper," this meal was actually a covenant meal that was eaten as part of the institution of the New Covenant that would be cut the next day in the body of Jesus on the Cross.

The celebration of the Passover supper in the time of Christ differed somewhat from the time of its institution.

1. The cup of wine was filled for everyone and he who presided over the table pronounced the blessing, after which the wine was drank.

2. The bitter herbs, the unleavened bread, the *charoseth* (vinegar and water), and the flesh of the *chagigah* (a special voluntary peace-offering), were then brought in.

3. When these were all

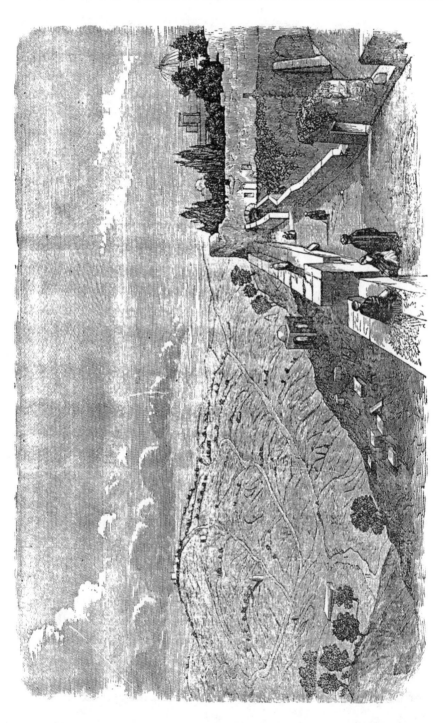

Mount of Olives

placed on the table, the head of the family, or president of the feast, took a portion of the bitter herbs in his hand, dipped it into the charoseth, and, after thanking God for the fruits of the earth, ate a small portion, and then gave a similar portion to all at the table. The unleavened bread was then distributed, and the paschal lamb placed on the table in front of the head of the family.

4. A second cup of wine was given, in accordance with Exodus 12:26-27. The first part of the "Hallel" (hymn of praise consisting of Psalms 113 and 114) was sung. Another blessing followed.

5. After the singing, unleavened bread and bitter herbs, dipped in charoseth, were eaten. Then the flesh of the chagigah was eaten, then the paschal lamb. A third cup of wine was poured out and drank, as well as a fourth. After the fourth cup, the rest of the "Hallel" was sung (Psalms 115 to 118). This is the hymn referred to in Matthew 26:30 and Mark 14:26. Many authorities believe that the specific verse that was sung was Psalm 118:24: "This is the day the LORD has made; let us rejoice and be glad

in it." It's part of the Messianic passage in that Psalm.

26:36 GETHSEMANE

Then Jesus went with his disciples to a place called Gethsemane.

Gethsemane is a garden east of Jerusalem near the foot of the Mount of Olives. It was the scene of Jesus' agony and betrayal.

In modern usage, "a person's gethsemane" is an instance or a place of great suffering. It may also be a place of decision to accept suffering in order to do what is right and needed.

26:39 CUP OF SUFFERING

"My Father, if it is possible, may (let, KJV) this cup be taken (pass, KJV) from me. Yet not as I will, but as you will."

The word "cup" is frequently used in the Bible in a figurative sense. The contents of the cup are accentuated, since symbolically God serves the drink. Thus the cup might represent blessings or prosperity for a righteous person. (Psalms 16:5; 23:5; 116:13.) It

Gethsemane

Jesus in the garden of agony

also represented the totality of divine judgment on the wicked. (Psalms 11:6; 75:8; Isaiah 51:17, 22; Jeremiah 25:15; 49:12; 51:7; Ezekiel 23:31-34; Revelation 14:10; 16:19; 17:4; 18:6.) Jesus voluntarily drank the cup of suffering. For Jesus that cup was His death and everything that it involved. See also Matthew 20:22; 26:42; Mark 10:38; 14:36; Luke 22:42; John 18:11.

Jesus' expression as rendered in the KJV, "let this cup pass from me," may also have been based upon one of the Romans' methods of executing soldiers who had been sentenced to death for various crimes. At times they would line them up on a high cliff and push them over one by one, or if the purpose was simply to instill discipline where it had been lacking in battle, they might push over only selected ones, such as every tenth man. A different method that involved the use of a cup was to line up the men who were to be executed and give the first man a full cup of hemlock, or some other deadly poison that created great pain in accordance to the amount that was drank. If this first man had the courage, heart, and compassion, he could drink the full measure of the cup, "to its

bitter dregs," and suffer all the pains of the poison himself. If he did, the rest of the men would go free. If he did not, the next man must drink the poison also—and he had the same choice as the first man, to drink the full measure of the poison and suffer its pains for the rest of his companions, or he could let them suffer the pains of their portions of the poison. Each man to whom the cup was passed had the same choice. If this was the cup our Lord spoke to His Father about in the Garden, then the symbolism is obvious. See 2 Chronicles **25:12 Executed by Being Thrown from a Cliff.**

26:47 Chief Priests - Elders

With him was a large crowd armed with swords and clubs, sent from the chief priests and the elders of the people.

1. Priest in charge of the Temple (or tabernacle) worship. A number of terms are used to refer to the high priest: *the priest* (Exodus 31:10); *the anointed priest* (Leviticus 4:3); *the priest who is chief among his brethren* (Leviticus 21:10); *chief priest* (2

Chronicles 26:20); and *high priest* (2 Kings 12:10).

2. In the Old Testament, "elder" usually translates the Hebrew word *zaqen* from a root that means "beard" or "chin." In the New Testament, the Greek word is *presbuteros*, from which we get our English word, "presbyter," and from which the word "priest" was derived.

From the beginning of Israelite history, the elders were the leaders of the various clans and tribes. When the tribes came together to form the nation of Israel, the elders of the tribes assumed important roles in governing the affairs of the nation.

Although elders were less prominent in the period after their exile and the term was apparently not much used in Jewish communities outside Palestine, the "council of elders" was an integral part of the Sanhedrin at Jerusalem. In the New Testament, frequent reference is made to the elders of the Jews, usually in conjunction with the chief priests or scribes. In this context the elders, apparently members of leading families, had some authority but were not the principal leaders in either religious or political affairs. Elders did have leading roles in the government of synagogues and, after the fall of the Temple, became even more central to Jewish religious life. Acts 15:2 speaks of Paul and Barnabas going "up to Jerusalem to see the apostles and elders." Paul also wrote about this in his letter to the Galatians.

26:59 SANHEDRIN

The chief priests and the whole Sanhedrin were looking for false evidence against Jesus so that they could put him to death.

The word *Sanhedrin* is usually translated "council." Because of the predominance of the chief priests in the Sanhedrin, at times the words *chief priests* seem to refer to the action of the Sanhedrin, even though the name itself is not used.

The Sanhedrin was the highest Jewish council in the first century. According to the Mishna, the first section of the Talmud, the council had 70 members and was presided over by the high priest. The Sanhedrin included both of the main Jewish parties among its membership. Since the high priest presided, the Sadducean priestly party seems to have predominated; but some leading Pharisees also were members (Acts 5:34; 23:1-9).

According to Jewish tradition, the Sanhedrin began with the 70 elders appointed by Moses in Numbers 11:16 and was reorganized by Ezra after the Exile. However, there is no scriptural evidence of a council that functioned like the Sanhedrin of later times. Thus, the Sanhedrin had its origin sometime during the centuries between the Testaments.

During the first century, the Sanhedrin exerted authority under the watchful eye of the Romans. Generally, the Roman governor allowed the Sanhedrin considerable autonomy and authority. The trial of Jesus, however, shows that the Sanhedrin did not have the authority to condemn people to death. (John 18:31) See Matthew 26:14-26; Mark 14:55-56; 15:1-5; Luke 22:66; John 11: 47-53; Acts 4:5-21; 5:21,27, 34-42; 6:12-15; 7:54-60; 22:30; 23:28.

27:6 "BLOOD MONEY"

The chief priests picked up the coins and said, "It is against the law to put this into the treasury, since it is blood money."

Blood money is money paid by a killer as compensation to the next of kin of a murder victim, or money gained at the cost of another person's life or livelihood.

27:7 "POTTER'S FIELD"

So they decided to use the money to buy the potter's field as a burial place for foreigners.

In modern usage a "Potter's Field" is a place for the burial of unknown or impoverished persons.

27:8 "FIELD OF BLOOD"

That is why it has been called the Field of Blood to this day.

Aramaic *Aceldama*. The name that the Jews gave to the field that was purchased with the money that had been given to Judas to betray Jesus. It was previously called "the potter's field," and was appropriated as the burial-place for strangers. It lies on a narrow level terrace on the south face of the valley of Hinnom. Its modern name is *Hak ed-damm*. See Acts 1:19.

27:15 ONE PRISONER RELEASED

Now it was the governor's custom at the Feast to release a prisoner chosen by the crowd.

It's not known whether this custom originated with the Jews or Gentiles. According to Maimonides, the Spanish-born Jewish philosopher and physician (1135-1204), the Jews were in the habit of punishing criminals at the three great feasts, because there would then be a greater multitude of people to witness the punishment than at other times. If the custom originated with the Gentiles, as many suppose, it's then a question of whether it was a Syrian or Roman custom. Grotius, the Dutch theologian (1583-1645), said that the Romans introduced it to gain the good will of the

Jews. There is, however, no historic mention of the practice aside from what we find in the Gospels.

It's believed that this privilege of demanding the release of a prisoner at the Feast of the Passover was expressly named in the instructions that Pilate received as pro praetor, since the governor had not the right himself to release a prisoner, the right of pardoning a condemned criminal being a prerogative of the emperor alone.

27:27 ROMAN COHORT

Then the governor's soldiers took Jesus into the Praetorium and gathered the whole company *(band, KJV)* of soldiers around him. (See Mark 15:16.)

Company or *band* in this Scripture is the Greek word, *speira* (spi'-rah), which means a mass of men or, more exactly, a Roman military *cohort*. A cohort was the tenth part of a legion, and consisted of three *maniples* (a subdivision containing 60 or 120 men), each having two *centuries* (a unit consisting of 100 men). Ordinarily the cohort

Roman soldier with Jesus

comprised six hundred men, but at times the number varied from three hundred to a thousand or more. Cornelius commanded a century in the Italian cohort in Acts 10:1. The cohort is also referred to in Acts 21:31; 27:1.

27:28 ROBE

They stripped him and put a scarlet robe on him.

The "scarlet robe" was probably the Roman *paludamentum*, which closely resembled the Greek *chlamys* (a

Robe

short mantle fastened at the shoulder). The paludamentum was an outer garment that hung loosely over the shoulders, was open in front, reached down to the knees or lower, and was fastened across the chest with a clasp, which, by the motions of the wearer, sometimes shifted to either shoulder. It was commonly either white or purple. Mark and John speak of this one as purple, and Matthew says it was scarlet. The two terms were convertible. The paludamentum was a military cloak, and, in mockery of the royalty of Jesus, was put upon him after he had been "stripped" of the outer garment that he usually wore. See Matthew 27:31.

27:33 GOLGOTHA

They came to a place called Golgotha (which means The Place of the Skull). (See Mark 15:22; Luke 23:33; John 19:17.)

The Road to Golgotha—Via Dolorosa

This name represents in Greek letters the Aramaic word *Gulgaltha*, which is the Hebrew *Gulgoleth.* The Latin equivalent is *calvaria.* Both words mean skull.

Golgotha was a little knoll rounded like a bare skull. It appears to be a well-known spot outside the gate (Hebrews 13:12), and near the city (Luke 23:26), containing a "garden" (John 19:41), and on a road that lead into the country. Therefore it's unlikely that it's within the present *"Church of the Holy Sepulchre."* The hill above *Jeremiah's Grotto*, to the north of the city, is in all probability the true site of Calvary. The rock in the southern precipice of the hill has a remarkable skull-like appearance. This would be in keeping with Hebrews 13:12, which says: "And so Jesus also suffered outside (without, KJV) the city gate to make the people holy through his own blood."

27:34 Wine Mixed with Gall

There they offered Jesus wine to drink, mixed with gall; but after tasting it, he refused to drink it. (See Mark 15:23; Luke 23:36.)

Greek, *chole*, a translation of the Hebrew *rosh* in Psalms 69:21, which foretells Christ's sufferings. The drink offered to Jesus was vinegar (made of light wine rendered acid, the common drink of Roman soldiers) "mingled with gall," or, according to Mark "mingled with myrrh." Both expressions mean that the vinegar was made bitter by the infusion of wormwood (any of several aromatic plants of the genus *Artemisia,* especially native to Europe, yielding a bitter extract used in making absinthe and in flavoring certain wines) or some other bitter substance. This mixture was commonly given as an anesthetic to those who were crucified to make them less sensitive to pain.

27:35 Crucifixion

When they had crucified him, they divided up his clothes by casting lots. (See Mark 15:25; Luke 23:33; John 19:18.)

A common method of punishment among heathen nations in early times. It's not certain whether it was known among the ancient Jews, since the methods of capital

Jesus crucified

punishment according to the Mosaic law were by the sword (Exodus 21), strangling, fire (Leviticus 20), and stoning (Deuteronomy 21). Originally a cross was a wooden pointed stake used to build a wall or to erect fortifications around a town. Beginning with the Assyrians and Persians, it was used to display the heads of captured enemies or criminals on the palisades above the gateway into a city. Later, crucifixion developed into a form of capital punishment, as enemies of the state were impaled on the stake itself.

The Greeks and Romans at first reserved the punishment only for slaves, saying it was too barbaric for freeborn or citizens. By the first century, however, it was used for any enemy of the state, though citizens could only be crucified by direct edict of Caesar. As time went on, the Romans began to use crucifixion more and more as a deterrent to criminal activity, so that by Jesus' time it was a common sight.

According to Jewish law (Deuteronomy 21:22-23) offenders "hung on a tree" were "accursed of God" and outside the covenant people. Such criminals were to be removed from the cross before nightfall lest they "defile the land." In 76 B.C. Alexander Janneus crucified 800 Pharisees, but on the whole the Jews condemned and seldom used the method. Even Herod the Great refused to crucify his enemies. The practice was abolished after the "conversion" of Constantine to Christianity.

A person crucified in Jesus' day was first scourged (beaten with a whip consisting of thongs with pieces of metal or bone attached to the end) or at least flogged until the blood flowed—but at other times until bones were exposed. This was not just done out of cruelty but, some say, was designed to hasten death and lessen the terrible ordeal.

Other say it was to decrease the victim's ability to withstand pain, which is more probable since most of us have experienced a decreasing ability to withstand pain on top of pain. During persecution of Christians in times past, and prisoners and others in recent wars, those being tortured would be inflicted with exactly the same tortures time after time. Remembering the pain that particular torture caused the last time would in many cases rapidly break the will of the victim.

After the beating, the victim was forced to bear the crossbeam to the execution site to signify his life was already over, to humiliate him before those who watched, and to be a warning to the onlookers.

A tablet detailing the crime(s) was often placed around the criminal's neck and then fastened to the cross. In Jesus' case, the tablet was inscribed, "THIS IS JESUS THE KING OF THE JEWS" (Matthew 27:37; Mark 15:26; Luke 23:38; John 19:19). At the site the prisoner was often tied (the normal method) or nailed (if greater pain was desired) to the crossbeam. The nail would be driven through the wrist, at the cluster of nerves feeding to the hand, rather than the palm, since the smaller bones of the hand could not support the weight of the body. The beam with the body was then lifted and tied to the upright pole that was already planted in the ground.

Pins or a small wooden block were sometimes placed halfway up to provide a seat for the body lest the nails tear open the wounds or the ropes pull the victim's arms from the sockets. At other times, no such seat was provided and the victim suffered not only dislocated shoulders but an inability to breath as his body sagged down on his hands and constricted his chest. The feet were tied or nailed to the post. Death usually occurred due to the loss of blood circulation, or suffocation and heart failure. Death did not come quickly, it could take days of hideous pain as the extremities turned slowly gangrenous, or the victim could no longer hold himself upright so that he could intake air. Often the soldiers would break the victim's legs with a club, thus preventing the victim from thrusting upward with his legs to expand his chest so that he could breath. Victim's were usually crucified in public

places, and the body left to rot for days, with carrion birds allowed to degrade the corpse further—all as a warning to anyone passing by.

Four types of crosses were used: 1) The Latin cross has the crossbeam about two-thirds of the way up the upright pole; 2) St. Anthony's cross (probably due to its similarity to his famous crutch) had the beam at the top of the upright pole like a T. 3) St. Andrew's cross (supposedly the form used to crucify Andrew) had the shape of the letter X; 4) the Greek cross has both beams equal in the shape of a plus sign. It is commonly believed that Jesus was crucified on the Latin cross.

27:51 Veil of the Temple

And, behold, the veil of the temple was rent in twain from the top to the bottom. (See Mark 15:38; Luke 23:45.)

This veil was the curtain that hung between the Holy Place and the Most Holy Place. It was sixty feet in length, and reached from floor to ceiling. Note that it wasn't torn in two from bottom to top as human hands would do

The temple veil is torn from top to bottom

it, but from top to bottom as only God could do it. (See Matthew **24:1 Herod's Temple.**)

27:60 DOOR OF THE TOMB

And placed it in his own new tomb that he had cut out of the rock. He rolled a big stone in front of the entrance to the tomb and went away.

Dr. Barclay, in his account of the "Tombs of the Kings," represents the outer door as consisting of a large stone disc like a millstone, and suggests that this may have been the case with Joseph's tomb, into which the Savior was put. He says, "Immediately in front of the doorway (the top of which is more than a foot below the floor of the porch) is a deep trench, commencing a foot or two west of the door, and extending three or four yards along the wall eastward. The bottom of this trench is a short distance below the sill of the door, and is probably an inclined plane. Along this channel a large thick stone disc traverses, fitting very accurately against its western end, which is made concave, so as to be exactly conformed to the convexity of this large millstone-like disc when rolled to that

Door of a tomb

end—thus closing the doorway most effectively." See Matthew 28:2; Mark 16:3-4; Luke 24:2; John 11:38-39, and Genesis **50:2-3 Embalming**.

27:66 SEALING THE TOMB

So they went and made the tomb secure by putting a seal on the stone and posting the guard.

The context shows that this was an official sealing that was intended to be so arranged that the seal could not be broken without detection. In the same way, the lion's den was sealed into which Daniel was thrown (Daniel 6:17). A cord stretched across the stone, with a lump of stamped clay fastening it at each end, would prevent any entrance without detection. Clay was often impressed with the stamp of seals for various purposes. (See Job **38:14 Impressions of Seals**.)

The Sea of Galilee

MARK

2:4 House Architecture

Since they could not get him to Jesus because of the crowd, they made an opening in the roof above Jesus and, after digging through it, lowered the mat the paralyzed man was lying on. (See Luke 5:19.)

Houses in Jesus' day usually followed a plan that arranged the rooms around an inner courtyard. A stairway on the outside of the house led to the upper stories. A stone or timber projected out from the wall at various places and supported the staircase. This technique is known as *corbelling*. The walls and ceiling were plastered, and arches sometimes supported the roof. Houses often had arches that came out from the walls to form the roof. After placing thin slabs of limestone over the arches, the entire roof was plastered. In the lower city of Jerusalem, houses were constructed with small stones and were crowded closely together; however, they still maintained small courtyards.

It is advocated by most commentators that, in this instance, the sticks, thorn-bush, mortar, and earth, that comprised the roofing plaster, were actually broken up and set aside until an aperture was made large enough to let the sick man through. One authority states that the roof could easily be broken up in this manner, and easily repaired, and that it was often done for the purpose of letting down grain, straw, and other articles. This authority, writing in the mid-1800s, stated: "I have often seen it done, and done it myself to houses in Lebanon, but there is always more dust made than is agreeable."

7:11 Corban

"But you say that if a man says to his father or mother: 'Whatever help you might otherwise have received from me is Corban' (that is, a gift devoted to God)." (See Matthew 15:5.)

Corban is a Hebrew word adopted into the Greek of the New Testament and left untranslated. It occurs only once, that being in our text-verse. It means a gift or offering consecrated to God. Anything over which this word was once pronounced was irrevocably dedicated to the temple. Land, however, so dedicated might be redeemed during the year of jubilee (Leviticus 27:16-24). Jesus rebukes the Pharisees for their false doctrine, because they had destroyed the commandment that requires children to honor their father and mother, teaching them to find excuse from helping their parents by the device of pronouncing "corban" over their goods, thus releasing them from all obligation to sustain their parents. It did not, however, bind them to consecrate their goods to sacred uses. These could be used for their own purposes, or given to whomever they pleased, except to those to whom they had said, "It is corban."

The widow's mite

12:42 MITE - FARTHING

And there came a certain poor widow, and she threw in two mites, which make a farthing *(KJV)*. (See Luke 21:2.)

1. Mite is a contraction of *minute*, from the Latin *minutum*, the translation of the Greek word *lepton*, the very smallest copper coin. Two mites made one *quadrans*, i.e., the fourth part of a Roman *as* (see Matthew **10:29 Sparrows - Farthings**). See Luke 7:59.

2. A farthing is from the Greek, *kodrantes*, the quadrant, the fourth of an *as*, equal to two *lepta* or mites.

13:35 NIGHT WATCHES

"Therefore keep watch because you do not know when the owner of the house will come back—whether in the evening, or at midnight, or when the rooster crows, or at dawn."

The earliest division of the night into watches is detailed in the Exodus **14:24 Night Watches**. After the Jews became subject to Roman power, they adopted the Roman method of dividing the watches. There were four watches: Sunset to 3 hours later; from this time until midnight; midnight to three hours before sunrise; and the last from this time until sunrise. These four watches are all alluded to in our text-verse. The first being "evening," the second "midnight," the third "rooster crowing," and the fourth "dawn"—the names indicating when the watch ended. See Matthew 14:24; 24:43; Mark 6:48; Luke 12:38.

14:14-15 THE UPPER ROOM

"Where is my guest room, where I may eat the Passover with my disciples?" He will show you a large upper room, furnished and ready. Make preparations for us there.

Some suppose this "guest chamber" and "upper room" to be the *aliyah*, or room above the porch or on the roof. (See 2 Kings **4:10 Prophet's Room**.) Others, however, think the words refer to a large open room fronting the court, on the side opposite to the entrance from the porch, and elevated above the level of the court.

More than a century after Christ's ministry on earth, the room believed to be the one in which the meal was eaten was made into a shrine and still is commemorated today. But whether God would allow such a room to be preserved—or any other such object—and eventually near-worshiped is doubtful. When the Israelites worshiped the bronze snake by which they were once healed, He had Hezekiah destroy it: "He broke into pieces the bronze snake (serpent, KJV) Moses had made, for up to that time the Israelites had been burning incense to it" (1 Kings 18:4).

14:20 MANNER OF EATING

"It is one of the Twelve," he replied, "one who dips bread into the bowl with me." (See Matthew 26:23.)

Knives, forks, and spoons were not used at table in biblical times. It was the custom to eat with one's fingers, most food being easily handled that way. When, however, the food was in a semi-fluid state, or so soft that the fingers could not conveniently hold it, a piece of bread was used to scoop the food out of the dish. This bread formed the "sop" mentioned in John 13:26. Even today it's a casual custom in many homes to use bread to "sop" up gravy or other food juices—it's not acceptable etiquette, however, in formal situations unless the ethnic tone of the meal allows it, such as in the case of Mediterranean-style meals, where it's the custom to dip bread in olive oil before eating, especially olive oil flavored with roasted garlic or other spices.

15:43 COUNSELOR

Joseph of Arimathaea, an honourable counsellor *(KJV).* (See Luke 23:50.)

The expression "counselor" means that Joseph was a member of the Jewish Sanhedrin or Great Council. See Matthew **26:59 Sanhedrin**.

LUKE

1:5 WIVES OF PRIESTS

There was a priest named Zechariah, who belonged to the priestly division of Abijah; his wife Elizabeth was also a descendant of Aaron.

Great care was taken in the selection of wives for the Jewish priests, so that the line of priests might be kept in every respect unsullied. One authority states: "It was lawful for a priest to marry a Levitess, or, indeed, a daughter of Israel; but it was most commendable of all to marry one of the priest's line." Zechariah was especially honored in having for his wife one of the descendants of Aaron (Leviticus, chapters 8 and 9).

1:59 NAMING A CHILD

On the eighth day they came to circumcise the child, and they were going to name him after his father Zechariah. (See Genesis **17:10-11 Circumcision.**)

In biblical times the task of naming a child generally fell to the mother (Genesis 29:31-30:24; 1 Samuel 1:20) but could be performed by the father (Genesis 16:15; Exodus 2:22) and, in some cases, by non-parental figures (Exodus 2:10; Ruth 4:17). The last son of Jacob and Rachel received a name from both parents—Jacob altered the name Rachel gave the boy (Genesis 35:18). Naming sometimes came through a divine birth announcement (Genesis 17:19; Luke 1:13). Naming took place near birth in the Old Testament and on the eighth day accompanying circumcision in New Testament narratives (Luke 1:59; 2:21).

Revealing character and destiny, personal names might express hopes for the child's future. Changing of name could occur at divine or human initiative, revealing a transformation in character or destiny (Genesis 17:5, 15; 32:28; Matthew 16:17-18).

Proper names consisting of one or more terms consciously chosen conveyed a readily understandable meaning within the biblical world. Reflecting the circumstances of her son's birth, Rachel called the child of her death, Ben-oni, "son of my sorrow" (Genesis 5:18). Jacob was named "the supplanter" for "he took hold on Esau's heel" (Genesis 25:26). Moses named his son Gershom because he had been a"stranger in a strange land" (Exodus 2:22). Conditions in the land at the time of birth proved to be fodder for names as well: Ichabod, "The glory has departed from Israel," (NRSV) came about by the ark of the covenant falling into Philistine hands (1 Samuel 4:21-22) as did the symbolic names of Isaiah's sons: Shear-jashub, "a remnant shall return," (Isaiah 7:3); Maher-Shalal-hash-baz, "swift is the booty, speedy is the prey," (Isaiah 8:3, NASB).

Personal or physical characteristics produced names: Esau means "hairy" and Careah means "bald" (Genesis 25:25; 2 Kings 25:23). Animal names were also used, perhaps as a testament to the child's temperament: Deborah means "bee," Jonah means "dove" and Rachel means "ewe." Less frequently occurring are names taken from plants: Tamar meaning "palm tree" and Susanna meaning "lily."

Simple names functioning as epithets, such as Nabal meaning "fool" and Sarah meaning "princess," gave way to compound names that were spiritually factual or hopeful in nature, such as Mattaniah meaning "gift of Yahweh" and Ezekiel meaning "may God strengthen."

The practice whereby a child received the name of a relative, especially the grandfather (Simon Bar-Jona is "son of Jona") was common by the Christian era. Geographical identities are in evidence also (Goliath of Gath and Jesus of Nazareth).

1:63 WRITING TABLETS

He asked for a writing tablet, and to everyone's astonishment he wrote, "His name is John."

Writing tablets were in use among various ancient nations.

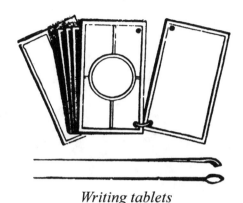

Writing tablets

They are referred to in Isaiah 30:8, Habakkuk 2:2, and metaphorically in Proverbs 3:3, Jeremiah 17:1, and 2 Corinthians 3:3. Among the Romans they were occasionally made of ivory or of citron-wood, but generally of beach, fir, or some other common wood. They were covered with a thin coating of wax, in which the letters were formed by a stylus, an instrument preceding the modern pen. It was made of gold, silver, brass, iron, copper, ivory, or bone. One end was pointed for writing, while the other was smooth, flat, and circular, for erasing, and for smoothing the wax surface that it might be used again. The outside part of the tablet held in the hand was not coated with wax, and around the edge of the inside was a thin, narrow ledge, so that when two tablets came together, the waxed surfaces would not touch each other and become marred.

A book was often made of several of these tablets combined, fastened together at the backs by means of wires that also served as hinges. Tablets were used for almost all writings where the document was not lengthy. Letters, or even wills, were written upon them. In order to seal the tablets, holes were made in the outer edge, through which tripled thread was passed and fastened with a seal.

2:7 "SWADDLING CLOTHES" - MANGER - INN

She wrapped him in cloths *(swaddling clothes, KJV)* and placed him in a manger, because there was no room for them in the inn.

1. The cloths in which Jesus was wrapped were commonly referred to as "swaddling clothes." These were bandages that were tightly wrapped around a newborn child to hold its legs and arms still. The custom is still

widely practiced in many countries. "Swaddling clothes" has also come to indicate restrictions imposed on the immature.

Bethlehem

2. A manger is a feeding trough used for cattle, sheep, donkeys, or horses. Archaeologists have discovered stone mangers in the horse stables of Ahab at Megiddo. They were cut out of limestone and were approximately three feet long, eighteen inches wide, and two feet deep. Other ancient mangers were made of masonry. Many Palestinian homes consisted of one large room that contained an elevated section and a lower section. The elevated section was the family's living quarters, while the lower section housed the family's animals. Usually a manger, in the form of a masonry box or a stone niche, was located in the lower section. Mangers were also put in cave stables or other

stalls. The manger referred to in our text-verse may have been in a cave stable or other shelter.

It is doubtful that inns, in the sense of public inns with a building, existed in Old Testament times. By the time of Christ, public inns could be found in Grecian and Roman lands. The Greek word for "inn" in the New Testament implies some type of stopping place for travelers. At times it refers to a public inn. Such an inn of the first century consisted primarily of a walled-in area with a well. A larger inn might have small rooms surrounding the court. People and animals stayed together. The primary services that could be depended upon were water for the family and

Christ's birth in a manger

animals and a place to spread a pallet.

In addition to referring to a public inn or lodging place, the same Greek word, *kataluma,* used in our text-verse, at times refers simply to a guest room in a private home (Mark 14:14; Luke 22:11).

The reference in Luke 10:34 is to a *pandocheion* or a public lodging-place, clearly a public place where the wounded could be fed and cared for by the innkeeper.

2:25 The Consolation

Now there was a man in Jerusalem called Simeon, who was righteous and devout. He was waiting for the consolation of Israel.

The consolation was a term used to designate the Messiah. Israel's ultimate hope was the consolation only the Messiah could bring.

2:44-45 "A Day's Journey"

Thinking he was in their company, they traveled on for a day *(went a day's journey, KJV)*. Then they began looking for him among their relatives and friends. When they did not find him, they went back to Jerusalem to look for him.

An ordinary day's journey varied from eighteen to thirty miles. But when a party started on a journey, the first day's journey was invariably shorter.

When everything was ready for the caravan, the travelers slowly marched on, but halted for the first night at a distance some three to eight miles from the place of their departure. Thus if anything was found to be left behind, someone could easily return and retrieve it and rejoin the caravan the next day.

In our text-verse, they made the short journey of the first day, and then halted for the night. So instead of traveling all day without missing Jesus, they only traveled a few hours.

Traditionally, the first stopping place of all traveling parties who left Jerusalem for the north was the ancient Beer, or Beeroth, now supposed to be the site of el-Bireh on the way to Nablus, ten miles north of Jerusalem, or, in ancient days, a three-hours' journey.

2:46 Jesus Questioning the Teachers

After three days they found him in the temple courts, sitting among the teachers, listening to them and asking them questions.

There were several places within the Temple area where teachers of the law met their disciples. One of these places was in the cloisters described in Matthew **24:1 Herod's Temple**. Another was in the synagogue that was in the Temple enclosure. After services, the teachers admitted any who wished to converse with them on matters pertaining to the law.

There is no reason to suppose that Jesus' conversation with the teachers was in any way controversial. He simply followed the custom of the time, which allowed anyone who chose to question the teachers on any points they desired. Although our text-verse is often twisted by some to say that the child Jesus was teaching these learned men, that is not what the verse says. He was asking them questions and learning from them. They were, however, amazed at His understanding and answers to questions that they asked Him—asking questions of students was a rabbinical method of teaching.

4:16 Public Reading

He went to Nazareth, where he had been brought up, and on the Sabbath day he went into the synagogue, as was his custom. And he stood up to read.

When the law and the prophets were read in the synagogue, those who read were expected to stand. Not only priests and Levites, but common Israelites were allowed to read the Scriptures publicly. Every Sabbath, seven persons read: a priest, a Levite, and five ordinary Israelites.

4:20 Attendant - Teaching While Seated.

Then he rolled up the scroll, gave it back to the attendant and sat down.

1. Translated from the Greek *huperetes*, an attendant is a subordinate such as an assistant, sexton, constable, minister, officer, or servant. This person had charge of the furniture, and kept the building in good order, preparing it for service and summoning the people at the appointed hour. It was also his duty to call out the names of those whom the ruler of the synagogue selected to read the lesson of the day, hand them the sacred scroll, and retrieve it from them when the reading was finished.

2. It was the customary posture of a teacher to be seated when instructing his disciples. After Jesus returned the scroll to the attendant, He sat down on the platform instead of going back into the congregation, because He wished to address the people. This custom is referred to in Matthew 5:1; 23:2; 26:55; John 8:2. See Acts 22:3.

6:38 Bosom

"Give, and it shall be given unto you; good measure, pressed down, and shaken together, and running over, shall men give into your bosom" *(KJV)*.

The term *bosom* refers to the folds of the garment as they extend beyond and droop over the girdle or belt (see Matthew **10:9 Belts**). This part of the dress is also called the "lap." It is used as a receptacle for various articles, just as pockets are now employed, though some of the things carried in the bosom would not fit in our pocket. Children were often carried in the bosom (Numbers 11:12), as were lambs by their shepherd (2 Samuel 12:3; Isaiah 40:11).

7:12 Funerals

As he approached the town gate, a dead person was being carried out—the only son of his mother, and she was a widow. And a large crowd from the town was with her.

When preparations for burial were completed, the body of the deceased was usually placed in a coffin and borne to the burial site in a procession of relatives, friends, and servants (Amos 6:10). The procession carried out the mourning ritual, which could include baldness and cutting of the beard, rending garments and wearing sackcloth, loud and agonized weeping, and putting dust on the head and sitting in ashes (2 Samuel 1:11-12; 13:31; 14:2; Isaiah 3:24, 22:12; Jeremiah 7:29; Ezekiel 7:18; Joel 1:8). The Canaanite practices of laceration and mutilation are forbidden in the Torah (Leviticus 19:27-28; 21:5; Deuteronomy 14:1).

7:38 Kissing the Feet

And as she stood behind him at his feet weeping, she . . . kissed them.

A customary practice among the Jews, Greeks, and Romans. It was a mark of affection and of reverence. It was also the practice of supplicants, and of those who had an important request to present. See Luke 7:45.

9:62 PLOW

"No one who puts his hand to the plow and looks back is fit for service in the kingdom of God."

It is evident from our text-verse that in Jesus' time the plow usually had but one handle. One hand guided the plow, while the other held the long *goad*—a long staff, pointed on the end—by which the oxen were spurred on to their work. Since the plow was fairly lightweight, it was necessary for the plowman to lean forward with all his weight on the handle to keep the *share*—the cutting blade—in the ground.

Many commentators suggest

for the plowman to pick an object at the far end of the field and keep the plow going directly toward it. If he turned to look behind him to see how he was doing, he would

A plow

lose sight of his objective and go off from his straight line. Jesus' spiritual lesson is that if we look back at our old life with longing,

Plowing and sowing

that by looking back, the laborer would be unable to make straight furrows. The usual method was

as the Israelites in the wilderness kept looking back at Egypt, then we aren't fit for service in His kingdom.

10:4 FORMAL SALUTATIONS

"Salute no man by the way" *(KJV)*.

A salutation is an act of greeting, addressing, blessing, or welcoming by gestures or words; a specific form of words serving as a greeting, especially in the opening and closing of letters.

In ancient times, a salutation covered a wide range of social practices: exchanging a greeting ("Hail"), asking politely about another person's welfare, expressing personal regard, and the speaking of a parting blessing ("Go in Peace"). Physical actions, such as kneeling, kissing, and embracing, were also involved. The salutation functioned to maintain close, personal contact and to foster good relations. Jesus criticized the Pharisees for practicing long, protracted, deferential salutations (Mark 12:37-40; Luke 20:45-47; Matthew 23:1-36) and forbade His disciples from practicing such public displays. Instead, Jesus endorsed a salutation when it signified the long-awaited presence of messianic "peace" (Hebrew, *shalom*), that is the "peace" of the kingdom of God (Luke 10:5-13; 19:42; John 14:27; 20:21; Mark 15:18)

Paul, as do other New Testament authors, also changed the salutation to speak of newness brought on by the Cross and resurrection. The typical greeting in Greek letters was the infinitive, "to rejoice" (*charein*). Paul fused the Greek word for the typical Hebrew blessing, "Peace" (*einrene*), with the noun form of the Greek blessing, "Grace" (*charis*), to yield the salutation: "Grace and Peace" (*charis kai eirene*). Paul was able to invoke the blessings found in Jesus: mercy from God ("grace") and eternal well-being from God's presence ("peace").

Paul used this expression at the beginning of most of his letters, not in a rote manner, but to teach those to whom he was writing that Christianity begins with grace from God and ends in peace through Jesus Christ. The purpose of Christianity, and therefore of all that Christ did, is peace with God, and so Paul states in Romans 5:1— "Therefore, since we have been justified through faith, we have peace with God through our Lord Jesus Christ." This coupled with Paul's statement in Ephesians 2:8, "For it is by grace you have been saved, through faith," is the essence of Christianity.

10:34 OIL AND WINE AS FIRST AID

He went to him and bandaged his wounds, pouring on oil and wine.

This was a favorite application for wounds in ancient medicine. It was considered a sovereign remedy, especially for wounds produced by violence; wool, lint, or pounded olive being first laid upon the wound. The wine—or, more specifically, the alcohol in the wine—was supposed to cleanse, and the oil to soothe and heal. The two were sometimes made into a compound.

11:7 SINGLE ROOM HOUSE

"The door is already locked, and my children are with me in bed. I can't get up and give you anything."

In Jesus' time, for the more fortunate poor, a multipurpose, one room house served as protection from the elements, and as a kitchen, work space, and sleeping quarters for all family members.

11:44 UNMARKED GRAVES

"Woe to you, because you are like unmarked graves, which men walk over without knowing it."

When the customary whitewashing of a flat tomb (see Matthew **23:27 Whitewashed Tombs**) was neglected, its presence was easily concealed from view, and the passerby might walk upon it and thus become ceremonially defiled.

12:34 "WHERE YOUR TREASURE IS, THERE YOUR HEART WILL BE ALSO."

"For where your treasure is, there your heart will be also." (See Matthew 6:21.)

In modern usage this expression means that whatever is most important to you has all your attention and care. This expression by Jesus also provides us a means of knowing whether we are laying up treasures in heaven, for if we are we will find that our hearts are naturally turning more and more toward heaven.

13:6 TREES IN THE VINEYARD

"A man had a fig tree, planted in his vineyard."

Vineyards were not devoted exclusively to vines. Fruit-trees of various kinds were planted within their limits. The ancient Egyptians planted their vines and fruit-trees in the same enclosure. This was done when a winemaker desired a subtle addition of another flavor, such as apple, or in this case, fig, in the wine. It was common knowledge that wine carried within its bouquet and taste, a hint, or subtle bouquet, of its neighboring plants and those plants that made use of the soil prior to the vine.

14:9-10 ARRANGEMENTS OF GUESTS' SEATS

"If so, the host who invited both of you will come and say to you, 'Give this man your seat.' Then, humiliated, you will have to take the least important place. But when you are invited, take the lowest place, so that when your host comes, he will say to you, 'Friend, move up to a better place.' Then you will be honored in the presence of all your fellow guests."

The host did not hesitate to regulate the position of his guests after they had seated themselves. He gave the highest rank the chief place, sending the guests up or down as circumstances required. Nowadays, the gracious host uses place cards for seating guests rather than embarrass someone needlessly by moving them publicly to a more appropriate seat. Guests have been known to switch place cards for their own purposes though.

15:12 DIVISION OF PROPERTY

"The younger one said to his father, 'Father, give me my share of the estate.' So he divided his property between them."

Neither Jewish nor Roman law permitted the father to have the arbitrary disposal of all his estate. The property was entailed on the sons at the father's death, the daughter's not being allowed to inherit unless there were no sons (Genesis 31:14; Numbers

27:8). The firstborn son received a double-share of the inheritance. The Hebrew words for inheritance did not necessarily presuppose a death, therefore it could have been of his own volition that the father in our text-verse chose to divide his estate between his sons. This is said to have been sometimes done among the Romans, and that it may have been an occasional custom among the Jews is evident from the example of Abraham, who "gave all that he had" to his son Isaac (Genesis 25:5).

15:15 Feeding Pigs

"So he went and hired himself out to a citizen of that country, who sent him to his fields to feed pigs."

This was considered one of the most degrading employments, not only by the Jews, but by other nations. Among the Egyptians, for example, the swineherd was completely shut off from society. See Matthew **7:6 "Do not cast your pearls before swine."**

16:1 Steward

"There was a certain rich man, which had a steward" (KJV) (manager, NIV).

Greek, *oikonomos*, a house-distributor or manager, or overseer, a fiscal agent (treasurer), chamberlain, or governor. The steward had general charge of the business of the house, and was also responsible for the care of the heir. This is referred to in Galatians 4:2, where the word elsewhere rendered "steward" is translated "governors." The honorable position of the steward is seen in the fact that he was considered to be ruler over the household (Luke 12:42). His duties are also referred to in the Parable of the Laborers (Matthew 20:8).

18:12 Semi-weekly Fasts

"I fast twice a week."

It is said that semi-weekly fasts were observed by the Jews because continuous fasting might be injurious. The days selected were the second and the fifth days of the week. The reason assigned for the selection of these days is because it was supposed to be on the second day of the week that Moses went up into Mount Sinai to receive the two tablets of the law, and it was on the fifth day of the week that he came down on account of the idolatry concerning the golden calf. These days were chosen, not only when public fasts were to be observed, but also when individuals fasted privately.

18:12 Tithe

"And give a tenth of all I get."

A tenth of the produce of the earth consecrated and set apart for special purposes. The dedication of a tenth to God was recognized as a duty before the time of Moses. Abraham paid tithes to Melchizedek (Genesis 14:20; Hebrews 7:6); and Jacob vowed unto the Lord and said, "Of all that thou shalt give me I will surely give the tenth unto thee."

The first Mosaic law on this subject is recorded in Leviticus 27:30-32. Subsequent legislation regulated the destination of the tithes (Numbers 18:21-24, 26-28; Deuteronomy 12:5, 6, 11, 17; 14:22, 23). The paying of the tithes was an important part of the Jewish religious worship. In the days of Hezekiah one of the first results of the reformation of religion was the eagerness with which the people brought in their tithes (2 Chronicles 31:5, 6). The neglect of this duty was sternly rebuked by the prophets (Amos 4:4; Malachi 3:8-10). It cannot be affirmed that the Old Testament law of tithes is binding on the Christian Church, nevertheless the principle of this law remains, and is incorporated in the gospel (1 Corinthians 9:13, 14). And if, as is the case, the motive that should prompt generosity in the cause of religion and service to God is greater now than in Old Testament times, then Christians should go beyond the ancient Hebrews in consecrating both themselves and their substance to God.

Every Jew was required by the Levitical law to pay three tithes of his property

1. One tithe for the Levites.

2. One for the use of the temple and the great feasts.

3. One for the poor of the land.

18:13 Beating the Breast

"But the tax collector stood at a distance. He would

not even look up to heaven, but beat his breast and said, 'God, have mercy on me, a sinner.'"

This is one mode of expressing great grief in some nations, especially in mourning the dead. Its insertion in the parable is very expressive of the deep sorrow of the penitent tax collector. His grief on account of his sins was like the grief of those who mourn the dead.

19:13 MINAS

"So he called ten of his servants and gave them ten minas *(pounds, KJV)*."

Greek, *mna, mnah*; a certain weight: a pound. The "mina" (the "pound" used in the KJV is the basic monetary unit of the United Kingdom) was not a coin, but a sum of silver reckoned by weight. Mina and talent were multiples of the shekel. According to the account of the sanctuary tax (Exodus 38:25-26), three thousand shekels were in a talent, probably sixty minas of fifty shekels each. See Matthew **26:15 Thirty Pieces of Silver**.

21:5 ORNAMENTS OF THE TEMPLE

Some of his disciples were remarking about how the temple was adorned with beautiful stones and with gifts dedicated to God.

The temple of Herod was built of stones so exceedingly white that Josephus, the Jewish historian, says the building from a distance looked like a mountain of snow. It was also gilded in many places, so that the reflection from the sun's rays was sometimes painful to the eye of the beholder. It was likewise adorned with the spoils of war, and with the voluntary offerings of those who desired in this way to express gratitude to God for past favors, or manifest a hope for future benefits. According to Josephus, there were among these costly gifts, golden vines from which hung clusters of grapes as tall as a man.

22:4 TEMPLE GUARD

And Judas went to the chief priests and the officers of the temple guard and discussed with them how he might betray Jesus.

These were not military guards, but the Levitical officers who had charge of the temple watch. See Acts 4:1; 5:26.

24:44 Division of Jewish Scriptures

"This is what I told you while I was still with you: Everything must be fulfilled that is written about me in the Law of Moses, the Prophets and the Psalms." (See Matthew 5:17.)

This is the ordinary division of the Jewish Scriptures. The *first* is the *Law*, which includes the Pentateuch; *secondly*, the *Prophets*, which includes Joshua, Judges, the two books of Samuel, the two books of Kings, and all the prophets except Daniel; and *thirdly*, the *Hagiographa* or Sacred Writings, which comprise, in the following order, the Psalms, Proverbs, Job, Song of Solomon, Ruth, Lamentations, Ecclesiastes, Esther, Daniel, Ezra, Nehemiah, and the two books of Chronicles. This third division was called "the Psalms" because that book was the first in the division. In our text-verse, Jesus refers to it by this name.

JOHN

2:6 FIRKIN

And there were set there six waterpots of stone, after the manner of the purifying of the Jews, containing two or three firkins apiece *(KJV)*.

A unit of liquid measure. The term is used in the Bible only in our text-verse. *Firkin* is an archaic English word that was used to translate a Greek term referring to a measure of approximately ten gallons.

2:8 MASTER OF THE BANQUET

"Now draw some out and take it to the master *(governor, KJV)* of the banquet."

Among the Greeks, at all formal feasts, there was a *symposiarch* who was one of the guests, and was selected to take charge of the feast. It was his duty to preserve order, to maintain liveliness among the guests, to assign each one his proper place, to decide which proportion of water should be mixed with the wine, and how much each of the company was to drink. Among the Romans was a corresponding officer who was called the *rex convivii* or *arbiter bibendi*. Some say that among the Romans this "master of the banquet" was not one of the guests, but a hired servant, whose business it was to take charge of the other servants and see that they performed their tasks properly. He had some duties in common with the *symposiarch*, among which was the tasting of the wine before it was offered to the guests.

3:29 FRIEND OF THE BRIDEGROOM

"The friend who attends the bridegroom waits and listens for him, and is full of joy when he hears the bridegroom's voice."

"The friend who attends the bridegroom" was the person selected by the bridegroom to conduct the marriage negotiations on his part. It was he who carried messages between the bridegroom and the bride during the time of the betrothal (see Matthew **1:18 Pledges of Marriage**). Today, the role of best man is loosely based upon this tradition.

This position John the Baptist claims for himself figuratively. He is not the Christ, but bears a relation to Him similar to that borne by the friend of the bridegroom. He makes the arrangements for bringing Christ, the Bridegroom, to the Church, His bride.

4:27 Contempt for Women

Just then his disciples returned and were surprised to find him talking with a woman.

The disciples astonishment was not only because of the non-intercourse of the Jews and Samaritans, but also because it was unusual for a Jewish teacher to converse with a woman in a public place. Women were not to be saluted or spoken to in the street, and they were not to be instructed in the law.

6:27 Seal of Approval

"On him God the Father has placed his seal of approval."

Herodotus gives an account of the ceremonies among the ancient Egyptians accompanying the selection of an animal for sacrifice. If, after careful search, the animal was found without blemish, the priest bound a label to his horns, applied wax to the label, and sealed it with his ring. This set it apart for sacrifice, and no animal could be offered unless it bore this seal.

References to the sealing or setting apart of the people of God are made in 2 Corinthians 1:22; Ephesians 1:13; 4:30; Revelation 7:2.

7:37 Ceremonies at the Feast of Tabernacles

On the last and greatest day of the Feast, Jesus stood and said in a loud voice, "If anyone is thirsty, let him come to me and drink."

Jesus with the woman from Samaria

In addition to the ceremonies originally prescribed at the institution of the Feast of Tabernacles {see Exodus **23:16 Pentecost (Feast of Harvest)**}, were several others of a later date. Among these was the daily drawing of water from the pool of Siloam. Every daybreak of the seven days of the feast, a priest went to the pool of Siloam and filled with water a golden pitcher, containing about two and one-half pints. He was accompanied by a procession of the people and musicians. On returning to the temple, he was welcomed with three blasts from a trumpet, and, going to the west side of the great altar, he poured the water from the golden pitcher into a silver basin, which had holes in the bottom through which the water was carried off. This ceremony was accompanied with songs and shouts from the people and the sound of trumpets. It is supposed to have been designed to represent three distinct things: 1. A memorial of the water provided for their fathers in the desert. 2. A symbol of the forthcoming "latter rain." 3. A representation of the outpouring of the Holy Spirit at the coming of the Messiah. To this last, reference is made in verses 38

and 39, and it's to this pouring out of water, or the Holy Spirit, that Jesus no doubt refers to in our text-verse.

8:48 JEWISH HATRED OF SAMARITANS

The Jews answered him, "Aren't we right in saying that you are a Samaritan and demon-possessed?"

The contempt and hatred that the Jews entertained toward the Samaritans was manifested, not only in their refusal to have any dealings with them beyond what was demanded by necessity (John 4:9), but also in the fact that the Jews made the name Samaritan a synonym for everything that was vile and contemptible. They could not, in this instance, have mistaken Jesus for a Samaritan literally, because, according to verse 20, Jesus was in the treasury of the temple, a place where no Samaritan was permitted to come. They used the term figuratively as a reproach.

The name *Samaritans* originally was identified with the Israelites of the Northern Kingdom (2 Kings 17:29). When the Assyrians conquered Israel and exiled 27,290 Israelites, a "remnant of Israel" remained in the land. Assyrian captives from distant places also settled there (2 Kings 17:24). This led to the inter-marrying of some Jews with Gentiles and to worship of foreign gods. Ezra and Nehemiah refused to let the Samaritans share in the rebuilding of the Temple and the walls of Jerusalem (Ezra 4:1-3; Nehemiah 4:7).

The Jewish inhabitants of Samaria identified Mount Gerizim as the chosen place of God and the only center of worship, calling it the "navel of the earth" because of a tradition that Adam sacrificed there. Their Scriptures were limited to the Pentateuch. Moses was regarded as the only prophet and intercessor in the final judgment. They also believed that 6,000 years after creation, a restorer would arise and would live on earth for 110 years. On the Judgment Day, the righteous would be resurrected in paradise and the wicked roasted in eternal fire. A small Samaritan community continues to this day to follow the traditional worship near Shechem.

9:22 EXCOMMUNICATION

The Jews had decided that anyone who acknowledged that Jesus was the Christ would be put out of the synagogue.

According to the Talmud, there were three grades of excommunication among the Jews. The first was called *niddin,* and those on whom it was pronounced were not permitted for thirty days to have any communication with any person unless at a distance over four cubits (about 6 feet). They were not prohibited from attending public worship, though they could not, during the thirty days, enter the temple by the ordinary gate. They were not allowed to shave during that time, and were required to wear garments of mourning.

The second was called *cherem,* and was pronounced on those who remained openly disobedient under the first. It was of greater severity than the other, and required the presence of at least ten members of the congregation to make it valid. The offender was formally cursed, was excluded from all intercourse with other people, and was prohibited from entering the temple or synagogue.

The third was *shammatha,* and was inflicted on those who persisted in their stubborn resistance to authority. By this they were cut off from all connection with the Jewish people, and were consigned to utter perdition.

The Talmud assigns as the two general causes for excommunication, money and epicurism. The first refers to those who refused to pay the moneys that the court directed them to pay; the second refers to those who despised the Word of God or of the scribes—both being put on an equal basis.

Excommunication is alluded to in Matthew 18:17; John 9:34; 12:42; 16:2. Some think Jesus in Luke 6:22 refers to the several grades of excommunication noted: "Blessed are ye, when men shall hate you, and when they shall separate you from their company, and shall reproach you, and cast out your name as evil, for the Son of man's sake" (KJV).

10:3-5 SHEPHERD AND SHEEP

"He calls his own sheep by name and leads them out. When he has brought out all his own, he goes on ahead of them, and his sheep follow him because they know his voice. But they will never follow a stranger; in fact, they will run away from him because they do not recognize a stranger's voice."

It is not unusual for shepherds to give names to their sheep just as we do with dogs, cats, horses, fish, etc. Every sheep recognizes his own name, and comes when called. Travelers in lands where old-fashioned sheep herding methods are still used, have noticed the readiness with which the sheep of a large flock will recognize the shepherd's voice. Though several flocks are mingled, they speedily separate at the command of the shepherd, while the command of a stranger would have no effect on them.

The Latin word transliterated "pastor" means shepherd. It is for that reason that a church's congregation is sometimes referred to as a "flock."

The Good Shepherd and His sheep

10:22 THE FEAST OF DEDICATION

Then came the Feast of Dedication at Jerusalem. It was winter.

This was a feast instituted in honor of the restoration of divine worship in the temple, and its formal rededication to sacred uses after it had been defiled by the heathen under Antiochus Epiphanes. This dedication took place in 164 B.C., and an account of it is given in the apocryphal book 1 Maccabees 4:52-59. The feast lasted two days, and could be celebrated not only in Jerusalem, but elsewhere.

In later times it was known by the name of the "Feast of Lamps," or the "Feast of Lights," because of the custom of illuminating the houses while celebrating it. The Jewish rabbis have a tradition that, when the Jews under Judas Maccabeus drove the heathen out of the temple and cleansed it from its pollution, they found a solitary bottle of sacred oil that had escaped the profane search of the heathen. This was all they had for lighting the sacred lamps, but by a miracle this was made to last eight days, and so this became the duration of the feast.

This is the holiday referred to now as Hanukkah, an eight-day festival beginning on the 25th day of Kislev. Hebrew *nukkâ*, dedication, from *nak*, to dedicate.

11:16 DOUBLE NAMES

Then Thomas (called Didymus).

Both these names have the same signification, a twin; Thomas being Aramaic, and Didymus being Greek. It is said to have been customary for the Jews when traveling into foreign countries, or familiarly conversing with the Greeks or Romans, to assume a Greek or Latin name of similar meaning to their own.

11:17 RABBINICAL BELIEFS ABOUT SOUL AND BODY

On his arrival, Jesus found that Lazarus had already been in the tomb for four days.

The three days after death were called "days of weeping," which were followed by four "days of lamentation," thus making up the seven "days of mourning" (see Genesis **27:41 Days of Mourning**).

According to rabbinical thought, the spirit wanders about the sepulcher for three days seeking an opportunity to return into the body; but when the aspect of the body changes, it hovers no more, but leaves the body to itself. The friends of the deceased were in the habit of visiting the sepulcher for three days after death and burial, probably because they supposed they would thus be nearer to the departed soul. When the fourth day came, and decomposition took place, and the soul, as they supposed, went away from the sepulcher, they beat their breast and made loud lamentations. This explains the allusion to the "four days" in this text and in verse 39. The saying that one had been in the grave four days was equivalent to saying that bodily corruption had begun.

11:18 Furlong

Now Bethany was nigh unto Jerusalem, about fifteen furlongs *(less than two miles, NIV)* off *(KJV)*.

The *stadion,* or furlong mentioned here and in Luke 24:13; John 6:19; Revelation 14:20; 21:16, was six hundred and six feet and nine inches in length.

18:17 Female Doorkeepers

The damsel that kept the door *(girl at the door, NIV)"* *(KJV)*.

Women were often employed in biblical times as porters. Classical writers make frequent allusion to the custom. It is also mentioned in the account of Peter's deliverance from prison, wherein it is stated that the house of Mary, the mother of John, also called Mark, had a female porter (Acts 12:13).

19:23 Tunic

The undergarment *(coat, KJV)* remaining. This garment was seamless, woven in one piece from top to bottom.

The tunic, or undergarment, was worn next to the skin. It usually had sleeves, was woven in one piece, and generally

Tunic

mentioned in Matthew 5:40; Luke 6:29; Acts 9:39. Sometimes for luxury two tunics were worn at the same time. This Jesus forbade His disciples (Matthew 10:10; Mark 6:9; Luke 3:11). When a person had on no garment but this, he was said to be naked (1 Samuel 19:24).

reached to the knees, though sometimes to the ankles. It is

Preparing Jesus for Burial

19:40 BURIAL PREPARATIONS

Taking Jesus' body, the two of them wrapped it, with the spices, in strips of linen. This was in accordance with Jewish burial customs.

Though the Bible does not systematically describe Hebrew burial practice, several features can be gleaned from individual passages. Joseph closed his father's eyelids soon after Jacob's death (Genesis 46:4). Jesus' body was prepared for burial by anointing it with aromatic oils and spices and wrapping it in a linen cloth (Mark 16:1; Luke 24:1; John 19:39). The arms and legs of Lazarus' body were bound with cloth, and the face covered by a napkin (John 11:44). The body of Tabitha was washed in preparation for burial (Acts 9:37). Putting them all together may give a picture of the Hebrew method of preparing bodies for burial.

Burial of Jesus

Jerusalem and the Mount of Olives

Rooftop prayer

ACTS

1:12 Sᴀʙʙᴀᴛʜ's Dᴀʏ Jᴏᴜʀɴᴇʏ

Then they returned to Jerusalem from the hill called the Mount of Olives, a Sabbath day's walk from the city.

This was the distance beyond which it was considered unlawful for a Jew to travel on the Sabbath day. Its limitation is supposed to have originated in Exodus 16:29, where every man is commanded to abide in his place on the Sabbath. The distance of a Sabbath's day journey was 2000 cubits, which was said to be the distance between the Ark and the Israelites when they crossed the Jordan. Two thousand cubits is less than half a mile.

10:9 Rᴏᴏғᴛᴏᴘ Pʀᴀʏᴇʀs

About noon the following day as they were on their journey and approaching the city, Peter went up on the roof to pray.

Rooftop prayers were popular among the heathen as well as the Jews. It's believed that in addition to acting as a screen from public observation, the person praying might also more readily look in the direction of the temple in Jerusalem (see Daniel **6:10 Time of Prayer**).

12:4 Mɪʟɪᴛᴀʀʏ Nɪɢʜᴛ-Wᴀᴛᴄʜ

After arresting him, he put him in prison, handing him over to be guarded by four squads of four soldiers each.

The usual number of a Roman military night-watch was four, and the watch was changed every three hours. Thus during the twelve hours of night, there would be four of these watchers, or "quarternions." Of these, two were in the prison (verse 6), and two were sentinels before the door (verses 6 and 10).

12:6 PRISONERS IN CHAINS

Peter was sleeping between two soldiers, bound with two chains, and sentries stood guard at the entrance.

The Roman custom was to bind the prisoner to the soldier who had charge of him by means of a chain, which joined the prisoner's right wrist to the left wrist of the soldier. For greater security the prisoner was sometimes chained to two soldiers, one on each side of him. This was the case with Peter, and with Paul in Acts 21:33.

13:15 RULERS OF THE SYNAGOGUE

After the reading from the Law and the Prophets, the synagogue rulers sent word to them.

The "ruler of the synagogue" occupied an important position. In the temple synagogue, he was the third officer in rank; the first officer being the high priest, and the second, the chief of the priests. In provincial synagogues, the "ruler" was supreme. No one was eligible for this office until he had a certificate from the Great Sanhedrin stating that he possessed the required qualifications. His election, however, was by the members of the synagogue. It was his duty to supervise all matters connected with worship.

Sometimes this office is

Peter chained between two guards

mentioned in the singular number, as if there were but one ruler to the synagogue (Mark 5:35, 36, 38; Luke 8:49; 13:14). At other times the plural form is used, as in our text-verse (Mark 5:22).

14:12 Zeus and Hermes

Barnabas they called Zeus *(Jupiter, KJV)*, and Paul they called Hermes *(Mercurius, KJV)* because he was the chief speaker.

Zeus, called Jupiter by the Romans, was the supreme head of all the heathen deities. He had a temple at Lystra. Hermes, called Mercury by the Romans, was a son of Zeus, and the herald or messenger of all the mythical gods. Hence he was the god of eloquence. There two deities were supposed to travel together.

Zeus

Thus the people, having decided that because of his eloquence Paul must be Hermes, inferred that his traveling companion was Zeus.

16:13 Places of Prayer

On the Sabbath we went outside the city gate to the river, where we expected to find a place of prayer.

The places of prayer, or *proseuche*, were in locations where there were no synagogues. These were places of prayer outside of towns where the Jews were too poor to have synagogues, or were not permitted to have them. they were generally located near the water for the convenience of ablution. sometimes a large building was erected; but frequently the *proseuche* was simply a retired place in the open air or in a grove.

Proseuche is translated "chapel." Even today it is not uncommon to find a chapel or similar structure in a grove, forest, or alongside a lake, or other peaceful body of water.

16:24 Stocks

Upon receiving such orders, he put them in the inner cell and fastened their feet in the stocks.

An instrument that secured the feet (and sometimes the neck and hands) of a prisoner (Job 13:27; Jeremiah 29:26). Stocks were usually constructed of wood with holes to secure the feet. They could also be used as an instrument of torture by stretching the legs apart and causing the prisoner to sit in unnatural positions. The Romans often added chains along with the stocks. Stocks were much used in medieval and later times during persecution of Christians.

16:27 Responsibilities of Jailers

He drew his sword and was about to kill himself because he thought the prisoners had escaped.

According to Roman law, if a prisoner escaped, the jailer who had charge of him was compelled to suffer the penalty that was to have been inflicted on the prisoner. This accounts for the despair of the jailer in this case. He preferred death by his own hands to the death by torture, which probably was the fate awaiting some of the prisoners whom he thought had escaped.

In the stocks

16:37 ROMAN CITIZENS NOT TO BE BEATEN

But Paul said to the officers: "They beat us publicly without a trial, even though we are Roman citizens, and threw us into prison."

The Roman forbade the binding or beating of a Roman citizen. Cicero, in his celebrated *Oration against Verres*, asserts: "It is a transgression of the law to bind a Roman citizen; it is wickedness to scourge him. Unheard, no man can be condemned."

17:17 PUBLIC DEBATES

So he reasoned in the synagogue with the Jews and the God-fearing Greeks, as well as in the marketplace day by day with those who happened to be there.

The marketplace was not only a place for buying and selling, for hiring and being hired (see Matthew **20:3 Marketplace**), it was also a public resort for all who wished to acquire news or hold disputations. For this reason, the Pharisees loved to go there, because amid the crowds assembled they would receive the ceremonious salutations in which they delighted. See also Matthew 23:7; Mark 12:38; Luke 11:43; 20:46.

17:18 EPICUREANS - STOICS

A group of Epicurean and Stoic philosophers began to dispute with him.

1. Epicureanism was a philosophy that emerged in Athens about 300 B.C. It was developed by Epicurus, who was born in 341 B.C. on the Greek island of Samos. Epicurus founded his school, "The Garden," in Athens. Epicurean thought had a significant impact on the *Hellenistic* (of or relating to post-classical Greek history and culture from the death of Alexander the Great to the accession of Augustus) world and later, Rome. The philosophy advanced by Epicurus considered happiness, or the avoidance of pain and emotional disturbance, to be the highest good.

2. The Stoics were a sect of Greek philosophers at Athens, so called from the Greek word *stoa*

(a "porch" or "portico"), which was their principle meeting place. They have been called "the Pharisees of Greek paganism." The founder of the Stoics was Zeno, who flourished about 300 B.C. He taught his disciples that a man's happiness consisted in bringing himself into harmony with the course of the universe. They were trained to bear evils with indifference, and so to be independent of externals. Materialism, pantheism, fatalism, and pride were the leading features of this philosophy.

18:3 TRADES

Because he was a tentmaker as they were, he stayed and worked with them.

Among the Jews, the boys were compelled to learn trades. It was considered disreputable not to be acquainted with some branch of handicraft, a practical knowledge of a trade being regarded as a prerequisite to personal independence.

19:24 SHRINES OF ARTEMIS

A silversmith named Demetrius, who made silver shrines of Artemis, brought in no little business for the craftsmen.

These shrines were miniature representations of the most sacred portion of the heathen temple; that part of it where the statue of the goddess was situated. They were made of wood or precious metal, and were worn as charms. A little door on one side concealed the image of the goddess within.

19:27 TEMPLE OF ARTEMIS

"The temple of the great goddess Artemis will be discredited, and the goddess herself, who is worshiped throughout the province of Asia and the world."

Temple of Artemis/Diana

Called Diana by the Romans; called Artemis by the Greeks. Her most noted temple was that at Ephesus. It was built outside the city walls, and was one of the seven wonders of the ancient world. One historian writes: "First and last it was the work of 220 years; built of shining marble; 342 feet long by 164 feet broad; supported by a forest of columns, each 56 feet high; a sacred museum of masterpieces of sculpture and painting. At the

as St. Paul saw it subsisted till A.D. 262, when it was ruined by the Goths" (Acts 19:23-41).

19:29 THEATER

Rushed as one man into the theater.

Public drama arrived with the Greeks after 400 B.C.. As a symbol of Greco-Roman culture, the presence of theaters in Palestine was a constant reminder of Greek and Roman control of the Jewish

The theater at Ephesus

centre, hidden by curtains, within a gorgeous shrine, stood the very ancient image of the goddess, on wood or ebony reputed to have fallen from the sky. Behind the shrine was a treasury, where, as in 'the safest bank in Asia,' nations and kings stored their most precious things. The temple

state. Herod I built numerous theaters in the Greek cities during his reign in Palestine (37- 4 B.C.). The presence of these theaters, especially near the Temple in Jerusalem, continually aroused anger in the Jews. Public performances began with a sacrifice to a heathen god, usually the patron god of the city. Dramas and comedies included historical or political themes and were often lewd and suggestive. The semicircular seats of the theater rose step fashion either up a natural hillside or on artificial tiers. A facade, several stories high, was decorated with sculptures and stood behind the stage. The general public sat in the higher seats, farther back, but wealthier patrons were given seats lower and closer to the stage. A large central area was reserved for the local governor or ruler. Theaters varied in size. Those in small towns held approximately 4,000 persons, while larger theaters, such as that in Ephesus where Paul was denounced, were capable of holding 25,000 or more.

19:31 Asiarche (Officials)

Even some of the officials of the province, friends of Paul

The Asiarche comprised the presidency of the public festivities in a city of Asia Minor. Every year ten of the most prominent citizens of the chief cities of proconsular Asia were chosen to the office of Asiarch for the term of one year, though eligible for reappointment. They were, of necessity, men of great wealth, since the games at which they officiated were very costly, and the Asiarche were themselves obliged to meet the entire expense. When officiating, they were clad in purple and crowned with garlands.

19:35 City Clerk - Artemis of Ephesus

The city clerk quieted the crowd and said "Men of Ephesus, doesn't all the world know that the city of Ephesus is the guardian of the temple of the great Artemis and of her image, which fell from heaven?"

1. The *grammateus*, scribe, or city clerk, as the word is here rendered, seems to have been charged with the duties of a higher order than those of the ordinary scribes among the Greeks. It is supposed that under Roman rule in Asia Minor the work of the scribes was not limited to recording the laws and reading them in public. They presided over assemblies, and

sometimes legally assumed the functions of magistrates. The title is preserved on ancient coins and

Statue of Diana of Ephesus

marbles, and the scribes were evidently regarded as governors of cities or districts.

2. While the Artemis of the Greeks corresponded to the Diana of the Romans, this Ephesian Diana or Artemis was a totally distinct divinity of Asiatic

origin. Her worship was found by the Greeks in Ionia when they settled there. There was in many respects a resemblance between the Ephesian Artemis and the Syrian Astarte (see 1 Kings **11:5 Ashtoreth and Molech**). Her worship extended over a vast region, and cities vied with each other for the honor of being called *neokoron,* sweeper, or keeper, of the temple—guardian in our text-verse. The original Ephesian image was said to have fallen from heaven, as was also asserted of images of other deities in other cities. This has given rise to the opinion that this and similar images were aerolites, chiefly siliceous meteorites, and were worshiped according to the ancient superstition that gave sanctity and divinity to certain stones.

21: 23-24 NAZARITE VOWS

"There are four men with us who have made a vow. Take these men, join in their purification rites and pay their expenses, so that they can have their heads shaved."

This institution was a symbol of a life devoted to God and

separated from all sin—a holy life (Numbers 6:2-21). The vow of a Nazarite involved these three things.

1. Abstinence from wine and strong drink.

2. Refraining from cutting their hair during the whole period of the continuance of the vow.

3. Avoidance of contact with the dead.

When the period of the continuance of the vow came to an end, the Nazarite had to present himself at the door of the sanctuary with three things.

1. A male lamb of the first year for a burnt-offering.

2. A ewe lamb of the first year for a sin-offering.

3. A ram for a peace-offering.

After these sacrifices were offered by the priest, the Nazarite cut off his hair at the door and threw it into the fire under the peace-offering.

For some reason, probably in the midst of his work at Corinth, Paul himself took on the Nazarite vow. This could only be terminated by his going up to Jerusalem to offer up his hair, which until then was to be left uncut. But it seems to have been allowable for persons at a distance to cut their hair, which was to be brought up to Jerusalem, where the ceremony was completed. This Paul did at Cenchrea just before setting out on his voyage into Syria (Acts 18:18).

In our text-verse, Paul took on the Nazarite vow again at the Feast of Pentecost. One commentator writes: "The ceremonies involved took a longer time than Paul had at his disposal, but the law permitted a man to share the vow if he could find companions who had gone through the prescribed ceremonies, and who permitted him to join their company. This permission was commonly granted if the newcomer paid all the fees required from the whole company (fees to the Levites for cutting the hair and fees for sacrifices), and finished the vow along with the others. Four Jewish Christians were performing the vow, and would admit Paul to their company, provided he paid their expenses.

Paul consented, paid the charges, and when the last seven days of the vow began he went with them to live in the temple, giving the usual notice to the priests that he had joined in regular fashion, was a sharer with the four men, and that his vow would end with theirs. Nazarites retired to the temple during the last period of seven days, because they could be secure there against any accidental defilement."

As to the duration of a Nazarite's vow, every one was left at liberty to fix his own time. There is mention made in the Scriptures of only three who were Nazarites for life, Samson, Samuel, and John the Baptist (Judges 13:4, 5; 1 Samuel 1:11; Luke 1:15). In its ordinary form, however, the Nazarite's vow lasted only thirty and, at most, one hundred, days.

The Apostle Paul

25:11-12 Appeal - Roman Councilors

"I appeal to Caesar!" After Festus had conferred with his council, he declared: "You have appealed to Caesar. To Caesar you will go!"

1. The Roman governors exercised supreme jurisdiction over the provinces but all Roman citizens had the inalienable right of appeal. This right Paul saw fit to use, and thereby took the case out of the hands of Festus and removed it to a higher court.

2. The *sumboulion*—provincial assessors, or councilors—were men learned in the law, whose business it was to sit in judgment with the governor, and advise him on points of law.

26:1 Hand Gestures

So Paul motioned with his hand and began his defense.

The gesture spoken of here is a customary form of dignified oratory, designed to show the earnestness of the speaker. The orator stretched forth the right hand, with the two lowest fingers shut in on the palm of the hand and the other fingers extended. It's said that Demosthenes (384-322 B.C., known mainly for *Philippics,* a series of orations exhorting the citizens of Athens to rise up against Philip II of Macedon), used this gesture quite eloquently.

27:17 UNDERGIRDING

When the men had hoisted it aboard, they passed ropes under the ship itself to hold it together.

Every ship carried large cables, which were used in case of necessity for passing around the hull, thus "undergirding" it, and saving it from the strain that resulted from the working of the mast in a storm.

27:29 ANCHORS

Fearing that we would be dashed against the rocks, they dropped four anchors from the stern.

Ancient vessels had lighter anchors than those on modern ships, therefore they carried more. It was customary to anchor ancient ships by the stern (rear section), through they were sometimes anchored at the bow (front section). The anchors were carried in the skiff (a flat bottomed open boat of shallow draft, having a pointed bow and a square stern and propelled by oars, or sail) to a suitable distance from the ship and there dropped.

27:40 RUDDERS - FORESAIL

Cutting loose the anchors, they left them in the sea and at the same time untied the ropes that held the rudders. Then they hoisted the foresail to the wind and made for the beach.

1. The rudder was a vertically hinged plate made of wood in ancient times, of metal or fiberglass in modern times—mounted at the stern of a vessel for directing its course.

2. The foresail was the principal square sail hung to the forward mast of a square-rigged vessel—that is, a vessel fitted with square sails as the principal sails.

ROMANS

7:24 CAPITAL PUNISHMENT

Who will rescue me from this body of death?

This is a reference to the Roman method of punishment in which the body of the murdered person was chained to the murderer. The murderer was then released to wander where he might, but no one was allowed to help or comfort him upon penalty of suffering the same punishment. In the hot Eastern sun the dead body would soon begin to decay, overwhelming the sentenced person not only with the smell but also with infection from the rotting flesh. It was perhaps the most horrible of all sentences that the imaginary Romans ever devised. To Paul our putrefying body of sinful flesh is like this, and only Christ can rescue us from it.

8:15 ADOPTION

Ye have received the Spirit of adoption, whereby we cry, Abba, Father.

Among the Greeks and Romans, when a man had no son, he was permitted to adopt one even though not related. He might, if he chose, adopt one of his slaves as a son. The adopted son took the name of the father, and was in every respect regarded and treated as a son. Among the Romans there were two parts to the act of adoption: one a private arrangement between the parties, and the other a formal public declaration of the fact. It is thought by some that the former is referred to in this verse, and the latter in verse 23, where the apostle speaks of "waiting for the adoption." The servant has been adopted privately, but he is waiting for a formal public declaration of the fact.

After adoption, the son, no longer a slave, had the privilege of addressing his former master by the title of "father." See Galatians 4:5-6.

16:16 HOLY KISS

Greet one another with a holy kiss.

The kiss was not only used among men as a token of friendship and of homage to a superior, but as one of the ceremonies connected with divine worship, and intended to express mutual love and equality. As such, it is supposed to have been used in the synagogues, and thence passed on to the Church. The holy kiss was widely practiced among the early Christians as a manner of greeting, a sign of acceptance, and an imparting of blessing. This custom could well have been used to express the unity of the Christian fellowship. See also Genesis **29:13 Men Kissing**.

1 CORINTHIANS

9:25 Temperance - Victors' Crowns

Everyone who competes in the games goes into strict training. They do it to get a crown that will not last; but we do it to get a crown that will last forever.

Among the four sacred games of the ancient Greeks, the Olympic and the Isthmian were the most celebrated, the former taking the precedence. To these familiar games the apostle makes many allusions in his writings (see Hebrews **12:1 Footrace**). There are two such in this text.

1. Every competitor in these games was obliged to undergo a severe and protracted training, sometimes lasting nearly a year. During this time he carefully avoided excesses of every kind. A passage from Epictetus, the Greek Stoic Philosopher, illustrates this text so well that it is cited by most commentators: "Would you be a victor in the Olympic games? so in good truth would I, for it is a glorious thing; but pray consider what must go before, and what may follow, and so proceed to the attempt. You must then live by rule, eat what will be disagreeable, refrain from delicacies; you must oblige yourself to constant exercises at the appointed hour, in heat and cold; you must abstain from wine and cold liquors; in a word, you must be as submissive to all direction of your master as to those of a physician." Thus Paul says in out text-verse, "Everyone who competes in the games goes into strict training."

2. The victor was rewarded with a crown or chaplet of leaves. The Olympic crown was made of leaves of the wild olive, the Isthmian crown was made of pine or ivy. From the earliest period of history, chaplets of leaves were bestowed upon heroes who had conquered on the field of battle. Thus the Psalmist says of the triumphant Messiah: "Upon himself shall his crown flourish"

(Psalm 132:18). The idea of the crown flourishing is very expressive when spoken of a leafy chaplet; though some commentators render the word *shine*. This is the sort of crown to which Paul refers in the text as "corruptible." The crown of thorns that was placed on the Savior's head was a mockery of these wreaths of triumph, as well as of the golden crowns of kings (Matthew 27:29; Mark 15:17; John 29:2, 5).

The leafy crown given to the victor in these ancient games doubtless furnished the metaphor that is used in 2 Timothy 2:5; 4:8; James 1:12; 1 Peter 5:4; Revelation 2:10; 3:11.

9:26 Boxing

I do not fight like a man beating the air.

The allusion here is to boxing. It was customary for the boxers while training to strike out at an imaginary adversary merely for exercise. This was "beating the air." The apostle struck real blows at a real adversary.

2 CORINTHIANS

2:14 ROMAN MILITARY TRIUMPHS

But thanks be to God, who always leads us in triumphal procession in Christ and through us spreads everywhere the fragrance of the knowledge of him.

A Roman military triumphal procession was one of the grandest spectacles of ancient times. It was granted to a conqueror only when certain conditions had been fully complied with. Among these it was required that the victory be complete and decisive, that it should be over a foreign foe, that at least five thousand of the enemy should be slain in a single battle, that the conquest should extend the territory of the state, and that it put an end to the war.

When the senate decided that all required conditions had been met, a day was appointed and every necessary arrangement was made for the splendid pageant. When the day arrived the people crowded the streets and filled every place from which a good view of the procession could be obtained. The temples were all open and decorated with flowers, and incense was burned on every altar. Fragrant odors from burning spices were profusely scattered through the temples and along the streets, filling the air with perfume.

In the procession were the senate and chief citizens of the state, who by their presence honored the conqueror. The richest spoils of war—gold, silver, weapons of every description, standards, rare and costly works of art, and everything that was deemed most valuable by either conqueror or vanquished—were carried in open view in the procession. The general in whose honor the triumph was decreed rode in a chariot that was of peculiar form and drawn by four horses. His robe was embroidered with gold, and his tunic with flowers. In his right hand was a laurel bough, and in his left, a scepter. On his brow there was a wreath of Delphic laurel. Amid the shouts of the soldiers and the applause of the populace, the conqueror was carried through the streets to the temple of Jupiter, where sacrifices were offered, after which there was a public feast in the temple.

To the splendors of such a scene the apostle doubtless alludes in our text-verse, and also in Colossians 2:15: "and having spoiled principalities and powers, he made a show of them openly, triumphing over them in it."

2 TIMOTHY

2:3 Roman Military Discipline

Endure hardship with us like a good soldier of Christ Jesus.

The discipline of the Roman army was severe. Every soldier was compelled to "endure hardship." The weapons were heavy, and in addition to them, the ordinary foot soldier was compelled to carry a saw, a basket, a pickax, an ax, a thong of leather, and a hook, together with three days of rations.

2:4 Singleness of Purpose

No one serving as a soldier gets involved in civilian affairs—he wants to please his commanding officer.

The Roman soldier was expected to keep one thing in his sights, and only one: the service of his commander. He was not allowed to marry, nor could he engage in agriculture, trade, or manufacture. He was a soldier and could not be anything else.

The figure is suggestive of the singleness of purpose that characterizes the true minister of Jesus Christ. He is not allowed to engage in an employment that will interfere with his usefulness to his Commander. This is what Paul, in our text-verse, intimates to Timothy.

2:5 No Cheating

Similarly, if anyone competes as an athlete, he does not receive the victor's crown unless he competes according to the rules.

No man could hope to obtain the reward in ancient games of running, leaping, boxing, or wrestling, unless he complied with the regulations that were prescribed, both in the necessary training and in the conduct of the games. It's believed by some that Paul refers to these rules of the games when he says in 1 Corinthians 9:26—"Therefore I do not run like a man running aimlessly." That is, "I have a knowledge of all the rules that regulate the race, and I know what I am engaged in."

2:19 MURAL INSCRIPTIONS

Nevertheless, God's solid foundation stands firm, sealed with this inscription: "The Lord knows those who are his," and, "Everyone who confesses the name of the Lord must turn away from wickedness."

The allusion here is to inscriptions that were placed on buildings. Besides writing on doors (see Deuteronomy **6:9 Doorposts Inscriptions**), it was customary to inscribe on some of the foundation stones of large buildings words indicating the purpose for which the building was erected, or containing some striking maxim. Allusion to this custom is made in Revelation 21:14: "The wall of the city had twelve foundations, and on them were the names of the twelve apostles of the Lamb."

4:13 CLOAK

When you come, bring the cloak that I left with Carpus at Troas.

The cloak was a thick outer garment used in traveling as a protection against the weather. It was sometimes worn by women as well as by the men. It was usually made of wool, though occasionally of leather, and was a long, sleeveless garment, made like a sack, with an opening for the head similar to the Spanish poncho.

Cloak

HEBREWS

11:37 SAWING IN TWO

They were sawed in two.

This terrible mode of punishment is said to have originated either with the Persians or the Chaldeans, and was occasionally practiced by other ancient nations. It is believed by some to be mentioned in 2 Samuel 12:31, and 1 Chronicles 20:3, though commentators by no means agree on this point. There is an ancient tradition that says Isaiah was tied inside a sack and then sawed in two. Jesus is thought to have referred to it in Matthew 24:51 and Luke 12:46.

12:1 FOOTRACE

Therefore, since we are surrounded by such a great cloud of witnesses, let us throw off everything that hinders and the sin that so easily entangles, and let us run with perseverance the race marked out for us.

Running was one of the most popular of the Olympic games. The place prepared for the race was called the *stadium* because

Ancient footrace

its length equaled a *stadion*, or six hundred Greek feet (see John **11:18 Furlong**). The stadium was an oblong area, with a straight wall across one end, where the entrances were, the other end being round and entirely closed. Tiers of seats were on either side for the spectators or witnesses. The starting place was at the entrance end and was marked by a square pillar. At the opposite end was the goal, where the judge sat and held the prize. The eyes of the competitors remained fixed on him: "Let us fix our eyes on Jesus" (Hebrews 12:2). The goal, as well as the starting point, was marked by a square pillar, and a third was placed midway between the two. This goal is referred to in Philippians 3:14. The competitors, through sever training, had no superfluous flesh, and ran unclothed. Flesh and clothing were laid aside as a "weight" that might hinder them in the race.

See Acts 20:24; 2 Thessalonians 3:1; Philippians 3:13,14; 1 Timothy 6:12; 2 Timothy 4:7 for other allusions to sports competitions.

1 PETER

5:4 CHIEF SHEPHERD

And when the Chief Shepherd appears.

In Hebrews 13:20, Jesus is called "that great Shepherd of the sheep." This corresponds to the "chief Shepherd" in our text-verse. Where the flocks were numerous and a large number of shepherds were necessary, one was placed in charge of all the others. This was true of the herdsmen also. Pharaoh told Joseph to take the most active of his kinsmen and make them "rulers" over his cattle (Genesis 47:6, KJV). Doeg was the "chiefest of the herdmen" of Saul (1 Samuel 21:7, KJV).

Thus we have an illustration of the text. Christian ministers are pastors, or shepherds, but there is one over them all. Jesus is the "chief Shepherd." He superintends them, cares for them, assigns them their several positions, and rewards or chastises them.

JUDE

1:12 Love Feasts

These men are blemishes at your love feasts.

The *agape* or love-feasts were celebrated in connection with the Lord's Supper. Joseph Bingham, writing in 1870, gives this account of it: "The first Christians had all things in common, as we see in the Acts of the Apostles; and when that ceased, as it did in the apostles' time, this came in its room, as an efflux or imitation of it. For though the rich did not make all their substance common, yet, upon certain days appointed, they made a common table; and when their service was ended and they had all communicated in the holy mysteries, they all met at a common feast: the rich bringing provisions, and the poor and those who had nothing being invited, they all feasted in common together."

Paradise lost and paradise found

REVELATION

2:7 "PARADISE"

He who has an ear, let him hear what the Spirit says to the churches. To him who overcomes, I will give the right to eat from the tree of life, which is in the paradise of God.

Paradise is often used metaphorically to mean any place or condition of pure happiness. Christians normally identify paradise with the Garden of Eden and with heaven, based upon Jesus saying to the thief on the Cross who believed in Him: "I tell you the truth, today you will be with me in paradise" (Luke 23:43), and after His resurrection saying to the churches through the apostle John: "To him who overcomes, I will give the right

to eat from the tree of life, which is in the paradise of God" (Revelation 2:7).

It's this connection between paradise and the Garden of Eden that is the theme of John Milton's *Paradise Lost*. The subject of his epic is the fall of man, but Milton also fictionalized the rebellion and punishment of Satan and the creation of Adam and Eve. Milton said that the intent of his poem is "to justify the ways of God to men," and so in the poem he attempts to explain why God allowed the fall of man.

7:9 PALM BRANCHES

They were wearing white robes and were holding palm branches in their hands.

Palm branches were used on occasions of festivity (Leviticus 23:40, Nehemiah 8:15). They were regarded as tokens of joy and triumph. Kings and conquerors were welcomed by having palm branches strewn before them and waved in the air. Thus they were waved before the Messiah on the occasion of His entry into Jerusalem (John 12:13). Conquerors in Grecian games returned to their homes

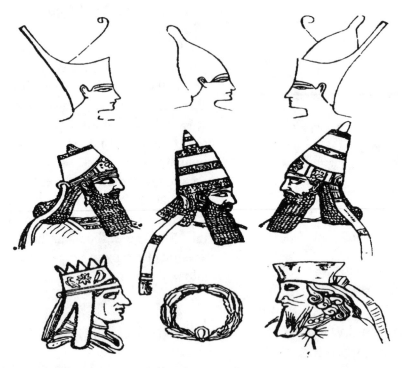

Various types of crowns

triumphantly waving palm branches in their hands. Thus in the New Jerusalem, John sees the triumphant followers of the Messiah with "palm branches in their hands."

19:12 MANY CROWNS

On his head are many crowns.

Monarchs who claimed authority over more than one country wore more than one crown. The kings of Egypt were crowned with the *Pshent*, or united crowns of Upper and Lower Egypt. When Ptolemy Philometer entered Antioch as a conqueror, he wore a triple crown, two for Egypt, and a third for Asia.

John saw Him who was "King of kings and Lord of lords," and "on His head were many crowns." Thus, in a beautiful figure, the universal dominion of our blessed Lord is set forth.

INDEX

A

Ab 287, 416
Abel 4
Abel-mizraim 96
Abib 121, 173
Abomination 83, 105
Absalom's Monument 186
abyss 322
acacia wood 130, 132, 135
Aceldama 481
Achor 186
Adam and Eve 1
Adar 284, 287
adder 320
Adrammelech 269
agalah 359
Agreeing with an Adversary 410
Aker 109

Akris 403
Alabaster 313, 471
aliyah 259, 495
Aliyoth 260
Alms and Trumpets 412
aloes 93
Am I my brother's keeper? 4
Ambushes Near Water 193
amethysts 344
ammah 125
Ammon 372
Amon 109, 121
amon 372
amon minno 372
Amon of No 372
amphora 259
Amphorae 259
Amun 373
Anammelech 269
anger 381
angle 353
anklets 349
Annual Pilgrimages 124
anoint 354
anointed 264
anointed priest 479
anointest 313
Anointing Guests 313
Anubis 109, 269
apex 409
aphar 150
Apis 109, 129
appiryone 345
aqueducts 105
arbeh 402
Ares 168

B

D

X

no entries

Y

Z

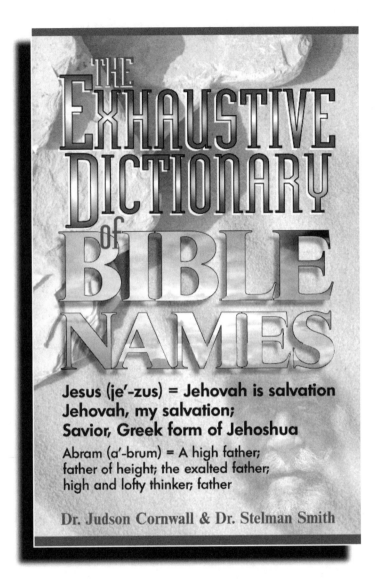

Timeline Guidelines

Covering the period from the time of Creation to 100 AD, the charts are designed to inform the reader of general world-wide events.

* The order of events is sequential—not chronological.
* Dates "anchor" specific events within paragraphs.
* Biblical history is in black, World history in blue.